D0080378

FREE Study Skills DVD Offer

Dear Customer,

Thank you for your purchase from Mometrix! We consider it an honor and a privilege that you have purchased our product and we want to ensure your satisfaction.

As a way of showing our appreciation and to help us better serve you, we have developed a Study Skills DVD that we would like to give you for <u>FREE</u>. This DVD covers our *best practices* for getting ready for your exam, from how to use our study materials to how to best prepare for the day of the test.

All that we ask is that you email us with feedback that would describe your experience so far with our product. Good, bad, or indifferent, we want to know what you think!

To get your FREE Study Skills DVD, email <u>freedvd@mometrix.com</u> with *FREE STUDY SKILLS DVD* in the subject line and the following information in the body of the email:

- The name of the product you purchased.
- Your product rating on a scale of 1-5, with 5 being the highest rating.
- Your feedback. It can be long, short, or anything in between. We just want to know your impressions and experience so far with our product. (Good feedback might include how our study material met your needs and ways we might be able to make it even better. You could highlight features that you found helpful or features that you think we should add.)
- Your full name and shipping address where you would like us to send your free DVD.

If you have any questions or concerns, please don't hesitate to contact me directly.

Thanks again!

Sincerely,

Jay Willis
Vice President
<u>jay.willis@mometrix.com</u>
1-800-673-8175

Secrets of the

TEAS® V

for Allied Health

SECRETS

Study Guide
Your Key to Exam Success

TEAS® V Test Review for the
Test of Essential Academic Skills

Library Discard
This item has been withdrawn.

Published by
Mometrix Test Preparation
Mometrix Healthcare Admissions Test Team

LIBRARIES
SOUTH CAMPUS LIBRARY
6665 S Howell Avenue - Oak Creek, WI
414-571-4720 - book.matc.edu

610.73069
S446
2017

Copyright © 2019 by Mometrix Media LLC

All rights reserved. This product, or parts thereof, may not be reproduced, stored in a retrieval system, or transmitted in any form or by any means—electronic, mechanical, photocopy, recording, scanning, or other—except for brief quotations in critical reviews or articles, without the prior written permission of the publisher.

Written and edited by the Mometrix Healthcare Admissions Test Team

Printed in the United States of America

This paper meets the requirements of ANSI/NISO Z39.48-1992 (Permanence of Paper).

Mometrix offers volume discount pricing to institutions. For more information or a price quote, please contact our sales department at sales@mometrix.com or 888-248-1219.

Mometrix Media LLC is not affiliated with or endorsed by any official testing organization. All organizational and test names are trademarks of their respective owners.

Paperback
ISBN 13: 978-1-63094-990-7
ISBN 10: 1-63094-990-6

Ebook
ISBN 13: 978-1-5167-0650-1
ISBN 10: 1-5167-0650-1

Dear Future Exam Success Story:

First of all, **THANK YOU** for purchasing Mometrix study materials!

Second, congratulations! You are one of the few determined test-takers who are committed to doing whatever it takes to excel on your exam. **You have come to the right place.** We developed these study materials with one goal in mind: to deliver you the information you need in a format that's concise and easy to use.

In addition to optimizing your guide for the content of the test, we've outlined our recommended steps for breaking down the preparation process into small, attainable goals so you can make sure you stay on track.

We've also analyzed the entire test-taking process, identifying the most common pitfalls and showing how you can overcome them and be ready for any curveball the test throws you.

Standardized testing is one of the biggest obstacles on your road to success, which only increases the importance of doing well in the high-pressure, high-stakes environment of test day. Your results on this test could have a significant impact on your future, and this guide provides the information and practical advice to help you achieve your full potential on test day.

Your success is our success

We would love to hear from you! If you would like to share the story of your exam success or if you have any questions or comments in regard to our products, please contact us at **800-673-8175** or **support@mometrix.com**.

Thanks again for your business and we wish you continued success!

Sincerely,
The Mometrix Test Preparation Team

Need more help? Check out our flashcards at: http://mometrixflashcards.com/TEAS

TABLE OF CONTENTS

Introduction

Thank you for purchasing this resource! You have made the choice to prepare yourself for a test that could have a huge impact on your future, and this guide is designed to help you be fully ready for test day. Obviously, it's important to have a solid understanding of the test material, but you also need to be prepared for the unique environment and stressors of the test, so that you can perform to the best of your abilities.

For this purpose, the first section that appears in this guide is the **Secret Keys**. We've devoted countless hours to meticulously researching what works and what doesn't, and we've boiled down our findings to the five most impactful steps you can take to improve your performance on the test. We start at the beginning with study planning and move through the preparation process, all the way to the testing strategies that will help you get the most out of what you know when you're finally sitting in front of the test.

We recommend that you start preparing for your test as far in advance as possible. However, if you've bought this guide as a last-minute study resource and only have a few days before your test, we recommend that you skip over the first two Secret Keys since they address a long-term study plan.

If you struggle with **test anxiety**, we strongly encourage you to check out our recommendations for how you can overcome it. Test anxiety is a formidable foe, but it can be beaten, and we want to make sure you have the tools you need to defeat it.

Copyright © Mometrix Media. You have been licensed one copy of this document for personal use only. Any other reproduction or redistribution is strictly prohibited. All rights reserved.

Secret Key #1 – Plan Big, Study Small

There's a lot riding on your performance. If you want to ace this test, you're going to need to keep your skills sharp and the material fresh in your mind. You need a plan that lets you review everything you need to know while still fitting in your schedule. We'll break this strategy down into three categories.

Information Organization

Start with the information you already have: the official test outline. From this, you can make a complete list of all the concepts you need to cover before the test. Organize these concepts into groups that can be studied together, and create a list of any related vocabulary you need to learn so you can brush up on any difficult terms. You'll want to keep this vocabulary list handy once you actually start studying since you may need to add to it along the way.

Time Management

Once you have your set of study concepts, decide how to spread them out over the time you have left before the test. Break your study plan into small, clear goals so you have a manageable task for each day and know exactly what you're doing. Then just focus on one small step at a time. When you manage your time this way, you don't need to spend hours at a time studying. Studying a small block of content for a short period each day helps you retain information better and avoid stressing over how much you have left to do. You can relax knowing that you have a plan to cover everything in time. In order for this strategy to be effective though, you have to start studying early and stick to your schedule. Avoid the exhaustion and futility that comes from last-minute cramming!

Study Environment

The environment you study in has a big impact on your learning. Studying in a coffee shop, while probably more enjoyable, is not likely to be as fruitful as studying in a quiet room. It's important to keep distractions to a minimum. You're only planning to study for a short block of time, so make the most of it. Don't pause to check your phone or get up to find a snack. It's also important to **avoid multitasking**. Research has consistently shown that multitasking will make your studying dramatically less effective. Your study area should also be comfortable and well-lit so you don't have the distraction of straining your eyes or sitting on an uncomfortable chair.

The time of day you study is also important. You want to be rested and alert. Don't wait until just before bedtime. Study when you'll be most likely to comprehend and remember. Even better, if you know what time of day your test will be, set that time aside for study. That way your brain will be used to working on that subject at that specific time and you'll have a better chance of recalling information.

Finally, it can be helpful to team up with others who are studying for the same test. Your actual studying should be done in as isolated an environment as possible, but the work of organizing the information and setting up the study plan can be divided up. In between study sessions, you can discuss with your teammates the concepts that you're all studying and quiz each other on the details. Just be sure that your teammates are as serious about the test as you are. If you find that your study time is being replaced with social time, you might need to find a new team.

Copyright © Mometrix Media. You have been licensed one copy of this document for personal use only. Any other reproduction or redistribution is strictly prohibited. All rights reserved.

Secret Key #2 – Make Your Studying Count

You're devoting a lot of time and effort to preparing for this test, so you want to be absolutely certain it will pay off. This means doing more than just reading the content and hoping you can remember it on test day. It's important to make every minute of study count. There are two main areas you can focus on to make your studying count:

Retention

It doesn't matter how much time you study if you can't remember the material. You need to make sure you are retaining the concepts. To check your retention of the information you're learning, try recalling it at later times with minimal prompting. Try carrying around flashcards and glance at one or two from time to time or ask a friend who's also studying for the test to quiz you.

To enhance your retention, look for ways to put the information into practice so that you can apply it rather than simply recalling it. If you're using the information in practical ways, it will be much easier to remember. Similarly, it helps to solidify a concept in your mind if you're not only reading it to yourself but also explaining it to someone else. Ask a friend to let you teach them about a concept you're a little shaky on (or speak aloud to an imaginary audience if necessary). As you try to summarize, define, give examples, and answer your friend's questions, you'll understand the concepts better and they will stay with you longer. Finally, step back for a big picture view and ask yourself how each piece of information fits with the whole subject. When you link the different concepts together and see them working together as a whole, it's easier to remember the individual components.

Finally, practice showing your work on any multi-step problems, even if you're just studying. Writing out each step you take to solve a problem will help solidify the process in your mind, and you'll be more likely to remember it during the test.

Modality

Modality simply refers to the means or method by which you study. Choosing a study modality that fits your own individual learning style is crucial. No two people learn best in exactly the same way, so it's important to know your strengths and use them to your advantage.

For example, if you learn best by visualization, focus on visualizing a concept in your mind and draw an image or a diagram. Try color-coding your notes, illustrating them, or creating symbols that will trigger your mind to recall a learned concept. If you learn best by hearing or discussing information, find a study partner who learns the same way or read aloud to yourself. Think about how to put the information in your own words. Imagine that you are giving a lecture on the topic and record yourself so you can listen to it later.

For any learning style, flashcards can be helpful. Organize the information so you can take advantage of spare moments to review. Underline key words or phrases. Use different colors for different categories. Mnemonic devices (such as creating a short list in which every item starts with the same letter) can also help with retention. Find what works best for you and use it to store the information in your mind most effectively and easily.

Copyright © Mometrix Media. You have been licensed one copy of this document for personal use only. Any other reproduction or redistribution is strictly prohibited. All rights reserved.

Secret Key #3 – Practice the Right Way

Your success on test day depends not only on how many hours you put into preparing, but also on whether you prepared the right way. It's good to check along the way to see if your studying is paying off. One of the most effective ways to do this is by taking practice tests to evaluate your progress. Practice tests are useful because they show exactly where you need to improve. Every time you take a practice test, pay special attention to these three groups of questions:

- The questions you got wrong
- The questions you had to guess on, even if you guessed right
- The questions you found difficult or slow to work through

This will show you exactly what your weak areas are, and where you need to devote more study time. Ask yourself why each of these questions gave you trouble. Was it because you didn't understand the material? Was it because you didn't remember the vocabulary? Do you need more repetitions on this type of question to build speed and confidence? Dig into those questions and figure out how you can strengthen your weak areas as you go back to review the material.

Additionally, many practice tests have a section explaining the answer choices. It can be tempting to read the explanation and think that you now have a good understanding of the concept. However, an explanation likely only covers part of the question's broader context. Even if the explanation makes sense, **go back and investigate** every concept related to the question until you're positive you have a thorough understanding.

As you go along, keep in mind that the practice test is just that: practice. Memorizing these questions and answers will not be very helpful on the actual test because it is unlikely to have any of the same exact questions. If you only know the right answers to the sample questions, you won't be prepared for the real thing. **Study the concepts** until you understand them fully, and then you'll be able to answer any question that shows up on the test.

It's important to wait on the practice tests until you're ready. If you take a test on your first day of study, you may be overwhelmed by the amount of material covered and how much you need to learn. Work up to it gradually.

On test day, you'll need to be prepared for answering questions, managing your time, and using the test-taking strategies you've learned. It's a lot to balance, like a mental marathon that will have a big impact on your future. Like training for a marathon, you'll need to start slowly and work your way up. When test day arrives, you'll be ready.

Start with the strategies you've read in the first two Secret Keys—plan your course and study in the way that works best for you. If you have time, consider using multiple study resources to get different approaches to the same concepts. It can be helpful to see difficult concepts from more than one angle. Then find a good source for practice tests. Many times, the test website will suggest potential study resources or provide sample tests.

Copyright © Mometrix Media. You have been licensed one copy of this document for personal use only. Any other reproduction or redistribution is strictly prohibited. All rights reserved.

Practice Test Strategy

When you're ready to start taking practice tests, follow this strategy:

Untimed and Open-Book Practice

Take the first test with no time constraints and with your notes and study guide handy. Take your time and focus on applying the strategies you've learned.

Timed and Open-Book Practice

Take the second practice test open-book as well, but set a timer and practice pacing yourself to finish in time.

Timed and Closed-Book Practice

Take any other practice tests as if it were test day. Set a timer and put away your study materials. Sit at a table or desk in a quiet room, imagine yourself at the testing center, and answer questions as quickly and accurately as possible.

Keep repeating timed and closed-book tests on a regular basis until you run out of practice tests or it's time for the actual test. Your mind will be ready for the schedule and stress of test day, and you'll be able to focus on recalling the material you've learned.

Copyright © Mometrix Media. You have been licensed one copy of this document for personal use only. Any other reproduction or redistribution is strictly prohibited. All rights reserved.

Secret Key #4 – Pace Yourself

Once you're fully prepared for the material on the test, your biggest challenge on test day will be managing your time. Just knowing that the clock is ticking can make you panic even if you have plenty of time left. Work on pacing yourself so you can build confidence against the time constraints of the exam. Pacing is a difficult skill to master, especially in a high-pressure environment, so **practice is vital**.

Set time expectations for your pace based on how much time is available. For example, if a section has 60 questions and the time limit is 30 minutes, you know you have to average 30 seconds or less per question in order to answer them all. Although 30 seconds is the hard limit, set 25 seconds per question as your goal, so you reserve extra time to spend on harder questions. When you budget extra time for the harder questions, you no longer have any reason to stress when those questions take longer to answer.

Don't let this time expectation distract you from working through the test at a calm, steady pace, but keep it in mind so you don't spend too much time on any one question. Recognize that taking extra time on one question you don't understand may keep you from answering two that you do understand later in the test. If your time limit for a question is up and you're still not sure of the answer, mark it and move on, and come back to it later if the time and the test format allow. If the testing format doesn't allow you to return to earlier questions, just make an educated guess; then put it out of your mind and move on.

On the easier questions, be careful not to rush. It may seem wise to hurry through them so you have more time for the challenging ones, but it's not worth missing one if you know the concept and just didn't take the time to read the question fully. Work efficiently but make sure you understand the question and have looked at all of the answer choices, since more than one may seem right at first.

Even if you're paying attention to the time, you may find yourself a little behind at some point. You should speed up to get back on track, but do so wisely. Don't panic; just take a few seconds less on each question until you're caught up. Don't guess without thinking, but do look through the answer choices and eliminate any you know are wrong. If you can get down to two choices, it is often worthwhile to guess from those. Once you've chosen an answer, move on and don't dwell on any that you skipped or had to hurry through. If a question was taking too long, chances are it was one of the harder ones, so you weren't as likely to get it right anyway.

On the other hand, if you find yourself getting ahead of schedule, it may be beneficial to slow down a little. The more quickly you work, the more likely you are to make a careless mistake that will affect your score. You've budgeted time for each question, so don't be afraid to spend that time. Practice an efficient but careful pace to get the most out of the time you have.

Copyright © Mometrix Media. You have been licensed one copy of this document for personal use only. Any other reproduction or redistribution is strictly prohibited. All rights reserved.

Secret Key #5 – Have a Plan for Guessing

When you're taking the test, you may find yourself stuck on a question. Some of the answer choices seem better than others, but you don't see the one answer choice that is obviously correct. What do you do?

The scenario described above is very common, yet most test takers have not effectively prepared for it. Developing and practicing a plan for guessing may be one of the single most effective uses of your time as you get ready for the exam.

In developing your plan for guessing, there are three questions to address:

- When should you start the guessing process?
- How should you narrow down the choices?
- Which answer should you choose?

When to Start the Guessing Process

Unless your plan for guessing is to select C every time (which, despite its merits, is not what we recommend), you need to leave yourself enough time to apply your answer elimination strategies. Since you have a limited amount of time for each question, that means that if you're going to give yourself the best shot at guessing correctly, you have to decide quickly whether or not you will guess.

Of course, the best-case scenario is that you don't have to guess at all, so first, see if you can answer the question based on your knowledge of the subject and basic reasoning skills. Focus on the key words in the question and try to jog your memory of related topics. Give yourself a chance to bring the knowledge to mind, but once you realize that you don't have (or you can't access) the knowledge you need to answer the question, it's time to start the guessing process.

It's almost always better to start the guessing process too early than too late. It only takes a few seconds to remember something and answer the question from knowledge. Carefully eliminating wrong answer choices takes longer. Plus, going through the process of eliminating answer choices can actually help jog your memory.

Summary: Start the guessing process as soon as you decide that you can't answer the question based on your knowledge.

Copyright © Mometrix Media. You have been licensed one copy of this document for personal use only. Any other reproduction or redistribution is strictly prohibited. All rights reserved.

How to Narrow Down the Choices

The next chapter in this book (**Test-Taking Strategies**) includes a wide range of strategies for how to approach questions and how to look for answer choices to eliminate. You will definitely want to read those carefully, practice them, and figure out which ones work best for you. Here though, we're going to address a mindset rather than a particular strategy.

Your chances of guessing an answer correctly depend on how many options you are choosing from.

How many choices you have	How likely you are to guess correctly
5	20%
4	25%
3	33%
2	50%
1	100%

You can see from this chart just how valuable it is to be able to eliminate incorrect answers and make an educated guess, but there are two things that many test takers do that cause them to miss out on the benefits of guessing:

- Accidentally eliminating the correct answer
- Selecting an answer based on an impression

We'll look at the first one here, and the second one in the next section.

To avoid accidentally eliminating the correct answer, we recommend a thought exercise called **the $5 challenge**. In this challenge, you only eliminate an answer choice from contention if you are willing to bet $5 on it being wrong. Why $5? Five dollars is a small but not insignificant amount of money. It's an amount you could afford to lose but wouldn't want to throw away. And while losing $5 once might not hurt too much, doing it twenty times will set you back $100. In the same way, each small decision you make—eliminating a choice here, guessing on a question there—won't by itself impact your score very much, but when you put them all together, they can make a big difference. By holding each answer choice elimination decision to a higher standard, you can reduce the risk of accidentally eliminating the correct answer.

The $5 challenge can also be applied in a positive sense: If you are willing to bet $5 that an answer choice *is* correct, go ahead and mark it as correct.

Summary: Only eliminate an answer choice if you are willing to bet $5 that it is wrong.

Copyright © Mometrix Media. You have been licensed one copy of this document for personal use only. Any other reproduction or redistribution is strictly prohibited. All rights reserved.

Which Answer to Choose

You're taking the test. You've run into a hard question and decided you'll have to guess. You've eliminated all the answer choices you're willing to bet $5 on. Now you have to pick an answer. Why do we even need to talk about this? Why can't you just pick whichever one you feel like when the time comes?

The answer to these questions is that if you don't come into the test with a plan, you'll rely on your impression to select an answer choice, and if you do that, you risk falling into a trap. The test writers know that everyone who takes their test will be guessing on some of the questions, so they intentionally write wrong answer choices to seem plausible. You still have to pick an answer though, and if the wrong answer choices are designed to look right, how can you ever be sure that you're not falling for their trap? The best solution we've found to this dilemma is to take the decision out of your hands entirely. Here is the process we recommend:

Once you've eliminated any choices that you are confident (willing to bet $5) are wrong, select the first remaining choice as your answer.

Whether you choose to select the first remaining choice, the second, or the last, the important thing is that you use some preselected standard. Using this approach guarantees that you will not be enticed into selecting an answer choice that looks right, because you are not basing your decision on how the answer choices look.

This is not meant to make you question your knowledge. Instead, it is to help you recognize the difference between your knowledge and your impressions. There's a huge difference between thinking an answer is right because of what you know, and thinking an answer is right because it looks or sounds like it should be right.

Summary: To ensure that your selection is appropriately random, make a predetermined selection from among all answer choices you have not eliminated.

Copyright © Mometrix Media. You have been licensed one copy of this document for personal use only. Any other reproduction or redistribution is strictly prohibited. All rights reserved.

Test-Taking Strategies

This section contains a list of test-taking strategies that you may find helpful as you work through the test. By taking what you know and applying logical thought, you can maximize your chances of answering any question correctly!

It is very important to realize that every question is different and every person is different: no single strategy will work on every question, and no single strategy will work for every person. That's why we've included all of them here, so you can try them out and determine which ones work best for different types of questions and which ones work best for you.

Question Strategies

Read Carefully

Read the question and answer choices carefully. Don't miss the question because you misread the terms. You have plenty of time to read each question thoroughly and make sure you understand what is being asked. Yet a happy medium must be attained, so don't waste too much time. You must read carefully, but efficiently.

Contextual Clues

Look for contextual clues. If the question includes a word you are not familiar with, look at the immediate context for some indication of what the word might mean. Contextual clues can often give you all the information you need to decipher the meaning of an unfamiliar word. Even if you can't determine the meaning, you may be able to narrow down the possibilities enough to make a solid guess at the answer to the question.

Prefixes

If you're having trouble with a word in the question or answer choices, try dissecting it. Take advantage of every clue that the word might include. Prefixes and suffixes can be a huge help. Usually they allow you to determine a basic meaning. Pre- means before, post- means after, pro - is positive, de- is negative. From prefixes and suffixes, you can get an idea of the general meaning of the word and try to put it into context.

Hedge Words

Watch out for critical hedge words, such as *likely, may, can, sometimes, often, almost, mostly, usually, generally, rarely,* and *sometimes.* Question writers insert these hedge phrases to cover every possibility. Often an answer choice will be wrong simply because it leaves no room for exception. Be on guard for answer choices that have definitive words such as *exactly* and *always.*

Switchback Words

Stay alert for *switchbacks.* These are the words and phrases frequently used to alert you to shifts in thought. The most common switchback words are *but, although,* and *however.* Others include *nevertheless, on the other hand, even though, while, in spite of, despite, regardless of.* Switchback words are important to catch because they can change the direction of the question or an answer choice.

Copyright © Mometrix Media. You have been licensed one copy of this document for personal use only. Any other reproduction or redistribution is strictly prohibited. All rights reserved.

Face Value

When in doubt, use common sense. Accept the situation in the problem at face value. Don't read too much into it. These problems will not require you to make wild assumptions. If you have to go beyond creativity and warp time or space in order to have an answer choice fit the question, then you should move on and consider the other answer choices. These are normal problems rooted in reality. The applicable relationship or explanation may not be readily apparent, but it is there for you to figure out. Use your common sense to interpret anything that isn't clear.

Answer Choice Strategies

Answer Selection

The most thorough way to pick an answer choice is to identify and eliminate wrong answers until only one is left, then confirm it is the correct answer. Sometimes an answer choice may immediately seem right, but be careful. The test writers will usually put more than one reasonable answer choice on each question, so take a second to read all of them and make sure that the other choices are not equally obvious. As long as you have time left, it is better to read every answer choice than to pick the first one that looks right without checking the others.

Answer Choice Families

An answer choice family consists of two (in rare cases, three) answer choices that are very similar in construction and cannot all be true at the same time. If you see two answer choices that are direct opposites or parallels, one of them is usually the correct answer. For instance, if one answer choice says that quantity x increases and another either says that quantity x decreases (opposite) or says that quantity y increases (parallel), then those answer choices would fall into the same family. An answer choice that doesn't match the construction of the answer choice family is more likely to be incorrect. Most questions will not have answer choice families, but when they do appear, you should be prepared to recognize them.

Eliminate Answers

Eliminate answer choices as soon as you realize they are wrong, but make sure you consider all possibilities. If you are eliminating answer choices and realize that the last one you are left with is also wrong, don't panic. Start over and consider each choice again. There may be something you missed the first time that you will realize on the second pass.

Avoid Fact Traps

Don't be distracted by an answer choice that is factually true but doesn't answer the question. You are looking for the choice that answers the question. Stay focused on what the question is asking for so you don't accidentally pick an answer that is true but incorrect. Always go back to the question and make sure the answer choice you've selected actually answers the question and is not merely a true statement.

Extreme Statements

In general, you should avoid answers that put forth extreme actions as standard practice or proclaim controversial ideas as established fact. An answer choice that states the "process should be used in certain situations, if…" is much more likely to be correct than one that states the "process should be discontinued completely." The first is a calm rational statement and doesn't even make a

- 11 -

Copyright © Mometrix Media. You have been licensed one copy of this document for personal use only. Any other reproduction or redistribution is strictly prohibited. All rights reserved.

definitive, uncompromising stance, using a hedge word *if* to provide wiggle room, whereas the second choice is a radical idea and far more extreme.

Benchmark

As you read through the answer choices and you come across one that seems to answer the question well, mentally select that answer choice. This is not your final answer, but it's the one that will help you evaluate the other answer choices. The one that you selected is your benchmark or standard for judging each of the other answer choices. Every other answer choice must be compared to your benchmark. That choice is correct until proven otherwise by another answer choice beating it. If you find a better answer, then that one becomes your new benchmark. Once you've decided that no other choice answers the question as well as your benchmark, you have your final answer.

Predict the Answer

Before you even start looking at the answer choices, it is often best to try to predict the answer. When you come up with the answer on your own, it is easier to avoid distractions and traps because you will know exactly what to look for. The right answer choice is unlikely to be word-for-word what you came up with, but it should be a close match. Even if you are confident that you have the right answer, you should still take the time to read each option before moving on.

General Strategies

Tough Questions

If you are stumped on a problem or it appears too hard or too difficult, don't waste time. Move on! Remember though, if you can quickly check for obviously incorrect answer choices, your chances of guessing correctly are greatly improved. Before you completely give up, at least try to knock out a couple of possible answers. Eliminate what you can and then guess at the remaining answer choices before moving on.

Check Your Work

Since you will probably not know every term listed and the answer to every question, it is important that you get credit for the ones that you do know. Don't miss any questions through careless mistakes. If at all possible, try to take a second to look back over your answer selection and make sure you've selected the correct answer choice and haven't made a costly careless mistake (such as marking an answer choice that you didn't mean to mark). This quick double check should more than pay for itself in caught mistakes for the time it costs.

Pace Yourself

It's easy to be overwhelmed when you're looking at a page full of questions; your mind is confused and full of random thoughts, and the clock is ticking down faster than you would like. Calm down and maintain the pace that you have set for yourself. Especially as you get down to the last few minutes of the test, don't let the small numbers on the clock make you panic. As long as you are on track by monitoring your pace, you are guaranteed to have time for each question.

Copyright © Mometrix Media. You have been licensed one copy of this document for personal use only. Any other reproduction or redistribution is strictly prohibited. All rights reserved.

Don't Rush

It is very easy to make errors when you are in a hurry. Maintaining a fast pace in answering questions is pointless if it makes you miss questions that you would have gotten right otherwise. Test writers like to include distracting information and wrong answers that seem right. Taking a little extra time to avoid careless mistakes can make all the difference in your test score. Find a pace that allows you to be confident in the answers that you select.

Keep Moving

Panicking will not help you pass the test, so do your best to stay calm and keep moving. Taking deep breaths and going through the answer elimination steps you practiced can help to break through a stress barrier and keep your pace.

Final Notes

The combination of a solid foundation of content knowledge and the confidence that comes from practicing your plan for applying that knowledge is the key to maximizing your performance on test day. As your foundation of content knowledge is built up and strengthened, you'll find that the strategies included in this chapter become more and more effective in helping you quickly sift through the distractions and traps of the test to isolate the correct answer.

Now it's time to move on to the test content chapters of this book, but be sure to keep your goal in mind. As you read, think about how you will be able to apply this information on the test. If you've already seen sample questions for the test and you have an idea of the question format and style, try to come up with questions of your own that you can answer based on what you're reading. This will give you valuable practice applying your knowledge in the same ways you can expect to on test day.

Good luck and good studying!

Copyright © Mometrix Media. You have been licensed one copy of this document for personal use only. Any other reproduction or redistribution is strictly prohibited. All rights reserved.

Copyright © Mometrix Media. You have been licensed one copy of this document for personal use only. Any other reproduction or redistribution is strictly prohibited. All rights reserved.

Introduction

Thank you for your purchase of *Secrets of the TEAS® V Exam*. This study manual includes comprehensive review sections on each of the four TEAS test sections: Reading, Mathematics, Science, and English and Language Usage. Following those review sections are three complete TEAS practice tests. Each practice test is followed by detailed answer explanations.

The TEAS is an important test, so it is essential that you adequately prepare for your test day. Be sure to set aside enough study time to be able to take each of the practice tests using only the amount of time that is specified. You are encouraged to minimize your external distractions in order to make the practice test conditions as similar to the real test conditions as possible.

Below is a breakdown of the four sections on the exam, including the subcategories, how many questions are in each section, and how much time will be allotted for you to complete that section. Each section of the test contains more questions than will actually be scored. The other questions are used for testing purposes.

Content Areas	Time Allowed	Number of Test Items	Percent of Test Items	Number of Scored Test Items
Reading	**58 min**	**48**	**28%**	**42**
Paragraph and Passage Comprehension				19
Informational Source Comprehension				23
Mathematics	**51 min**	**34**	**20%**	**30**
Numbers and Operations				19
Measurement				4
Data Interpretation				3
Algebraic Applications				4
Science	**66 min**	**54**	**32%**	**48**
Scientific Reasoning				11
Human Body Science				15
Life Science				14
Earth and Physical Science				8
English and Language Usage	**34 min**	**34**	**20%**	**30**
Grammar and Word Meanings in Context				15
Spelling and Punctuation				9
Structure				6
Total	**209 min**	**170**		**150**

Copyright © Mometrix Media. You have been licensed one copy of this document for personal use only. Any other reproduction or redistribution is strictly prohibited. All rights reserved.

Reading

Paragraph and Passage Comprehension

Primary sources

When conducting research, it is important to depend on reputable primary sources. A primary source is the documentary evidence closest to the subject being studied. For instance, the primary sources for an essay about penguins would be photographs and recordings of the birds, as well as accounts of people who have studied penguins in person. A secondary source would be a review of a movie about penguins or a book outlining the observations made by others. A primary source should be credible and, if it is on a subject that is still being explored, recent. One way to assess the credibility of a work is to see how often it is mentioned in other books and articles on the same subject. Just by reading the works cited and bibliographies of other books, one can get a sense of what the reliable sources authorities in the field are.

Internet sources

The Internet was once considered a poor place to find sources for an essay or article, but its credibility has improved greatly over the years. Still, students need to exercise caution when performing research online. The best sources are those affiliated with established institutions, such as universities, public libraries, and think tanks. Most newspapers are available online, and many of them allow the public to browse their archives. Magazines frequently offer similar services. When obtaining information from an unknown website, however, one must exercise considerably more caution. A website can be considered trustworthy if it is referenced by other sites that are known to be reputable. Also, credible sites tend to be properly maintained and frequently updated. A site is easier to trust when the author provides some information about himself, including some credentials that indicate expertise in the subject matter.

Topic and summary sentences

Topic and summary sentences are a convenient way to encapsulate the main idea of a text. In some textbooks and academic articles, the author will place a topic or summary sentence at the beginning of each section as a means of preparing the reader for what is to come. Research suggests that the brain is more receptive to new information when it has been prepared by the presentation of the main idea or some key words. The phenomenon is somewhat akin to the primer coat of paint that allows subsequent coats of paint to absorb more easily. A good topic sentence will be clear and not contain any jargon. When topic or summary sentences are not provided, good readers can jot down their own so that they can find their place in a text and refresh their memory.

Fact and opinion

Readers must always be conscious of the distinction between fact and opinion. A fact can be subjected to analysis and can be either proved or disproved. An opinion, on the other hand, is the author's personal thoughts or feelings which may not be alterable by research or evidence. If the author writes that the distance from New York to Boston is about two hundred miles, then he or she is stating a fact. If an author writes that New York is too crowded, then he or she is giving an opinion because there is no objective standard for overpopulation.

An opinion may be indicated by words like *believe*, *think*, or *feel*. Readers must be aware that an opinion may be supported by facts. For instance, the author might give the population density of

Copyright © Mometrix Media. You have been licensed one copy of this document for personal use only. Any other reproduction or redistribution is strictly prohibited. All rights reserved.

New York as a reason for an overcrowded population. An opinion supported by fact tends to be more convincing. On the other hand, when authors support their opinions with other opinions, readers should not be persuaded by the argument to any degree.

> **Review Video: Fact or Opinion**
> Visit mometrix.com/academy and enter code: 870899

Biases and stereotypes

Every author has a point-of-view, but authors demonstrate a bias when they ignore reasonable counterarguments or distort opposing viewpoints. A bias is evident whenever the author is unfair or inaccurate in his or her presentation. Bias may be intentional or unintentional, and readers should be skeptical of the author's argument. Remember that a biased author may still be correct; however, the author will be correct in spite of his or her bias, not because of the bias. A stereotype is like a bias, yet a stereotype is applied specifically to a group or place. Stereotyping is considered to be particularly abhorrent because the practice promotes negative generalizations about people. Readers should be very cautious of authors who stereotype in their writing. These faulty assumptions typically reveal the author's ignorance and lack of curiosity.

> **Review Video: Bias**
> Visit mometrix.com/academy and enter code: 456336

Identifying the logical conclusion

Identifying a logical conclusion can help you determine whether you agree with the writer or not. Coming to this conclusion is much like making an inference: the approach requires you to combine the information given by the text with what you already know in order to make a logical conclusion. If the author intended the reader to draw a certain conclusion, then you can expect the author's argumentation and detail to be leading in that direction. One way to approach the task of drawing conclusions is to make brief notes of all the points made by the author. When the notes are arranged on paper, they may clarify the logical conclusion. Another way to approach conclusions is to consider whether the reasoning of the author raises any pertinent questions. Sometimes you will be able to draw several conclusions from a passage. On occasion these will be conclusions that were never imagined by the author. Therefore, be aware that these conclusions must be supported directly by the text.

Topics and main ideas

One of the most important skills in reading comprehension is the identification of **topics** and **main ideas.** There is a subtle difference between these two features. The topic is the subject of a text (i.e., what the text is all about). The main idea, on the other hand, is the most important point being made by the author. The topic is usually expressed in a few words at the most while the main idea often needs a full sentence to be completely defined. As an example, a short passage might have the topic of penguins and the main idea could be written as *Penguins are different from other birds in many ways*. In most nonfiction writing, the topic and the main idea will be stated directly and often appear in a sentence at the very beginning or end of the text. When being tested on an understanding of the author's topic, you may be able to skim the passage for the general idea, by reading only the first sentence of each paragraph. A body paragraph's first sentence is often--but not always--the main topic sentence which gives you a summary of the content in the paragraph.

Copyright © Mometrix Media. You have been licensed one copy of this document for personal use only. Any other reproduction or redistribution is strictly prohibited. All rights reserved.

However, there are cases in which the reader must figure out an unstated topic or main idea. In these instances, you must read every sentence of the text and try to come up with an overarching idea that is supported by each of those sentences.

Review Video: Topics and Main Ideas
Visit mometrix.com/academy and enter code: 407801

Supporting details

Supporting details provide evidence and backing for the main point. In order to show that a main idea is correct, or valid, authors add details that prove their point. All texts contain details, but they are only classified as supporting details when they serve to reinforce some larger point. Supporting details are most commonly found in informative and persuasive texts. In some cases, they will be clearly indicated with terms like *for example* or *for instance*, or they will be enumerated with terms like *first*, *second*, and *last*. However, you need to be prepared for texts that do not contain those indicators. As a reader, you should consider whether the author's supporting details really back up his or her main point. Supporting details can be factual and correct, yet they may not be relevant to the author's point. Conversely, supporting details can seem pertinent, but they can be ineffective because they are based on opinion or assertions that cannot be proven.

Review Video: Supporting Details
Visit mometrix.com/academy and enter code: 396297

Themes

Themes are seldom expressed directly in a text and can be difficult to identify. A theme is an issue, an idea, or a question raised by the text. For instance, a theme of *Cinderella* (the Charles Perrault version) is perseverance as the title character serves her step-sisters and step-mother, and the prince seeks to find the girl with the missing slipper. A passage may have many themes, and you--as a dedicated reader--must take care to identify only themes that you are asked to find. One common characteristic of themes is that they raise more questions than they answer. In a good piece of fiction, authors are trying to elevate the reader's perspective and encourage him or her to consider the themes in a deeper way. In the process of reading, one can identify themes by constantly asking about the general issues that the text is addressing. A good way to evaluate an author's approach to a theme is to begin reading with a question in mind (e.g., How does this text approach the theme of love?) and to look for evidence in the text that addresses that question.

Review Video: Theme
Visit mometrix.com/academy and enter code: 732074

Persuasive writing

In a persuasive essay, the author is attempting to change the reader's mind or convince him or her of something that he or she did not believe previously. There are several identifying characteristics of persuasive writing. One is opinion presented as fact. When authors attempt to persuade readers, they often present their opinions as if they were fact. Readers must be on guard for statements that sound factual but which cannot be subjected to research, observation, or experiment. Another characteristic of persuasive writing is emotional language. An author will often try to play on the emotions of readers by appealing to their sympathy or sense of morality. When an author uses colorful or evocative language with the intent of arousing the reader's passions, then the author

Copyright © Mometrix Media. You have been licensed one copy of this document for personal use only. Any other reproduction or redistribution is strictly prohibited. All rights reserved.

may be attempting to persuade. Finally, in many cases, a persuasive text will give an unfair explanation of opposing positions, if these positions are mentioned at all.

Appeal to emotion

Sometimes, authors will appeal to the reader's emotion in an attempt to persuade or to distract the reader from the weakness of the argument. For instance, the author may try to inspire the pity of the reader by delivering a heart-rending story. An author also might use the bandwagon approach, in which he suggests that his opinion is correct because it is held by the majority. Some authors resort to name-calling, in which insults and harsh words are delivered to the opponent in an attempt to distract. In advertising, a common appeal is the celebrity testimonial, in which a famous person endorses a product. Of course, the fact that a famous person likes something should not really mean anything to the reader. These and other emotional appeals are usually evidence of poor reasoning and a weak argument.

> **Review Video: Appeal to Emotion**
> Visit mometrix.com/academy and enter code: 163442

Informative texts

An informative text is written to educate and enlighten readers. Informative texts are almost always nonfiction and are rarely structured as a story. The intention of an informative text is to deliver information in the most comprehensible way. So, look for the structure of the text to be very clear. In an informative text, the thesis statement is one sentence (or sometimes two sentences) that normally appears at the end of the first paragraph. The author may use some colorful language, but he or she is likely to put more emphasis on clarity and precision. Informative essays do not typically appeal to the emotions. They often contain facts and figures and rarely include the opinion of the author; however, readers should remain aware of the possibility for a bias as those facts are presented. Sometimes a persuasive essay can resemble an informative essay, especially if the author maintains an even tone and presents his or her views as if they were established fact.

> **Review Video: Informative Text**
> Visit mometrix.com/academy and enter code: 924964

Entertaining texts

The success or failure of an author's intent to **entertain** is determined by those who read the author's work. Entertaining texts may be either fiction or nonfiction, and they may describe real or imagined people, places, and events. Entertaining texts are often narratives or poems. A text that is written to entertain is likely to contain colorful language that engages the imagination and the emotions. Such writing often features a great deal of figurative language, which typically enlivens the subject matter with images and analogies.

Though an entertaining text is not usually written to persuade or inform, authors may accomplish both of these tasks in their work. An entertaining text may appeal to the reader's emotions and cause him or her to think differently about a particular subject. In any case, entertaining texts tend to showcase the personality of the author more than other types of writing.

Copyright © Mometrix Media. You have been licensed one copy of this document for personal use only. Any other reproduction or redistribution is strictly prohibited. All rights reserved.

Expression of feelings

When an author intends to **express feelings,** he or she may use expressive and bold language. An author may write with emotion for any number of reasons. Sometimes, authors will express feelings because they are describing a personal situation of great pain or happiness. In other situations, authors will attempt to persuade the reader and will use emotion to stir up the passions. This kind of expression is easy to identify when the writer uses phrases like *I felt* and *I sense.* However, readers may find that the author will simply describe feelings without introducing them. As a reader, you must know the importance of recognizing when an author is expressing emotion and not to become overwhelmed by sympathy or passion. Readers should maintain some detachment so that they can still evaluate the strength of the author's argument or the quality of the writing.

Predictions based on prior knowledge

A prediction is a guess about what will happen next. Readers constantly make predictions based on what they have read and what they already know. Consider the following sentence: *Staring at the computer screen in shock, Kim blindly reached over for the brimming glass of water on the shelf to her side.* The sentence suggests that Kim is agitated, and that she is not looking at the glass that she is going to pick up. So, a reader might predict that Kim is going to knock over the glass. Of course, not every prediction will be accurate: perhaps Kim will pick the glass up cleanly. Nevertheless, the author has certainly created the expectation that the water might be spilled. Predictions are always subject to revision as the reader acquires more information.

Making inferences

Readers are often required to understand a text that claims and suggests ideas without stating them directly. An **inference** is a piece of information that is implied but not written outright by the author. For instance, consider the following sentence: *After the final out of the inning, the fans were filled with joy and rushed the field.* From this sentence, a reader can infer that the fans were watching a baseball game and their team won the game. Readers should take great care to avoid using information beyond the provided passage before making inferences. As you practice drawing inferences, you will find that they require concentration and attention.

Drawing conclusions

In addition to inference and prediction, readers must often **draw conclusions** about the information they have read. When asked for a *conclusion* that may be drawn, look for critical "hedge" phrases, such as *likely, may, can, will often,* among many others. When you are being tested on this knowledge, remember the question that writers insert into these hedge phrases to cover every possibility. Often an answer will be wrong simply because there is no room for exception. Extreme positive or negative answers (such as always or never) are usually not correct. The reader should not use any outside knowledge that is not gathered from the passage to answer the related questions. Correct answers can be derived straight from the passage.

Problem-solution text structure

Some nonfiction texts are organized to present a problem followed by a solution. For this type of text, the problem is often explained before the solution is offered. In some cases, as when the problem is well known, the solution may be introduced briefly at the beginning. Other passages may focus on the solution, and the problem will be referenced only occasionally. Some texts will outline multiple solutions to a problem, leaving readers to choose among them. If the author has an

Copyright © Mometrix Media. You have been licensed one copy of this document for personal use only. Any other reproduction or redistribution is strictly prohibited. All rights reserved.

interest or an allegiance to one solution, he or she may fail to mention or describe accurately some of the other solutions. Readers should be careful of the author's agenda when reading a problem-solution text. Only by understanding the author's perspective and interests can one develop a proper judgment of the proposed solution.

Descriptive text

In a sense, almost all writing is descriptive, insofar as an author seeks to describe events, ideas, or people to the reader. Some texts, however, are primarily concerned with **description**. A descriptive text focuses on a particular subject and attempts to depict the subject in a way that will be clear to readers. Descriptive texts contain many adjectives and adverbs (i.e., words that give shades of meaning and create a more detailed mental picture for the reader). A descriptive text fails when it is unclear to the reader. A descriptive text will certainly be informative, and the passage may be persuasive and entertaining as well.

> **Review Video: Descriptive Texts**
> Visit mometrix.com/academy and enter code: 174903

Sequence

Readers must be able to identify a text's **sequence**, or the order in which things happen. Often, when the sequence is very important to the author, the text is indicated with signal words like *first*, *then*, *next*, and *last*. However, a sequence can be merely implied and must be noted by the reader. Consider the sentence *He walked through the garden and gave water and fertilizer to the plants*. Clearly, the man did not walk through the garden before he collected water and fertilizer for the plants. So, the implied sequence is that he first collected water, then he collected fertilizer, next he walked through the garden, and last he gave water or fertilizer as necessary to the plants. Texts do not always proceed in an orderly sequence from first to last. Sometimes they begin at the end and start over at the beginning. As a reader, you can enhance your understanding of the passage by taking brief notes to clarify the sequence.

> **Review Video: Sequence**
> Visit mometrix.com/academy and enter code: 489027

Comparison and contrast

Authors will use different stylistic and writing devices to make their meaning clear for readers. One of those devices is comparison and contrast. As mentioned previously, when an author describes the ways in which two things are alike, he or she is comparing them. When the author describes the ways in which two things are different, he or she is contrasting them. The "compare and contrast" essay is one of the most common forms in nonfiction. These passages are often signaled with certain words: a comparison may have indicating terms such as *both*, *same*, *like*, *too*, and *as well*; while a contrast may have terms like *but*, *however*, *on the other hand*, *instead*, and *yet*. Of course, comparisons and contrasts may be implicit without using any such signaling language. A single sentence may both compare and contrast. Consider the sentence *Brian and Sheila love ice cream, but Brian prefers vanilla and Sheila prefers strawberry*. In one sentence, the author has described both a similarity (love of ice cream) and a difference (favorite flavor).

> **Review Video: Compare and Contrast**
> Visit mometrix.com/academy and enter code: 798319

- 21 -

Copyright © Mometrix Media. You have been licensed one copy of this document for personal use only. Any other reproduction or redistribution is strictly prohibited. All rights reserved.

Cause and effect

One of the most common text structures is cause and effect. A cause is an act or event that makes something happen, and an effect is the thing that happens as a result of the cause. A cause-and-effect relationship is not always explicit, but there are some terms in English that signal causes, such as *since*, *because*, and *due to*. Furthermore, terms that signal effects include *consequently, therefore, this lead(s) to*. As an example, consider the sentence *Because the sky was clear, Ron did not bring an umbrella*. The cause is the clear sky, and the effect is that Ron did not bring an umbrella. However, readers may find that sometimes the cause-and-effect relationship will not be clearly noted. For instance, the sentence *He was late and missed the meeting* does not contain any signaling words, but the sentence still contains a cause (he was late) and an effect (he missed the meeting).

> **Review Video:** Rhetorical Strategy of Cause-and-Effect Analysis
> Visit mometrix.com/academy and enter code: 725944

Identifying an author's position

In order to be an effective reader, one must pay attention to the author's **position** and purpose. Even those texts that seem objective and impartial, like textbooks, have a position and bias. Readers need to take these positions into account when considering the author's message. When an author uses emotional language or clearly favors one side of an argument, his or her position is clear. However, the author's position may be evident not only in what he or she writes, but also in what he or she doesn't write. In a normal setting, a reader would want to review some other texts on the same topic in order to develop a view of the author's position. If this was not possible, then you would want to acquire some background about the author. However, since you are in the middle of an exam and the only source of information is the text, you should look for language and argumentation that seems to indicate a particular stance on the subject.

Purpose

Usually, identifying the **purpose** of an author is easier than identifying his or her position. In most cases, the author has no interest in hiding his or her purpose. A text that is meant to entertain, for instance, should be written to please the reader. Most narratives, or stories, are written to entertain, though they may also inform or persuade. Informative texts are easy to identify, while the most difficult purpose of a text to identify is persuasion because the author has an interest in making this purpose hard to detect. When a reader discovers that the author is trying to persuade, he or she should be skeptical of the argument. For this reason persuasive texts often try to establish an entertaining tone and hope to amuse the reader into agreement. On the other hand, an informative tone may be implemented to create an appearance of authority and objectivity.

An author's purpose is evident often in the organization of the text (e.g., section headings in bold font points to an informative text). However, you may not have such organization available to you in your exam. Instead, if the author makes his or her main idea clear from the beginning, then the likely purpose of the text is to inform. If the author begins by making a claim and provides various arguments to support that claim, then the purpose is probably to persuade. If the author tells a story or seems to want the attention of the reader more than to push a particular point or deliver information, then his or her purpose is most likely to entertain. As a reader, you must judge authors on how well they accomplish their purpose. In other words, you need to consider the type of

Copyright © Mometrix Media. You have been licensed one copy of this document for personal use only. Any other reproduction or redistribution is strictly prohibited. All rights reserved.

passage (e.g., technical, persuasive, etc.) that the author has written and whether the author has followed the requirements of the passage type.

Review Video: Purpose
Visit mometrix.com/academy and enter code: 511819

Narrative passage

A **narrative** passage is a story that can be fiction or nonfiction. However, there are a few elements that a text must have in order to be classified as a narrative. First, the text must have a plot (i.e., a series of events). Narratives often proceed in a clear sequence, but this is not a requirement. If the narrative is good, then these events will be interesting to readers. Second, a narrative has characters. These characters could be people, animals, or even inanimate objects--so long as they participate in the plot. Third, a narrative passage often contains figurative language which is meant to stimulate the imagination of readers by making comparisons and observations. For instance, a metaphor, a common piece of figurative language, is a description of one thing in terms of another. *The moon was a frosty snowball* is an example of a metaphor. In the literal sense this is obviously untrue, but the comparison suggests a certain mood for the reader.

Expository passage

An **expository** passage aims to inform and enlighten readers. The passage is nonfiction and usually centers around a simple, easily defined topic. Since the goal of exposition is to teach, such a passage should be as clear as possible. Often, an expository passage contains helpful organizing words, like *first*, *next*, *for example*, and *therefore*. These words keep the reader oriented in the text. Although expository passages do not need to feature colorful language and artful writing, they are often more effective with these features. For a reader, the challenge of expository passages is to maintain steady attention. Expository passages are not always about subjects that will naturally interest a reader, and the writer is often more concerned with clarity and comprehensibility than with engaging the reader. By reading actively, you will ensure a good habit of focus when reading an expository passage.

Technical passage

A **technical** passage is written to describe a complex object or process. Technical writing is common in medical and technological fields, in which complex ideas of mathematics, science, and engineering need to be explained simply and clearly. To ease comprehension, a technical passage usually proceeds in a very logical order. Technical passages often have clear headings and subheadings, which are used to keep the reader oriented in the text. Additionally, you will find that these passages divide sections up with numbers or letters. Many technical passages look more like an outline than a piece of prose. The amount of jargon or difficult vocabulary will vary in a technical passage depending on the intended audience. As much as possible, technical passages try to avoid language that the reader will have to research in order to understand the message, yet readers will find that jargon cannot always be avoided.

Persuasive passage

A **persuasive** passage is meant to change the mind of readers and lead them into agreement with the author. The persuasive intent may be very obvious or quite difficult to discern. In some cases, a persuasive passage will be indistinguishable from one that is informative. Both passages make an assertion and offer supporting details. However, a persuasive passage is more likely to appeal to the

Copyright © Mometrix Media. You have been licensed one copy of this document for personal use only. Any other reproduction or redistribution is strictly prohibited. All rights reserved.

reader's emotions and to make claims based on opinion. Persuasive passages may not describe alternate positions, but--when they do--they often display significant bias. Readers may find that a persuasive passage is giving the author's viewpoint, or the passage may adopt a seemingly objective tone. A persuasive passage is successful if it can make a convincing argument and win the trust of the reader.

Historical context

Historical context affects literature: the events, knowledge base, and assumptions of an author's time influence every aspect of his or her work. Sometimes, authors hold opinions and use language that would be considered inappropriate or immoral in a modern setting, but those ideas were acceptable in the author's time. As a reader, one should consider how the historical context influenced a work and how today's opinions and ideas shape the way that modern readers approach the works of the past. For instance, in most societies of the past, women were treated as second-class citizens. An author who wrote in 18th-century England might sound sexist to modern readers even if that author could be considered a feminist in his time. Readers should not have to excuse the faulty assumptions and prejudices of the past, but they should acknowledge that a person's thoughts and words are--in part--a result of the time and culture in which they lived.

> **Review Video: Historical Context**
> Visit mometrix.com/academy and enter code: 169770

Similar themes across cultures

A brief study of world literature suggests that writers from vastly different cultures address similar themes. For instance, works like the *Odyssey* and *Hamlet* both consider the individual's battle for self-control and independence. In most cultures, authors address themes of personal growth and the struggle for maturity. Another universal theme is the conflict between the individual and society. Works that are as culturally disparate as *Native Son*, the *Aeneid*, and *1984* dramatize how people struggle to maintain their personalities and dignity in large (sometimes) oppressive groups. Finally, many cultures have versions of the hero's or heroine's journey in which an adventurous person must overcome many obstacles in order to gain greater knowledge, power, and perspective. Some famous works that treat this theme are the *Epic of Gilgamesh*, Dante's *Divine Comedy*, and Cervantes' *Don Quixote*.

Difference in addressing themes in various cultures and genres

Authors from different genres and cultures may address similar themes, but they do so in different ways. For instance, poets are likely to address subject matter indirectly through the use of images and allusions. In a play, the author is more likely to dramatize themes by using characters to express opposing viewpoints--this disparity is known as a dialectical approach. In a passage, the author does not need to express themes directly; indeed, they can be expressed through events and actions. In some regional literatures, such as Greece or England, authors use more irony: their works have characters that express views and make decisions that are clearly disapproved of by the author. In Latin America, there is a great tradition of using supernatural events to illustrate themes about real life. Chinese and Japanese authors frequently use well-established regional forms (e.g., haiku poetry in Japan) to organize their treatment of universal themes.

Copyright © Mometrix Media. You have been licensed one copy of this document for personal use only. Any other reproduction or redistribution is strictly prohibited. All rights reserved.

Informational Source Comprehension

Following directions

Technical passages often require the reader to follow a set of directions. For many people, especially those who are tactile or visual learners, this can be a difficult process. It is important to approach a set of directions differently than other texts. First, it is a good idea to scan the directions to determine whether special equipment or preparations are needed. Sometimes in a recipe, for instance, the author fails to mention that the oven should be preheated first, and then halfway through the process, the cook is supposed to be baking. After briefly reading the directions, the reader should return to the first step. When following directions, it is appropriate to complete each step before moving on to the next. If this is not possible, it is useful at least to visualize each step before reading the next.

Word meaning from context

One of the benefits of reading is the expansion of one's vocabulary. In order to obtain this benefit, however, one needs to know how to identify the definition of a word from its context. This means defining a word based on the words around it and the way it is used in a sentence. Consider the following sentence: *The elderly scholar spent his evenings hunched over arcane texts that few other people even knew existed.* The adjective *arcane* is uncommon, but you can obtain significant information about it based on its use in the sentence. The fact that few other people know of their existence allows you to assume that "arcane texts" must be rare and be of interest to a few people. Also, the texts are being read by an elderly scholar. So, you can assume that they focus on difficult academic subjects. Sometimes, words can be defined by what they are not. Consider the following sentence: *Ron's fealty to his parents was not shared by Karen, who disobeyed their every command.* Someone who disobeys is not demonstrating *fealty*. So, you can infer that the word means something like *obedience* or *respect*.

Dictionary entry

Dictionary entries are in alphabetical order. Many words have more than one definition. These different definitions are numbered. Also, some words can be used as different parts of speech. The definitions for each part of speech are separated. A simple entry might look like this:

WELL: (adverb) 1. in a good way | (noun) 1. a hole drilled into the earth

The correct definition of a word depends on how the word is used in a sentence. To know that you are using the word correctly, you can try to replace the dictionary's definitions for the word in the passage. Then, choose the definition that seems to be the best fit.

Food and medicine labels

The Food and Drug Administration has strict mandates for the information that must be included on food and medicine labels. For instance, a food label must list the corresponding food's number of calories, total fat, cholesterol, sodium, protein, and carbohydrates, among other requirements. Also, a food label will usually contain a list of the vitamins that can be found in the product.

Most importantly, a food label lists the serving size, which is the portion of the product for which the vitamin and nutrient values are true. Some food manufacturers use odd serving sizes to make it look as if a product is healthier than it is. When making a comparison, one should always calculate

Copyright © Mometrix Media. You have been licensed one copy of this document for personal use only. Any other reproduction or redistribution is strictly prohibited. All rights reserved.

the amount of nutrients per unit of measure (grams or fluid ounces, for example) to account for these serving size distortions.

Medicine labels contain a wealth of information that can be used to make comparisons and informed purchases. Every medicine label must have detailed and comprehensive instructions regarding dosage, including how much and how often the medicine should be taken. A label will also include warning information, and what to do in case of overdose or adverse reaction. Medicine labels will have a complete list of ingredients, but will isolate the active ingredients, which are those that accomplish the advertised purpose of the product. Generic versions of a medicine have the same active ingredients as more expensive name-brand versions. Finally, a label will specify when a medication should not be taken by certain people, like the elderly or pregnant women. When comparing medicines, it is important to isolate the most crucial information: dosage schedule, active ingredients, and counter-indications.

Information from printed communication

Memo

A memo (short for *memorandum*) is a common form of written communication. There is a standard format for these documents. It is typical for there to be a heading at the top indicating the author, date, and recipient. In some cases, this heading will also include the author's title and the name of his or her institution. Below this information will be the body of the memo. These documents are typically written by and for members of the same organization. They usually contain a plan of action, a request for information on a specific topic, or a response to such a request. Memos are considered to be official documents, and so are usually written in a formal style. Many memos are organized with numbers or bullet points, which make it easier for the reader to identify key ideas.

Posted announcement

People post announcements for all sorts of occasions. Many people are familiar with notices for lost pets, yard sales, and landscaping services. In order to be effective, these announcements need to contain all of the information the reader requires to act on the message. For instance, a lost pet announcement needs to include a good description of the animal and a contact number for the owner. A yard sale notice should include the address, date, and hours of the sale, as well as a brief description of the products that will be available there. When composing an announcement, it is important to consider the perspective of the audience -- what will they need to know in order to respond to the message? Although a posted announcement can have color and decoration to attract the eye of the passerby, it must also convey the necessary information clearly.

Classified advertisement

Classified advertisements, or *ads*, are used to sell or buy goods, to attract business, to make romantic connections, and to do countless other things. They are an inexpensive, and sometimes free, way to make a brief pitch. Classified ads used to be found only in newspapers or special advertising circulars, but there are now online listings as well. The style of these ads has remained basically the same. An ad usually begins with a word or phrase indicating what is being sold or sought. Then, the listing will give a brief description of the product or service. Because space is limited and costly in newspapers, classified ads there will often contain abbreviations for common attributes. For instance, two common abbreviations are *bk* for *black*, and *obo* for *or best offer*. Classified ads will then usually conclude by listing the price (or the amount the seeker is willing to pay), followed by contact information like a telephone number or email address.

Copyright © Mometrix Media. You have been licensed one copy of this document for personal use only. Any other reproduction or redistribution is strictly prohibited. All rights reserved.

Index

Normally, a nonfiction book will have an **index** at the end. The index is for you to find information about specific topics. An index lists the topics in alphabetical order (i.e., a, b, c, d…). The names of people are listed by last name. For example, *Adams, John* would come before *Washington, George*. To the right of a topic, the page numbers are listed for that topic. When a topic is spread over several pages, the index will connect these pages with a dash. For example, the topic is said to be on pages 35 to 42 and again on 53. The topic will be labeled as 35-42, 53. Some topics will have subtopics. These subtopics are listed below the main topic, indented slightly, and placed in alphabetical order. This is common for subjects that are covered over several pages in the book. For example, you have a book about Elizabethan drama; William Shakespeare is an important topic. Beneath Shakespeare's name in the index, you may find listings for *death of, dramatic works of, life of*, etc. These specific sub-topics help you narrow your search.

Table of contents

Most books, magazines, and journals have a **table of contents** at the beginning. The table of contents lists the different subjects or chapter titles with a page number. This information allows you to find what you need with ease. Normally, the table of contents is found a page or two after the title page in a book or in the first few pages of a magazine. In a book, the table of contents will have the chapters listed on the left side. The page number for each chapter comes on the right side. Many books have a preface (i.e., a note that explains the background of the book) or introduction. The preface and introduction come with Roman numerals. The chapters are listed in order from the beginning to the end.

Road atlas

A road atlas is a collection of maps specially designed for drivers. It is useful for finding the distances between places, the correct roads and highways for reaching a given destination, and the relative positions of places in a certain geographic area. Most road atlases have a table at the beginning that illustrates the distance in miles between any two major cities. These tables are set up like a grid, with cities listed along the left and top sides. To find the distance between two places, follow the row of the first place perpendicular from the left until it intersects with the column of the second place. Some atlases have similar tables indicating the estimated travel time from one location to another.

Card catalog

Although physical card catalogs are rarely seen anymore, they still exist in most libraries in an online, digital format. These catalogs contain a wealth of information about the items in the library. A typical card catalog entry contains the title of the work, name of the author, year of publication, publisher, number of pages, and reference number in the Library of Congress. Most importantly, perhaps, card catalogs contain a brief summary of the book, so that a potential reader or researcher can get an idea of its contents. Many online card catalogs allow easy navigation to books on the same subject, by the same author, or close by on the library shelves. In any case, the card catalog entry will contain the library call number so that the researcher can find the book.

Dictionary

Dictionaries have information about the definition and use of words. A standard dictionary word begins with a pronunciation guide for the word. The entry will also give the word's part of speech. A good dictionary will have the word's origins. This information is known as the word's etymology.

Copyright © Mometrix Media. You have been licensed one copy of this document for personal use only. Any other reproduction or redistribution is strictly prohibited. All rights reserved.

Owner's manual

An owner's manual is the appropriate source of information for a purchased product. An owner's manual is mainly devoted to the operation and maintenance of the product. It will often begin with a brief outline of the product's parts and method of operation. Most manuals will contain the product's specifications -- that is, the precise details about its components and features. For the most part, though, the owner's manual will be devoted to the routine repairs and care that a non-expert owner can be expected to provide. In the owner's manual for a car, for instance, there will be instructions for tasks like changing the oil, replacing windshield wipers, and presetting stations on the radio. An owner's manual is unlikely to contain instructions for complex repairs that require special equipment. Finally, the owner's manual will often detail the service warranty associated with the product.

Database information

Databases are systems for storing and organizing large amounts of information. As personal computers have become more common and accessible, databases have, too. The standard layout of a database is as a grid, with labels down the left side and across the top. The horizontal rows and vertical columns that make up the grid are usually numbered or lettered, so that a particular square within the database might have a name like A3 or G5. Databases are good for storing information that can be expressed succinctly. They are most commonly used to store numerical data, but they also can be used to store the answers to yes/no questions and other brief data points. Information that has multiple possible meanings or is difficult to express in a few words is not appropriate for a database.

Encyclopedia

Encyclopedias are an excellent source for general information on a range of common subjects. A good encyclopedia remains a great place to get basic information about a well-known topic. Finding general information for subjects like ostriches, Pennsylvania, or the Crimean War, is welcome for an encyclopedia.

Headings and subheadings

Many informative texts--especially textbooks--use headings and subheadings for organization. Headings and subheadings are printed in larger and bolder fonts. Sometimes, they are in a different color than the main body of the book. Headings may be larger than subheadings. Also, headings and subheadings are not always complete sentences. A heading gives the topic that will be addressed in the paragraphs below. Headings are meant to alert you about what is coming next. Subheadings give the topics of smaller sections. For example, the heading of a section in a science textbook might be *AMPHIBIANS*. Within that section, you may have subheadings for *Frogs*, *Salamanders*, and *Newts*. Pay close attention to headings and subheadings. They make it easy to go back and find specific details in a book.

Bold text and underlining

Authors will often incorporate text features like bold text and underlining to communicate meaning to the reader. When text is made bold, it is often because the author wants to emphasize the point that is being made. Bold text indicates importance. Also, many textbooks place key terms in bold. This not only draws the reader's attention, but also makes it easy to find these terms when reviewing before a test. Underlining serves a similar purpose. It is often used to suggest emphasis. However, underlining is also used on occasion beneath the titles of books, magazines, and works of

Copyright © Mometrix Media. You have been licensed one copy of this document for personal use only. Any other reproduction or redistribution is strictly prohibited. All rights reserved.

art. This was more common when people used typewriters, which weren't able to create italics. Now that word processing software is nearly universal, italics are generally used for longer works.

Italics

Italics, like bold text and underlines, are used to emphasize important words, phrases, and sentences in a text. However, italics have other uses as well. A word is placed in italics when it is being discussed *as* a word; that is, when it is being defined or its use in a sentence is being described. For instance, it is appropriate to use italics when saying that *esoteric* is an unusual adjective. Italics are also used for long or large works, like books, magazines, long operas, and epic poems. Shorter works are typically placed within quotation marks. A reader should note how an author uses italics, as this is a marker of style and tone. Some authors use them frequently, creating a tone of high emotion, while others are more restrained in their use, suggesting calm and reason.

Line graph

A line graph is a type of graph that is typically used for measuring trends over time. The graph is set up along a vertical and a horizontal axis. The variables being measured are listed along the left side and the bottom side of the axes. Points are then plotted along the graph as they correspond with their values for each variable. For instance, imagine a line graph measuring a person's income for each month of the year. If the person earned $1500 in January, there should be a point directly above January (perpendicular to the horizontal axis) and directly to the right of $1500 (perpendicular to the vertical axis). Once all of the lines are plotted, they are connected with a line from left to right. This line provides a nice visual illustration of the general trends. For instance, using the earlier example, if the line sloped up, then one would see that the person's income had increased over the course of the year.

Bar graph

The bar graph is one of the most common visual representations of information. Bar graphs are used to illustrate sets of numerical data. The graph has a vertical axis (along which numbers are listed), and a horizontal axis (along which categories, words, or some other indicators are placed). One example of a bar graph is a depiction of the respective heights of famous basketball players: the vertical axis would contain numbers ranging from five to eight feet, and the horizontal axis would contain the names of the players. The length of the bar above the player's name would illustrate his height, and the top of the bar would stop perpendicular to the height listed along the left side. In this representation, one would see that Yao Ming is taller than Michael Jordan because Yao's bar would be higher.

Pie chart

A **pie chart**, also known as a circle graph, is useful for depicting how a single unit or category is divided. The standard pie chart is a circle with designated wedges. Each wedge is proportional in size to a part of the whole. For instance, consider a pie chart representing a student's budget. If the student spends half of his or her money on rent, then the pie chart will represent that amount with a line through the center of the pie. If she spends a quarter of her money on food, there will be a line extending from the edge of the circle to the center at a right angle to the line depicting rent. This illustration would make it clear that the student spends twice the amount of money on rent as she does on food.

A pie chart is effective at showing how a single entity is divided into parts. They are not effective at demonstrating the relationships between parts of different wholes. For example, an unhelpful use

Copyright © Mometrix Media. You have been licensed one copy of this document for personal use only. Any other reproduction or redistribution is strictly prohibited. All rights reserved.

of a pie chart would be to compare the respective amounts of state and federal spending devoted to infrastructure since these values are only meaningful in the context of the entire budget.

Scale readings of standard measurement instruments

The scales used on standard measurement instruments are fairly easy to read with a little practice. Take the ruler as an example. A typical ruler has different units along each long edge. One side measures inches, and the other measures centimeters. The units are specified close to the zero reading for the ruler. Note that the ruler does not begin measuring from its outermost edge. The zero reading is a black line a tiny distance inside of the edge. On the inches side, each inch is indicated with a long black line and a number. Each half-inch is noted with a slightly shorter line. Quarter-inches are noted with still shorter lines, eighth-inches are noted with even shorter lines, and sixteenth-inches are noted with the shortest lines of all. On the centimeter side, the second-largest black lines indicate half-centimeters, and the smaller lines indicate tenths of centimeters, otherwise known as millimeters.

Legend or key of a map

Almost all maps contain a key, or legend, that defines the symbols used on the map for various landmarks. This key is usually placed in a corner of the map. It should contain listings for all of the important symbols on the map. Of course, these symbols will vary depending on the nature of the map. A road map uses different colored lines to indicate roads, highways, and interstates. A legend might also show different dots and squares that are used to indicate towns of various sizes. The legend may contain information about the map's scale, though this may be elsewhere on the map. Many legends will contain special symbols, such as a picnic table indicating a campground.

Calculating the most economical buy

When deciding between similar products, it can be difficult to discern the most economical choice. Before making a final decision, one should evaluate the itemized price of each product. That is, one should break down the price into its components: base cost, tax, and delivery charges, if any. When purchasing a product that is sold in different sizes or amounts (like cereal or shampoo), one should calculate and compare price per unit. As an example, imagine one set of blank CDs costs $15 for 10, while another costs $20 for 12. The per-unit cost can be calculated by dividing the total cost by the number of units: 15/10 = 1.5 and 20/12 = about 1.67, so the first set of CDs costs $1.50 per disc and the second costs approximately $1.67 per disc. By this measure, the pack of 10 is the more economical choice.

Yellow Pages

The Yellow Pages of the phone book contain commercial listings for businesses that provide services to the general public. The listings are organized according to the type of service being offered. For example, there are sections for florists, auto mechanics, and pizza restaurants. These categories are placed in alphabetical order, and within each category, the listings are in alphabetical order. A basic listing in the yellow pages will include the name of the business, the address, and the phone number. However, some merchants elect to pay extra and have large advertisements alongside their listing in the yellow pages. For instance, a restaurant might buy enough space to print their entire menu.

Copyright © Mometrix Media. You have been licensed one copy of this document for personal use only. Any other reproduction or redistribution is strictly prohibited. All rights reserved.

Items and costs

Reading a table, such as a menu or a set of movie listings takes practice. In a typical menu format, the price is listed directly across from the item. However, in some cases all of the items in a category (desserts, for example) have the same price, and this price is given at the top of the section. Sometimes, the prices of extras (like 75 cents for cheese on a hamburger) are listed at the bottom of the section. In some restaurants, prices are listed without the dollar sign ($). Also, some restaurants automatically add a certain amount of money for the server's tip, and this information is usually listed at the bottom of the menu page. On a set of movie listings, it is typical for the times at which a picture is showing to be listed in chronological order, as in the following example: *Harold Goes to Mars – 1:15, 3:30, 5:45, 8, 10:30*. Note that times that are exactly on the hour do not include minutes. Also, in some places a period is used instead of a colon to separate hours and minutes.

Copyright © Mometrix Media. You have been licensed one copy of this document for personal use only. Any other reproduction or redistribution is strictly prohibited. All rights reserved.

Mathematics

Numbers and their Classifications

Numbers are the basic building blocks of mathematics. Specific features of numbers are identified by the following terms:

Integers – The set of whole positive and negative numbers, including zero. Integers do not include fractions ($\frac{1}{3}$), decimals (0.56), or mixed numbers ($7\frac{3}{4}$).

Prime number – A whole number greater than 1 that has only two factors, itself and 1; that is, a number that can be divided evenly only by 1 and itself.

Composite number – A whole number greater than 1 that has more than two different factors; in other words, any whole number that is not a prime number. For example: The composite number 8 has the factors of 1, 2, 4, and 8.

Even number – Any integer that can be divided by 2 without leaving a remainder. For example: 2, 4, 6, 8, and so on.

Odd number – Any integer that cannot be divided evenly by 2. For example: 3, 5, 7, 9, and so on.

Decimal number – a number that uses a decimal point to show the part of the number that is less than one. Example: 1.234.

Decimal point – a symbol used to separate the ones place from the tenths place in decimals or dollars from cents in currency.

Decimal place – the position of a number to the right of the decimal point. In the decimal 0.123, the 1 is in the first place to the right of the decimal point, indicating tenths; the 2 is in the second place, indicating hundredths; and the 3 is in the third place, indicating thousandths.

The decimal, or base 10, system is a number system that uses ten different digits (0, 1, 2, 3, 4, 5, 6, 7, 8, 9). An example of a number system that uses something other than ten digits is the binary, or base 2, number system, used by computers, which uses only the numbers 0 and 1. It is thought that the decimal system originated because people had only their 10 fingers for counting.

Rational, irrational, and real numbers can be described as follows:

Rational numbers include all integers, decimals, and fractions. Any terminating or repeating decimal number is a rational number.

Irrational numbers cannot be written as fractions or decimals because the number of decimal places is infinite and there is no recurring pattern of digits within the number. For example, pi (π) begins with 3.141592 and continues without terminating or repeating, so pi is an irrational number.

Real numbers are the set of all rational and irrational numbers.

> **Review Video: Numbers and Their Classifications**
> Visit mometrix.com/academy and enter code: 461071

Copyright © Mometrix Media. You have been licensed one copy of this document for personal use only. Any other reproduction or redistribution is strictly prohibited. All rights reserved.

Operations

There are four basic mathematical operations:

Addition increases the value of one quantity by the value of another quantity. Example: $2 + 4 = 6$; $8 + 9 = 17$. The result is called the sum. With addition, the order does not matter. $4 + 2 = 2 + 4$.

Subtraction is the opposite operation to addition; it decreases the value of one quantity by the value of another quantity. Example: $6 - 4 = 2$; $17 - 8 = 9$. The result is called the difference. Note that with subtraction, the order does matter. $6 - 4 \neq 4 - 6$.

Multiplication can be thought of as repeated addition. One number tells how many times to add the other number to itself. Example: 3×2 (three times two) $= 2 + 2 + 2 = 6$. With multiplication, the order does not matter. $2 \times 3 = 3 \times 2$ or $3 + 3 = 2 + 2 + 2$.

Division is the opposite operation to multiplication; one number tells us how many parts to divide the other number into. Example: $20 \div 4 = 5$; if 20 is split into 4 equal parts, each part is 5. With division, the order of the numbers does matter. $20 \div 4 \neq 4 \div 20$.

Exponents and Parentheses

An exponent is a superscript number placed next to another number at the top right. It indicates how many times the base number is to be multiplied by itself. Exponents provide a shorthand way to write what would be a longer mathematical expression. Example: $a^2 = a \times a$; $2^4 = 2 \times 2 \times 2 \times 2$. A number with an exponent of 2 is said to be "squared," while a number with an exponent of 3 is said to be "cubed." The value of a number raised to an exponent is called its power. So, 8^4 is read as "8 to the 4th power," or "8 raised to the power of 4." A negative exponent is the same as the reciprocal of a positive exponent. Example: $a^{-2} = \frac{1}{a^2}$.

Parentheses are used to designate which operations should be done first when there are multiple operations. Example: $4 - (2 + 1) = 1$; the parentheses tell us that we must add 2 and 1, and then subtract the sum from 4, rather than subtracting 2 from 4 and then adding 1 (this would give us an answer of 3).

Order of Operations

Order of Operations is a set of rules that dictates the order in which we must perform each operation in an expression so that we will evaluate it accurately. If we have an expression that includes multiple different operations, Order of Operations tells us which operations to do first. The most common mnemonic for Order of Operations is PEMDAS, or "Please Excuse My Dear Aunt Sally." PEMDAS stands for Parentheses, Exponents, Multiplication, Division, Addition, Subtraction. It is important to understand that multiplication and division have equal precedence, as do addition and subtraction, so those pairs of operations are simply worked from left to right in order.

Copyright © Mometrix Media. You have been licensed one copy of this document for personal use only. Any other reproduction or redistribution is strictly prohibited. All rights reserved.

Example: Evaluate the expression $5 + 20 \div 4 \times (2 + 3)^2 - 6$ using the correct order of operations.

P: Perform the operations inside the parentheses, $(2 + 3) = 5$.

E: Simplify the exponents, $(5)^2 = 25$.

The equation now looks like this: $5 + 20 \div 4 \times 25 - 6$.

MD: Perform multiplication and division from left to right, $20 \div 4 = 5$; then $5 \times 25 = 125$.

The equation now looks like this: $5 + 125 - 6$.

AS: Perform addition and subtraction from left to right, $5 + 125 = 130$; then $130 - 6 = 124$.

> **Review Video: Order of Operations**
> Visit mometrix.com/academy and enter code: 259675

Laws of exponents

The laws of exponents are as follows:

1. Any number to the power of 1 is equal to itself: $a^1 = a$.
2. The number 1 raised to any power is equal to 1: $1^n = 1$.
3. Any number raised to the power of 0 is equal to 1: $a^0 = 1$.
4. Add exponents to multiply powers of the same base number: $a^n \times a^m = a^{n+m}$.
5. Subtract exponents to divide powers of the same number; that is $a^n \div a^m = a^{n-m}$.
6. Multiply exponents to raise a power to a power: $(a^n)^m = a^{n \times m}$.
7. If multiplied or divided numbers inside parentheses are collectively raised to a power, this is the same as each individual term being raised to that power: $(a \times b)^n = a^n \times b^n$; $(a \div b)^n = a^n \div b^n$.

Note: Exponents do not have to be integers. Fractional or decimal exponents follow all the rules above as well. Example: $5^{\frac{1}{4}} \times 5^{\frac{3}{4}} = 5^{\frac{1}{4} + \frac{3}{4}} = 5^1 = 5$.

Roots, square roots, and perfect squares

A root, such as a square root, is another way of writing a fractional exponent. Instead of using a superscript, roots use the radical symbol ($\sqrt{}$) to indicate the operation. A radical will have a number underneath the bar, and may sometimes have a number in the upper left: $\sqrt[n]{a}$, read as "the nth root of a." The relationship between radical notation and exponent notation can be described by this equation: $\sqrt[n]{a} = a^{\frac{1}{n}}$. The two special cases of $n = 2$ and $n = 3$ are called square roots and cube roots. If there is no number to the upper left, it is understood to be a square root ($n = 2$). Nearly all of the roots you encounter will be square roots. A square root is the same as a number raised to the one-half power. When we say that a is the square root of b ($a = \sqrt{b}$), we mean that a multiplied by itself equals b: ($a \times a = b$).

A perfect square is a number that has an integer for its square root. There are 10 perfect squares from 1 to 100: 1, 4, 9, 16, 25, 36, 49, 64, 81, 100 (the squares of integers 1 through 10).

Copyright © Mometrix Media. You have been licensed one copy of this document for personal use only. Any other reproduction or redistribution is strictly prohibited. All rights reserved.

Scientific notation

Scientific notation is a way of writing large numbers in a shorter form. The form $a \times 10^n$ is used in scientific notation, where a is greater than or equal to 1, but less than 10, and n is the number of places the decimal must move to get from the original number to a. Example: The number 230,400,000 is cumbersome to write. To write the value in scientific notation, place a decimal point between the first and second numbers, and include all digits through the last non-zero digit ($a = 2.304$). To find the appropriate power of 10, count the number of places the decimal point had to move ($n = 8$). The number is positive if the decimal moved to the left, and negative if it moved to the right. We can then write 230,400,000 as 2.304×10^8. If we look instead at the number 0.00002304, we have the same value for a, but this time the decimal moved 5 places to the right ($n = -5$). Thus, 0.00002304 can be written as 2.304×10^{-5}. Using this notation makes it simple to compare very large or very small numbers. By comparing exponents, it is easy to see that 3.28×10^4 is smaller than 1.51×10^5, because 4 is less than 5.

Rounding and estimation

Rounding is reducing the digits in a number while still trying to keep the value similar. The result will be less accurate, but will be in a simpler form, and will be easier to use. Whole numbers can be rounded to the nearest ten, hundred or thousand.

<u>Example</u>

Round each number:

1. Round each number to the nearest ten: 11, 47, 118
2. Round each number to the nearest hundred: 78, 980, 248
3. Round each number to the nearest thousand: 302, 1274, 3756

Answer

1. Remember, when rounding to the nearest ten, anything ending in 5 or greater rounds up. So, 11 rounds to 10, 47 rounds to 50, and 118 rounds to 120
2. Remember, when rounding to the nearest hundred, anything ending in 50 or greater rounds up. So, 78 rounds to 100, 980 rounds to 1000, and 248 rounds to 200.
3. Remember, when rounding to the nearest thousand, anything ending in 500 or greater rounds up. So, 302 rounds to 0, 1274 rounds to 1000, and 3756 rounds to 4000.

When you are asked for the solution a problem, you may need to provide only an approximate figure or estimation for your answer. In this situation, you can round the numbers that will be calculated to a non-zero number. This means that the first digit in the number is not zero, and the following numbers are zeros.

<u>Example</u>

Estimate the solution to 345,932 + 96,369.

Start by rounding each number to have only one digit as a non-zero number: 345,932 becomes 300,000 and 96,369 becomes 100,000.

Then, add the rounded numbers: 300,000 + 100,000 = 400,000. So, the answer is approximately 400,000.

- 35 -

Copyright © Mometrix Media. You have been licensed one copy of this document for personal use only. Any other reproduction or redistribution is strictly prohibited. All rights reserved.

The exact answer would be $345{,}932 + 96{,}369 = 442{,}301$. So, the estimate of 400,000 is a similar value to the exact answer.

Copyright © Mometrix Media. You have been licensed one copy of this document for personal use only. Any other reproduction or redistribution is strictly prohibited. All rights reserved.

Positive and Negative Numbers

A precursor to working with negative numbers is understanding what absolute values are. A number's *Absolute Value* is simply the distance away from zero a number is on the number line. The absolute value of a number is always positive and is written $|x|$.

<u>Example</u>

Show that $|3|=|-3|$.

The absolute value of 3, written as $|3|$, is 3 because the distance between 0 and 3 on a number line is three units. Likewise, the absolute value of -3, written as $|-3|$, is 3 because the distance between 0 and -3 on a number line is three units. So, $|3|=|-3|$.

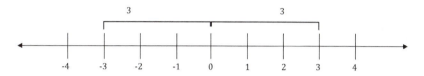

When adding signed numbers, if the signs are the same simply add the absolute values of the addends and apply the original sign to the sum. For example, $(+4) + (+8) = +12$ and $(-4) + (-8) = -12$. When the original signs are different, take the absolute values of the addends and subtract the smaller value from the larger value, then apply the original sign of the larger value to the difference. For instance, $(+4) + (-8) = -4$ and $(-4) + (+8) = +4$.

For subtracting signed numbers, change the sign of the number after the minus symbol and then follow the same rules used for addition. For example, $(+4)- (+8) = (+4) + (-8) = -4$.

If the signs are the same the product is positive when multiplying signed numbers. For example, $(+4) \times (+8) = +32$ and $(-4) \times (-8) = +32$. If the signs are opposite, the product is negative. For example, $(+4) \times (-8) = -32$ and $(-4) \times (+8) = -32$. When more than two factors are multiplied together, the sign of the product is determined by how many negative factors are present. If there are an odd number of negative factors then the product is negative, whereas an even number of negative factors indicates a positive product. For instance, $(+4) \times (-8) \times (-2) = +64$ and $(-4) \times (-8) \times (-2) = -64$.

The rules for dividing signed numbers are similar to multiplying signed numbers. If the dividend and divisor have the same sign, the quotient is positive. If the dividend and divisor have opposite signs, the quotient is negative. For example, $(-4) \div (+8) = -0.5$.

Copyright © Mometrix Media. You have been licensed one copy of this document for personal use only. Any other reproduction or redistribution is strictly prohibited. All rights reserved.

Factors and Multiples

Factors are numbers that are multiplied together to obtain a product. For example, in the equation $2 \times 3 = 6$, the numbers 2 and 3 are factors. A prime number has only two factors (1 and itself), but other numbers can have many factors.

A common factor is a number that divides exactly into two or more other numbers. For example, the factors of 12 are 1, 2, 3, 4, 6, and 12, while the factors of 15 are 1, 3, 5, and 15. The common factors of 12 and 15 are 1 and 3.

A prime factor is also a prime number. Therefore, the prime factors of 12 are 2 and 3. For 15, the prime factors are 3 and 5.

> **Review Video: Factors**
> Visit mometrix.com/academy and enter code: 920086

The greatest common factor (GCF) is the largest number that is a factor of two or more numbers. For example, the factors of 15 are 1, 3, 5, and 15; the factors of 35 are 1, 5, 7, and 35. Therefore, the greatest common factor of 15 and 35 is 5.

The least common multiple (LCM) is the smallest number that is a multiple of two or more numbers. For example, the multiples of 3 include 3, 6, 9, 12, 15, etc.; the multiples of 5 include 5, 10, 15, 20, etc. Therefore, the least common multiple of 3 and 5 is 15.

> **Review Video: Multiples**
> Visit mometrix.com/academy and enter code: 626738

Copyright © Mometrix Media. You have been licensed one copy of this document for personal use only. Any other reproduction or redistribution is strictly prohibited. All rights reserved.

Fractions, Percentages, and Related Concepts

A fraction is a number that is expressed as one integer written above another integer, with a dividing line between them ($\frac{x}{y}$). It represents the quotient of the two numbers "x divided by y." It can also be thought of as x out of y equal parts.

The top number of a fraction is called the numerator, and it represents the number of parts under consideration. The 1 in $\frac{1}{4}$ means that 1 part out of the whole is being considered in the calculation. The bottom number of a fraction is called the denominator, and it represents the total number of equal parts. The 4 in $\frac{1}{4}$ means that the whole consists of 4 equal parts. A fraction cannot have a denominator of zero; this is referred to as "undefined."

Fractions can be manipulated, without changing the value of the fraction, by multiplying or dividing (but not adding or subtracting) both the numerator and denominator by the same number. If you divide both numbers by a common factor, you are reducing or simplifying the fraction. Two fractions that have the same value, but are expressed differently are known as equivalent fractions. For example, $\frac{2}{10}, \frac{3}{15}, \frac{4}{20}$, and $\frac{5}{25}$ are all equivalent fractions. They can also all be reduced or simplified to $\frac{1}{5}$.

When two fractions are manipulated so that they have the same denominator, this is known as finding a common denominator. The number chosen to be that common denominator should be the least common multiple of the two original denominators. Example: $\frac{3}{4}$ and $\frac{5}{6}$; the least common multiple of 4 and 6 is 12. Manipulating to achieve the common denominator: $\frac{3}{4} = \frac{9}{12}; \frac{5}{6} = \frac{10}{12}$.

If two fractions have a common denominator, they can be added or subtracted simply by adding or subtracting the two numerators and retaining the same denominator. Example: $\frac{1}{2} + \frac{1}{4} = \frac{2}{4} + \frac{1}{4} = \frac{3}{4}$. If the two fractions do not already have the same denominator, one or both of them must be manipulated to achieve a common denominator before they can be added or subtracted.

Two fractions can be multiplied by multiplying the two numerators to find the new numerator and the two denominators to find the new denominator. Example: $\frac{1}{3} \times \frac{2}{3} = \frac{1 \times 2}{3 \times 3} = \frac{2}{9}$.

Two fractions can be divided by flipping the numerator and denominator of the second fraction and then proceeding as though it were a multiplication. Example: $\frac{2}{3} \div \frac{3}{4} = \frac{2}{3} \times \frac{4}{3} = \frac{8}{9}$.

A fraction whose denominator is greater than its numerator is known as a proper fraction, while a fraction whose numerator is greater than its denominator is known as an improper fraction. Proper fractions have values less than one and improper fractions have values greater than one.

A mixed number is a number that contains both an integer and a fraction. Any improper fraction can be rewritten as a mixed number. Example: $\frac{8}{3} = \frac{6}{3} + \frac{2}{3} = 2 + \frac{2}{3} = 2\frac{2}{3}$. Similarly, any mixed number can be rewritten as an improper fraction. Example: $1\frac{3}{5} = 1 + \frac{3}{5} = \frac{5}{5} + \frac{3}{5} = \frac{8}{5}$.

> **Review Video: Fractions**
> Visit mometrix.com/academy and enter code: 262335

Copyright © Mometrix Media. You have been licensed one copy of this document for personal use only. Any other reproduction or redistribution is strictly prohibited. All rights reserved.

Percentages can be thought of as fractions that are based on a whole of 100; that is, one whole is equal to 100%. The word percent means "per hundred." Fractions can be expressed as percents by finding equivalent fractions with a denomination of 100. Example: $\frac{7}{10} = \frac{70}{100} = 70\%$; $\frac{1}{4} = \frac{25}{100} = 25\%$.

To express a percentage as a fraction, divide the percentage number by 100 and reduce the fraction to its simplest possible terms. Example: $60\% = \frac{60}{100} = \frac{3}{5}$; $96\% = \frac{96}{100} = \frac{24}{25}$.

Converting decimals to percentages and percentages to decimals is as simple as moving the decimal point. To convert from a decimal to a percent, move the decimal point two places to the right. To convert from a percent to a decimal, move it two places to the left. Example: 0.23 = 23%; 5.34 = 534%; 0.007 = 0.7%; 700% = 7.00; 86% = 0.86; 0.15% = 0.0015.

It may be helpful to remember that the percentage number will always be larger than the equivalent decimal number.

A percentage problem can be presented three main ways: (1) Find what percentage of some number another number is. Example: What percentage of 40 is 8? (2) Find what number is some percentage of a given number. Example: What number is 20% of 40? (3) Find what number another number is a given percentage of.

Example: What number is 8 20% of? The three components in all of these cases are the same: a whole (W), a part (P), and a percentage (%). These are related by the equation: $P = W \times \%$. This is the form of the equation you would use to solve problems of type (2). To solve types (1) and (3), you would use these two forms:

$$\% = \frac{P}{W} \text{ and } W = \frac{P}{\%}$$

The thing that frequently makes percentage problems difficult is that they are most often also word problems, so a large part of solving them is figuring out which quantities are what. Example: In a school cafeteria, 7 students choose pizza, 9 choose hamburgers, and 4 choose tacos. Find the percentage that chooses tacos. To find the whole, you must first add all of the parts: 7 + 9 + 4 = 20. The percentage can then be found by dividing the part by the whole ($\% = \frac{P}{W}$): $\frac{4}{20} = \frac{20}{100} = 20\%$.

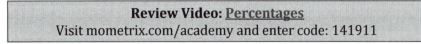

Review Video: Percentages
Visit mometrix.com/academy and enter code: 141911

A ratio is a comparison of two quantities in a particular order. Example: If there are 14 computers in a lab, and the class has 20 students, there is a student to computer ratio of 20 to 14, commonly written as 20:14. Ratios are normally reduced to their smallest whole number representation, so 20:14 would be reduced to 10:7 by dividing both sides by 2.

A proportion is a relationship between two quantities that dictates how one changes when the other changes. A direct proportion describes a relationship in which a quantity increases by a set amount for every increase in the other quantity, or decreases by that same amount for every decrease in the other quantity. Example: Assuming a constant driving speed, the time required for a car trip increases as the distance of the trip increases. The distance to be traveled and the time required to travel are directly proportional.

Inverse proportion is a relationship in which an increase in one quantity is accompanied by a decrease in the other, or vice versa. Example: the time required for a car trip decreases as the

Copyright © Mometrix Media. You have been licensed one copy of this document for personal use only. Any other reproduction or redistribution is strictly prohibited. All rights reserved.

speed increases, and increases as the speed decreases, so the time required is inversely proportional to the speed of the car.

Copyright © Mometrix Media. You have been licensed one copy of this document for personal use only. Any other reproduction or redistribution is strictly prohibited. All rights reserved.

Numbers and Operations

Converting percents, fractions, and decimals

<u>Example 1</u>

15% can be written as a fraction and as a decimal. 15% written as a fraction is $\frac{15}{100}$ which equals $\frac{3}{20}$. 15% written as a decimal is 0.15.

To convert a percent to a fraction, follow these steps:

1) Write the percent over 100 because percent means "per one hundred." So, 15% can be written as $\frac{15}{100}$.

2) Fractions should be written in simplest form, which means that the numbers in the numerator and denominator should be reduced if possible. Both 15 and 100 can be divided by 5.

3) Therefore, $\frac{15 \div 5}{100 \div 5} = \frac{3}{20}$.

To convert a percent to a decimal, follow these steps:

1) Write the percent over 100 because percent means "per one hundred." So, 15% can be written as $\frac{15}{100}$.

2) 15 divided by 100 equals 0.15, so 15% = 0.15. In other words, when converting from a percent to a decimal, drop the percent sign and move the decimal two places to the left.

<u>Example 2</u>

Write 24.36% as a fraction and then as a decimal. Explain how you made these conversions.

24.36% written as a fraction is $\frac{24.36}{100}$, or $\frac{2436}{10,000}$, which reduces to $\frac{609}{2500}$. 24.36% written as a decimal is 0.2436. Recall that dividing by 100 moves the decimal two places to the left.

> **Review Video:** <u>Converting Percentages to Decimals and Fractions</u>
> Visit mometrix.com/academy and enter code: 287297

<u>Example 3</u>

Convert $\frac{4}{5}$ to a decimal and to a percent.

To convert a fraction to a decimal, simply divide the numerator by the denominator in the fraction. The numerator is the top number in the fraction and the denominator is the bottom number in a fraction. So $\frac{4}{5} = 4 \div 5 = 0.80 = 0.8$.

Percent means "per hundred." $\frac{4 \cdot 20}{5 \cdot 20} = \frac{80}{100} = 80\%$.

<u>Example 4</u>

Convert $3\frac{2}{5}$ to a decimal and to a percent.

- 42 -

Copyright © Mometrix Media. You have been licensed one copy of this document for personal use only. Any other reproduction or redistribution is strictly prohibited. All rights reserved.

The mixed number $3\frac{2}{5}$ has a whole number and a fractional part. The fractional part, namely $\frac{2}{5}$, can be written as a decimal by dividing 5 into 2, which gives 0.4. Adding the whole to the part gives 3.4. Alternatively, note that $3\frac{2}{5} = 3\frac{4}{10} = 3.4$

To change a decimal to a percent, multiply it by 100.
3.4(100) = 340%. Notice that this percentage is greater than 100%. This makes sense because the original mixed number $3\frac{2}{5}$ is greater than 1.

> **Review Video:** <u>**Converting Fractions to Percentages and Decimals**</u>
> Visit mometrix.com/academy and enter code: 306233
>
> **Review Video:** <u>**Converting Decimals to Fractions and Percentages**</u>
> Visit mometrix.com/academy and enter code: 986765

Product with decimals

When numbers are multiplied, the resulting number is the product. For example, the product of 2 and 4 is 8 because 2 × 4 = 8. When finding the product of numbers containing decimals, it is often helpful to multiply the numbers as if neither contains a decimal and then to adjust the product afterwards.

For instance,

```
   25
×   4
  100
```

In order to change 2.5 to a whole number to make multiplying easier, you essentially multiply it by ten, which moves the decimal one place to the right. Because 25 is ten times 2.5, the product of 25 and 4 (100) is ten times the product of 2.5 and 4. To adjust for the initial change, you must divide the product by ten, which moves the decimal one place back to the left. So, the product of 2.5 and 4 is 10 (or 10.0).

Percentage

Example 1

What is 30% of 120?

The word "of" indicates multiplication, so 30% of 120 is found by multiplying 30% by 120. First, change 30% to a fraction or decimal. Recall that "percent" means per hundred, so 30% $= \frac{30}{100} = 0.30$. 120 times 0.3 is 36.

Example 2

What is 150% of 20?

150% of 20 is found by multiplying 150% by 20. First, change 150% to a fraction or decimal. Recall that "percent" means per hundred, so 150% $= \frac{150}{100} = 1.50$. So, (1.50)(20) =

- 43 -

Copyright © Mometrix Media. You have been licensed one copy of this document for personal use only. Any other reproduction or redistribution is strictly prohibited. All rights reserved.

30. Notice that 30 is greater than the original number of 20. This makes sense because you are finding a number that is more than 100% of the original number.

Example 3

According to a hospital survey, 82% of nurses were highly satisfied at their job. Of 145 nurses, how many were highly satisfied?

82% of 145 = 0.82 · 145 = 118.9. Because you can't have 0.9 of a person, the answer is "about 119 nurses are highly satisfied with their jobs."

Example 4

What is 14.5% of 96?

Change 14.5% to a decimal before multiplying. 0.145 · 96 = 13.92. Notice that 13.92 is much smaller than the original number of 96. This makes sense because you are finding a small percentage of the original number.

Example 5

Find 275% of 33.

Change 275% to a decimal before multiplying: 275% of 33 = (275%)(33) = (2.75)(33) = 90.75. Notice that 90.75 is greater than the original number of 33. This makes sense because you are finding a number that is more than 100% of the original number.

Mathematical reasoning and computational procedures

Example 1

By what percentage does $\frac{3}{4}$ exceed $\frac{1}{3}$?

$$\frac{\text{new fraction} - \text{original fraction}}{\text{original fraction}} \cdot 100\% = \text{percent increase.}$$

$$\frac{\frac{3}{4} - \frac{1}{3}}{\frac{1}{3}} \cdot 100\% = \frac{\frac{5}{12}}{\frac{1}{3}} \cdot 100\% = \frac{5}{12} \cdot \frac{3}{1} \cdot 100\% = \frac{15}{12} \cdot 100\% = 125\%.$$

Example 2

A patient's age is thirteen more than half of 60. How old is the patient?

"More than" indicates addition, and "of" indicates multiplication. The expression can be written as "1/2(60) + 13". So, the patient's age is equal to $\frac{1}{2}(60) + 13 = 30 + 13 = 43$. The patient is 43 years old.

Simplifying

Example 1

How to simplify:

$$\frac{\frac{2}{5}}{\frac{4}{7}}$$

- 44 -

Copyright © Mometrix Media. You have been licensed one copy of this document for personal use only. Any other reproduction or redistribution is strictly prohibited. All rights reserved.

Dividing a fraction by a fraction may appear tricky, but it's not if you write out your steps carefully. Follow these steps to divide a fraction by a fraction.

Step 1: Rewrite the problem as a multiplication problem. Dividing by a fraction is the same as multiplying by its reciprocal, also known as its multiplicative inverse. The product of a number and its reciprocal is 1. Because $\frac{4}{7}$ times $\frac{7}{4}$ is 1, these numbers are reciprocals. Note that reciprocals can be found by simply interchanging the numerators and denominators. So, rewriting the problem as a multiplication problem gives $\frac{2}{5} \times \frac{7}{4}$.

Step 2: Perform multiplication of the fractions by multiplying the numerators by each other and the denominators by each other. In other words, multiply across the top and then multiply across the bottom.

$$\frac{2}{5} \times \frac{7}{4} = \frac{2 \times 7}{5 \times 4} = \frac{14}{20}$$

Step 3: Make sure the fraction is reduced to lowest terms. Both 14 and 20 can be divided by 2.

$$\frac{14}{20} = \frac{14 \div 2}{20 \div 2} = \frac{7}{10}$$

The answer is $\frac{7}{10}$.

Example 2

How to simplify:

$$\frac{1}{4} + \frac{3}{6}$$

Fractions with common denominators can be easily added or subtracted. Recall that the denominator is the bottom number in the fraction and that the numerator is the top number in the fraction.

The denominators of $\frac{1}{4}$ and $\frac{3}{6}$ are 4 and 6, respectively. The lowest common denominator of 4 and 6 is 12 because 12 is the least common multiple of 4 (multiples 4, 8, 12, 16, …) and 6 (multiples 6, 12, 18, 24, …). Convert each fraction to its equivalent with the newly found common denominator of 12.

$\frac{1 \times 3}{4 \times 3} = \frac{3}{12}; \frac{3 \times 2}{6 \times 2} = \frac{6}{12}$.

Now that the fractions have the same denominator, you can add them.

$\frac{3}{12} + \frac{6}{12} = \frac{9}{12}$.

Be sure to write your answer in lowest terms. Both 9 and 12 can be divided by 3, so the answer is $\frac{3}{4}$.

Copyright © Mometrix Media. You have been licensed one copy of this document for personal use only. Any other reproduction or redistribution is strictly prohibited. All rights reserved.

Example 3

How to simplify:

$$\frac{7}{8} - \frac{8}{16}$$

Fractions with common denominators can be easily added or subtracted. Recall that the denominator is the bottom number in the fraction and that the numerator is the top number in the fraction.

The denominators of $\frac{7}{8}$ and $\frac{8}{16}$ are 8 and 16, respectively. The lowest common denominator of 8 and 16 is 16 because 16 is the least common multiple of 8 (multiples 8, 16, 24 ...) and 16 (multiples 16, 32, 48, ...). Convert each fraction to its equivalent with the newly found common denominator of 16.

$$\frac{7 \times 2}{8 \times 2} = \frac{14}{16} \qquad \frac{8 \times 1}{16 \times 1} = \frac{8}{16}$$

Now that the fractions have the same denominator, you can subtract them.

$$\frac{14}{16} - \frac{8}{16} = \frac{6}{16}$$

Be sure to write your answer in lowest terms. Both 6 and 16 can be divided by 2, so the answer is $\frac{3}{8}$.

Example 4

How to simplify:

$$\frac{1}{2} + \left(3\left(\frac{3}{4}\right) - 2\right) + 4^2$$

When simplifying expressions, first perform operations within groups. Within the set of parentheses are multiplication and subtraction operations. Perform the multiplication first to get $\frac{1}{2} + \left(\frac{9}{4} - 2\right) + 4^2$. Then, subtract two to obtain $\frac{1}{2} + \frac{1}{4} + 4^2$.

Next, evaluate the exponent: $\frac{1}{2} + \frac{1}{4} + 16$. Finally, perform addition from left to right.

$\frac{1}{2} + \frac{1}{4} + 16 = \frac{2}{4} + \frac{1}{4} + \frac{64}{4} = \frac{67}{4}$.

Example 5

How to simplify:

$$0.22 + 0.5^2 - (5.5 + 3.3 \div 3)$$

First, evaluate the terms in the parentheses $(5.5 + 3.3 \div 3)$ using order of operations. $3.3 \div 3 = 1.1$, and $5.5 + 1.1 = 6.6$. Rewrite the problem: $0.22 + 0.5^2 - 6.6$. Next, evaluate the exponent of $0.5^2 = 0.5 \times 0.5 = 0.25$.

Rewrite the problem: $0.22 + 0.25 - 6.6$. Finally, add and subtract from left to right. $0.22 + 0.25 = 0.47$; $0.47 - 6.6 = -6.13$. The answer is -6.13.

Copyright © Mometrix Media. You have been licensed one copy of this document for personal use only. Any other reproduction or redistribution is strictly prohibited. All rights reserved.

<u>Example 6</u>

How to simplify:

$$\frac{3}{2} + (4(0.5) - 0.75) + 2^2$$

First, simplify within the parentheses:

$$\frac{3}{2} + (2 - 0.75) + 2^2$$

$$\frac{3}{2} + 1.25 + 2^2$$

Next, evaluate the exponent:

$$\frac{3}{2} + 1.25 + 4$$

Finally, change the fraction to a decimal and perform addition from left to right:

$$1.5 + 1.25 + 4 = 6.75$$

<u>Example 7</u>

How to simplify:

$$1.45 + 1.5^2 + (6 - 9 \div 2) + 45$$

First, evaluate the terms in the parentheses using proper order of operations.

$$1.45 + 1.5^2 + (6 - 4.5) + 45$$

$$1.45 + 1.5^2 + 1.5 + 45$$

Next, evaluate the exponent.

$$1.45 + 2.25 + 1.5 + 45$$

Finally, add from left to right.

$$1.45 + 2.25 + 1.5 + 45 = 50.2$$

Word problems

<u>Event and Material Planning</u>

To organize an event or to build something, you need to consider the materials that you will need to reach the goal. Also, you will need to consider the cost of having enough material for your project. For your exam, you will be asked to evaluate the goal of a project. The goal may be to find the amount of material needed for something or the goal may be to learn the expenses of hosting an event. So, consider the following examples for planning an event or having the right amount of material.

Copyright © Mometrix Media. You have been licensed one copy of this document for personal use only. Any other reproduction or redistribution is strictly prohibited. All rights reserved.

<u>Example 1</u>

Frank's Bakery sells cupcakes for $2.25 each, cookies for $1.50 each, slices of cake for $3.50 each, cups of tea for $2, and cups of coffee for $2.75. Frank calculates that it costs about $1 to make a cupcake, 75 cents to make a cookie, $2 to make each slice of cake, 50 cents for each cup of tea, and $1.15 to make each cup of coffee. At his bakery, the majority of his customers come in the morning. Yesterday, he sold 35 cupcakes, 20 cookies, 15 slices of cake, 3 dozen cups of tea, and 5 dozen cups of coffee. What was Frank's profit yesterday morning?

Answer

First, find the cost of making each item for each customer:

$$35 \text{ cupcakes} \times \$1 = \$35$$

$$20 \text{ cookies} \times \$0.75 = \$15$$

15 slices of cake $\times \$2 = \$30$

3 dozen cups of tea $\times \$0.50 = \$18$

$$5 \text{ dozen cups of coffee} \times \$1.15 = \$69$$

Second, add up the total cost of making each item:

$$\$35 + \$15 + \$30 + \$18 + \$69 = \$167$$

Third, find the cost to all of the customers:

$$35 \text{ cupcakes} \times \$2.25 = \$78.75$$

$$20 \text{ cookies} \times \$1.50 = \$30$$

15 slices of cake $\times \$3.50 = \$52.50$

3 dozen cups of tea $\times \$2 = \$72$

$$5 \text{ dozen cups of coffee} \times \$2.75 = \$165$$

Fourth, add up the total cost to all of the customers:

$$\$78.75 + \$30 + \$52.50 + \$72 + \$165 = \$398.25$$

Fifth, subtract the total cost of making each item from the total cost to all of the customers:

$\$398.25 - \$167 = \$231.25$

So, Frank's profit during the morning was $231.25

Copyright © Mometrix Media. You have been licensed one copy of this document for personal use only. Any other reproduction or redistribution is strictly prohibited. All rights reserved.

Perimeter formulas

Triangle

The perimeter of any triangle is found by summing the three side lengths; $P = a + b + c$. For an equilateral triangle, this is the same as $P = 3s$, where s is any side length, since all three sides are the same length.

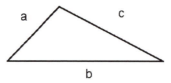

Square

The perimeter of a square is found by using the formula $P = 4s$, where s is the length of one side. Because all four sides are equal in a square, it is faster to multiply the length of one side by 4 than to add the same number four times. You could use the formulas for rectangles and get the same answer.

Rectangle

The perimeter of a rectangle is found by the formula $P = 2l + 2w$ or $P = 2(l + w)$, where l is the length, and w is the width. It may be easier to add the length and width first and then double the result, as in the second formula.

Parallelogram

The perimeter of a parallelogram is found by the formula $P = 2a + 2b$ or $P = 2(a + b)$, where a and b are the lengths of the two sides.

Trapezoid

The perimeter of a trapezoid is found by the formula $P = a + b_1 + c + b_2$, where a, b_1, c, and b_2 are the four sides of the trapezoid.

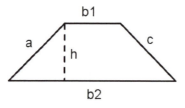

Circle

The circumference of a circle is found by the formula $C = 2\pi r$, where r is the radius. Again, remember to convert the diameter if you are given that measure rather than the radius.

Copyright © Mometrix Media. You have been licensed one copy of this document for personal use only. Any other reproduction or redistribution is strictly prohibited. All rights reserved.

<u>Example 2</u>

Dwight has a beach ball with a radius of 9 inches. He is planning to wrap the ball with wrapping paper. Which of the following is the best estimate for the number of square feet of wrapping paper he will need?

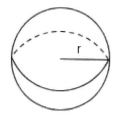

Answer

The surface area of a sphere may be calculated using the formula $SA = 4\pi r^2$. Substituting 9 for r gives $SA = 4\pi(9)^2$, which simplifies to $SA \approx 1017.36$. So the surface area of the ball is approximately 1017.36 square inches. There are twelve inches in a foot. So, there are $12^2 = 144$ square inches in a square foot. To convert this measurement to square feet, the following proportion may be written and solved for x: $\frac{1}{144} = \frac{x}{1017.36}$. So, $x \approx 7.07$. He needs approximately 7.07 square feet of wrapping paper.

Work/Unit rate

Unit rate expresses a quantity of one thing in terms of one unit of another. For example, if you travel 30 miles every two hours, a unit rate expresses this comparison in terms of one hour: in one hour you travel 15 miles, so your unit rate is 15 miles per hour. Other examples are how much one ounce of food costs (price per ounce), or figuring out how much one egg costs out of the dozen (price per 1 egg, instead of price per 12 eggs). The denominator of a unit rate is always 1. Unit rates are used to compare different situations to solve problems. For example, to make sure you get the best deal when deciding which kind of soda to buy, you can find the unit rate of each. If Soda #1 costs $1.50 for a 1-liter bottle, and soda #2 costs $2.75 for a 2-liter bottle, it would be a better deal to buy Soda #2, because its unit rate is only $1.375 per 1-liter, which is cheaper than Soda #1. Unit rates can also help determine the length of time a given event will take. For example, if you can paint 2 rooms in 4.5 hours, you can determine how long it will take you to paint 5 rooms by solving for the unit rate per room and then multiplying that by 5.

<u>Example 1</u>

Janice made $40 during the first 5 hours she spent babysitting. She will continue to earn money at this rate until she finishes babysitting in 3 more hours. Find how much money Janice earned babysitting and how much she earns per hour.

Janice will earn $64 babysitting in her 8 total hours (adding the first 5 hours to the remaining 3 gives the 8 hour total). This can be found by setting up a proportion comparing money earned to babysitting hours. Since she earns $40 for 5 hours and since the rate is constant, she will earn a proportional amount in 8 hours: $\frac{40}{5} = \frac{x}{8}$. Cross-multiplying will yield $5x = 320$, and division by 5 shows that $x = 64$.

Copyright © Mometrix Media. You have been licensed one copy of this document for personal use only. Any other reproduction or redistribution is strictly prohibited. All rights reserved.

Janice earns $8 per hour. This can be found by taking her total amount earned, $64, and dividing it by the total number of hours worked, 8. Since $\frac{64}{8} = 8$, Janice makes $8 in one hour. This can also be found by finding the unit rate, money earned per hour: $\frac{64}{8} = \frac{x}{1}$. Since cross-multiplying yields $8x = 64$, and division by 8 shows that $x = 8$, Janice earns $8 per hour.

Example 2

The McDonalds are taking a family road trip, driving 300 miles to their cabin. It took them 2 hours to drive the first 120 miles. They will drive at the same speed all the way to their cabin. Find the speed at which the McDonalds are driving and how much longer it will take them to get to their cabin.

The McDonalds are driving 60 miles per hour. This can be found by setting up a proportion to find the unit rate, the number of miles they drive per one hour: $\frac{120}{2} = \frac{x}{1}$. Cross-multiplying yields $2x = 120$ and division by 2 shows that $x = 60$.

Since the McDonalds will drive this same speed, it will take them another 3 hours to get to their cabin. This can be found by first finding how many miles the McDonalds have left to drive, which is 300 – 120 = 180. The McDonalds are driving at 60 miles per hour, so a proportion can be set up to determine how many hours it will take them to drive 180 miles: $\frac{180}{x} = \frac{60}{1}$. Cross-multiplying yields $60x = 180$, and division by 60 shows that $x = 3$. This can also be found by using the formula $D = r \times t$ (or $Distance = rate \times time$), where $180 = 60 \times t$, and division by 60 shows that $t = 3$.

Example 3

It takes Andy 10 minutes to read 6 pages of his book. He has already read 150 pages in his book that is 210 pages long. Find how long it takes Andy to read 1 page and also find how long it will take him to finish his book if he continues to read at the same speed.

It takes Andy 1 minute and 40 seconds to read one page in his book. This can be found by finding the unit rate per one page, by dividing the total time it takes him to read 6 pages by 6. Since it takes him 10 minutes to read 6 pages, $\frac{10}{6} = 1\,^2/_3$ minutes, which is 1 minute and 40 seconds.

It will take Andy another 100 minutes, or 1 hour and 40 minutes to finish his book. This can be found by first figuring out how many pages Andy has left to read, which is 210-150 = 60. Since it is now known that it takes him $1\,^2/_3$ minutes to read each page, then that rate must be multiplied by however many pages he has left to read (60) to find the time he'll need: $60 \times 1\,^2/_3 = 100$, so it will take him 100 minutes, or 1 hour and 40 minutes, to read the rest of his book.

Copyright © Mometrix Media. You have been licensed one copy of this document for personal use only. Any other reproduction or redistribution is strictly prohibited. All rights reserved.

Other word problems

Example 1

A patient was given pain medicine at a dosage of 0.22 grams. The patient's dosage was then increased to 0.80 grams. By how much was the patient's dosage increased?

The first step is to determine what operation (addition, subtraction, multiplication, or division) the problem requires. Notice the key words and phrases "by how much" and "increased." "Increased" means that you go from a smaller amount to a larger amount. This change can be found by subtracting the smaller amount from the larger amount: 0.80 grams – 0.22 grams = 0.58 grams.

Remember to line up the decimal when subtracting.

$$\begin{array}{r} 0.80 \\ -\,0.22 \\ \hline 0.58 \end{array}$$

Example 2

At a hospital, $\frac{3}{4}$ of the 100 beds are occupied today. Yesterday, $\frac{4}{5}$ of the 100 beds were occupied. On which day were more of the hospital beds occupied and by how much more?

First, find the actual number of beds that were occupied each day. To do so, multiply the fraction of beds occupied by the number of beds available:

Actual number of beds occupied = fraction of beds occupied × number of beds available

Today: Actual number of beds occupied = $\frac{3}{4}$ × 100.

$$\frac{3}{4} \times \frac{100}{1} = \frac{3 \times 100}{4 \times 1} = \frac{300}{4}$$

Then, write the fraction in lowest terms. $\frac{300}{4} \div \frac{4}{4} = \frac{75}{1} = 75$.

Today, 75 beds are occupied.

Yesterday: Actual number of beds occupied = $\frac{4}{5}$ × 100.

$$\frac{4}{5} \times \frac{100}{1} = \frac{4 \times 100}{5 \times 1} = \frac{400}{5}$$

Then, write the fraction in lowest terms.

$$\frac{400}{5} \div \frac{5}{5} = \frac{80}{1} = 80.$$

Yesterday, 80 beds were occupied.

The difference in the number of beds occupied is 80 – 75 = 5 beds.

Therefore, five more beds were occupied yesterday than today.

Copyright © Mometrix Media. You have been licensed one copy of this document for personal use only. Any other reproduction or redistribution is strictly prohibited. All rights reserved.

Example 3

A patient complaining of fatigue and weight gain was diagnosed with hypothyroidism and was prescribed 125 mcg of medication. Three months later, her symptoms had improved, and her thyroid stimulation hormone (TSH) level was found to be 0.5 mIU/L. The doctor reduced the patient's thyroid medication dosage to 100 mcg, after which the patient's TSH level was found to be 1.5 mIU/L, which is within the normal range. By what percentage did the doctor reduce the patient's thyroid medication?

In this problem you must determine which information is necessary to answer the question. The question asks by what percentage the doctor reduced the patient's thyroid medication dosage. Find the two dosage amounts and perform subtraction to find their difference. The first dosage amount is 125 mcg. The second dosage amount is 100 mcg. Therefore, the difference is 125 mcg – 100 mcg = 25 mcg. The percentage reduction can then be calculated as $\frac{\text{change}}{\text{original}} = \frac{25 \text{ mcg}}{125 \text{ mcg}} = \frac{1}{5} = 20\%$.

Example 4

In a hospital emergency room, there are 4 nurses for every 12 patients. What is the ratio of nurses to patients? If the nurse-to-patient ratio remains constant, how many nurses must be present to care for 24 patients?

The ratio of nurses to patients can be written as 4 to 12, 4:12, or $\frac{4}{12}$. Because four and twelve have a common factor of four, the ratio should be reduced to 1:3, which means that there is one nurse present for every three patients. If this ratio remains constant, there must be eight nurses present to care for 24 patients.

Example 5

In an intensive care unit, the nurse-to-patient ratio is 1:2. If seven nurses are on duty, how many patients are currently in the ICU?

Use proportional reasoning or set up a proportion to solve. Because there are twice as many patients as nurses, there must be fourteen patients when seven nurses are on duty. Setting up and solving a proportion gives the same result:

$$\frac{\text{number of nurses}}{\text{number of patients}} = \frac{1}{2} = \frac{7}{\text{number of patients}}$$

Represent the unknown number of patients as the variable x.

$$\frac{1}{2} = \frac{7}{x}$$

To solve for x, cross multiply:

$1 \cdot x = 7 \cdot 2$, so x = 14.

Example 6

During a shift, a new nurse spent five hours of her time observing procedures, three hours working in the oncology department, and four hours doing paperwork. During the next shift, she spent four hours observing procedures, six hours in the

- 53 -

Copyright © Mometrix Media. You have been licensed one copy of this document for personal use only. Any other reproduction or redistribution is strictly prohibited. All rights reserved.

oncology department, and two hours doing paperwork. What was the percent change for each task between the two shifts?

The three tasks are observing procedures, working in the oncology department, and doing paperwork. To find the amount of change, compare the first amount with the second amount for each task. Then, write this difference as a percentage compared to the initial amount.

Amount of change for observing procedures: 5 hours – 4 hours = 1 hour.

The percent of change is $\frac{\text{amount of change}}{\text{original amount}} \cdot 100\%$. $\frac{1 \text{ hour}}{5 \text{ hours}} \cdot 100\% = 20\%$. The nurse spent 20% less time observing procedures on her second shift than on her first.

Amount of change for working in the oncology department: 6 hours – 3 hours = 3 hours.

The percent of change is $\frac{\text{amount of change}}{\text{original amount}} \cdot 100\%$. $\frac{3 \text{ hours}}{3 \text{ hours}} \cdot 100\% = 100\%$. The nurse spent 100% more time (or twice as much time) working in the oncology department during her second shift than she did in her first.

Amount of change for doing paperwork: 4 hours – 2 hours = 2 hours.

The percent of change is $\frac{\text{amount of change}}{\text{original amount}} \cdot 100\%$. $\frac{2 \text{ hours}}{4 \text{ hours}} \cdot 100\% = 50\%$. The nurse spent 50% less time (or half as much time) working on paperwork during her second shift than she did in her first.

Example 7

A patient's heart beat 422 times over the course of six minutes. About how many times did the patient's heart beat during each minute?

"About how many" indicates that you need to estimate the solution. In this case, look at the numbers you are given. 422 can be rounded down to 420, which is easily divisible by 6. A good estimate is 420 ÷ 6 = 70 beats per minute. More accurately, the patient's heart rate was just over 70 beats per minute since his heart actually beat a little more than 420 times in six minutes.

Example 8

At a hospital, 40% of the nurses work in labor and delivery. If 20 nurses work in labor and delivery, how many nurses work at the hospital?

To answer this problem, first think about the number of nurses that work at the hospital. Will it be more or less than the number of nurses who work in a specific department such as labor and delivery? More nurses work at the hospital, so the number you find to answer this question will be greater than 20.

40% of the nurses are labor and delivery nurses. "Of" indicates multiplication, and words like "is" and "are" indicate equivalence. Translating the problem into a

Copyright © Mometrix Media. You have been licensed one copy of this document for personal use only. Any other reproduction or redistribution is strictly prohibited. All rights reserved.

mathematical sentence gives 40% · n = 20, where n represents the total number of nurses. Solving for n gives

$$n = \frac{20}{40\%} = \frac{20}{0.40} = 50.$$

Fifty nurses work at the hospital.

Example 9

A patient was given 40 mg of a certain medicine. Later, the patient's dosage was increased to 45 mg. What was the percent increase in his medication? To find the percent increase, first compare the original and increased amounts. The original amount was 40 mg, and the increased amount is 45 mg, so the dosage of medication was increased by 5 mg (45 − 40 = 5). Note, however, that the question asks not by how much the dosage increased but by what percentage it increased. Percent increase $= \frac{\text{new amount}-\text{original amount}}{\text{original amount}} \cdot 100\%$.

So, $\frac{45\text{ mg}-40\text{ mg}}{40\text{ mg}} \cdot 100\% = \frac{5}{40} \cdot 100\% = 0.125 \cdot 100\% \approx 12.5\%$

The percent increase is approximately 12.5%.

Example 10

A patient was given 100 mg of a medicine every two hours. How much medication will the patient receive in four hours?

Using proportional reasoning, since four hours is twice as long as two hours, the patient will receive twice as much medication, 2·100 mg = 200 mg, within that time period.

To write an equation, first, write the amount of medicine per 2 hours as a ratio.

$$\frac{100\text{ mg}}{2\text{ hours}}$$

Next create a proportion to relate the different time increments of 2 hours and 4 hours.

$\frac{100\text{ mg}}{2\text{ hours}} = \frac{x\text{ mg}}{4\text{ hours}}$, where x is the amount of medicine the patient receives in four hours. Make sure to keep the same units in either the numerator or denominator. In this case the numerator units must be mg for both ratios and the denominator units must be hours for both ratios.

Use cross multiplication and division to solve for x.

$$\frac{100\text{ mg}}{2\text{ hours}} = \frac{x\text{ mg}}{4\text{ hours}}$$

$$100(4) = 2(x)$$
$$400 = 2x$$
$$400 \div 2 = 2x \div 2$$
$$200 = x$$

- 55 -

Copyright © Mometrix Media. You have been licensed one copy of this document for personal use only. Any other reproduction or redistribution is strictly prohibited. All rights reserved.

Therefore, the patient receives 200 mg every four hours.

Example 11

Jane ate lunch at a local restaurant. She ordered a $4.99 appetizer, a $12.50 entrée, and a $1.25 soda. If she wants to tip her server 20%, how much money will she spend in all?

To find total amount, first find the sum of the items she ordered from the menu and then add 20% of this sum to the total.

In other words:

$4.99 + $12.50 + $1.25 = $18.74.

Then 20% of $18.74 is (20%)($18.74) = (0.20)($18.74) = $3.75.

So, the total she spends is cost of the meal plus the tip or $18.74 + $3.75 = $22.49.

Another way to find this sum is to multiply 120% by the cost of the meal.

$18.74(120%) = $18.74(1.20) = $22.49.

Example 12

A patient was given 100 mg of a certain medicine. The patient's dosage was later decreased to 88mg. What was the percent decrease?

The medication was decreased by 12 mg (100 mg - 88 mg = 12 mg). To find by what percent the medication was decreased, this change must be written as a percentage when compared to the original amount.

In other words, $\frac{\text{original amount} - \text{new amount}}{\text{original amount}} \cdot 100\% = \text{percent decrease}$

$\frac{12 \text{ mg}}{100 \text{ mg}} \cdot 100\% = 0.12 \cdot 100\% = 12\%$.

The percent decrease is 12%.

Example 13

A patient was given blood pressure medicine at a dosage of 2 grams. The patient's dosage was then decreased to 0.45 grams. By how much was the patient's dosage decreased?

The decrease is represented by the difference between the two amounts:

2 grams – 0.45 grams = 1.55 grams.

Remember to line up the decimal point before subtracting.

```
  2.00
- 0.45
  1.55
```

- 56 -

Copyright © Mometrix Media. You have been licensed one copy of this document for personal use only. Any other reproduction or redistribution is strictly prohibited. All rights reserved.

Example 14

Two weeks ago, $\frac{2}{3}$ of the 60 patients at a hospital were male. Last week, $\frac{3}{6}$ of the 80 patients were male. During which week were there more male patients?

First, you need to find the number of male patients that were in the hospital each week. You are given this amount in terms of fractions. To find the actual number of male patients, multiply the fraction of male patients by the number of patients in the hospital.

Actual number of male patients = fraction of male patients × total number of patients.

Two weeks ago: Actual number of male patients = $\frac{2}{3}$ × 60.

$$\frac{2}{3} \times \frac{60}{1} = \frac{2 \times 60}{3 \times 1} = \frac{120}{3} = 40.$$

Two weeks ago, 40 of the patients were male.

Last week: Actual number of male patients = $\frac{3}{6}$ × 80.

$$\frac{3}{6} \times \frac{80}{1} = \frac{3 \times 80}{6 \times 1} = \frac{240}{6} = 40.$$

Last week, 40 of the patients were male.

The number of male patients was the same both weeks.

Example 15

At a hospital, for every 20 female patients there are 15 male patients. This same patient ratio happens to exist at another hospital. If there are 100 female patients at the second hospital, how many male patients are there?

One way to find the number of male patients is to set up and solve a proportion.

$$\frac{\text{number of female patients}}{\text{number of male patients}} = \frac{20}{15} = \frac{100}{\text{number of male patients}}.$$

Represent the unknown number of male patients as the variable x.

$$\frac{20}{15} = \frac{100}{x}.$$

Follow these steps to solve for x:

1) Cross multiply. $20 \times x = 15 \times 100$.
$20x = 1500$

2) Divide each side of the equation by 20.
$x = 75$

Or, notice that

$$\frac{20 \cdot 5}{15 \cdot 5} = \frac{100}{75}, \text{ so } x = 75.$$

- 57 -

Copyright © Mometrix Media. You have been licensed one copy of this document for personal use only. Any other reproduction or redistribution is strictly prohibited. All rights reserved.

<u>Example 16</u>

In a performance review, an employee received a score of 70 out of 100 for efficiency and 90 out of 100 for meeting project deadlines. Six months later, the employee received a score of 65 out of 100 for efficiency and 96 out of 100 for meeting project deadlines. What was the percent change for each score on the performance review?

To find the percent change, compare the first amount with the second amount for each score; then, write this difference as a percentage compared to the initial amount. Or, write the original amounts as percentages and then subtract.

Percent change for efficiency score:

70% – 65% = 5%.

The employee's efficiency decreased by 5%.

Percent change for meeting project deadlines score:

96% – 90% = 6%

The employee increased his ability to meet project deadlines by 6%.

<u>Example 17</u>

A patient's total bill is about $128 for the same procedure repeated each month for 5 months. About how much does the procedure cost?

"About how much" indicates that you need to estimate the solution. In this case, look at the numbers you are given which are $128 and 5. 128 can be rounded up to 130 which is easily divisible by 5. So a good estimate is 130 ÷ 5 = $26 per procedure. More accurately, the procedure costs a little less than $26.

Subtracting fractions

Fractions with common denominators can be easily added or subtracted. Recall that the denominator is the bottom number in the fraction and that the numerator is the top number in the fraction. For example, subtract $\frac{1}{5}$ from $\frac{3}{4}$:

The denominators of $\frac{3}{4}$ and $\frac{1}{5}$ are 4 and 5, respectively. The lowest common denominator of 4 and 5 is 20 because 20 is the least common multiple of 4 (multiples 4, 8, 16, 20 …) and 5 (multiples 5, 10, 15, 20, …). Convert each fraction to its equivalent with the newly found common denominator of 20.

$\frac{3 \times 5}{4 \times 5} = \frac{15}{20}; \frac{1 \times 4}{5 \times 4} = \frac{4}{20}.$

Now that the fractions have the same denominator, you can subtract them.

$\frac{15}{20} - \frac{4}{20} = \frac{11}{20}.$

Copyright © Mometrix Media. You have been licensed one copy of this document for personal use only. Any other reproduction or redistribution is strictly prohibited. All rights reserved.

Subtracting with regrouping

<u>Example 1</u>

Demonstrate how to subtract 189 from 525 using regrouping.

First, set up the subtraction problem:

```
  525
- 189
```

Notice that the numbers in the ones and tens columns of 525 are smaller than the numbers in the ones and tens columns of 189. This means you will need to use regrouping to perform subtraction.

```
 5  2  5
-1  8  9
```

To subtract 9 from 5 in the ones column you will need to borrow from the 2 in the tens columns:

```
 5  1  15
-1  8   9
         6
```

Next, to subtract 8 from 1 in the tens column you will need to borrow from the 5 in the hundreds column:

```
 4  11  15
-1   8   9
     3   6
```

Last, subtract the 1 from the 4 in the hundreds column:

```
 4  11  15
-1   8   9
 3   3   6
```

<u>Example 2</u>

Demonstrate how to subtract 477 from 620 using regrouping.

First, set up the subtraction problem:

```
  620
- 477
```

Notice that the numbers in the ones and tens columns of 620 are smaller than the numbers in the ones and tens columns of 477. This means you will need to use regrouping to perform subtraction.

```
 6  2  0
-4  7  7
```

Copyright © Mometrix Media. You have been licensed one copy of this document for personal use only. Any other reproduction or redistribution is strictly prohibited. All rights reserved.

To subtract 7 from 0 in the ones column you will need to borrow from the 2 in the tens column.

```
  6  1  10
- 4  7   7
            3
```

Next, to subtract 7 from the 1 that's still in the tens column you will need to borrow from the 6 in the hundreds column.

```
  5  11  10
- 4   7   7
         4   3
```

Lastly, subtract 4 from the 5 remaining in the hundreds column to get:

```
  5  11  10
- 4   7   7
    1  4   3
```

Calculation of salary after deductions

<u>Example 1</u>

Before taxes, a monthly paycheck was $2,160. However, the following deductions were taken from the paycheck: Federal Withholding, $154; Social Security, $90.72; Medicare $31.22; and State Withholding, $126.20. What is actual amount of the paycheck after these deductions?

Notice the key words in the problem: the words "deduction" and "from" indicate subtraction. To determine the amount of the paycheck after the deductions, or expenses, use either of these methods.

Method 1: Add all the deductions. Then, subtract this amount from the original amount.

Total Deductions = $154 + $90.72 + $31.22 + $126.20 = $402.14

Subtract this total amount from the original amount. $2,160 - $402.14 = $1,757.86.

Method 2: Subtract each amount from the original amount.

$2,160 - $154 - $90.72 - $31.22 - $126.20 = $1,757.86

<u>Example 2</u>

Before taxes, a monthly paycheck was $787.57. However, the following deductions were taken from the paycheck: Federal Withholding, $78.42; Social Security, $36.99; Medicare, $7.04; and State Withholding, $45.86. What is amount of the paycheck after these deductions?

Deductions, or expenses, are subtracted from the original amount. There are two ways to answer this problem.

- 60 -

Copyright © Mometrix Media. You have been licensed one copy of this document for personal use only. Any other reproduction or redistribution is strictly prohibited. All rights reserved.

Method 1: Add all the deductions. Then subtract this amount from the original amount.

Total Deductions = $78.42 + $36.99 + $7.04 + $45.86 = $168.31

Subtract this total amount from the original amount. $787.57 - $168.31 = $619.26.

Method 2: Subtract each amount from the original amount.

$787.57 - $78.42 - $36.99 - $7.04 - $45.86 = $619.26

Calculation of balance after transactions

Example 1

Two weeks ago, a checking account had a balance of $7,809.45. The transactions for the last two weeks are shown in table below.

Water Bill	$36.78	Expense
Paycheck	$2,891.45	Income
Cell Phone Bill	$98.99	Expense
Credit Card Bill	$375.17	Expense
Refund for returned clothing items	$45.28	Refund

What is the new account balance after these transactions?

When reconciling a checking account balance, you need to know what operation (addition or subtraction) to use for each transaction. An expense is a deduction from the account balance. Therefore, you subtract the expense amount from the account balance. A transaction labeled "income" means that you are adding the amount to your account balance. Lastly, a refund means that you are receiving, or adding money back, to your account

To find the new account balance, perform the following operations:

$7,809.45 - $36.78 + $2,891.45 - $98.99 - $375.17 + $45.28 = $10,235.24

Example 2

Two months ago, a checking account had a balance of $4,009.67. The transactions for the last two months are shown in table below.

Electric Bill	$189.45	Expense
Paycheck	$1,000.31	Income
Internet Bill	$68.77	Expense
Paycheck	$1,000.31	Income
Sold items on Ebay	$201.55	Income

What is the new account balance after these transactions?

When reconciling a checking account balance, you need to know what operation (addition or subtraction) to use for each transaction. An expense is a deduction from

- 61 -

Copyright © Mometrix Media. You have been licensed one copy of this document for personal use only. Any other reproduction or redistribution is strictly prohibited. All rights reserved.

the account balance. Therefore, you would subtract the expense amount from the account balance. An income is added to the account balance.

To find the new account balance, perform the following operations:

$4,009.67 - $189.45 + $1,000.31 - $68.77 + $1,000.31 + $201.55 = $5953.62

Solving for x in a proportion

Solve for x in this proportion: $\frac{10}{15} = \frac{x}{30}$.

There are two ways to solve for x.

Method 1: Cross multiply; then, solve for x.

$$\frac{10}{15} = \frac{x}{30}$$
$$10(30) = 15(x)$$
$$300 = 15x$$
$$300 \div 15 = 15x \div 15$$
$$x = 20$$

Method 2: Notice that 30 is twice as much as 15, so x should be twice as much as 10. Therefore, $x = 10 \times 2 = 20$.

Roman numerals

Roman numerals are numbers represented by a combination of the letters I, V, X, L, C, D, and M. These letters individually represent the numbers 1, 5, 10, 50, 100, 500, and 1000. When there is a string of letters together, as long as they are written in order of value from greatest to smallest, they represent the sum of the individual letters. For instance, LVI represents 50 + 5 + 1 = 56 because they are written in order 50, 5, 1. If the symbol for a smaller number comes before the symbol for a larger number, the smaller number is subtracted from the larger number. For instance, LIV represents 50 + (5-1) = 54 since I represents a smaller number than V. The only letter pairs that will be used in this way are IV, IX, XL, XC, CD, and CM. For the test, you can either memorize and be on the lookout for these six letter pairs or check the entire string to make sure it is written in order of value.

Decimal placement in a product

Example

What is 3.52 × 5? How did you find this answer?

When finding the product of numbers containing decimals, it is often helpful to multiply the numbers as if neither contains a decimal and then to adjust the product afterwards. For instance, 352 × 5 = 1760.

In order to change 3.52 to a whole number to make multiplying easier, you essentially multiply it by 100, which moves the decimal two places to the right. Because 352 is 100 times 3.52, the product of 352 and 5 (1760) is 100 times the product of 3.52 and 5. To adjust for the initial change, you must divide the product by 100, which moves the decimal two places back to the left. So, the product of 3.52

Copyright © Mometrix Media. You have been licensed one copy of this document for personal use only. Any other reproduction or redistribution is strictly prohibited. All rights reserved.

and 5 is 17.6 (or 17.60). An easier way to think about this may be to count the total number of digits after each decimal in the original problem and make sure the answer contains the same number of digits after its decimal. Since there are two numbers after a decimal in the problem, there should be two numbers after the decimal in the answer. So, the answer must be 17.60. (Note that a decimal was inserted in the number 1760 such that there are two numbers, namely the six and zero, after the decimal in the adjusted answer just as there are two numbers, namely the five and two, after a decimal in the problem.) It is also important to ensure that your answer makes sense. 3.52 is between 3 and 4, so 3.52 × 5 should be between 3 × 5 and 4 × 5. Indeed, 17.6 is between 15 and 20, so it is a sensible answer.

Equivalent ratios

<u>Example</u>

Write two ratios that are equivalent to 5:25.

5:25 can be reduced to 1:5. Any ratio in which the second term is five times the first is equivalent to the given ratio. Two additional examples are 3:15 and 25:125.

Rational numbers from least to greatest

<u>Example</u>

Order the following rational numbers from least to greatest: 0.55, 17%, $\sqrt{25}$, $\frac{64}{4}$, $\frac{25}{50}$, 3.

The term "rational" simply means that the number can be expressed as a ratio, or fraction. The set of rational numbers includes integers, of which whole numbers are a subset, because these numbers can be written as ratios. Notice that each of the numbers in the problem can be written as fractions:

$\sqrt{25} = 5 = \frac{5}{1}$
$0.55 = \frac{55}{100}$

$17\% = 0.17 = \frac{17}{100}$

To order the numbers from least to greatest, compare their values.

Notice that $\frac{64}{4}$ is equal to 16, and $\frac{25}{50}$ can be written as $\frac{1}{2}$.

So, the answer is 17%, $\frac{25}{50}$, 0.55, 3, $\sqrt{25}$, $\frac{64}{4}$.

Rational numbers from greatest to least

<u>Example</u>

Order the following rational numbers from greatest to least:

0.3, 27%, $\sqrt{100}$, $\frac{72}{9}$, $\frac{1}{9}$, 4.5

The term "rational" simply means that the number can be expressed as a ratio, or fraction. The set of rational numbers includes integers, of which whole numbers are

- 63 -

Copyright © Mometrix Media. You have been licensed one copy of this document for personal use only. Any other reproduction or redistribution is strictly prohibited. All rights reserved.

a subset, because these numbers can be written as ratios. Notice that each of the numbers in the problem can be written as fractions:

$\sqrt{100} = 10 = \frac{10}{1}$

$0.3 = \frac{3}{10}$

$27\% = 0.27 = \frac{27}{100}$

Also notice that $\frac{72}{9}$ is equal to 8 and that $\frac{1}{9}$ is approximately 0.11.

So, the answer is $\sqrt{100}, \frac{72}{9}, 4.5, 0.3, 27\%, \frac{1}{9}$.

Copyright © Mometrix Media. You have been licensed one copy of this document for personal use only. Any other reproduction or redistribution is strictly prohibited. All rights reserved.

Algebraic Applications

Equations with one unknown

Example 1

$\frac{45\%}{12\%} = \frac{15\%}{x}$. Solve for x.

First, cross multiply; then, solve for x: $\frac{45\%}{12\%} = \frac{15\%}{x}$

$\frac{0.45}{0.12} = \frac{0.15}{x}$.

$0.45(x) = 0.12(0.15)$

$0.45\,x = 0.0180$
$0.45x \div 0.45 = 0.0180 \div 0.45$

$x = 0.04 = 4\%$

Alternatively, notice that $\frac{45\% \div 3}{12\% \div 3} = \frac{15\%}{4\%}$. So, x = 4%.

Example 2

How do you solve for x in the proportion $\frac{0.50}{2} = \frac{1.50}{x}$?

First, cross multiply; then, solve for x.

$\frac{0.50}{2} = \frac{1.50}{x}$.
$0.50(x) = 2(1.50)$

$0.50x = 3$
$0.50x \div 0.50 = 3 \div 0.50$

$x = 6$

Or, notice that $\frac{0.50 \cdot 3}{2 \cdot 3} = \frac{1.50}{6}$, so x = 6.

Example 3

$\frac{40}{8} = \frac{x}{24}$. Find x.

One way to solve for x is to first cross multiply.

$\frac{40}{8} = \frac{x}{24}$.

$40(24) = 8(x)$

$960 = 8x$

$960 \div 8 = 8x \div 8$

$x = 120$

Copyright © Mometrix Media. You have been licensed one copy of this document for personal use only. Any other reproduction or redistribution is strictly prohibited. All rights reserved.

Or, notice that:

$\frac{40 \cdot 3}{8 \cdot 3} = \frac{120}{24}$, so x = 120

Example 4

x = $\frac{1}{4}$ + 70%. Write your answer as a percent and as a fraction in lowest terms.

The key is to write the two values in the same format. You can write both of them as percents and then perform addition, or you can write both of them as fractions and then perform addition.

Method 1: Write both numbers as percents and then perform addition.

To convert $\frac{1}{4}$ to a percent simply divide the numerator by the denominator in the fraction and then multiply by 100%. $\frac{1}{4}$ = 0.25. Then 0.25(100%) = 25%.

Then perform addition: x = 25% + 70% = 95%.

95% $= \frac{95}{100} = \frac{19}{20}$.

Method 2: Write both numbers as fractions and then perform addition.

70% $= \frac{70}{100} = \frac{7}{10}$.

x $= \frac{7}{10} + \frac{1}{4} = \frac{14}{20} + \frac{5}{20} = \frac{19}{20}$.

$\frac{19}{20} = \frac{95}{100} = 95\%$.

Polynomials and monomials

To multiply two binomials, follow the *FOIL* method. FOIL stands for:

- First: Multiply the first term of each binomial
- Outer: Multiply the outer terms of each binomial
- Inner: Multiply the inner terms of each binomial
- Last: Multiply the last term of each binomial

Using FOIL $(Ax + By)(Cx + Dy) = ACx^2 + ADxy + BCxy + BDy^2$.

> **Review Video: Multiplying Terms Using the FOIL Method**
> Visit mometrix.com/academy and enter code: 854792

Example 1

Simplify $10c^2 + 25c - 3c^2 - 10$.

This is an example of a polynomial. To perform addition and subtraction on a polynomial you must first identify "like" terms. "Like" terms have the same variable with the same exponent. For example $10c^2$ and $-3c^2$ are "like" terms because they both have the variable c with exponent of 2, so they both have c^2.

- 66 -

Copyright © Mometrix Media. You have been licensed one copy of this document for personal use only. Any other reproduction or redistribution is strictly prohibited. All rights reserved.

After you identify "like" terms, add or subtract their coefficients.

$10c^2 - 3c^2 = (10 - 3)\ c^2 = 7c^2$

There are no other "like" terms in the polynomial, so the answer written in descending powers of c is $7c^2 + 25c - 10$.

Example 2

Simplify $4b(2b^3 - 5f^4 + 3b^2 + 7)$.

This is an example of multiplying monomial and polynomial terms. Use the distributive property by multiplying the term 4b by each term in the parentheses:

$4b(2b^3) - 4b(5f^4) + 4b(3b^2) + 4b(7)$

When multiplying monomials, first multiply the coefficients: $(4 \times 2)(b \times b^3) - (4 \times 5)(b \times f^4) + (4 \times 3)(b \times b^2) + (4 \times 7)(b)$

When multiplying powers with the same base, add their exponents:

$8b^{1+3} - 20bf^4 + 12b^{1+2} + 28b$

$8b^4 - 20bf^4 + 12b^3 + 28b$

Notice that the exponents for b and f can't be combined since the variables are not the same.

Example 3

What is $6x^8y^3z$ divided by $3x^3y^5z^2$?

This is an example of dividing the monomials $6x^8y^3z$ and $3x^3y^5z^2$: When simplifying $6x^8y^3z \div 3x^3y^5z^2$, first divide the coefficients of the variables: $6 \div 3 = 2$.

For each variable, subtract the exponent in the second term from the exponent in the first term.

$x^{8-3} = x^5$

$y^{3-5} = y^{-2}$

$z^{1-2} = z^{-1}$ Note: $z = z^1$.

The resulting $2x^5y^{-2}z^{-1}$ should be written with only positive exponents. Because $y^{-2} = \frac{1}{y^2}$ and $z^{-1} = \frac{1}{z}$, $2x^5y^{-2}z^{-1}$ is the same as $\frac{2x^5}{y^2z}$.

Translating

Words to mathematical expression

Write "four less than twice *x*" as a mathematical expression.

Remember that an expression does not have an equals sign. "Less" indicates subtraction, and "twice" indicates multiplication by two. Four less than 2*x* is 2*x* – 4. Notice how this is

Copyright © Mometrix Media. You have been licensed one copy of this document for personal use only. Any other reproduction or redistribution is strictly prohibited. All rights reserved.

different than 4 – 2x. You can plug in values for x to see how these expressions would yield different values.

Words to mathematical equation

Translate "three hundred twenty-five increased by six times 3x equals three hundred forty-three" into a mathematical equation.

The key words and phrases are "increased by," "times," and "equals."

Three hundred twenty-five increased by six times 3x equals three hundred forty-three:

$$325 \ + \ 6(3x) \ = \ 343.$$

The mathematical sentence is $325 + 6(3x) = 343$.

Words to inequality

Write an inequality that represents "64 plus 25f is less than or equal to 23 plus the quantity x minus 44."

The key words and phrases are "plus," "less than or equal to," "the quantity," and "minus." The first part of the number sentence is 64 plus 25f. "Plus" indicates addition. So this can be written as 64 + 25f which will go on the left hand side of the inequality sign.

"Less than or equal to" is represented with the inequality symbol ≤.

The second part of the number sentence is 23 plus the quantity x minus 44. "Plus" indicates addition. "The quantity x minus 44" means that 44 must be subtracted from x before it is added to the 23; in other words, the "x minus 44" needs to be grouped together inside parentheses. All together, this can be written as 23 + (x – 44), which goes on the right hand side of the inequality sign.

The final answer is $64 + 25f \leq 23 + (x – 44)$.

Mathematical expression to a phrase

Write a phrase which represents this mathematical expression: $75 – 3t + 14^2$.

Because there are many words which indicate various operations, there are several ways to write this expression, including "seventy-five minus three times t plus fourteen squared."

Copyright © Mometrix Media. You have been licensed one copy of this document for personal use only. Any other reproduction or redistribution is strictly prohibited. All rights reserved.

Data Interpretation

Consistency between studies

Example

In a drug study containing 100 patients, a new cholesterol drug was found to decrease low-density lipoprotein (LDL) levels in 25% of the patients. In a second study containing 50 patients, the same drug administered at the same dosage was found to decrease LDL levels in 50% of the patients. Are the results of these two studies consistent with one another?

Even though in both studies 25 people (25% of 100 is 25 and 50% of 50 is 25) showed improvements in their LDL levels, the results of the studies are inconsistent. The results of the second study indicate that the drug has a much higher efficacy (desired result) than the results of the first study. Because 50 out of 150 total patients showed improvement on the medication, one could argue that the drug is effective in one-third (or approximately 33%) of patients. However, one should be wary of the reliability of results when they're not reproducible from one study to the next and when the sample size is fairly low.

Data organization

Example

A nurse found the heart rates of eleven different patients to be 76, 80, 90, 86, 70, 76, 72, 88, 88, 68, and 88 beats per minutes. Organize this information in a table.

There are several ways to organize data in a table. The table below is an example.

Patient Number	1	2	3	4	5	6	7	8	9	10	11
Heart Rate (bpm)	76	80	90	86	70	76	72	88	88	68	88

When making a table, be sure to label the columns and rows appropriately.

Interpretation of graphs

Example 1

The following graph shows the ages of five patients a nurse is caring for in the hospital:

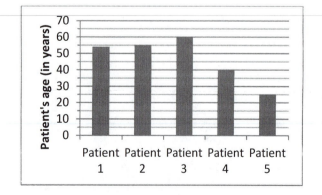

Copyright © Mometrix Media. You have been licensed one copy of this document for personal use only. Any other reproduction or redistribution is strictly prohibited. All rights reserved.

Use this graph to determine the age range of the patients for which the nurse is caring.

Use the graph to find the age of each patient: Patient 1 is 54 years old; Patient 2 is 55 years old; Patient 3 is 60 years old; Patient 4 is 40 years old; and Patient 5 is 25 years old. The age range is the age of the oldest patient minus the age of the youngest patient. In other words, 60 – 25 = 35. The age range is 35 years.

Example 2

Following is a line graph representing the heart rate of a patient during the day. Use the graph to answer the following questions:

The patient's minimum measured heart rate occurred at what time? The patient's maximum measured heart rate occurred at what time? At what times during the day did the patient have the same measured heart rate? What trends, if any, can you find about the patient's heart rate throughout the day?

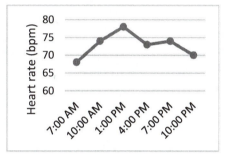

The patient's minimum measured heart rate occurred at the lowest data point on the graph, which is 68 bpm at 7:00 AM. The patient's maximum measured heart rate occurred at the highest data point on the graph, which is 78 bpm at 1:00 PM. The patient had the same measured heart rate of 74 bpm at 10:00 AM and 7:00 PM. The patient's heart rate increased through the morning to early afternoon, and generally declined as the afternoon progressed.

Independent and dependent variables

A variable is a symbol, usually an alphabetic character, designating a value that may change within the scope of a given problem. Variables can be described as either independent or dependent variables. An independent variable is an input into a system that may take on values freely. Dependent variables are those that change as a consequence of changes in other values in the equation.

Example 1

If Ray earns $10 an hour, this can be represented by the expression $10x$, where x is equal to the number of hours that Ray works. The value of x represents the number of hours because it is the independent variable, or the amount that you can choose and can manipulate. To find out how much money ,y, he earns in x hours, you would write the equation,$10x=y$. The variable y is the dependent variable because it depends on x and cannot be manipulated. Once you have the equation for the function, you can choose any number of hours to find the corresponding amount that he earns. For example, if you want to know how much he would earn working

- 70 -

Copyright © Mometrix Media. You have been licensed one copy of this document for personal use only. Any other reproduction or redistribution is strictly prohibited. All rights reserved.

36 hours, you would substitute 36 in for x and multiply to find that he would earn $360.

Example 2

A patient told a doctor she feels fine after running one mile but that her knee starts hurting after running two miles. Her knee throbs after running three miles and swells after running four. Identify the independent and dependent variables with regard to the distance she runs and her level of pain.

An independent variable is one that does not depend on any other variables in the situation. In this case, the distance the patient runs would be considered the independent variable. The dependent variable would be her level of pain because it depends on how far she runs.

Copyright © Mometrix Media. You have been licensed one copy of this document for personal use only. Any other reproduction or redistribution is strictly prohibited. All rights reserved.

Measurement

Measurement conversion

<u>Example</u>

Convert the following measurements from the given unit of measurement to the unit measurement indicated:

1 foot = ___ yards

3 inches = ___ foot

5 inches = ___ centimeters

450 centimeters = ___ meters

32 ounces = ___ pounds

4 tons = ___ pounds

1 foot = 1/3 yard

There are 12 inches in 1 foot, so 3 inches = 1/4 foot.

There are 2.54 centimeters in 1 inch, so 5 inches = 5(2.54) = 12.7 centimeters.

There are 100 centimeters in 1 meter, so 450 centimeters = 450/100 = 4.50 meters.

There are 16 ounces in 1 pound, so 32 ounces = 2 pounds.

There are 2,000 pounds in 1 ton, so 4 tons = 8,000 pounds.

Appropriate measurement unit

<u>Example</u>

Determine the most appropriate measurement unit given the situation:

1. The volume of a tissue box: cubic inches, cubic feet, or square yards
2. The area of a floor in a room: centimeters, square feet, or cubic meters
3. The perimeter of an office building: inches, pounds, feet

To determine the appropriate unit of measurement, first you must determine what is being measured; for instance, perimeter is measured in units, area in square units, and volume in cubic units. Next, you must determine the magnitude of the measurements: for example, it would make sense to measure the distance between two cities in miles rather than inches and the weight of a car in tons rather than ounces.

1. The volume of a tissue box is best measured in cubic inches.
2. The area of a floor in a room is best measured in square feet.
3. The perimeter of an office building is best measured in feet.

Copyright © Mometrix Media. You have been licensed one copy of this document for personal use only. Any other reproduction or redistribution is strictly prohibited. All rights reserved.

Science

Human Body Science

Animal tissues

Animal tissues may be divided into seven categories:

- Epithelial - Tissue in which cells are joined together tightly. Skin tissue is an example.
- Connective - Connective tissue may be dense, loose or fatty. It protects and binds body parts.
- Cartilage - Cushions and provides structural support for body parts. It has a jelly-like base and is fibrous.
- Blood - Blood transports oxygen to cells and removes wastes. It also carries hormones and defends against disease.
- Bone - Bone is a hard tissue that supports and protects softer tissues and organs. Its marrow produces red blood cells.
- Muscle - Muscle tissue helps support and move the body. The three types of muscle tissue are smooth, cardiac, and skeletal.
- Nervous - Cells called neurons form a network through the body that control responses to changes in the external and internal environment. Some send signals to muscles and glands to trigger responses.

Vitamins

Humans need dietary vitamins, which can be classified as either water soluble or fat soluble. Vitamins A, D, E, and K are fat soluble. Vitamins C and B are water soluble. Vitamin A (retinol) can be found in milk, eggs, liver, and some vegetables and fruits. It plays a role in immune system function, cell growth, and eye function.

Vitamin C (ascorbic acid) is in berries, peppers, and citrus fruits. It helps promote cell cohesiveness and healthy bones, teeth, and gums. It also improves brain function and aids in the absorption of some minerals. Other vitamins include: D (calciferol), which strengthens bones; vitamin B_2 (riboflavin), which is found in eggs; vitamin E (tocopherol); B_{12} (cyanocobalamin), which plays a role in red blood cell and nerve function; K (phylloquinone), which is found in alfalfa; B_5 (pantothenic acid); B_7 (biotin); B_6 (pyridoxine); B_3 (niacin); B_9 (folic acid); and B_1 (thiamine), which is needed to convert carbohydrates and plays a role in heart, muscle and nervous system function.

The Three Primary Body Planes

The **Transverse (or horizontal) plane** divides the patient's body into imaginary upper (superior) and lower (inferior or caudal) halves.

The **Sagittal plane** divides the body, or any body part, vertically into right and left sections. The sagittal plane runs parallel to the midline of the body.

The **Coronal (or frontal) plane** divides the body, or any body structure, vertically into front and back (anterior and posterior) sections. The coronal plane runs vertically through the body at right angles to the midline.

Copyright © Mometrix Media. You have been licensed one copy of this document for personal use only. Any other reproduction or redistribution is strictly prohibited. All rights reserved.

Terms of Direction

Medial means nearer to the midline of the body. In anatomical position, the little finger is medial to the thumb.

Lateral is the opposite of medial. It refers to structures further away from the body's midline, at the sides. In anatomical position, the thumb is lateral to the little finger.

Proximal refers to structures closer to the center of the body. The hip is proximal to the knee.

Distal refers to structures further away from the center of the body. The knee is distal to the hip.

Anterior refers to structures in front.

Posterior refers to structures behind.

Cephalad and cephalic are adverbs meaning towards the head. Cranial is the adjective, meaning of the skull.

Caudad is an adverb meaning towards the tail or posterior. Caudal is the adjective, meaning of the hindquarters.

Superior means above, or closer to the head.

Inferior means below, or closer to the feet.

Integumentary system

The skin and its associated structures are called the integumentary system. It provides the following key functions:

- Protects the body from abrasion and bacterial attack.
- Serves as a control mechanism for internal temperature.
- Provides a reserve of blood vessels that can be used as necessary.
- Produces vitamin D for metabolic purposes.

The top layer of the skin is the epidermis and the layer beneath that is the dermis. The dermis consists of dense connective tissue which protects the body. Skin structure varies widely among animals according to the needs of the particular species. Pigments determine skin color. The process of keratinization results in a new layer of top skin in humans every month or so. This process helps the skin heal itself after minor injuries and forms a barrier against toxic substances and bacterial infections.

Skeletal system

The skeletal system has an important role in the following body functions:

- Movement - The action of skeletal muscles on bones moves the body.
- Mineral Storage - Bones serve as storage facilities for essential mineral ions.
- Support - Bones act as a framework and support system for the organs.
- Protection - Bones surround and protect key organs in the body.
- Blood Cell Formation - Red blood cells are produced in the marrow of certain bones.

Copyright © Mometrix Media. You have been licensed one copy of this document for personal use only. Any other reproduction or redistribution is strictly prohibited. All rights reserved.

Bones are classified as either long, short, flat, or irregular. They are a connective tissue with a base of pulp containing collagen and living cells. Red marrow, an important site of red blood cell production, fills the spongy tissue of many bones. Bone tissue is constantly regenerating itself as the mineral composition changes. This allows for special needs during growth periods and maintains calcium levels for the body. Bone regeneration can deteriorate in old age, particularly among women, leading to osteoporosis.

The skeletal structure in humans contains both bones and cartilage. There are 206 bones in the human body, divided into two parts:

- Axial skeleton - Includes the skull, sternum, ribs, and vertebral column (the spine).
- Appendicular skeleton - Includes the bones of the arms, feet, hands, legs, hips, and shoulders.

The flexible and curved backbone is supported by muscles and ligaments. Intervertebral discs are stacked one above another and provide cushioning for the backbone. Trauma or shock may cause these discs to herniate and cause pain. The sensitive spinal cord is enclosed in a cavity which is well protected by the bones of the vertebrae.

Joints are areas of contact adjacent to bones. Synovial joints are the most common, and are freely moveable. These may be found at the shoulders and knees. Cartilaginous joints fill the spaces between some bones and restrict movement. Examples of cartilaginous joints are those between vertebrae. Fibrous joints have fibrous tissue connecting bones and no cavity is present.

Muscular system

There are three types of muscle tissue: skeletal, cardiac, and smooth. There are over 600 muscles in the human body. All muscles have these three properties in common:

- Excitability - All muscle tissues have an electric gradient which can reverse when stimulated.
- Contraction - All muscle tissues have the ability to contract, or shorten.
- Elongate – All muscle tissues share the capacity to elongate, or relax.

Only skeletal muscle interacts with the skeleton to move the body. When they contract, the muscles transmit force to the attached bones. Working together, the muscles and bones act as a system of levers which move around the joints. A small contraction of a muscle can produce a large movement. A limb can be extended and rotated around a joint due to the way the muscles are arranged.

Digestive system

Most digestive systems function by the following means:

- Movement - Movement mixes and passes nutrients through the system and eliminates waste.
- Secretion - Enzymes, hormones, and other substances necessary for digestion are secreted into the digestive tract.
- Digestion - Includes the chemical breakdown of nutrients into smaller units that enter the internal environment.
- Absorption - The passage of nutrients through plasma membranes into the blood or lymph and then to the body.

Copyright © Mometrix Media. You have been licensed one copy of this document for personal use only. Any other reproduction or redistribution is strictly prohibited. All rights reserved.

The human digestive system consists of the mouth, pharynx, esophagus, stomach, small and large intestine, rectum, and anus. Enzymes and other secretions are infused into the digestive system to assist the absorption and processing of nutrients. The nervous and endocrine systems control the digestive system. Smooth muscle moves the food by peristalsis, contracting and relaxing to move nutrients along.

Mouth and stomach

Digestion begins in the mouth with the chewing and mixing of nutrients with saliva. Only humans and other mammals actually chew their food. Salivary glands are stimulated and secrete saliva. Saliva contains enzymes that initiate the breakdown of starch in digestion. Once swallowed, the food moves down the pharynx into the esophagus en route to the stomach.

The stomach is a flexible, muscular sac. It has three main functions:

- Mixing and storing food
- Dissolving and degrading food via secretions
- Controlling passage of food into the small intestine

Protein digestion begins in the stomach. Stomach acidity helps break down the food and make nutrients available for absorption. Smooth muscle contractions move nutrients into the small intestine where the absorption process begins.

Liver

The liver is the largest solid organ of the body. It is also the largest gland. It weighs about three pounds and is located below the diaphragm on the right side of the chest. The liver is made up of four lobes. They are called the right, left, quadrate, and caudate lobes. The liver is secured to the diaphragm and abdominal walls by five ligaments. They are called the falciform (that forms a membrane-like barrier between the right and left lobes), coronary, right triangular, left triangular, and round ligaments. Nutrient-rich blood is supplied to the liver via the hepatic portal vein. The hepatic artery supplies oxygen-rich blood. Blood leaves the liver through the hepatic veins. The liver's functional units are called lobules (made up of layers of liver cells). Blood enters the lobules through branches of the portal vein and hepatic artery. The blood then flows through small channels called sinusoids.

The liver is responsible for performing many vital functions in the body including:

- Production of bile
- Production of certain blood plasma proteins
- Production of cholesterol (and certain proteins needed to carry fats)
- Storage of excess glucose in the form of glycogen (that can be converted back to glucose when needed)
- Regulation of amino acids.
- Processing of hemoglobin (to store iron)
- Conversion of ammonia (that is poisonous to the body) to urea (a waste product excreted in urine)
- Purification of the blood (clears out drugs and other toxins)
- Regulation of blood clotting
- Controlling infections by boosting immune factors and removing bacteria.

Copyright © Mometrix Media. You have been licensed one copy of this document for personal use only. Any other reproduction or redistribution is strictly prohibited. All rights reserved.

The liver processes all of the blood that passes through the digestive system. The nutrients (and drugs) that pass through the liver are converted into forms that are appropriate for the body to use.

Small intestine

In the digestive process, most nutrients are absorbed in the small intestine. Enzymes from the pancreas, liver, and stomach are transported to the small intestine to aid digestion. These enzymes act on fats, carbohydrates, nucleic acids, and proteins. Bile is a secretion of the liver and is particularly useful in breaking down fats. It is stored in the gall bladder between meals.

By the time food reaches the lining of the small intestine, it has been reduced to small molecules. The lining of the small intestine is covered with villi, tiny absorptive structures that greatly increase the surface area for interaction with chyme (the semi-liquid mass of partially digested food). Epithelial cells at the surface of the villi, called microvilli, further increase the ability of the small intestine to serve as the main absorption organ of the digestive tract.

Large intestine

Also called the colon, the large intestine concentrates, mixes, and stores waste material. A little over a meter in length, the colon ascends on the right side of the abdominal cavity, cuts across transversely to the left side, then descends and attaches to the rectum, a short tube for waste disposal.

When the rectal wall is distended by waste material, the nervous system triggers an impulse in the body to expel the waste from the rectum. A muscle sphincter at the end of the anus is stimulated to facilitate the expelling of waste matter.

The speed at which waste moves through the colon is influenced by the volume of fiber and other undigested material present. Without adequate bulk in the diet, it takes longer to move waste along, sometimes with negative effects. Lack of bulk in the diet has been linked to a number of disorders.

Pancreas

The pancreas is six to ten inches long and located at the back of the abdomen behind the stomach. It is a long, tapered organ. The wider (right) side is called the head and the narrower (left) side is called the tail. The head lies near the duodenum (the first part of the small intestine) and the tail ends near the spleen. The body of the pancreas lies between the head and the tail. The pancreas is made up of exocrine and endocrine tissues. The exocrine tissue secretes digestive enzymes from a series of ducts that collectively form the main pancreatic duct (that runs the length of the pancreas). The main pancreatic duct connects to the common bile duct near the duodenum. The endocrine tissue secretes hormones (such as insulin) into the bloodstream. Blood is supplied to the pancreas from the splenic artery, gastroduodenal artery, and the superior mesenteric artery.

Digestive role of pancreas

The pancreas assists in the digestion of foods by secreting enzymes (to the small intestine) that help to break down many foods, especially fats and proteins. The precursors to these enzymes (called zymogens) are produced by groups of exocrine cells (called acini). They are converted, through a chemical reaction in the gut, to the active enzymes (such as pancreatic lipase and amylase) once they enter the small intestine. The pancreas also secretes large amounts of sodium bicarbonate to neutralize the stomach acid that reaches the small intestine. The exocrine functions of the pancreas are controlled by hormones released by the stomach and small intestine (duodenum) when food is present. The exocrine secretions of the pancreas flow into the main pancreatic duct (Wirsung's duct) and are delivered to the duodenum through the pancreatic duct.

Copyright © Mometrix Media. You have been licensed one copy of this document for personal use only. Any other reproduction or redistribution is strictly prohibited. All rights reserved.

Renal/Urinary system

The renal/urinary system is capable of eliminating excess substances while preserving the substances needed by the body to function. The urinary system consists of the kidneys, urinary ducts, and bladder. The mammalian kidney is a bean-shaped organ attached to the body near the peritoneum. The kidney helps to eliminate water and waste from the body. Within the kidney, there are various tubes and capillaries. Substances exit the bloodstream if they are not needed, and those that are needed are reabsorbed. The unnecessary substances are filtered out into the tubules that form urine. From theses tubes, urine flows into the bladder and then out of the body through the urethra.

Kidneys

The kidneys are bean-shaped structures that are located at the back of the abdominal cavity just under the diaphragm. Each kidney consists of three layers: the renal cortex (outer layer), renal medulla (inner layer), and renal pelvis (innermost portion). The renal cortex is composed of approximately one million nephrons, which are the tiny, individual filters of the kidneys. Each nephron contains a cluster of capillaries called a glomerulus surrounded by the cup-shaped Bowman's capsule, which leads to a tubule. The kidneys receive blood from the renal arteries, which branch off the aorta.

In general, the kidneys filter the blood, reabsorb needed materials, and secrete wastes and excess water in the urine. More specifically, blood flows from the renal arteries into arterioles into the glomerulus, where it is filtered. The glomerular filtrate enters the proximal convoluted tubule where water, glucose, ions, and other organic molecules are resorbed back into the bloodstream. Additional substances such as urea and drugs are removed from the blood in the distal convoluted tubule. Also, the pH of the blood can be adjusted in the distal convoluted tubule by the secretion of hydrogen ions. Finally, the unabsorbed materials flow out from the collecting tubules located in the renal medulla to the renal pelvis as urine. Urine is drained from the kidneys through the ureters to the urinary bladder, where it is stored until expulsion from the body through the urethra.

Circulatory system

The circulatory system is responsible for the internal transport of substances to and from the cells. The circulatory system usually consists of the following three parts:

- Blood - Blood is composed of water, solutes, and other elements in a fluid connective tissue.
- Blood Vessels - Tubules of different sizes that transport blood.
- Heart - The heart is a muscular pump providing the pressure necessary to keep blood flowing.

Circulatory systems can be either open or closed. Most animals have closed systems, where the heart and blood vessels are continually connected. As the blood moves through the system from larger tubules through smaller ones, the rate slows down. The flow of blood in the capillary beds, the smallest tubules, is quite slow.

A supplementary system, the lymph vascular system, cleans up excess fluids and proteins and returns them to the circulatory system.

Copyright © Mometrix Media. You have been licensed one copy of this document for personal use only. Any other reproduction or redistribution is strictly prohibited. All rights reserved.

Blood

Blood helps maintain a healthy internal environment in animals by carrying raw materials to cells and removing waste products. It helps stabilize internal pH and hosts various kinds of infection fighters.

An adult human has about five quarts of blood. Blood is composed of red and white blood cells, platelets, and plasma. Plasma constitutes over half of the blood volume. It is mostly water and serves as a solvent. Plasma contains plasma proteins, ions, glucose, amino acids, hormones, and dissolved gases.

Red blood cells transport oxygen to cells. Red blood cells form in the bone marrow and can live for about four months. These cells are constantly being replaced by fresh ones, keeping the total number relatively stable.

White blood cells defend the body against infection and remove various wastes. The types of white blood cells include lymphocytes, neutrophils, monocytes, eosinophils, and basophils. Platelets are fragments of stem cells and serve an important function in blood clotting.

Heart

The heart is a muscular pump made of cardiac muscle tissue. It has four chambers; each half contains both an atrium and a ventricle, and the halves are separated by a valve, known as the AV valve. It is located between the ventricle and the artery leading away from the heart. Valves keep blood moving in a single direction and prevent any backwash into the chambers.

The heart has its own circulatory system with its own coronary arteries. The heart functions by contracting and relaxing. Atrial contraction fills the ventricles and ventricular contraction empties them, forcing circulation. This sequence is called the cardiac cycle. Cardiac muscles are attached to each other and signals for contractions spread rapidly. A complex electrical system controls the heartbeat as cardiac muscle cells produce and conduct electric signals. These muscles are said to be self-exciting, needing no external stimuli.

> **Review Video: The Heart**
> Visit mometrix.com/academy and enter code: 451399

Cardiac cycle

The cardiac cycle consists of diastole and systole phases, which can be further divided into the first and second phases to describe the events of the right and left sides of the heart. However, these events are simultaneously occurring. During the first diastole phase, blood flows through the superior and inferior venae cavae. Because the heart is relaxed, blood flows passively from the atrium through the open atrioventricular valve (tricuspid valve) to the right ventricle. The sinoatrial (SA) node, the cardiac pacemaker located in the wall of the right atrium, generates electrical signals, which are carried by the Purkinje fibers to the rest of the atrium, stimulating it to contract and fill the right ventricle with blood. The impulse from the SA node is transmitted to the ventricle through the atrioventricular (AV) node, signaling the right ventricle to contract and initiating the first systole phase. The tricuspid valve closes, and the pulmonary semilunar valve opens. Blood is pumped out the pulmonary arteries to the lungs. Blood returning from the lungs fills the left atrium as part of the second diastole phase. The SA node triggers the mitral valve to open, and blood fills the left ventricle. During the second systole phase, the mitral valve closes and the aortic semilunar valve opens. The left ventricle contracts, and blood is pumped out of the aorta to the rest of the body.

Copyright © Mometrix Media. You have been licensed one copy of this document for personal use only. Any other reproduction or redistribution is strictly prohibited. All rights reserved.

Types of circulation

The circulatory system includes coronary circulation, pulmonary circulation, and systemic circulation. Coronary circulation is the flow of blood to the heart tissue. Blood enters the coronary arteries, which branch off the aorta, supplying major arteries, which enter the heart with oxygenated blood. The deoxygenated blood returns to the right atrium through the cardiac veins, which empty into the coronary sinus. Pulmonary circulation is the flow of blood between the heart and the lungs. Deoxygenated blood flows from the right ventricle to the lungs through pulmonary arteries. Oxygenated blood flows back to the left atrium through the pulmonary veins. Systemic circulation is the flow of blood to the entire body with the exception of coronary circulation and pulmonary circulation. Blood exits the left ventricle through the aorta, which branches into the carotid arteries, subclavian arteries, common iliac arteries, and the renal artery. Blood returns to the heart through the jugular veins, subclavian veins, common iliac veins, and renal veins, which empty into the superior and inferior venae cavae. Included in systemic circulation is portal circulation, which is the flow of blood from the digestive system to the liver and then to the heart, and renal circulation, which is the flow of blood between the heart and the kidneys.

Blood pressure

Blood pressure is the fluid pressure generated by the cardiac cycle.

Arterial blood pressure functions by transporting oxygen-poor blood into the lungs and oxygen-rich blood to the body tissues. Arteries branch into smaller arterioles which contract and expand based on signals from the body. Arterioles are where adjustments are made in blood delivery to specific areas based on complex communication from body systems.

Capillary beds are diffusion sites for exchanges between blood and interstitial fluid. A capillary has the thinnest wall of any blood vessel, consisting of a single layer of endothelial cells.

Capillaries merge into venules which in turn merge with larger diameter tubules called veins. Veins transport blood from body tissues back to the heart. Valves inside the veins facilitate this transport. The walls of veins are thin and contain smooth muscle and also function as blood volume reserves.

Lymphatic system

The main function of the lymphatic system is to return excess tissue fluid to the bloodstream. This system consists of transport vessels and lymphoid organs. The lymph vascular system consists of lymph capillaries, lymph vessels, and lymph ducts. The major functions of the lymph vascular system are:

- The return of excess fluid to the blood.
- The return of protein from the capillaries.
- The transport of fats from the digestive tract.
- The disposal of debris and cellular waste.

Lymphoid organs include the lymph nodes, spleen, appendix, adenoids, thymus, tonsils, and small patches of tissue in the small intestine. Lymph nodes are located at intervals throughout the lymph vessel system. Each node contains lymphocytes and plasma cells. The spleen stores macrophages which help to filter red blood cells. The thymus secretes hormones and is the major site of lymphocyte production.

Copyright © Mometrix Media. You have been licensed one copy of this document for personal use only. Any other reproduction or redistribution is strictly prohibited. All rights reserved.

<u>Spleen</u>

The spleen is in the upper left of the abdomen. It is located behind the stomach and immediately below the diaphragm. It is about the size of a thick paperback book and weighs just over half a pound. It is made up of lymphoid tissue. The blood vessels are connected to the spleen by splenic sinuses (modified capillaries). The following peritoneal ligaments support the spleen:

- The gastrolienal ligament that connects the stomach to the spleen.
- The lienorenal ligament that connects the kidney to the spleen.
- The middle section of the phrenicocolic ligament (connects the left colic flexure to the thoracic diaphragm).

The main functions of the spleen are to filter unwanted materials from the blood (including old red blood cells) and to help fight infections. Up to ten percent of the population has one or more accessory spleens that tend to form at the hilum of the original spleen.

Immune system

The body's general immune defenses include:

- Skin - An intact epidermis and dermis form a formidable barrier against bacteria.
- Ciliated Mucous Membranes - Cilia sweep pathogens out of the respiratory tract.
- Glandular Secretions - Secretions from exocrine glands destroy bacteria.
- Gastric Secretions - Gastric acid destroys pathogens.
- Normal Bacterial Populations - Compete with pathogens in the gut and vagina.

In addition, phagocytes and inflammation responses mobilize white blood cells and chemical reactions to stop infection. These responses include localized redness, tissue repair, and fluid-seeping healing agents. Additionally, plasma proteins act as the complement system to repel bacteria and pathogens.

Three types of white blood cells form the foundation of the body's immune system. They are:

- Macrophages - Phagocytes that alert T cells to the presence of foreign substances.
- T Lymphocytes - These directly attack cells infected by viruses and bacteria.
- B Lymphocytes - These cells target specific bacteria for destruction.

Memory cells, suppressor T cells, and helper T cells also contribute to the body's defense. Immune responses can be anti-body mediated when the response is to an antigen, or cell-mediated when the response is to already infected cells. These responses are controlled and measured counter-attacks that recede when the foreign agents are destroyed. Once an invader has attacked the body, if it returns it is immediately recognized and a secondary immune response occurs. This secondary response is rapid and powerful, much more so than the original response. These memory lymphocytes circulate throughout the body for years, alert to a possible new attack.

<u>Active and Passive Immunity</u>

At birth, an innate immune system protects an individual from pathogens. When an individual encounters infection or has an immunization, the individual develops an adaptive immunity that reacts to pathogens. So, this adaptive immunity is acquired. Active and passive immunities can be acquired naturally or artificially.

Copyright © Mometrix Media. You have been licensed one copy of this document for personal use only. Any other reproduction or redistribution is strictly prohibited. All rights reserved.

A naturally acquired active immunity is natural because the individual is exposed and builds immunity to a pathogen without an immunization. An artificially acquired active immunity is artificial because the individual is exposed and builds immunity to a pathogen by a vaccine.

A naturally acquired passive immunity is natural because it happens during pregnancy as antibodies move from the mother's bloodstream to the bloodstream of the fetus. The antibodies can also be transferred from a mother's breast milk. During infancy, these antibodies provide temporary protection until childhood. An artificially acquired passive immunity is an immunization that is given in recent outbreaks or emergency situations. This immunization provides quick and short-lived protection to disease by the use of antibodies that can come from another person or animal.

Nervous system

The human nervous system senses, interprets, and issues commands as a response to conditions in the body's environment. This process is made possible by a very complex communication system organized as a grid of neurons.

Messages are sent across the plasma membrane of neurons through a process called action potential. These messages occur when a neuron is stimulated past a necessary threshold. These stimulations occur in a sequence from the stimulation point of one neuron to its contact with another neuron. At the point of contact, called a chemical synapse, a substance is released that stimulates or inhibits the action of the adjoining cell. This network fans out across the body and forms the framework for the nervous system. The direction the information flows depends on the specific organizations of nerve circuits and pathways.

> **Review Video:** The Nervous System
> Visit mometrix.com/academy and enter code: 708428

Central nervous system

There are two primary components of the central nervous system:

Spinal cord

The spinal cord is encased in the bony structure of the vertebrae, which protects and supports it. Its nervous tissue functions mainly with respect to limb movement and internal organ activity. Major nerve tracts ascend and descend from the spinal cord to the brain.

Brain

The brain consists of the hindbrain, which includes the medulla oblongata, cerebellum, and pons. The midbrain integrates sensory signals and orchestrates responses to these signals. The forebrain includes the cerebrum, thalamus, and hypothalamus. The cerebral cortex is a thin layer of gray matter covering the cerebrum. The brain is divided into two hemispheres, with each responsible for multiple functions.

The brain is divided into four main lobes, the frontal lobe, the parietal lobe, the occipital lobe, and the temporal lobes. The frontal lobe located in the front of the brain is responsible for a short term and working memory and information processing as well as decision-making, planning, and judgment. The parietal lobe is located slightly toward the back of the brain and the top of the head and is responsible for sensory input as well as spatial positioning of the body. The occipital lobe is located at the back of the head just above the brain stem. This lobe is responsible for visual input, processing, and output; specifically nerves from the eyes enter directly into this lobe. Finally, the

Copyright © Mometrix Media. You have been licensed one copy of this document for personal use only. Any other reproduction or redistribution is strictly prohibited. All rights reserved.

temporal lobes are located at the left and right sides of the brain. These lobes are responsible for all auditory input, processing, and output.

The cerebellum plays a role in the processing and storing of implicit memories. Specifically, for those memories developed during classical conditioning learning techniques. The role of the cerebellum was discovered by exploring the memory of individuals with damaged cerebellums. These individuals were unable to develop stimulus responses when presented via a classical conditioning technique. Researcher found that this was also the case for automatic responses. For example, when these individuals where presented with a puff or air into their eyes, they did not blink, which would have been the naturally occurring and automatic response in an individual with no brain damage.

The posterior area of the brain that is connected to the spinal cord is known as the brain stem. The midbrain, the pons, and the medulla oblongata are the three parts of the brain stem. Information from the body is sent to the brain through the brain stem, and information from the brain is sent to the body through the brain stem. The brain stem is an important part of respiratory, digestive, and circulatory functions.

The midbrain lies above the pons and the medulla oblongata. The parts of the midbrain include the tectum, the tegmentum, and the ventral tegmentum. The midbrain is an important part of vision and hearing. The pons comes between the midbrain and the medulla oblongata. Information is sent across the pons from the cerebrum to the medulla and the cerebellum. The medulla oblongata (or medulla) is beneath the midbrain and the pons. The medulla oblongata is the piece of the brain stem that connects the spinal cord to the brain. So, it has an important role with the autonomous nervous system in the circulatory and respiratory system.

In addition, the peripheral nervous system consists of the nerves and ganglia throughout the body and includes sympathetic nerves which trigger the "fight or flight" response, and the parasympathetic nerves which control basic body function.

Autonomic nervous system

The autonomic nervous system (ANS) maintains homeostasis within the body. In general, the ANS controls the functions of the internal organs, blood vessels, smooth muscle tissues, and glands. This is accomplished through the direction of the hypothalamus, which is located above the midbrain. The hypothalamus controls the ANS through the brain stem. With this direction from the hypothalamus, the ANS helps maintain a stable body environment (homeostasis) by regulating numerous factors including heart rate, breathing rate, body temperature, and blood pH. The ANS consists of two divisions: the sympathetic nervous system and the parasympathetic nervous system. The sympathetic nervous system controls the body's reaction to extreme, stressful, and emergency situations. For example, the sympathetic nervous system increases the heart rate, signals the adrenal glands to secrete adrenaline, triggers the dilation of the pupils, and slows digestion. The parasympathetic nervous system counteracts the effects of the sympathetic nervous system. For example, the parasympathetic nervous system decreases heart rate, signals the adrenal glands to stop secreting adrenaline, constricts the pupils, and returns the digestion process to normal.

The Somatic nervous system and the reflex arc

The somatic nervous system (SNS) controls the five senses and the voluntary movement of skeletal muscle. So, this system has all of the neurons that are connected to sense organs. Efferent (motor) and afferent (sensory) nerves help the somatic nervous system operate the senses and the movement of skeletal muscle. Efferent muscles bring signals from the central nervous system to the

Copyright © Mometrix Media. You have been licensed one copy of this document for personal use only. Any other reproduction or redistribution is strictly prohibited. All rights reserved.

sensory organs and the muscles. Afferent muscles bring signals from the sensory organs and the muscles to the central nervous system. The somatic nervous system also performs involuntary movements which are known as reflex arcs.

A reflex, the simplest act of the nervous system, is an automatic response without any conscious thought to a stimulus via the reflex arc. The reflex arc is the simplest nerve pathway, which bypasses the brain and is controlled by the spinal cord. For example, in the classic knee-jerk response (patellar tendon reflex), the stimulus is the reflex hammer hitting the tendon, and the response is the muscle contracting, which jerks the foot upward. The stimulus is detected by sensory receptors, and a message is sent along a sensory (afferent) neuron to one or more interneurons in the spinal cord. The interneuron(s) transmit this message to a motor (efferent) neuron, which carries the message to the correct effector (muscle).

Respiration

Connected airways of the body (including the nasal cavities, pharynx, larynx, trachea, bronchi, and bronchioles) provide a transport highway for respiration. Alveoli at the end of this system serve as the gas exchange mechanism of the system.

As air is inhaled, oxygen brought into the lungs diffuses from the alveoli into pulmonary capillaries. It then diffuses into red blood cells and fuses with hemoglobin. When the oxygen-rich blood reaches the body tissues, the hemoglobin releases its oxygen, which diffuses out of the capillaries, through the interstitial fluid, and into the cells. The hemoglobin releases oxygen in response to body signals. Carbon dioxide then diffuses from cells, through interstitial fluid, into the bloodstream, completing the cycle.

Endocrine system

The endocrine system is responsible for secreting the hormones and other molecules that help regulate the entire body in both the short and the long term. There is a close working relationship between the endocrine system and the nervous system. The hypothalamus and the pituitary gland coordinate to serve as a neuroendocrine control center.

Hormone secretion is triggered by a variety of signals, including hormonal signs, chemical reactions, and environmental cues. Only cells with particular receptors can benefit from hormonal influence. This is the "key in the lock" model for hormonal action. Steroid hormones trigger gene activation and protein synthesis in some target cells. Protein hormones change the activity of existing enzymes in target cells. Hormones such as insulin work quickly when the body signals an urgent need. Slower acting hormones afford longer, gradual, and sometimes permanent changes in the body.

The eight major endocrine glands and their functions are:

- Adrenal cortex - Monitors blood sugar level; helps in lipid and protein metabolism.
- Adrenal medulla - Controls cardiac function; raises blood sugar and controls the size of blood vessels.
- Thyroid gland - Helps regulate metabolism and functions in growth and development.
- Parathyroid - Regulates calcium levels in the blood.
- Pancreas islets - Raises and lowers blood sugar; active in carbohydrate metabolism.
- Thymus gland - Plays a role in immune responses.

- 84 -

Copyright © Mometrix Media. You have been licensed one copy of this document for personal use only. Any other reproduction or redistribution is strictly prohibited. All rights reserved.

- Pineal gland - Has an influence on daily biorhythms and sexual activity.
- Pituitary gland - Plays an important role in growth and development.

Endocrine glands are intimately involved in a myriad of reactions, functions, and secretions that are crucial to the well-being of the body.

<u>Endocrine functions of the pancreas</u>

Located amongst the groupings of exocrine cells (acini) are groups of endocrine cells (called islets of Langerhans). The islets of Langerhans are primarily made up of insulin-producing beta cells (fifty to eighty percent of the total) and glucagon-releasing alpha cells. The major hormones produced by the pancreas are insulin and glucagon. The body uses insulin to control carbohydrate metabolism by lowering the amount of sugar (glucose) in the blood. Insulin also affects fat metabolism and can change the liver's ability to release stored fat. The body also uses glucagon to control carbohydrate metabolism. Glucagon has the opposite effect of insulin in that the body uses it to increase blood sugar (glucose) levels. The levels of insulin and glucagon are balanced to maintain the optimum level of blood sugar (glucose) throughout the day.

<u>Thyroid and parathyroid glands</u>

The thyroid and parathyroid glands are located in the neck just below the larynx. The parathyroid glands are four small glands that are embedded on the posterior side of the thyroid gland. The basic function of the thyroid gland is to regulate metabolism. The thyroid gland secretes the hormones thyroxine, triiodothyronine, and calcitonin. Thyroxine and triiodothyronine increase metabolism, and calcitonin decreases blood calcium by storing calcium in bone tissue. The hypothalamus directs the pituitary gland to secrete thyroid-stimulating hormone (TSH), which stimulates the thyroid gland to release these hormones as needed via a negative-feedback mechanism. The parathyroid glands secrete parathyroid hormone, which can increase blood calcium by moving calcium from the bone to the blood.

Animal reproduction

As a rule, animals produce sexually. Evolution has ensured that separation into male and female structures maximizes the chances for successful fertilization and nutritional support to the offspring. It has also played a role in shaping behaviors of animals to assure these goals.

Humans have a pair of primary reproductive organs, one for each gender: the sperm-producing testes in males and the egg-producing ovaries in females. These organs have supplementary ducts, glands, and supporting structures. Human males produce sperm continually from puberty onward. Females produce and release eggs on a monthly cycle. Hormones such as estrogen, progesterone, FSH, and LH control this cycle.

The six stages of development are gamete formation, fertilization, cleavage, gastrulation, organ formation, and the growth and development of specialized tissues. All tissues and organs arise from three germ layers: the endoderm, ectoderm, and mesoderm of the early embryo. Embryonic development requires the help of some embryonic membranes including the yolk sac, amnion, chorion, and allantois.

Demographic transition model

The demographic transition model is a representation of changes in population in industrial societies, created by demographer Warren Thompson. This model describes variations (transitions) in birth and death rates in developed nations over the past 200 years.

Copyright © Mometrix Media. You have been licensed one copy of this document for personal use only. Any other reproduction or redistribution is strictly prohibited. All rights reserved.

The demographic transition model encompasses four transitional phases:

- Stage One is associated with pre-modern (that is, pre-industrialized) society; it characterizes most regions of the world through the 17th century. In this stage (the high stationary stage), birth and death rates are high and nearly equivalent, indicating that population growth is slow. The second stage in the demographic transition model is differentiated by a sharp increase in a society's population due to a dramatic decrease in the death rate. This transition occurred in the late 18th century in Western Europe and spread outward.
- Stage Two is associated with advances in public health such as the creation of food handling regulations and sewage disposal, as well as advances in agricultural practices (including crop rotation) that helped to create a stable food source.
- Stage Three of the demographic transition model involves a decrease in a society's birth rate (following the rapid population growth in Stage Two). Most developed nations entered this phase late in the 19th century. Many hypotheses have been advanced to explain this phenomenon. For example, some have suggested that the decline in birth rates observed in developed societies is related to urbanization, which dilutes the high value traditionally placed on fertility; also, the costs attendant to urbanization make it less financially desirable for a family to have many children. The decline in birth rates has also been said to relate to medical advancements that decreased the rate of childhood mortality, or to improvements in contraceptive technology (though this occurred later, in the second half of the 20th century).
- In Stage Four of the demographic transition model, the populations of societies are either stable or declining. After the decline in birth rates, the general population grows older. If the fertility rate dips below replacement, the population experiences a rapid decline.

Population

Fertility Rate

A fertility rate is the average number of children that a woman will have over a lifetime during her childbearing years which can range from 15 to 44 or 15 to 49. This should not be confused with birth rate. An important tie in to fertility rate is the replacement rate.

The replacement fertility rate is the fertility rate at which women on average are having just enough females to replace themselves in the population. Many developed countries have replacement rates that range between 2 and 3 births per woman. While some less-developed countries can have replacement rates as high as 6 or 7 births per woman.

Population momentum is the phenomenon whereby a society's population persists after the attainment of replacement fertility. This occurs at the end of Stage Three in the demographic transition model, due to the relatively high concentration of people of the same age in their childbearing years.

Population Growth and Decline

The birth rate of a society refers to the number of births per 1,000 people in that society. This figure, usually expressed as the crude birth rate (CBR), is calculated without consideration of the sex or age of the population. The death rate of a society is figured in the same manner but with regard to deaths rather than births and is expressed as the crude death rate (CDR). Immigration is when a person comes to another country to stay permanently. Emigration is when a person leaves their current country of residence to live in another country.

Copyright © Mometrix Media. You have been licensed one copy of this document for personal use only. Any other reproduction or redistribution is strictly prohibited. All rights reserved.

Populations vary over time due to deaths, births, immigration, and emigration. In most situations, resources such as food, water, and shelter are limited. Each environment or habitat can only support a limited number of individuals. This is known as the carrying capacity. There are many things that can influence the population of an area. The culture, economy, education, number of medical facilities, and government are all important factors that can change the rates of a population. As you reflect on expanding and diminishing populations, be sure to think about climate, natural resources, and land as reasons for the growth or decline of a population.

In the coming decades, developed countries could see a greater decrease in their population. Also, less-developed countries could see a greater increase in their population. A decrease in population can be dangerous to a society that needs to maintain or to expand a workforce. An increase in population can be dangerous to a society that does not have the resources to provide for so many people. These dangers can be avoided if a society with a decreasing population has an increase in immigration or a society that has an increasing population has an increase in emigration.

Copyright © Mometrix Media. You have been licensed one copy of this document for personal use only. Any other reproduction or redistribution is strictly prohibited. All rights reserved.

Life Science

Natural Selection, Adaptations, and Mutations

Natural selection acts continually on an organism's phenotype and this activity affects the organism's genotype. This process is the way in which a population can change over generations. Every population has variations in individual heritable traits. However, not all individuals of a population reproduce. The organisms best suited for survival typically reproduce and pass on their genetic traits. Traits that are more advantageous become more common in a population. Natural selection brings about evolutionary adaptations and is responsible for biological diversity.

Although there are multiple factors that affect gene pools, natural selection best explains the adaptations organisms make to survive in different environments. As Darwin recognized, natural selection is a key mechanism in evolution; it affects the phenotypes of microbes, plants, and animals over time and, in doing so, determines the way present day organisms look and behave. Major considerations in the understanding of natural selection include the following topics:

- The concept of fitness.
- How genotypes are affected by phenotypes.
- The varieties of natural selection.
- The mechanisms of evolution.

Adaptations

An adaptation is a change for an organism that allows it become better suited for its surroundings. These adaptations come from the natural selection process. Organisms must be able to adapt to their environment in order to thrive or survive. For example, an insect that can use natural camouflage to protect itself from predators. Individual organisms must be able to recognize stimuli in their surroundings and adapt quickly. For example, an individual euglena can sense light and respond by moving toward the light. Individual organisms must also be able to adapt to changes in the environment on a larger scale. For example, plants must be able to respond to the change in the length of the day to flower at the correct time. Populations must also be able to adapt to a changing environment. For example, wooly mammoths were unable to adapt to a warming climate and are now extinct, but many species of deer did adapt and are abundant today.

Adaptive radiation is an evolutionary process in which a species branches out and adapts and fills numerous unoccupied ecological niches. The adaptations occur relatively quickly, driven by natural selection and resulting in new phenotypes and possibly new species eventually. An example of adaptive radiation is the finches that Darwin studied on the Galápagos Islands. Darwin recorded 13 different varieties of finches, which differed in the size and shape of their beaks. Through the process of natural selection, each type of finch adapted to the specific environment and specifically the food sources of the island to which it belonged. On newly formed islands with many unoccupied ecological niches, the adaptive radiation process occurred quickly due to the lack of competing species and predators. These differences in finches on the Galápagos Islands were the result of random mutations in the genome of a finch that were passed on to future generations.

Mutations

Mutations are one of the main sources of genetic variation. Mutations are changes in DNA. The changes can be gene mutations such as the point mutations of substitution, addition, or deletion, or the changes can be on the chromosomal level such as the chromosomal aberrations of translocations, deletions, inversions, and duplications. Mutations are random and can benefit, harm,

Copyright © Mometrix Media. You have been licensed one copy of this document for personal use only. Any other reproduction or redistribution is strictly prohibited. All rights reserved.

or have no effect on the individual. Most mutations are harmful. It is a rare occurrence for a mutation to have a benefit to the organism. Somatic mutations do not affect inheritance and therefore do not affect genetic variation with regard to evolution. Germline mutations that occur in gametes (eggs and sperm) can be passed to offspring and therefore are very important to genetic variation and evolution. Mutations introduce new genetic information into the genome. These mutations that are favorable to the organism's environment will bring about adaptive changes.

It is important to understand that natural selection and adaptation are not random processes. The process of natural selection is not random because predators are always in pursuit of prey. Adaptation is not random because the prey is always in pursuit of protection. Mutations are the random piece because of the changes that can occur on the chromosomal level. These changes can bring about beneficial or damaging traits that develop in organisms.

Fitness

Geneticists have a specialized definition of fitness. They use the term to denote an organism's capacity to survive, mate, and reproduce. This ultimately equates to the probability or likelihood that the organism will be able to pass on its genetic information to the next generation. Fitness does not mean the strongest, biggest, or most dangerous individual. A more subtle combination of anatomy, physiology, biochemistry, and behavior determine genetic fitness.

Another way to understand genetic fitness is knowing that phenotypes affect survival and the ability to successfully reproduce. Phenotypes are genetically determined and genes contributing to fitness tend to increase over time.

Thus, the "fittest" organisms survive and pass on their genetic makeup to the next generation. This is what Darwin meant by "survival of the fittest," which is the cornerstone of Darwin's theory of evolution.

Influence of phenotype on genotype

Natural selection provides processes that tend to increase a population's adaptive abilities. The strongest phenotypes survive, prosper, and pass on their genetic code to the next generation. The new generation of phenotypes has a fitter genotype because they have inherited more adaptive characteristics.

Thus, the fit thrive while the weak become extinct over time. This pattern, when repeated over many generations, develops strong, fit phenotypes that survive and reproduce offspring who are as fit as or fitter than their parents. Sometimes this apparently inexorable movement can be modified by drastic external conditions such as wide variations in climate. It is important to remember that all extinct species were once fit and adapted to their environments. Unforeseen circumstances always have the potential to cause chaos in the physical world.

Selective processes

There are four major selective processes which may produce evolutionary change or preserve existing adaptive traits. They are:

- Normalizing or stabilizing selection simply protects and preserves a fit existing phenotype. This type of selection is strongest in environments that have remained stable for long periods of time. Examples include arid desert areas and Antarctic glaciers.
- Directional variation occurs when an environment favors a genetic variant which grows in frequency over a period of time.

Copyright © Mometrix Media. You have been licensed one copy of this document for personal use only. Any other reproduction or redistribution is strictly prohibited. All rights reserved.

- Disrupting or diversifying selection occurs when a population is confronted with extreme new conditions that are so diverse that no one phenotype can prosper except at the expense of others. This selective process can lead to two or more phenotypes adapting to a different extreme condition of the environment.
- Balanced selection is when a heterozygote has a higher fitness level than either homozygote. This is also called hybrid advantage, such as when mongrel dogs are heartier than purebred dogs.

Classification for living organisms

The main characteristic by which living organisms are classified is the degree to which they are related, not the degree to which they resemble each other. The science of classification is called taxonomy; it's a difficult science since the division lines between groups are not always clear. Some animals have characteristics of two separate groups.

The basic system of taxonomy involves placing an organism into a major kingdom (Moneran, Protist, Fungi, Plants, and Animals), and then dividing those kingdoms into phyla, then classes, then orders, then families, and finally genera. For example, the domestic cat is in the kingdom of animals, the phylum of chordates, the class of mammals, the order of carnivores, the family of felidae, and the genus of felis. All species of living beings can be identified with Latin scientific names that are assigned by the worldwide binomial system. The genus name comes first, and is followed by the name of the species. The domestic cat is *felis domesticus*.

Although not part of taxonomy, behavior is also considered in identifying living beings. For example, birds are identified according to their songs or means of flight.

Cell

The cell is the basic organizational unit of all living things. Each piece within a cell has a function that helps organisms grow and survive. There are many different types of cells, but cells are unique to each type of organism. The one thing that all cells have in common is a membrane, which is comparable to a semi-permeable plastic bag. The membrane is composed of phospholipids. There are also some transport holes, which are proteins that help certain molecules and ions move in and out of the cell. The cell is filled with a fluid called cytoplasm or cytosol.

Within the cell are a variety of organelles, groups of complex molecules that help a cell survive, each with its own unique membrane that has a different chemical makeup from the cell membrane. The larger the cell, the more organelles it will need to live.

Nuclear parts of a cell

- Nucleus (pl. nuclei): This is a small structure that contains the chromosomes and regulates the DNA of a cell. The nucleus is the defining structure of eukaryotic cells, and all eukaryotic cells have a nucleus. The nucleus is responsible for the passing on of genetic traits between generations. The nucleus contains a nuclear envelope, nucleoplasm, a nucleolus, nuclear pores, chromatin, and ribosomes.
- Chromosomes: These are highly condensed, threadlike rods of DNA. Short for deoxyribonucleic acid, DNA is the genetic material that stores information about the plant or animal.
- Chromatin: This consists of the DNA and protein that make up chromosomes.

- 90 -

Copyright © Mometrix Media. You have been licensed one copy of this document for personal use only. Any other reproduction or redistribution is strictly prohibited. All rights reserved.

- Nucleolus: This structure contained within the nucleus consists of protein. It is small, round, does not have a membrane, is involved in protein synthesis, and synthesizes and stores RNA (ribonucleic acid).
- Nuclear envelope: This encloses the structures of the nucleus. It consists of inner and outer membranes made of lipids.
- Nuclear pores: These are involved in the exchange of material between the nucleus and the cytoplasm.
- Nucleoplasm: This is the liquid within the nucleus, and is similar to cytoplasm.

Cell membranes

The cell membrane, also referred to as the plasma membrane, is a thin semipermeable membrane of lipids and proteins. The cell membrane isolates the cell from its external environment while still enabling the cell to communicate with that outside environment. It consists of a phospholipid bilayer, or double layer, with the hydrophilic ends of the outer layer facing the external environment, the inner layer facing the inside of the cell, and the hydrophobic ends facing each other. Cholesterol in the cell membrane adds stiffness and flexibility. Glycolipids help the cell to recognize other cells of the organisms. The proteins in the cell membrane help give the cells shape. Special proteins help the cell communicate with its external environment. Other proteins transport molecules across the cell membrane.

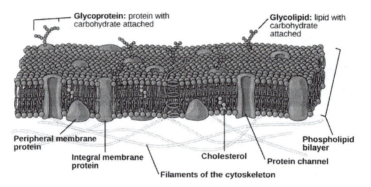

Selective permeability

The cell membrane, or plasma membrane, has selective permeability with regard to size, charge, and solubility. With regard to molecule size, the cell membrane allows only small molecules to diffuse through it. Oxygen and water molecules are small and typically can pass through the cell membrane. The charge of the ions on the cell's surface also either attracts or repels ions. Ions with like charges are repelled, and ions with opposite charges are attracted to the cell's surface. Molecules that are soluble in phospholipids can usually pass through the cell membrane. Many molecules are not able to diffuse the cell membrane, and, if needed, those molecules must be moved through by active transport and vesicles.

Prokaryotes and Eukaryotes

Cells of the domains of Bacteria and Archaea are prokaryotes. Bacteria cells and Archaea cells are much smaller than cells of eukaryotes. Prokaryote cells are usually only 1 to 2 micrometers in diameter, but eukaryotic cells are usually at least 10 times and possibly 100 times larger than prokaryotic cells. Eukaryotic cells are usually 10 to 100 micrometers in diameter. Most prokaryotes are unicellular organisms, although some prokaryotes live in colonies. Because of their large surface-area-to-volume ratios, prokaryotes have a very high metabolic rate. Eukaryotic cells are

Copyright © Mometrix Media. You have been licensed one copy of this document for personal use only. Any other reproduction or redistribution is strictly prohibited. All rights reserved.

much larger than prokaryotic cells. Due to their larger sizes, they have a much smaller surface-area-to-volume ratio and consequently have much lower metabolic rates.

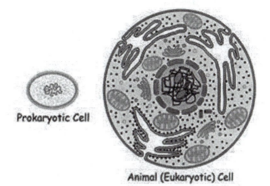

Prokaryotic cells are much simpler than eukaryotic cells. Prokaryote cells do not have a nucleus due to their small size. Their DNA is located in the center of the cell in a region referred to as a nucleoid. Eukaryote cells have a nucleus bound by a double membrane. Eukaryotic cells typically have hundreds or thousands of additional membrane-bound organelles that are independent of the cell membrane. Prokaryotic cells do not have any membrane-bound organelles that are independent of the cell membrane. Once again, this is probably due to the much larger size of the eukaryotic cells. The organelles of eukaryotes give them much higher levels of intracellular division than is possible in prokaryotic cells.

Not all cells have cell walls. Most prokaryotes have cell walls. Most bacteria have cell walls outside of the plasma membrane that contains the molecule peptidoglycan. Peptidoglycan is a large polymer of amino acids and sugars. The peptidoglycan helps maintain the strength of the cell wall. Plant cell walls contain cellulose, and woody plants are further strengthened by lignin. Some algae also contain lignin. Animal cells do not have cell walls.

Prokaryote cells have DNA arranged in a circular structure that should not be referred to as a chromosome. Due to the small size of a prokaryote cell, the DNA material is simply located near the center of the cell in a region called the nucleoid. Prokaryote cells lack histone proteins, and therefore the DNA is not actually packaged into chromosomes. Therefore, the DNA molecule located in a prokaryote cell floats freely within the cell. The DNA in a eukaryotic cell is located in the membrane-bound nucleus. Eukaryote cells have linear chromosomes and histone proteins. During mitosis, the chromatin is tightly wound on the histone proteins and packaged as a chromosome. A prokaryotic cell contains only one large DNA molecule, but it also contains tiny rings of DNA called plasmids. Eukaryotic cells may contain several large DNA molecules or chromosomes. Eukaryotes reproduce by mitosis, and prokaryotes reproduce by binary fission.

Cell cycle

The term cell cycle refers to the process by which a cell reproduces, which involves cell growth, the duplication of genetic material, and cell division. Complex organisms with many cells use the cell cycle to replace cells as they lose their functionality and wear out. The entire cell cycle in animal cells can take 24 hours. The time required varies among different cell types. Human skin cells, for example, are constantly reproducing. Some other cells only divide infrequently. Once neurons are mature, they do not grow or divide. The two ways that cells can reproduce are through meiosis and mitosis. When cells replicate through mitosis, the "daughter cell" is an exact replica of the parent cell. When cells divide through meiosis, the daughter cells have different genetic coding than the parent cell. Meiosis only happens in specialized reproductive cells called gametes.

Copyright © Mometrix Media. You have been licensed one copy of this document for personal use only. Any other reproduction or redistribution is strictly prohibited. All rights reserved.

Mitosis

The primary events that occur during mitosis are:

- Interphase: The cell prepares for division by replicating its genetic and cytoplasmic material. Interphase can be further divided into G_1, S, and G_2.
- Prophase: The chromatin thickens into chromosomes and the nuclear membrane begins to disintegrate. Pairs of centrioles move to opposite sides of the cell and spindle fibers begin to form. The mitotic spindle, formed from cytoskeleton parts, moves chromosomes around within the cell.
- Metaphase: The spindle moves to the center of the cell and chromosome pairs align along the center of the spindle structure.
- Anaphase: The pairs of chromosomes, called sisters, begin to pull apart, and may bend. When they are separated, they are called daughter chromosomes. Grooves appear in the cell membrane.
- Telophase: The spindle disintegrates, the nuclear membranes reform, and the chromosomes revert to chromatin. In animal cells, the membrane is pinched. In plant cells, a new cell wall begins to form.
- Cytokinesis: This is the physical splitting of the cell (including the cytoplasm) into two cells. Some believe this occurs following telophase. Others say it occurs from anaphase, as the cell begins to furrow, through telophase, when the cell actually splits into two.

> **Review Video: Mitosis**
> Visit mometrix.com/academy and enter code: 849894

Meiosis

Meiosis has the same phases as mitosis, but they happen twice. In addition, different events occur during some phases of meiosis than mitosis. The events that occur during the first phase of meiosis are interphase (I), prophase (I), metaphase (I), anaphase (I), telophase (I), and cytokinesis (I). During this first phase of meiosis, chromosomes cross over, genetic material is exchanged, and tetrads of four chromatids are formed. The nuclear membrane dissolves. Homologous pairs of chromatids are separated and travel to different poles. At this point, there has been one cell division resulting in two cells. Each cell goes through a second cell division, which consists of prophase (II), metaphase (II), anaphase (II), telophase (II), and cytokinesis (II). The result is four daughter cells with different sets of chromosomes. The daughter cells are haploid, which means they contain half the genetic material of the parent cell. The second phase of meiosis is similar to the process of mitosis. Meiosis encourages genetic diversity.

> **Review Video: Meiosis**
> Visit mometrix.com/academy and enter code: 247334

Cell Differentiation

The human body is filled with many different types of cells. The process that helps to determine the cell type for each cell is known as differentiation. Another way to say this is when a less-specialized cell becomes a more-specialized cell. This process is controlled by the genes of each cell among a group of cells known as a zygote. Following the directions of the genes, a cell builds certain proteins and other pieces that set it apart as a specific type of cell.

Copyright © Mometrix Media. You have been licensed one copy of this document for personal use only. Any other reproduction or redistribution is strictly prohibited. All rights reserved.

An example occurs with gastrulation--an early phase in the embryonic development of most animals. During gastrulation, the cells are organized into three primary germ layers: ectoderm, mesoderm, and endoderm. Then, the cells in these layers differentiate into special tissues and organs. For example, the nervous system develops from the ectoderm. The muscular system develops from the mesoderm. Much of the digestive system develops from the endoderm.

Passive transport mechanisms

Transport mechanisms allow for the movement of substances through membranes. Passive transport mechanisms include simple and facilitated diffusion and osmosis. They do not require energy from the cell. Diffusion occurs when particles are transported from areas of higher concentration to areas of lower concentration. When equilibrium is reached, diffusion stops. Examples are gas exchange (carbon dioxide and oxygen) during photosynthesis and the transport of oxygen from air to blood and from blood to tissue. Facilitated diffusion occurs when specific molecules are transported by a specific carrier protein. Carrier proteins vary in terms of size, shape, and charge. Glucose and amino acids are examples of substances transported by carrier proteins. Osmosis is the diffusion of water through a semi-permeable membrane from an area of lower solute concentration to one of higher solute concentration. Examples of osmosis include the absorption of water by plant roots and the alimentary canal. Plants lose and gain water through osmosis. A plant cell that swells because of water retention is said to be turgid.

Active transport mechanisms

Active transport mechanisms include exocytosis and endocytosis. Active transport involves transferring substances from areas of lower concentration to areas of higher concentration. Active transport requires energy in the form of ATP. Endocytosis is the ingestion of large particles into a cell, and can be categorized as phagocytosis (ingestion of a particle), pinocytosis (ingestion of a liquid), or receptor mediated. Endocytosis occurs when a substance is too large to cross a cell membrane. Endocytosis is a process by which eukaryotes ingest food particles. During phagocytosis, cell eating vesicles used during ingestion are quickly formed and unformed. Pinocytosis is also known as cell drinking. Exocytosis is the opposite of endocytosis. It is the expulsion or discharge of substances from a cell. A lysosome digests particles with enzymes, and can be expelled through exocytosis. A vacuole containing the substance to be expelled attaches to the cell membrane and expels the substance.

Photosynthesis

Photosynthesis is the conversion of sunlight into energy in plant cells (it also occurs in some types of bacteria and protists). Carbon dioxide and water are converted into glucose during photosynthesis, and light is required during this process. Cyanobacteria are thought to be the descendants of the first organisms to use photosynthesis about 3.5 billion years ago. Photosynthesis is a form of cellular respiration. It occurs in chloroplasts that use thylakoids, which are structures in the membrane that contain light reaction chemicals. Chlorophyll is a pigment that absorbs light.

During the process, water is used and oxygen is released. The equation for the chemical reaction that occurs during photosynthesis is $6H_2O + 6CO_2 \rightarrow C_6H_{12}O_6 + 6O_2$. During photosynthesis, six molecules of water and six molecules of carbon dioxide react to form one molecule of sugar and six molecules of oxygen.

> **Review Video: Photosynthesis**
> Visit mometrix.com/academy and enter code: 227035

- 94 -

Copyright © Mometrix Media. You have been licensed one copy of this document for personal use only. Any other reproduction or redistribution is strictly prohibited. All rights reserved.

Heterotrophs and Autotrophs

Heterotrophic refers to the method of getting energy by eating food that has energy releasing substances. Zooplankton are heterotrophic organisms, meaning they do not synthesize their own food. Plants, on the other hand, are autotrophs, which mean they make their own energy. In a sense, they are self sufficient. Phytoplankton are typically single-celled organisms that are nourished by the Sun. They are photosynthetic autotrophs, meaning they convert water, carbon dioxide, and solar energy into food.

Cellular respiration

Cellular respiration refers to a set of metabolic reactions that convert chemical bonds into energy stored in the form of ATP. Respiration includes many oxidation and reduction reactions that occur thanks to the electron transport system within the cell. Oxidation is a loss of electrons and reduction is a gain of electrons. Electrons in C-H (carbon/hydrogen) and C-C (carbon/carbon) bonds are donated to oxygen atoms. Processes involved in cellular respiration include glycolysis, the Krebs cycle, the electron transport chain, and chemiosmosis. The two forms of respiration are aerobic and anaerobic. Aerobic respiration is very common, and oxygen is the final electron acceptor. In anaerobic respiration, the final electron acceptor is not oxygen. Aerobic respiration results in more ATP than anaerobic respiration. Fermentation is another process by which energy is converted.

Gene, genotype, phenotype, and allele

A gene is a portion of DNA that identifies how traits are expressed and passed on in an organism. A gene is part of the genetic code. Collectively, all genes form the genotype of an individual. The genotype includes genes that may not be expressed, such as recessive genes. The phenotype is the physical, visual manifestation of genes. It is determined by the basic genetic information and how genes have been affected by their environment. An allele is a variation of a gene. Also known as a trait, it determines the manifestation of a gene. This manifestation results in a specific physical appearance of some facet of an organism, such as eye color or height. For example the genetic information for eye color is a gene. The gene variations responsible for blue, green, brown, or black eyes are called alleles. Locus (pl. loci) refers to the location of a gene or alleles.

DNA

Chromosomes consist of genes, which are single units of genetic information. Genes are made up of deoxyribonucleic acid (DNA). DNA is a nucleic acid located in the cell nucleus. There is also DNA in the mitochondria. DNA replicates to pass on genetic information. The DNA in almost all cells is the same. It is also involved in the biosynthesis of proteins. The model or structure of DNA is described as a double helix. A helix is a curve, and a double helix is two congruent curves connected by horizontal members. The model can be likened to a spiral staircase. It is right-handed. The British scientist Rosalind Elsie Franklin is credited with taking the x-ray diffraction image in 1952 that was used by Francis Crick and James Watson to formulate the double-helix model of DNA and speculate about its important role in carrying and transferring genetic information.

Structure

DNA has a double helix shape, resembles a twisted ladder, and is compact. It consists of nucleotides. Nucleotides consist of a five-carbon sugar (pentose), a phosphate group, and a nitrogenous base. Two bases pair up to form the rungs of the ladder. The "side rails" or backbone consists of the covalently bonded sugar and phosphate. The bases are attached to each other with hydrogen bonds, which are easily dismantled so replication can occur. Each base is attached to a phosphate and to a

Copyright © Mometrix Media. You have been licensed one copy of this document for personal use only. Any other reproduction or redistribution is strictly prohibited. All rights reserved.

sugar. There are four types of nitrogenous bases: adenine (A), guanine (G), cytosine (C), and thymine (T). There are about 3 billion bases in human DNA. The bases are mostly the same in everybody, but their order is different. It is the order of these bases that creates diversity in people. Adenine (A) pairs with thymine (T), and cytosine (C) pairs with guanine (G).

Replication

Pairs of chromosomes are composed of DNA, which is tightly wound to conserve space. When replication starts, it unwinds. The steps in DNA replication are controlled by enzymes. The enzyme helicase instigates the deforming of hydrogen bonds between the bases to split the two strands. The splitting starts at the A-T bases (adenine and thymine) as there are only two hydrogen bonds. The cytosine-guanine base pair has three bonds. The term "origin of replication" is used to refer to where the splitting starts. The portion of the DNA that is unwound to be replicated is called the replication fork. Each strand of DNA is transcribed by an mRNA. It copies the DNA onto itself, base by base, in a complementary manner. The exception is that uracil replaces thymine.

> **Review Video: DNA**
> Visit mometrix.com/academy and enter code: 639552

RNA

RNA is short for ribonucleic acid, which is a type of molecule that consists of a long chain (polymer) of nucleotide units. RNA and DNA differ in terms of structure and function. RNA has a different sugar than DNA. It has ribose rather than deoxyribose sugar. The RNA nitrogenous bases are adenine (A), guanine (G), cytosine (C), and uracil (U). Uracil is found only in RNA and thymine in found only in DNA. RNA consists of a single strand and DNA has two strands. If straightened out, DNA has two side rails. RNA only has one "backbone," or strand of sugar and phosphate group components. RNA uses the fully hydroxylated sugar pentose, which includes an extra oxygen compared to deoxyribose, which is the sugar used by DNA. RNA supports the functions carried out by DNA. It aids in gene expression, replication, and transportation.

RNA acts as a helper to DNA and carries out a number of other functions. Types of RNA include ribosomal RNA (rRNA), transfer RNA (tRNA), and messenger RNA (mRNA). Viruses can use RNA to carry their genetic material to DNA. Ribosomal RNA is not believed to have changed much over time. For this reason, it can be used to study relationships in organisms. Messenger RNA carries a copy of a strand of DNA and transports it from the nucleus to the cytoplasm. Transcription is the process in which RNA polymerase copies DNA into RNA. DNA unwinds itself and serves as a template while RNA is being assembled. The DNA molecules are copied to RNA. Translation is the process whereby ribosomes use transcribed RNA to put together the needed protein. Transfer RNA is a molecule that helps in the translation process, and is found in the cytoplasm. Ribosomal RNA is in the ribosomes.

> **Review Video: RNA**
> Visit mometrix.com/academy and enter code: 888852

Purines and Pyrimidines (Future Repetition)

The five bases in DNA and RNA can be categorized as either pyrimidine or purine according to their structure. The pyrimidine bases include cytosine, thymine, and uracil. They are six-sided and have a single ring shape. The purine bases are adenine and guanine, which consist of two attached rings. One ring has five sides and the other has six. When combined with a sugar, any of the five bases become nucleosides. Nucleosides formed from purine bases end in "osine" and those formed from

Copyright © Mometrix Media. You have been licensed one copy of this document for personal use only. Any other reproduction or redistribution is strictly prohibited. All rights reserved.

pyrimidine bases end in "idine." Adenosine and thymidine are examples of nucleosides. Bases are the most basic components, followed by nucleosides, nucleotides, and then DNA or RNA.

Codons

Codons are groups of three nucleotides on the messenger RNA, and can be visualized as three rungs of a ladder. A codon has the code for a single amino acid. There are 64 codons but 20 amino acids. More than one combination, or triplet, can be used to synthesize the necessary amino acids. For example, AAA (adenine-adenine-adenine) or AAG (adenine-adenine-guanine) can serve as codons for lysine. These groups of three occur in strings, and might be thought of as frames. For example, AAAUCUUCGU, if read in groups of three from the beginning, would be AAA, UCU, UCG, which are codons for lysine, serine, and serine, respectively. If the same sequence was read in groups of three starting from the second position, the groups would be AAU (asparagine), CUU (proline), and so on. The resulting amino acids would be completely different. For this reason, there are start and stop codons that indicate the beginning and ending of a sequence (or frame). AUG (methionine) is the start codon. UAA, UGA, and UAG, also known as ocher, opal, and amber, respectively, are stop codons.

Translation

Ribosomes synthesize proteins from mRNA in a process called translation. Sequences of three amino acids called codons make up the strand of mRNA. Each codon codes for a specific amino acid. The ribosome is composed of two subunits, a larger subunit and a smaller subunit, which are composed of ribosomal RNA (rRNA). The smaller subunit of RNA attaches to the mRNA near the cap. The smaller subunit slides along the mRNA until it reaches the first codon. Then, the larger subunit clamps onto the smaller subunit of the ribosome. Transfer RNA (tRNA) has codons complementary to the mRNA codons. The tRNA molecules attach at the site of translation. Amino acids are joined together by peptide bonds. The ribosome moves along the mRNA strand repeating this process until the protein is complete. Proteins are polymers of amino acids joined by peptide bonds.

Transcription

Transcription is the process by which a segment of DNA is copied onto a working blueprint called RNA. Each gene has a special region called a promoter that guides the beginning of the transcription process. RNA polymerase unwinds the DNA at the promoter of the needed gene. After the DNA is unwound, one strand or template is copied by the RNA polymerase by adding the complementary nucleotides, G with C , C with G, T with A, and A with U. Then, the sugar phosphate backbone forms

Copyright © Mometrix Media. You have been licensed one copy of this document for personal use only. Any other reproduction or redistribution is strictly prohibited. All rights reserved.

with the aid of RNA polymerase. Finally, the hydrogen bonds joining the strands of DNA and RNA together are broken. This forms a single strand of messenger RNA or mRNA.

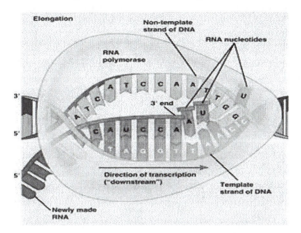

Mutations

A DNA mutation occurs when the normal gene sequence is altered. Mutations can happen when DNA is damaged as a result of environmental factors, such as chemicals, radiation, or ultraviolet rays from the sun. It can also happen when errors are made during DNA replication. The phosphate-sugar side rail of DNA can be damaged if the bonds between oxygen and phosphate groups are disassociated.

Translocation happens when the broken bonds attempt to bond with other DNA. This repair can cause a mutation. The nucleotide itself can be altered. A C, for example, might look like a T. During replication, the damaged C is replicated as a T and paired with a G, which is incorrect base pairing. Another way mutations can occur is if an error is made by the DNA polymerase while replicating a base. This happens about once for every 100,000,000 bases. A repair protein proofreads the code, however, so the mistake is usually repaired.

Gene disorders are the result of DNA mutations. DNA mutations lead to unfavorable gene disorders, but also provide genetic variability. This diversity can lead to increased survivability of a species. Mutations can be neutral, beneficial, or harmful. Mutations can be hereditary, meaning they are passed from parent to child. Polymorphism refers to differences in humans, such as eye and hair color, that may have originally been the result of gene mutations, but are now part of the normal variation of the species.

Mutations can be de novo, meaning they happen either only in sex cells or shortly after fertilization. They can also be acquired, or somatic. These are the kinds that happen as a result of DNA changes due to environmental factors or replication errors. Mosaicism is when a mutation happens in a cell during an early embryonic stage. The result is that some cells will have the mutation and some will not.

Review Video: Gene Mutation
Visit mometrix.com/academy and enter code: 955485

Dominant and recessive

Gene traits are represented in pairs with an uppercase letter for the dominant trait (A) and a lowercase letter for the recessive trait (a). Genes occur in pairs (AA, Aa, or aa). There is one gene on

- 98 -

Copyright © Mometrix Media. You have been licensed one copy of this document for personal use only. Any other reproduction or redistribution is strictly prohibited. All rights reserved.

each chromosome half supplied by each parent organism. Since half the genetic material is from each parent, the offspring's traits are represented as a combination of these. A dominant trait only requires one gene of a gene pair for it to be expressed in a phenotype, whereas a recessive requires both genes in order to be manifested. For example, if the mother's genotype is Dd and the father's is dd, the possible combinations are Dd and dd. The dominant trait will be manifested if the genotype is DD or Dd. The recessive trait will be manifested if the genotype is dd. Both DD and dd are homozygous pairs. Dd is heterozygous.

Monohybrid and hybrid crosses

Genetic crosses are the possible combinations of alleles, and can be represented using Punnett squares. A monohybrid cross refers to a cross involving only one trait. Typically, the ratio is 3:1 (DD, Dd, Dd, dd), which is the ratio of dominant gene manifestation to recessive gene manifestation. This ratio occurs when both parents have a pair of dominant and recessive genes. If one parent has a pair of dominant genes (DD) and the other has a pair of recessive (dd) genes, the recessive trait cannot be expressed in the next generation because the resulting crosses all have the Dd genotype. A dihybrid cross refers to one involving more than one trait, which means more combinations are possible. The ratio of genotypes for a dihybrid cross is 9:3:3:1 when the traits are not linked. The ratio for incomplete dominance is 1:2:1, which corresponds to dominant, mixed, and recessive phenotypes.

Mendel's laws and Punnett squares

Mendel's laws are the law of segregation (the first law) and the law of independent assortment (the second law). The law of segregation states that there are two alleles and that half of the total number of alleles are contributed by each parent organism. The law of independent assortment states that traits are passed on randomly and are not influenced by other traits. The exception to this is linked traits. A Punnett square can illustrate how alleles combine from the contributing genes to form various phenotypes. One set of a parent's genes are put in columns, while the genes from the other parent are placed in rows. The allele combinations are shown in each cell. When two different alleles are present in a pair, the dominant one is expressed. A Punnett square can be used to predict the outcome of crosses.

Important terms

- Cytosol: This is the liquid material in the cell. It is mostly water, but also contains some floating molecules.
- Cytoplasm: This is a general term that refers to cytosol and the substructures (organelles) found within the plasma membrane, but not within the nucleus.
- Cell membrane (plasma membrane): This defines the cell by acting as a barrier. It helps keeps cytoplasm in and substances located outside the cell out. It also determines what is allowed to enter and exit the cell.
- Endoplasmic reticulum: The two types of endoplasmic reticulum are rough (has ribosomes on the surface) and smooth (does not have ribosomes on the surface). It is a tubular network that includes the transport system of a cell. It is fused to the nuclear membrane and extends through the cytoplasm to the cell membrane.
- Mitochondrion (pl. mitochondria): These cell structures vary in terms of size and quantity. Some cells may have one mitochondrion, while others have thousands. This structure performs various functions such as generating ATP, and is also involved in cell growth and death. Mitochondria contain their own DNA that is separate from that contained in the nucleus.

- 99 -

Copyright © Mometrix Media. You have been licensed one copy of this document for personal use only. Any other reproduction or redistribution is strictly prohibited. All rights reserved.

- Ribosomes: Ribosomes are involved in synthesizing proteins from amino acids. They are numerous, making up about one quarter of the cell. Some cells contain thousands of ribosomes. Some are mobile and some are embedded in the rough endoplasmic reticulum.
- Golgi complex (Golgi apparatus): This is involved in synthesizing materials such as proteins that are transported out of the cell. It is located near the nucleus and consists of layers of membranes.
- Vacuoles: These are sacs used for storage, digestion, and waste removal. There is one large vacuole in plant cells. Animal cells have small, sometimes numerous vacuoles.
- Vesicle: This is a small organelle within a cell. It has a membrane and performs varying functions, including moving materials within a cell.
- Cytoskeleton: This consists of microtubules that help shape and support the cell.
- Microtubules: These are part of the cytoskeleton and help support the cell. They are made of protein.
- Centrosome: This is composed of the pair of centrioles located at right angles to each other and surrounded by protein. The centrosome is involved in mitosis and the cell cycle.
- Centriole: These are cylinder-shaped structures near the nucleus that are involved in cellular division. Each cylinder consists of nine groups of three microtubules. Centrioles occur in pairs.
- Lysosome: This digests proteins, lipids, and carbohydrates, and also transports undigested substances to the cell membrane so they can be removed. The shape of a lysosome depends on the material being transported.
- Cilia (singular: cilium): These are appendages extending from the surface of the cell, the movement of which causes the cell to move. They can also result in fluid being moved by the cell.
- Flagella: These are tail-like structures on cells that use whip-like movements to help the cell move. They are similar to cilia, but are usually longer and not as numerous. A cell usually only has one or a few flagella.
- Cell wall: Made of cellulose and composed of numerous layers, the cell wall provides plants with a sturdy barrier that can hold fluid within the cell. The cell wall surrounds the cell membrane.
- Chloroplast: This is a specialized organelle that plant cells use for photosynthesis, which is the process plants use to create food energy from sunlight. Chloroplasts contain chlorophyll, which has a green color.
- Plastid: This is a membrane-bound organelle found in plant cells that is used to make chemical compounds and store food. It can also contain pigments used during photosynthesis. Plastids can develop into more specialized structures such as chloroplasts, chromoplasts (make and hold yellow and orange pigments), amyloplasts (store starch), and leucoplasts (lack pigments, but can become differentiated).
- Plasmodesmata (sing. plasmodesma): These are channels between the cell walls of plant cells that allow for transport between cells.
- Lipid: Lipids take many forms and have varying functions, such as storing energy and acting as a building block of cell membranes..
- Organelle: This is a general term that refers to an organ or smaller structure within a cell. Membrane-bound organelles are found in eukaryotic cells.
- Polymer: This is a compound of large molecules formed by repeating monomers.
- Monomer: A monomer is a small molecule. It is a single compound that forms chemical bonds with other monomers to make a polymer.

Copyright © Mometrix Media. You have been licensed one copy of this document for personal use only. Any other reproduction or redistribution is strictly prohibited. All rights reserved.

- Nucleotides: These are molecules that combine to form DNA and RNA. They can be easily stained to make them more visible.
- Nucleoid: This is the nucleus-like, irregularly-shaped mass of DNA that contains the chromatin in a prokaryotic cell.

Copyright © Mometrix Media. You have been licensed one copy of this document for personal use only. Any other reproduction or redistribution is strictly prohibited. All rights reserved.

Earth and Physical Science

Proton, electron, and neutron

The three most important subatomic particles are the proton, electron, and neutron. Protons are the positively charged particles in the nucleus, with a mass of 1.67252×10^{-24} g. This is approximately 1,840 times the mass of the oppositely charged electron, 9.1095×10^{-28} g. Neutrons are also present in the nucleus, are electrically neutral, and have a mass slightly greater than that of protons, 1.67497×10^{-24} g. The electrons are attracted to the positively charged nucleus by the electrostatic or Coulomb force, which is directly proportional to the charge of the nucleus and inversely proportional to the square of the distance from the nucleus. The protons and neutrons are held together in the nucleus by the strong nuclear force. This nuclear force is known to be much stronger than the electrostatic force since the protons do not repel one another.

Atomic number, atomic mass number, and isotope

All atoms can be identified by the number of protons and neutrons they contain. The atomic number, often denoted as Z, is the number of protons in the nucleus of each atom of an element. In an electrically neutral atom, the number of protons is equal to the number of electrons. The atomic mass number, often denoted as A, is the total number of nucleons (neutrons and protons present in the nucleus) in each atom of an element. Atoms that have the same atomic number but different mass numbers are called isotopes. A similar term is nuclide, which refers to an atom with a given number of protons and neutrons. Atoms of a given element typically do not all have the same mass. For example, there are three hydrogen isotopes: protium, which has one proton and no neutrons; deuterium, which has one proton and one neutron; and tritium, which has one proton and two neutrons. Isotopes are denoted by the element symbol, preceded in superscript and subscript by the mass number and atomic number, respectively. For instance, the notations for protium, deuterium, and tritium are, respectively:

$_1^1H$, $_1^2H$, and $_1^3H$.

Matter

Matter is defined as anything that occupies space and has mass. Categories of matter include atoms, elements, molecules, compounds, substances and mixtures:

- An atom is the basic unit of an element that can enter into a chemical reaction.
- An element is a substance that cannot be separated into simpler substances by chemical means.
- A molecule is the smallest division of a compound that can exist in a natural state.
- A compound is a substance composed of atoms of two or more elements chemically united in fixed proportions.
- A substance is a form of matter that has a definite or constant composition and distinct properties.
- A mixture is a combination of two or more substances in which the substances retain their unique identities.

Organization of matter

An element is the most basic type of matter. It has unique properties and cannot be broken down into other elements. The smallest unit of an element is the atom. A chemical combination of two or more types of elements is called a compound. Compounds often have properties that are very

Copyright © Mometrix Media. You have been licensed one copy of this document for personal use only. Any other reproduction or redistribution is strictly prohibited. All rights reserved.

different from those of their constituent elements. The smallest independent unit of an element or compound is known as a molecule. Most elements are found somewhere in nature in single-atom form, but a few elements only exist naturally in pairs. These are called diatomic elements, of which some of the most common are hydrogen, nitrogen, and oxygen. Elements and compounds are represented by chemical symbols, one or two letters, most often the first in the element name. More than one atom of the same element in a compound is represented with a subscript number designating how many atoms of that element are present. Water, for instance, contains two hydrogens and one oxygen. Thus, the chemical formula is H_2O. Methane contains one carbon and four hydrogens, so its formula is CH_4.

States of matter

The three states in which matter can exist are solid, liquid, and gas. They differ from each other in the motion of and attraction between individual molecules. In a solid, the molecules have little or no motion and are heavily attracted to neighboring molecules, giving them a definite structure.

This structure may be ordered/crystalline or random/amorphous. Liquids also have considerable attraction between molecules, but the molecules are much more mobile, having no set structure. In a gas, the molecules have little or no attraction to one another and are constantly in motion. They are separated by distances that are very large in comparison to the size of the molecules. Gases easily expand to fill whatever space is available. Unlike solids and liquids, gases are easily compressible.

The three states of matter can be traversed by the addition or removal of heat. For example, when a solid is heated to its melting point, it can begin to form a liquid. However, in order to transition from solid to liquid, additional heat must be added at the melting point to overcome the latent heat of fusion. Upon further heating to its boiling point, the liquid can begin to form a gas, but again, additional heat must be added at the boiling point to overcome the latent heat of vaporization.

In the solid state, water is less dense than in the liquid state. This can be observed quite simply by noting that an ice cube floats at the surface of a glass of water. Were this not the case, ice would not form on the surface of lakes and rivers in those regions of the world where the climate produces temperatures below the freezing point. If water behaved as other substances do, lakes and rivers would freeze from the bottom up, which would be detrimental to many forms of aquatic life. The lower density of ice occurs because of a combination of the unique structure of the water molecule and hydrogen bonding. In the case of ice, each oxygen atom is bound to four hydrogen atoms, two covalently and two by hydrogen bonds. This forms an ordered, roughly tetrahedral structure that prevents the molecules from getting close to each other. As such, there are empty spaces in the structure that account for the low density of ice.

> **Review Video: States of Matter**
> Visit mometrix.com/academy and enter code: 742449

Physical and chemical properties of matter

If a property of a substance can be observed and measured without change it is a physical property. Density, melting point and boiling point are examples of physical properties.

If a chemical change must be carried out in order to observe and measure a property, then the property is a chemical property. For example, when hydrogen gas is burned in oxygen, it forms water. This is a chemical property of hydrogen because after burning, a different chemical

Copyright © Mometrix Media. You have been licensed one copy of this document for personal use only. Any other reproduction or redistribution is strictly prohibited. All rights reserved.

substance – water – is all that remains. The hydrogen cannot be recovered from the water by means of a physical change such as freezing or boiling.

The table below outlines the characteristic properties of the three states of matter:

State of matter	Volume/ shape	Density	Compressibility	Molecular motion
Gas	Assumes volume and shape of its container	Low	High	Very free motion
Liquid	Volume remains constant but it assumes shape of its container	High	Slightly	Move past each other freely
Solid	Definite volume and shape	High	Incompressible	Vibrates around fixed positions

Types of phase change

A substance that is undergoing a change from a solid to a liquid is said to be melting. If this change occurs in the opposite direction, from liquid to solid, this change is called freezing. A liquid which is being converted to a gas is undergoing vaporization. The reverse of this process is known as condensation. Direct transitions from gas to solid and solid to gas are much less common in everyday life, but they can occur given the proper conditions. Solid to gas conversion is known as sublimation, while the reverse is called deposition.

Evaporation: Evaporation is the change of state in a substance from a liquid to a gaseous form at a temperature below its boiling point (the temperature at which all of the molecules in a liquid are changed to gas through vaporization). Some of the molecules at the surface of a liquid always maintain enough heat energy to escape the cohesive forces exerted on them by neighboring molecules. At higher temperatures, the molecules in a substance move more rapidly, increasing their number with enough energy to break out of the liquid form. The rate of evaporation is higher when more of the surface area of a liquid is exposed (as in a large water body, such as an ocean). The amount of moisture already in the air also affects the rate of evaporation—if there is a significant amount of water vapor in the air around a liquid, some evaporated molecules will return to the liquid. The speed of the evaporation process is also decreased by increased atmospheric pressure.

Condensation: Condensation is the phase change in a substance from a gaseous to liquid form; it is the opposite of evaporation or vaporization. When temperatures decrease in a gas, such as water vapor, the material's component molecules move more slowly. The decreased motion of the molecules enables intermolecular cohesive forces to pull the molecules closer together and, in water, establish hydrogen bonds. Condensation can also be caused by an increase in the pressure exerted on a gas, which results in a decrease in the substance's volume (it reduces the distance between particles). In the hydrologic cycle, this process is initiated when warm air containing water vapor rises and then cools. This occurs due to convection in the air, meteorological fronts, or lifting over high land formations.

Formation of molecules

Electrons in an atom can orbit different levels around the nucleus. They can absorb or release energy, which can change the location of their orbit or even allow them to break free from the atom. The outermost layer is the valence layer, which contains the valence electrons. The valence layer tends to have or share eight electrons. Molecules are formed by a chemical bond between atoms, a

- 104 -

Copyright © Mometrix Media. You have been licensed one copy of this document for personal use only. Any other reproduction or redistribution is strictly prohibited. All rights reserved.

bond which occurs at the valence level. Two basic types of bonds are covalent and ionic. A covalent bond is formed when atoms share electrons. An ionic bond is formed when an atom transfers an electron to another atom. A hydrogen bond is a weak bond between a hydrogen atom of one molecule and an electronegative atom (such as nitrogen, oxygen, or fluorine) of another molecule. The Van der Waals force is a weak force between molecules. This type of force is much weaker than actual chemical bonds between atoms.

Interaction of atoms to form compounds

Atoms interact by transferring or sharing the electrons furthest from the nucleus. Known as the outer or valence electrons, they are responsible for the chemical properties of an element. Bonds between atoms are created when electrons are paired up by being transferred or shared. If electrons are transferred from one atom to another, the bond is ionic. If electrons are shared, the bond is covalent. Atoms of the same element may bond together to form molecules or crystalline solids. When two or more different types of atoms bind together chemically, a compound is made. The physical properties of compounds reflect the nature of the interactions among their molecules. These interactions are determined by the structure of the molecule, including the atoms they consist of and the distances and angles between them.

Chemical bonds between atoms

A union between the electron structures of atoms is called chemical bonding. An atom may gain, surrender, or share its electrons with another atom it bonds with. Listed below are three types of chemical bonding.

- Ionic bonding - When an atom gains or loses electrons it becomes negatively or positively charged, turning it into an ion. An ionic bond is a relationship between two oppositely charged ions.
- Covalent bonding - Atoms that share electrons have what is called a covalent bond. Electrons shared equally have a non-polar bond, while electrons shared unequally have a polar bond.
- Hydrogen bonding - The atom of a molecule interacts with a hydrogen atom in the same area. Hydrogen bonds can also form between two different parts of the same molecule, as in the structure of DNA and other large molecules.

Ionic bonding

The transfer of electrons from one atom to another is called ionic bonding. Atoms that lose or gain electrons are referred to as ions. The gain or loss of electrons will result in an ion having a positive or negative charge. Here is an example:

Take an atom of sodium (Na) and an atom of chlorine (Cl). The sodium atom has a total of 11 electrons (including one electron in its outer shell). The chlorine has 17 electrons (including 7 electrons in its outer shell). From this, the atomic number, or number of protons, of sodium can be calculated as 11 because the number of protons equals the number of electrons in an atom. When sodium chloride (NaCl) is formed, one electron from sodium transfers to chlorine. Ions have charges. They are written with a plus (+) or minus (-) symbol. Ions in a compound are attracted to each other because they have opposite charges.

Copyright © Mometrix Media. You have been licensed one copy of this document for personal use only. Any other reproduction or redistribution is strictly prohibited. All rights reserved.

Covalent bonding

Covalent bonding is characterized by the sharing of one or more pairs of electrons between two atoms or between an atom and another covalent bond. This produces an attraction to repulsion stability that holds these molecules together. Atoms have the tendency to share electrons with each other so that all outer electron shells are filled. The resultant bonds are always stronger than the intermolecular hydrogen bond and are similar in strength to ionic bonds. Covalent bonding occurs most frequently between atoms with similar electronegativities. Nonmetals are more likely to form covalent bonds than metals since it is more difficult for nonmetals to liberate an electron. Electron sharing takes place when one species encounters another species with similar electronegativity. Covalent bonding of metals is important in both process chemistry and industrial catalysis.

Periodicity

Periodicity describes the predictable and incremental nature of elements' properties and places them on the periodic table accordingly. An atom of every element has unique properties such as number of electrons, density, and mass. The periodic table is arranged such that elements near each other are more alike in these properties than those that are far apart on the table. Periodicity enables the prediction of properties and atomic configurations based on known trends represented by the position of elements on the table. One such trend is the number of electrons; reading from left to right on any given row of the table, each element contains one more electron than the one immediately preceding it. On row 4, for example, K contains 19 electrons and the next element, Ca, contains 20.

Periodic table

The periodic table is a tabular arrangement of the elements and is organized according to periodic law. The properties of the elements depend on their atomic structure and vary with atomic number. It shows periodic trends of physical and chemical properties and identifies families of elements with similar properties. In the periodic table, the elements are arranged by atomic number in horizontal rows called periods and vertical columns called groups or families. They are further categorized as metals, metalloids, or nonmetals. The majority of known elements are metals; there are seventeen nonmetals and eight metalloids. Metals are situated at the left end of the periodic table, nonmetals to the right and metalloids between the two.

Most periodic tables contain the element's atomic weight, number, and symbol in each box. The position of an element in the table reveals its group, its block, and whether it is a representative, transition, or inner transition element. Its position also shows the element as a metal, nonmetal, or metalloid. For the representative elements, the last digit of the group number reveals the number of outer-level electrons. Roman numerals for the A groups also reveal the number of outer level electrons within the group. The position of the element in the table reveals its electronic configuration and how it differs in atomic size from neighbors in its period or group. In this example, Boron has an atomic number of 5 and an atomic weight of 10.811. It is found in group 13, in which all atoms of the group have 3 valence electrons; the group's Roman numeral representation is IIIA.

> **Review Video:** Periodic Table
> Visit mometrix.com/academy and enter code: 154828

Copyright © Mometrix Media. You have been licensed one copy of this document for personal use only. Any other reproduction or redistribution is strictly prohibited. All rights reserved.

<u>Important features and structure</u>

The most important feature of the table is its arrangement according to periodicity, or the predictable trends observable in atoms. The arrangement enables classification, organization, and prediction of important elemental properties. The table is organized in horizontal rows called Periods, and vertical columns called groups or families. Groups of elements share predictable characteristics, the most important of which is that their outer energy levels have the same configuration of electrons. For example, the highest group is group 18, the noble gases. Each element in this group has a full complement of electrons in its outer level, making the reactivity low. Elements in periods also share some common properties, but most classifications rely more heavily on groups. A typical periodic table shows the elements' symbols and atomic number, which is the number of protons in the atomic nucleus. Some more detailed tables also list atomic mass, electronegativity, and other data.

<u>Chemical reactivity</u>

Reactivity refers to the tendency of a substance to engage in chemical reactions. If that tendency is high, the substance is said to be highly reactive, or to have high reactivity. Because the basis of a chemical reaction is the transfer of electrons, reactivity depends upon the presence of uncommitted electrons which are available for transfer. Periodicity allows us to predict an element's reactivity based on its position on the periodic table. High numbered groups on the right side of the table have a fuller complement of electrons in their outer levels, making them less likely to react. Noble gases, on the far right of the table, each have eight electrons in the outer level, with the exception of He, which has two. Because atoms tend to lose or gain electrons to reach an ideal of eight in the outer level, these elements have very low reactivity.

<u>Groups and periods in terms of reactivity</u>

Reading left to right within a period, each element contains one more electron than the one preceding it. (Note that H and He are in the same period, though nothing is between them and they are in different groups.) As electrons are added, their attraction to the nucleus increases, meaning that as we read to the right in a period, each atom's electrons are more densely compacted, more strongly bound to the nucleus, and less likely to be pulled away in reactions. As we read down a group, each successive atom's outer electrons are less tightly bound to the nucleus, thus increasing their reactivity, because the principal energy levels are increasingly full as we move downward within the group. Principal energy levels shield the outer energy levels from nuclear attraction, allowing the valence electrons to react. For this reason, noble gases farther down the group can react under certain circumstances.

Chemical reactions

The classic chemical reaction is a transfer of electrons resulting in a transformation of the substances involved in the reaction. The changes may be in composition or configuration of a compound or substance, and result in one or more products being generated which were not present in isolation before the reaction occurred. For instance, when oxygen reacts with methane (CH_4), water and carbon dioxide are the products; one set of substances ($CH_4 + O$) was transformed into a new set of substances ($CO_2 + H_2O$). Reactions are classified in many ways, some of which are as follows: as combination or synthesis, in which two or more compounds unite to form a more complex compound; decomposition, in which a compound is broken down into its constituent compounds or elements; and isomerization, in which compounds undergo structural changes without changing their atomic composition.

Copyright © Mometrix Media. You have been licensed one copy of this document for personal use only. Any other reproduction or redistribution is strictly prohibited. All rights reserved.

Chemical reactions measured in human time can take place quickly or slowly. They can take a fraction of a second or billions of years. The rates of chemical reactions are determined by how frequently reacting atoms and molecules interact. Rates are also influenced by the temperature and various properties (such as shape) of the reacting materials. Catalysts accelerate chemical reactions, while inhibitors decrease reaction rates. Some types of reactions release energy in the form of heat and light. Some types of reactions involve the transfer of either electrons or hydrogen ions between reacting ions, molecules, or atoms. In other reactions, chemical bonds are broken down by heat or light to form reactive radicals with electrons that will readily form new bonds. Processes such as the formation of ozone and greenhouse gases in the atmosphere and the burning and processing of fossil fuels are controlled by radical reactions.

Basic mechanisms

Chemical reactions normally occur when electrons are transferred from one atom or molecule to another. Reactions and reactivity depend on the octet rule, which describes the tendency of atoms to gain or lose electrons until their outer energy levels contain eight. Reactions always result in a change in composition or constitution of a compound. They depend on the presence of a reactant, or substance undergoing change, a reagent, or partner in the reaction less transformed than the reactant (such as a catalyst), and products, or the final result of the reaction. Reaction conditions, or environmental factors, are also important components in reactions. These include conditions such as temperature, pressure, concentration, whether the reaction occurs in solution, the type of solution, and presence or absence of catalysts. Chemical reactions are usually written in the following format:

$$\text{Reactants} \rightarrow \text{Products}$$

Exothermic, endothermic, activation energy, and reaction equilibrium

Exothermic reactions are chemical reactions in which energy is released or produced, such as in combustion. In endothermic reactions, external energy is required for the reaction to occur and is absorbed from the surroundings. Some reactions require energy to start the reaction. This energy is called activation energy. A match applied to tissue paper is an example of activation energy. When the same number of atoms is present on the reactant side of an equation as on the product side, the reaction is said to be in equilibrium. All atoms of a substance must be accounted for after it undergoes a chemical reaction. For instance, methane reacting with oxygen produces water and carbon dioxide, but all atoms in the original substances are still present, albeit in different combinations.

Catalysis

Catalysis occurs when a catalyst is added to a reaction to increase its rate and efficiency. Catalysts change the rate of a reaction without being changed *by* the reaction and are important elements of chemical and biological processes. They function by decreasing the activation energy required for a reaction to occur. Homogeneous catalysis occurs when the catalyst is in the same state of matter as the reactant(s) and product(s). Heterogeneous catalysis occurs when the catalyst is in a different state. For example, hydrogen peroxide (H_2O_2) breaks down naturally to produce water and oxygen; this is normally a very slow reaction. Liquid hydrogen bromide can be added to the H_2O_2 to speed up the reaction considerably; because all compounds in question are liquid, this is an example of homogeneous catalysis. Solid manganese dioxide crystals (MnO_2) can also be added to the H_2O_2 as a catalyst to demonstrate heterogeneous catalysis.

Copyright © Mometrix Media. You have been licensed one copy of this document for personal use only. Any other reproduction or redistribution is strictly prohibited. All rights reserved.

Enzymes

Enzymes are proteins with strong catalytic power. They greatly accelerate the speed at which specific reactions approach equilibrium. Although enzymes do not start chemical reactions that would not eventually occur by themselves, they do make these reactions happen faster and more often. This acceleration can be substantial, sometimes making reactions happen a million times faster. Each type of enzyme deals with reactants, also called substrates. Each enzyme is highly selective, only interacting with substrates that are a match for it at an active site on the enzyme. This is the "key in the lock" analogy: a certain enzyme only fits with certain substrates. Even with a matching substrate, Sometimes an enzyme must reshape itself to fit well with the substrate, forming a strong bond that aids in catalyzing a reaction before it returns to its original shape. Sometimes an enzyme must reshape itself to fit well with the substrate, forming a strong bond that aids in catalyzing a reaction before it returns to its original shape. An unusual quality of enzymes is that they are not permanently consumed in the reactions they speed up. They can be used again and again, providing a constant source of energy accelerants for cells. This allows for a tremendous increase in the number and rate of reactions in cells.

Types of chemical reactions

Electron transfer, or redox reaction, occurs when electrons move from one atom to another, changing the charge of the ion. Because the charge has changed, the oxidation number also changes. Oxidation is an important class of redox reactions in which the oxidation number increases. Commonly, any reaction in which oxygen combines with other substances is oxidation. Rusting iron and burning wood are both examples of oxidation.

Precipitation, (ion combination reaction), occurs when positive and negative compounds in solution combine to form an insoluble ionic compound.

Acid-base reactions occur when an acid reacts with a base and an ion of hydrogen transfers to the base.

Polymerization reactions occur when simple molecules, also called monomers, combine to form complex molecules, or polymers.

Combination reactions occur when pairs of reactants combine to produce a single substance. The reactions take place when it the energy is favorable to do so. For instance:

$C_{(s)} + O_{2(g)} \rightarrow CO_{2(g)}$

$N_{2(g)} + 3H_{2(g)} \rightarrow 2NH_{3(g)}$

$CaO_{(s)} + H_2O_{(l)} \rightarrow Ca(OH)_{2(s)}$

Decomposition refers to the reaction involving those molecules which are stable at room temperature and decompose when heated:

$2KClO_{3(s)} \rightarrow 2KCl_{(s)} + 3O_{3(g)}$

$PbCO_{3(s)} \rightarrow 2PbO_{(s)} + CO_{2(g)}$

Copyright © Mometrix Media. You have been licensed one copy of this document for personal use only. Any other reproduction or redistribution is strictly prohibited. All rights reserved.

Single substitution is when a reaction involves an element that displaces another in a compound such as when a copper strip displaces silver atoms and produces copper nitrate and precipitating silver crystals of metal:

$$Cu_{(s)} + 2AgNO_{3(aq)} \rightarrow 2Ag_{(s)} + Cu(NO_3)_{2(aq)}$$

Double substitution is when a reaction looks as if it is exchanging parts of the reactants. An example:

$$2KI_{(aq)} + Pb(NO_3)_{2(aq)} \rightarrow 2KNO_{3(aq)} + PbI_{(s)}$$

Oxidation/reduction reactions

One way to organize chemical reactions is to sort them into two categories: oxidation/reduction reactions (also called redox reactions) and metathesis reactions (which include acid/base reactions). Oxidation/reduction reactions can involve the transfer of one or more electrons, or they can occur as a result of the transfer of oxygen, hydrogen, or halogen atoms. The species that loses electrons is oxidized and is referred to as the reducing agent. The species that gains electrons is reduced and is referred to as the oxidizing agent. The element undergoing oxidation experiences an increase in its oxidation number, while the element undergoing reduction experiences a decrease in its oxidation number. Single replacement reactions are types of oxidation/reduction reactions. In a single replacement reaction, electrons are transferred from one chemical species to another. The transfer of electrons results in changes in the nature and charge of the species.

Metathesis (acid/base) reactions

Double replacement reactions are metathesis reactions. In a double replacement reaction, the chemical reactants exchange ions but the oxidation state stays the same. One of the indicators of this is the formation of a solid precipitate. In acid/base reactions, an acid is a compound that can donate a proton, while a base is a compound that can accept a proton. In these types of reactions, the acid and base react to form a salt and water. When the proton is donated, the base becomes water and the remaining ions form a salt. One way of determining whether a reaction is an oxidation/reduction or a metathesis reaction is to remember that the oxidation number of atoms does not change during a metathesis reaction.

Oxidizing agent, reduction agent, and rate-determining step

An oxidizing agent is the reactant in oxidation reactions which gains electrons, causing oxidation of the other reactant(s). Peroxides, iodine and other halogens, and sulfoxides are common oxidizing agents. A reduction, or reducing agent, is the reactant oxidized in an oxidation reaction; it loses electrons to the oxidizing agent. In rusting iron, a common oxidation reaction, iron is the reducing agent, losing electrons to oxygen. In multi-step reactions, each of the steps has different reaction rates which are often very different. The rate-determining step is the slowest portion of such reactions. Because the reaction can only go as fast as its slowest step, that step determines overall reaction rate.

Law of Conservation of Mass

The Law of Conservation of Mass in a chemical reaction is commonly stated as follows:

In a chemical reaction, matter is neither created nor destroyed.

What this means is that there will always be the same total mass of material after a reaction as before. This allows for predicting how molecules will combine by balanced equations in which the number of each type of atom is the same on either side of the equation. For example, two hydrogen

- 110 -

Copyright © Mometrix Media. You have been licensed one copy of this document for personal use only. Any other reproduction or redistribution is strictly prohibited. All rights reserved.

molecules combine with one oxygen molecule to form water. This is a balanced chemical equation because the number of each type of atom is same on both sides of the arrow. It has to balance because the reaction obeys the Law of Conservation of Mass.

Reading and balancing chemical equations

Chemical equations describe chemical reactions. The reactants are on the left side before the arrow and the products are on the right side after the arrow. The arrow indicates the reaction or change. The coefficient, or stoichiometric coefficient, is the number before the element, and indicates the ratio of reactants to products in terms of moles. The equation for the formation of water from hydrogen and oxygen, for example, is $2H_{2(g)} + O_{2(g)} \rightarrow 2H_2O_{(l)}$. The 2 preceding hydrogen and water is the coefficient, which means there are 2 moles of hydrogen and 2 of water. There is 1 mole of oxygen, which does not have to be indicated with the number 1. In parentheses, g stands for gas, l stands for liquid, s stands for solid, and aq stands for aqueous solution (a substance dissolved in water). Charges are shown in superscript for individual ions, but not for ionic compounds. Polyatomic ions are separated by parentheses so the ion will not be confused with the number of ions.

An unbalanced equation is one that does not follow the law of conservation of mass, which states that matter can only be changed, not created. If an equation is unbalanced, the numbers of atoms indicated by the stoichiometric coefficients on each side of the arrow will not be equal. Start by writing the formulas for each species in the reaction. Count the atoms on each side and determine if the number is equal. Coefficients must be whole numbers. Fractional amounts, such as half a molecule, are not possible. Equations can be balanced by multiplying the coefficients by a constant that will produce the smallest possible whole number coefficient. $H_2 + O_2 \rightarrow H_2O$ is an example of an unbalanced equation. The balanced equation is $2H_2 + O_2 \rightarrow 2H_2O$, which indicates that it takes two moles of hydrogen and one of oxygen to produce two moles of water.

Hydrocarbons

Hydrocarbons are molecules containing only C and H and form the basis of organic chemistry. They bond together with strong covalent bonds in chains or rings to form the backbone of organic molecules which may have any number of a large variety of functional groups attached. Hydrocarbons are classified into two large groups based on the bonds between their C atoms; if only C—C single bonds are present, the hydrocarbon is saturated because other electrons will then form bonds with surrounding H atoms. If the C atoms are bound with multiple bonds (C=C or CÐC), fewer electrons are available to form bonds with H atoms and the hydrocarbon is unsaturated. Hydrocarbons are very stable molecules because of the tetravalency of C; it has four valence electrons making its octet requirement easy to satisfy, which results in very strong bonds.

> **Review Video: Basics of Hydrocarbons**
> Visit mometrix.com/academy and enter code: 824749

Properties of water

The important properties of water (H_2O) are high polarity, hydrogen bonding, cohesiveness, adhesiveness, high specific heat, high latent heat, and high heat of vaporization. It is essential to life as we know it, as water is one of the main if not the main constituent of many living things. Water is a liquid at room temperature. The high specific heat of water means it resists the breaking of its hydrogen bonds and resists heat and motion, which is why it has a relatively high boiling point and high vaporization point. It also resists temperature change. In its solid state, water floats. (Most substances are heavier in their solid forms.) Water is cohesive, which means it is attracted to itself.

- 111 -

Copyright © Mometrix Media. You have been licensed one copy of this document for personal use only. Any other reproduction or redistribution is strictly prohibited. All rights reserved.

It is also adhesive, which means it readily attracts other molecules. If water tends to adhere to another substance, the substance is said to be hydrophilic. Water makes a good solvent. Substances, particularly those with polar ions and molecules, readily dissolve in water.

Review Video: Properties of Water
Visit mometrix.com/academy and enter code: 279526

Solutions and molarity

When a substance (solute) is mixed with a liquid (solvent) and is dissolved into the liquid, a solution has been created. Solutions are homogeneous and symmetrical because any portion of a solution has the same composition and contents as any other portion. When the solution can hold no more of a solute, the solution is said to be saturated.

The amount of solute that is present in a solution is described by a quantity called molar concentration or molarity, usually given in units of moles per liter $\left(\frac{mol}{L}\right)$. It is calculated by taking the number of moles of solute and dividing that by the volume of the solution (not just the solvent). For instance, if 2 mol of NaCl were dissolved in a 5 liter solution, the molarity of the solution would be calculated as follows:

$$\frac{2\ mol}{5\ L} = 0.4\frac{mol}{L}$$

Mixtures

A mixture is made of two or more substances that are combined in various proportions with each retaining its own specific properties. A mixture's components may be separated by physical means, without making and breaking chemical bonds. An example would be table salt being completely dissolved in water. Heterogeneous mixtures are those in which the composition and properties are not uniform throughout the entire sample. Examples include concrete and wood. Homogeneous mixtures are those in which the composition and properties are uniform throughout the entire sample.

pH

The potential of hydrogen (pH) is a measurement of the concentration of hydrogen ions in a substance in terms of the number of moles of H^+ per liter of solution. All substances fall between 0 and 14 on the pH scale. A lower pH indicates a higher H^+ concentration, while a higher pH indicates a lower H^+ concentration.

Pure water has a neutral pH, which is 7. Anything with a pH lower than pure water (<7) is considered acidic. Anything with a pH higher than pure water (>7) is a base. Drain cleaner, soap, baking soda, ammonia, egg whites, and sea water are common bases. Urine, stomach acid, citric acid, vinegar, hydrochloric acid, and battery acid are acids. A pH indicator is a substance that acts as a detector of hydrogen or hydronium ions. It is halochromic, meaning it changes color to indicate that hydrogen or hydronium ions have been detected.

Review Video: pH
Visit mometrix.com/academy and enter code: 187395

Copyright © Mometrix Media. You have been licensed one copy of this document for personal use only. Any other reproduction or redistribution is strictly prohibited. All rights reserved.

Bases

Basic chemicals are usually in aqueous solution and have the following traits: a bitter taste; a soapy or slippery texture to the touch; the capacity to restore the blue color of litmus paper which had previously been turned red by an acid; the ability to produce salts in reaction with acids. The word alkaline is used to describe bases.

While acids yield hydrogen ions (H^+)when dissolved in solution, bases yield hydroxide ions (OH^-); the same models used to describe acids can be inverted and used to describe bases— Arrhenius, Brønsted-Lowry, and Lewis.

Some nonmetal oxides (such as Na_2O) are classified as bases even though they do not contain hydroxides in their molecular form. However, these substances easily produce hydroxide ions when reacted with water, which is why they are classified as bases.

Acids

Acids are a unique class of compounds characterized by consistent properties. The most significant property of an acid is not readily observable and is what gives acids their unique behaviors: the ionization of H atoms, or their tendency to dissociate from their parent molecules and take on an electrical charge. Carboxylic acids are also characterized by ionization, but of the O atoms. Some other properties of acids are easy to observe without any experimental apparatus. These properties include the following:

- They have a sour taste
- They change the color of litmus paper to red
- They produce gaseous H_2 in reaction with some metals
- They produce salt precipitates in reaction with bases

Other properties, while no more complex, are less easily observed. For instance, most inorganic acids are easily soluble in water and have high boiling points.

Strong or weak acids and bases

The characteristic properties of acids and bases derive from the tendency of atoms to ionize by donating or accepting charged particles. The strength of an acid or base is a reflection of the degree to which its atoms ionize in solution. For example, if all of the atoms in an acid ionize, the acid is said to be strong. When only a few of the atoms ionize, the acid is weak. Acetic acid ($HC_2H_3O_2$) is a weak acid because only its O_2 atoms ionize in solution. Another way to think of the strength of an acid or base is to consider its reactivity. Highly reactive acids and bases are strong because they tend to form and break bonds quickly and most of their atoms ionize in the process.

> **Review Video: Strong and Weak Acids and Bases**
> Visit mometrix.com/academy and enter code: 268930

Energy

Some discussions of energy consider only two types of energy: kinetic energy (the energy of motion) and potential energy (which depends on relative position). There are, however, other types of energy. Electromagnetic waves, for example, are a type of energy contained by a field. Gravitational energy is a form of potential energy. Objects perched any distance from the ground have gravitational energy, or the potential to move. Another type of potential energy is electrical

Copyright © Mometrix Media. You have been licensed one copy of this document for personal use only. Any other reproduction or redistribution is strictly prohibited. All rights reserved.

energy, which is the energy it takes to pull apart positive and negative electrical charges. Chemical energy refers to the manner in which atoms form into molecules, and this energy can be released or absorbed when molecules regroup. Solar energy comes in the form of visible light and non-visible light, such as infrared and ultraviolet rays. Sound energy refers to the energy in sound waves.

Kinetic and potential energy

Kinetic and potential energy are two commonly known types of energy. Kinetic energy refers to the energy of an object in motion. The following formula is used to calculate kinetic energy: $KE = \frac{1}{2}mv^2$, where KE is kinetic energy, m is mass, and v is velocity. Even though an object may appear to be motionless, its atoms are always moving. Since these atoms are colliding and moving, they have kinetic energy. Potential energy refers to a capacity for doing work that is based upon position or configuration. The following formula can be used to calculate potential energy: $PE = mgh$, where PE is potential energy, m is mass, g is the acceleration due to gravity, and h is the height.

> **Review Video: Potential and Kinetic Energy**
> Visit mometrix.com/academy and enter code: 491502

Chemical potential energy and electromagnetic potential energy

Everything has molecules. Energy is required to make these molecules and hold them together. The energy stored in molecules is called chemical potential energy. An example is the energy stored in gasoline. Bonds are broken and reformed during combustion and new products are made. The energy stored in gasoline is released when it is burned, which is combustion. Gasoline is changed into byproducts during combustion such as water and carbon dioxide, and energy is released. An airplane motor will use the energy that is released to turn a propeller. A battery has chemical potential energy as well as electrical potential energy. When a flashlight is turned on, the electrical potential energy stored in the battery is converted into other forms of energy such as light. With an electrical appliance that is plugged in, electrical potential energy is maintained in a power plant's generator, a windmill or a hydroelectric dam.

The Sun

Features and characteristics

The Sun is at the center of the solar system. It is composed of 70% hydrogen (H) and 28% helium (He). The remaining 2% is made up of metals. The Sun is one of 100 billion stars in the Milky Way galaxy. Its diameter is 1,390,000 km, its mass is 1.989×10^{30} kg, its surface temperature is 5,800 K, and its core temperature is 15,600,000 K. The Sun represents more than 99.8% of the total mass of the solar system.

At the core, the temperature is 15.6 million K, the pressure is 250 billion atmospheres, and the density is more than 150 times that of water. The surface is called the photosphere. The chromosphere lies above this, and the corona, which extends millions of kilometers into space, is next. Sunspots are relatively cool regions on the surface with a temperature of 3,800 K. Temperatures in the corona are over 1,000,000 K. Its magnetosphere, or heliosphere, extends far beyond Pluto.

> **Review Video: The Sun**
> Visit mometrix.com/academy and enter code: 699233

Copyright © Mometrix Media. You have been licensed one copy of this document for personal use only. Any other reproduction or redistribution is strictly prohibited. All rights reserved.

<u>Energy</u>

The Sun's energy is produced by nuclear fusion reactions. Each second, about 700,000,000 tons of hydrogen are converted (or fused) to about 695,000,000 tons of helium and 5,000,000 tons of energy in the form of gamma rays. In nuclear fusion, four hydrogen nuclei are fused into one helium nucleus, resulting in the release of energy. In the Sun, the energy proceeds towards the surface and is absorbed and re-emitted at lower and lower temperatures. Energy is mostly in the form of visible light when it reaches the surface. It is estimated that the Sun has used up about half of the hydrogen at its core since its birth. It is expected to radiate in this fashion for another 5 billion years. Eventually, it will deplete its hydrogen fuel, grow brighter, expand to about 260 times its diameter, and become a red giant. The outer layers will ablate and become a dense white dwarf the size of the Earth.

Renewable energy: Renewable energy can be used without being used up. Most of it comes from the Sun and its effects on Earth. Examples:

- Solar power - Active and passive solar heating of water and building materials uses the Sun's energy directly. Solar energy also can be captured and concentrated to make steam to run electricity-generating turbines or for use in solar cookers. Photovoltaic (solar) cells can convert sunlight to electricity.
- Biomass - The Sun's energy is stored in trees and other plants and in plant and animal wastes that we can burn or process to make biofuels, such as biodiesel.
- Hydropower - The water cycle is powered by the Sun. The kinetic energy in water moving through the cycle can be converted to electricity with dams and by small-scale hydroelectric machinery in flowing rivers. There are also devices to harvest the movement of tides and waves.

Important terms

- Atom - An atom is one of the most basic units of matter. An atom consists of a central nucleus surrounded by electrons.
- Nucleus - The nucleus of an atom consists of protons and neutrons. It is positively charged, dense, and heavier than the surrounding electrons. The plural form of nucleus is nuclei.
- Electrons - These are atomic particles that are negatively charged and orbit the nucleus of an atom.
- Protons - Along with neutrons, protons make up the nucleus of an atom. The number of protons in the nucleus usually determines the atomic number of an element. Carbon atoms, for example, have six protons. The atomic number of carbon is 6. The number of protons also indicates the charge of an atom.
- Atomic number (proton number) - The atomic number of an element, also known as the proton number, refers to the number of protons in the nucleus of an atom. It is a unique identifier. It can be represented as "Z." Atoms with a neutral charge have an atomic number that is equal to the number of electrons. The number of protons in the atomic nucleus also determines its electric charge, which in turn determines the number of electrons the atom has in its non-ionized state.
- Neutrons - Neutrons are the uncharged atomic particles contained within the nucleus. The number of neutrons in a nucleus can be represented as "N."
- Nucleon - This refers to the collective number of neutrons and protons.
- Element - An element is matter with one type of atom. It can be identified by its atomic number. There are 117 elements, 94 of which occur naturally on Earth.

Copyright © Mometrix Media. You have been licensed one copy of this document for personal use only. Any other reproduction or redistribution is strictly prohibited. All rights reserved.

Scientific Reasoning

Scientific method of inquiry

The scientific method of inquiry is a general method by which ideas are tested and either confirmed or refuted by experimentation. The first step in the scientific method is formulating the problem that is to be addressed. It is essential to clearly define the limits of what is to be observed, since that allows for a more focused analysis. Once the problem has been defined, it is necessary to form a hypothesis. This educated guess should be a possible solution to the problem that was formulated in the first step. The next step is to test that hypothesis by experimentation. This often requires the scientist to design a complete experiment. The key to making the best possible use of an experiment is observation. Observations may be quantitative, that is, when a numeric measurement is taken, or they may be qualitative, that is, when something is evaluated based on feeling or preference. This measurement data will then be examined to find trends or patterns that are present. From these trends, the scientist will draw conclusions or make generalizations about the results, intended to predict future results. If these conclusions support the original hypothesis, the experiment is complete and the scientist will publish his conclusions to allow others to test them by repeating the experiment. If they do not support the hypothesis, the results should then be used to develop a new hypothesis, which can then be verified by a new or redesigned experiment.

Scientific process skills

Perhaps the most important skill in science is that of observation. A scientist must be able to take accurate data from his experimental setup or from nature without allowing bias to alter the results. Another important skill is hypothesizing. A scientist must be able to combine his knowledge of theory and of other experimental results to logically determine what should occur in his own tests. The data-analysis process requires the twin skills of ordering and categorizing. Gathered data must be arranged in such a way that it is readable and readily shows the key results. A skill that may be integrated with the previous two is comparing. A scientist should be able to compare his own results with other published results. He must also be able to infer, or draw logical conclusions, from his results. He must be able to apply his knowledge of theory and results to create logical experimental designs and determine cases of special behavior. Lastly, a scientist must be able to communicate his results and his conclusions. The greatest scientific progress is made when scientists are able to review and test one another's work and offer advice or suggestions.

Scientific statements

Hypotheses are educated guesses about what is likely to occur, and are made to provide a starting point from which to begin design of the experiment. They may be based on results of previously observed experiments or knowledge of theory, and follow logically forth from these. Assumptions are statements that are taken to be fact without proof for the purpose of performing a given experiment. They may be entirely true, or they may be true only for a given set of conditions under which the experiment will be conducted. Assumptions are necessary to simplify experiments; indeed, many experiments would be impossible without them. Scientific models are mathematical statements that describe a physical behavior. Models are only as good as our knowledge of the actual system. Often models will be discarded when new discoveries are made that show the model to be inaccurate. While a model can never perfectly represent an actual system, they are useful for simplifying a system to allow for better understanding of its behavior. Scientific laws are statements of natural behavior that have stood the test of time and have been found to produce accurate and repeatable results in all testing. A theory is a statement of behavior that consolidates all current observations. Theories are similar to laws in that they describe natural behavior, but are

- 116 -

Copyright © Mometrix Media. You have been licensed one copy of this document for personal use only. Any other reproduction or redistribution is strictly prohibited. All rights reserved.

more recently developed and are more susceptible to being proved wrong. Theories may eventually become laws if they stand up to scrutiny and testing.

Experimental design

Designing relevant experiments that allow for meaningful results is not a simple task. Every stage of the experiment must be carefully planned to ensure that the right data can be safely and accurately taken. Ideally, an experiment should be controlled so that all of the conditions except the ones being manipulated are held constant. This helps to ensure that the results are not skewed by unintended consequences of shifting conditions. A good example of this is a placebo group in a drug trial. All other conditions are the same, but that group is not given the medication. In addition to proper control, it is important that the experiment be designed with data collection in mind. For instance, if the quantity to be measured is temperature, there must be a temperature device such as a thermocouple integrated into the experimental setup. While the data are being collected, they should periodically be checked for obvious errors. If there are data points that are orders of magnitude from the expected value, then it might be a good idea to make sure that no experimental errors are being made, either in data collection or condition control. Once all the data have been gathered, they must be analyzed. The way in which this should be done depends on the type of data and the type of trends observed. It may be useful to fit curves to the data to determine if the trends follow a common mathematical form. It may also be necessary to perform a statistical analysis of the results to determine what effects are significant. Data should be clearly presented.

Changing nature of scientific knowledge

Perhaps the greatest peculiarity of scientific knowledge is that, at the same time that it is taken as fact, it may be disproved. Current scientific knowledge is the basis from which new discoveries are made. Yet even knowledge that has stood for hundreds of years is not considered too infallible to be challenged. If someone can create an experiment whose results consistently and reproducibly defy a law that has been in place for generations, that law will be nullified. It is absolutely essential, however, that these reproductions of the experiment be conducted by many different scientists who are in isolation from one another so there is no bias or interacting effects on the results.

Applications of science and technology

Scientific and technological developments have led to the widespread availability of technologies heretofore unheard of, including cellular phones, satellite-based applications, and a worldwide network of connected computers. Some of the notable recent applications include:

- Health care: Antibiotics, genetic screening for diseases, the sequencing of the human genome. Issues include problems with health care distribution on an increasingly industrialized planet.
- The environment: Computerized models of climate change and pollution monitoring. Issues include increased pollution of the water, air, and soil, and the over-harvesting of natural resources with mechanized equipment.
- Agriculture: Genetic improvements in agricultural practices, including increased output on the same amount of arable land. Issues include unknown environmental effects of hybrid species, cross-pollination with organic species, and pollution caused by synthetic chemical fertilizers.
- Information technology: New Internet-based industries, increased worldwide collaboration, and access to information. Issues include the depletion of natural resources for electronics production.

Copyright © Mometrix Media. You have been licensed one copy of this document for personal use only. Any other reproduction or redistribution is strictly prohibited. All rights reserved.

Social impacts of recent developments in science and technology

Recent developments in science and technology have had both positive and negative effects on human society. The issue of sustainable growth is an increasingly important one, as humans realize that the resources they use are not unlimited. Genetic research into diseases, stem cell research, and cloning technology have created great controversies as they have been introduced, and an increasing number of people reject the morality of scientific practices like animal testing in the pursuit of scientific advancement. In addition, an increasingly technology-based world has produced a new social inequality based on access to computers and Internet technology.

These issues are beginning to be debated at all levels of human government, from city councils to the United Nations. Does science provide the authoritative answer to all human problems, or do ethics carry weight in scientific debates as well? Ultimately, humans must weigh the competing needs of facilitating scientific pursuits and maintaining an ethical society as they face new technological questions.

Copyright © Mometrix Media. You have been licensed one copy of this document for personal use only. Any other reproduction or redistribution is strictly prohibited. All rights reserved.

English and Language Usage

Grammar and Word Meanings in Context

Grammar

Grammar may be practically defined as the study of how words are put together, or the study of sentences. There are multiple approaches to grammar in modern linguistics. Any systematic account of the structure of a language and the patterns it describes is grammar. Modern definitions state that grammar is the knowledge of a language developed in the minds of the speakers.

A grammar, in the broadest sense, is a set of rules internalized by members of a speech community, and an account, by a linguist, of such a grammar. This internalized grammar is what is commonly called a language. The expanded scope of grammar includes morphology and syntax and a lexicon. Grammatical meaning is described as part of the syntax and morphology of a language, as distinct from its lexicon.

Verbs

The *verb* of a sentence usually expresses action or being. It is composed of a main verb and sometimes supporting verbs. These helping verbs are forms of *have, do, and be*, and nine modals. The modals are *can, could, may, might, shall, should, will, would*, and *ought*. Some verbs are followed by words that look like prepositions but are so closely associated with the verb as to be part of its meaning. These words are known as particles, and examples include *call off, look up, and drop off*.

The main verb of a sentence is always one that would change form from base form to past tense, past participle, present participle, and –*s* forms. When both the past-tense and past-participle forms of a verb end in –*ed*, the verb is regular. In all other cases, the verb is irregular. The verb *to be* is highly irregular, having eight forms instead of the usual five.

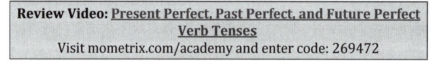

Review Video: Present Perfect, Past Perfect, and Future Perfect Verb Tenses
Visit mometrix.com/academy and enter code: 269472

Nouns and pronouns

Nouns name persons, places, things, animals, objects, time, feelings, concepts, and actions, and are usually signaled by an article (*a, an, the*). Nouns sometimes function as adjectives modifying other nouns. Nouns used in this manner are called noun/adjectives. Nouns are classified for a number of purposes: capitalization, word choice, count/no count nouns, and collective nouns are examples.

A pronoun is a word used in place of a noun. Usually the pronoun substitutes for the specific noun, called the antecedent. Although most pronouns function as substitutes for nouns, some can function as adjectives modifying nouns. Pronouns may be classed as personal, possessive, intensive, relative (*which, that, who, whoever*), interrogative, demonstrative (*this, that, these, those*), indefinite (*anybody, somebody, everybody*), and reciprocal. Personal pronouns (*he, she, they*) refer to specific people, places, or things and can be either singular or plural. Possessive pronouns (*his, hers, theirs, ours*) are used to show ownership. Pronouns can cause a number of problems for writers, including pronoun-antecedent agreement, distinguishing between who and whom, and differentiating pronouns, such as *I* and *me*.

- 119 -

Copyright © Mometrix Media. You have been licensed one copy of this document for personal use only. Any other reproduction or redistribution is strictly prohibited. All rights reserved.

Functions of pronouns

A *pronoun* always refers back to a noun. That noun is the pronoun's antecedent. Example: She bought some (antecedent) furniture yesterday, but (pronoun) it hasn't arrived. Pronoun and antecedent must agree in number and gender.

Example: We were happy when our *relatives* came. It was great seeing *them* again. *Relatives* in the first sentence is the antecedent of the pronoun *them* in the second sentence.

A *personal pronoun* refers to a person or thing. A personal pronoun can be a subject, an object, or a possessive. Personal pronouns usually change their form depending on if they are used as the subject or object of a sentence.

1st Person: I, we, me, us, mine, ours
2nd Person: you, yours
3rd Person: he, she, it, they, him, her, them, his, hers, theirs

Interrogative pronouns (who, whom, which, what, and whose) ask questions.

Relative pronouns (*who, whom, which, that, whose*) introduce adjective and noun clauses. The relative pronoun, *what*, introduces noun clauses only. Within an adjective or noun clause, the relative pronoun can function as a subject, object, or possessive. Relative pronouns of the *-ever* form (*whatever, whichever, whoever, whomever*) have an indefinite meaning: they do not refer back to a specific noun.

Indefinite pronouns

The rules of subject-verb agreement state that singular subjects need singular verb forms, while plural subjects need plural verb forms. This rule seems simple, but it can become confusing when sentences have complex structures. For indefinite pronouns (*whoever, anyone, someone, everyone, everybody*), the writer should use singular verb forms. For the indefinite pronouns *all* and *some*, whether the writer should use a singular or plural verb form depends on what the pronoun is referring to. The indefinite pronoun *none* can be used with either a singular or plural verb form. In this case, another word in the sentence may help the writer determine which form to use. For example, in the sentence *"None of the towels are clean,"* the indefinite pronoun *none* refers to *towels*, so the verb takes a plural form. In the sentence *"None of the building is repaired,"* the word *none* refers to *the building*, which is singular, and so the verb becomes singular.

Problems with pronouns

Pronouns are words that substitute for nouns: *he, it, them, her, me*, and so on. Four frequently encountered problems with pronouns include the following:

- Pronoun-antecedent agreement: The antecedent of a pronoun is the word the pronoun refers to. A pronoun and its antecedent agree when they are both singular or plural, or of the same gender.
- Pronoun reference: A pronoun should refer clearly to its antecedent. A pronoun's reference will be unclear if it is ambiguous, implied, vague, or indefinite.
- Personal pronouns: Some pronouns change their case form according to their grammatical structure in a sentence. Pronouns functioning as subjects appear in the subjective case, those functioning as objects appear in the objective case, and those functioning as possessives appear in the possessive case.

Copyright © Mometrix Media. You have been licensed one copy of this document for personal use only. Any other reproduction or redistribution is strictly prohibited. All rights reserved.

- Who or whom: *Who*, a subjective-case pronoun, can be used only as a subject or subject complement. *Whom*, an objective-case pronoun, can be used only for objects. The words *who* and *whom* appear primarily in subordinate clauses or in questions.

Pronoun-antecedent agreement

An antecedent is the word or phrase to which a pronoun refers. An antecedent must come before a pronoun in a sentence, and a pronoun and its antecedent must agree. Plural antecedents require plural pronouns, while singular antecedents require singular pronouns. The antecedent and pronoun must also agree in gender and person, as in the following examples: *The <u>man</u> used <u>his</u> glasses. The <u>three children</u> were eating <u>their</u> ice cream.* In the first example, *man* is the antecedent, and *his* is the pronoun. In the second example, *three children* is the antecedent, while *their* is the pronoun. In both examples, antecedents and pronouns agree in gender and person.

Noun-pronoun agreement in number

A pronoun must agree with its antecedent in number. If the antecedent is singular, the pronoun referring to it must be singular; if the antecedent is plural, the pronoun referring to it must be plural.

Use singular pronouns to refer to the singular indefinite pronouns: *each, either, neither, one, everyone, everybody, no one, nobody, anyone, anybody, someone, somebody.*

Example:
Each of the students bought their own lunch. (incorrect)
Each of the students bought his own lunch. (correct)

Use plural nouns to refer to the plural indefinite pronouns: *both, few, several, many.*

Example:
Both were within *their* boundaries.

The indefinite pronouns *some, any, none, all, most* may be referred to by singular or plural pronouns, depending on the sense of the sentence.

Examples:
Some of the children have misplaced *their* toy. (plural)
Some of the carpet has lost *its* nap. (singular)

Pronouns that refer to compound antecedents joined by *and* are usually plural.

Example:
Bill and Joe cook *their* own meals.

Pronoun-noun agreement in gender

A pronoun agrees with its antecedent in gender.

- Antecedents of *masculine* gender (male sex) are referred to by *he, him, his.*
- Antecedents of *feminine* gender (female sex) are referred to by *she, her, hers.*
- Antecedents of *neuter* gender (no sex) are referred to by *it, its.*
- Antecedents of *common* gender (sex not known) are referred to by *he, him, his.* It is understood that the masculine pronouns include both male and female.

- 121 -

Copyright © Mometrix Media. You have been licensed one copy of this document for personal use only. Any other reproduction or redistribution is strictly prohibited. All rights reserved.

- Antecedents that are names of animals are generally referred to by the neuter pronouns unless the writer wishes to indicate special interest in the animal, in which case the masculine pronouns are often used. When a feminine role is naturally suggested, the feminine pronouns are used.

Adjectives, articles, and adverbs

An *adjective* is a word used to modify or describe a noun or pronoun. An adjective usually answers one of these questions: Which one? What kind? How many? Adjectives usually precede the words they modify although they sometimes follow linking verbs, in which case they describe the subject.

Articles, sometimes classed as adjectives, are used to mark nouns. There are only three: the definite article *the* and the indefinite articles *a* and *an*.

An *adverb* is a word used to modify or qualify a verb, adjective, or another adverb. It usually answers one of these questions: When? Where? How? Why? Adverbs modifying adjectives or other adverbs usually intensify or limit the intensity of words they modify. The negators *not* and *never* are classified as adverbs.

Writers often misuse adverbs, and multilingual speakers can have trouble placing them correctly.

Prepositions and conjunctions

A *preposition* is a word placed before a noun or pronoun to form a phrase modifying another word in the sentence. The prepositional phrase usually functions as an adjective or adverb. There are a limited number of prepositions in English, perhaps around 80. Some prepositions are more than one word long. *Along with, listen to,* and *next to* are some examples.

Conjunctions join words, phrases, or clauses, and they indicate the relationship between the elements that are joined. There are coordinating conjunctions that connect grammatically equal elements, correlative conjunctions that connect pairs, subordinating conjunctions that introduce a subordinate clause, and conjunctive adverbs, which may be used with a semicolon to connect independent clauses. The most common conjunctive adverbs include *then, thus,* and *however.* Using conjunctions correctly helps avoid sentence fragments and run-on sentences.

> **Review Video: What is a Preposition?**
> Visit mometrix.com/academy and enter code: 946763

Subject of a sentence

The *subject* of a sentence names who or what the sentence is about. The complete subject is composed of the simple subject and all of its modifiers. To find the complete subject, ask *who* or *what.* Insert the verb to complete the question. The answer is the complete subject. To find the simple subject, strip away all the modifiers in the complete subject.

In imperative sentences, the verb's subject is understood, but not actually present in the sentence. Although the subject ordinarily comes before the verb, in sentences that begin with *There are* or *There was*, the subject follows the verb. The ability to recognize the subject of a sentence helps in

Copyright © Mometrix Media. You have been licensed one copy of this document for personal use only. Any other reproduction or redistribution is strictly prohibited. All rights reserved.

editing a variety of problems, such as sentence fragments and subject-verb agreement, as well as the using the correct pronouns.

Review Video: Subjects
Visit mometrix.com/academy and enter code: 444771

Subject-verb agreement

In the present tense, verbs agree with their subjects in number, (singular or plural) and in person (first, second, or third). The present tense ending –s is used with a verb if its subject is third person singular; otherwise, the verb takes no ending. The verb *to be* varies from this pattern, and, alone among verbs, it has special forms in both the present and past tense.

Review Video: Subject Verb Agreement
Visit mometrix.com/academy and enter code: 479190

Problems with subject-verb agreement tend to arise in certain contexts:

- Words between subject and verbs
- Subjects joined by *and*
- Subjects joined by *or* or *nor*
- Indefinite pronouns, such as *someone*
- Collective nouns
- Subject after the verb
- Pronouns who, which, and that
- Plural form, singular meaning
- Titles, company names, and words mentioned as words

Common grammatical mistakes

Subjects and verbs must agree in number. Often students, particularly those rushing to complete a test, make errors in subject-verb agreement. Even if the subject and verb of a sentence are separated by other words, they should still agree in number. Singular subjects require singular verbs, while plural subjects require plural verbs. Sometimes a subject will be a collective noun that represents a group. If the group acts as a single being, a singular verb should be used. If the group acts separately, a plural verb should be used. When there are two subjects separated by the word *and*, a plural verb should be used. When multiple subjects are separated by *or, either/or,* or *neither/nor*, a singular verb should be used.

Appositive

An *appositive* is a word or phrase that restates or modifies an immediately preceding noun. An appositive is often useful as a context clue for determining or refining the meaning of the word or words to which it refers. For example, consider *"My dad, James Brown, is a lawyer."* In this sentence the appositive is *James Brown* since it restates the subject.

Words and tone

A writer's choice of words is a signature of his or her style. A careful analysis of the use of words can improve a piece of writing. Attention to the use of specific nouns rather than general ones can enliven language. Verbs should be active whenever possible to keep the writing stronger and

Copyright © Mometrix Media. You have been licensed one copy of this document for personal use only. Any other reproduction or redistribution is strictly prohibited. All rights reserved.

energetic, and there should be an appropriate balance between numbers of nouns and verbs. Too many nouns can result in heavy, boring sentences.

Tone may be defined as the writer's attitude toward the topic, and to the audience. This attitude is reflected in the language used in the writing. The tone of a work should be appropriate to the topic and to the intended audience. Some texts should not contain slang or jargon, although these may be fine in a different piece. Tone can range from humorous to serious and all levels in between. It may be more or less formal, depending on the purpose of the writing and its intended audience. All these nuances in tone can flavor the entire writing and should be kept in mind as the work evolves.

Point of view

Point of view is the perspective from which writing occurs. There are several possibilities:

- *First person* is written so that the *I* of the story is a participant or observer.
- *Second person* is a device to draw the reader in more closely. It is really a variation or refinement of the first-person narrative.
- *Third person*, the most traditional form of point of view, is the omniscient narrator, in which the narrative voice, presumed to be the writer's, is presumed to know everything about the characters, plot, and action. Most novels use this point of view.
- A multiple point of view is narration delivered from the perspective of several characters.

In modern writing, the stream-of-consciousness technique is often used. Developed fully by James Joyce, this technique uses an interior monologue that provides the narration through the thoughts, impressions, and fantasies of the narrator.

> **Review Video: Point of View**
> Visit mometrix.com/academy and enter code: 383336

Context

Learning new words is an important part of comprehending and integrating unfamiliar information. When a reader encounters a new word, he can stop and find it in the dictionary or the glossary of terms but sometimes those reference tools aren't readily available or using them at the moment is impractical (e.g., during a test). Furthermore, most readers are usually not willing to take the time. Another way to determine the meaning of a word is by considering the context in which it is being used. These indirect learning hints are called context clues. They include definitions, descriptions, examples, and restatements. Because most words are learned by listening to conversations, people use this tool all the time even if they do it unconsciously. But to be effective in written text, context clues must be used judiciously because the unfamiliar word may have several subtle variations, and therefore the context clues could be misinterpreted.

Context refers to how a word is used in a sentence. Identifying context can help determine the definition of unknown words. There are different contextual clues such as definition, description, example, comparison, and contrast. The following are examples:

- Definition: the unknown word is clearly defined by the previous words. - "When he was painting, his instrument was a ___." (paintbrush)
- Description: the unknown word is described by the previous words. - "I was hot, tired, and thirsty; I was ___." (dehydrated)

Copyright © Mometrix Media. You have been licensed one copy of this document for personal use only. Any other reproduction or redistribution is strictly prohibited. All rights reserved.

- Example: the unknown word is part of a series of examples. - "Water, soda, and __ were the offered beverages." (coffee)
- Comparison: the unknown word is compared to another word. - "Barney is agreeable and happy like his __ parents." (positive)
- Contrast: the unknown word is contrasted with another word. - "I prefer cold weather to __ conditions." (hot)

On standardized tests, as well as in everyday life, you may be faced with words that you are not familiar with. In most cases, the definition of an unknown word can be derived from context clues. The term "context clues" refers to the ways or manner in which a word is used. When reading a passage, students should carefully examine the unfamiliar word and the words and sentences that surround it. The writer may have provided a definition in parentheses following the word, or the writer may have provided a synonym. Synonyms are useful because they offer a common substitute for the unfamiliar word. Also, the author may have provided an antonym, or opposite, for the unfamiliar word. Finally, a context clue might be found in the prior or later restatement of the idea that contained the word, and sometimes the writer may have even provided a detailed explanation of the unfamiliar word.

> **Review Video: Context**
> Visit mometrix.com/academy and enter code: 613660

Word usage

Word usage, or diction, refers to the use of words with meanings and forms that are appropriate for the context and structure of a sentence. A common error in word usage occurs when a word's meaning does not fit the context of the sentence.

Incorrect: Susie likes chips better then candy.
Correct: Susie likes chips better than candy.

Incorrect: The cat licked it's coat.
Correct: The cat licked its coat.

Commonly misused words include *than/then, it's/its, there/their/they're, your/you're, except/accept, and affect/effect.*

> **Review Video: Word Usage**
> Visit mometrix.com/academy and enter code: 197863

Prefixes

Here are some common prefixes, their meanings, and some examples of their use:

Prefix	Meaning	Examples
ab	from, away, off	abdicate, abjure
ad	to, toward	advance
ante	before, previous	antecedent, antedate
anti	against, opposing	antipathy, antidote
de	from	depart
epi	upon	epilogue
hyper	excessive, over	hypercritical, hypertension

Copyright © Mometrix Media. You have been licensed one copy of this document for personal use only. Any other reproduction or redistribution is strictly prohibited. All rights reserved.

Prefix	Meaning	Examples
hypo	under, beneath	hypodermic, hypothesis
inter	among, between	intercede, interrupt
intra	within	intramural, intrastate
mal	bad, poorly, not	malfunction
mor	die, death	mortality, mortuary
ob	against, opposing	objection
omni	all, everywhere	omniscient
pan	all, entire	panorama, pandemonium
per	through	perceive, permit
pre	before, previous	prevent, preclude
pro	forward, in place of	propel, pronoun
super	above, extra	supersede, supernumerary
supra	above, over	supraorbital, suprasegmental
trans	across, beyond, over	transact, transport
uni	one	uniform, unity

Review Video: Prefixes
Visit mometrix.com/academy and enter code: 361382

Suffixes

Suffixes are a group of letters, placed behind a root word, that carry a specific meaning. Suffixes can perform one of two possible functions. They can be used to create a new word, or they can shift the tense of a word without changing its original meaning.

For example, the suffix -*ability* can be added to the end of the word *account* to form the new word *accountability*. *Account* means a written narrative or description of events, while *accountability* means the state of being liable. The suffix -*ed* can be added to *account* to form the word *accounted*, which simply shifts the word from present tense to past tense.

Sometimes adding a suffix can change the spelling of a root word. If the suffix begins with a vowel, the final consonant of the root word must be doubled. This rule applies only if the root word has one syllable or if the accent is on the last syllable.

For example, when adding the suffix -*ery* to the root word *rob*, the final word becomes *robbery*. The letter *b* is doubled because *rob* has only one syllable. However, when adding the suffix -*able* to the root word *profit*, the final word becomes *profitable*. The letter t is not doubled because the root word *profit* has two syllables.

Spelling is not changed when the suffixes -*less, -ness, -ly*, or -*en* are used. The only exception to this rule occurs when the suffix -*ness* or -*ly* is added to a root word ending in *y*. In this case, the *y* changes to *i*. For example, *happy* becomes *happily*.

Certain suffixes require that the root word be modified. If the suffix begins with a vowel, e.g., -*ing*, and the root word ends in the letter *e*, the *e* must be dropped before adding the suffix. For example, the word *write* becomes *writing*. If the suffix begins with a consonant instead of a vowel, the letter *e* at the end of the root word does not need to be dropped. For example, *hope* becomes *hopeless*. The only exceptions to this rule are the words *judgment, acknowledgment,* and *argument*. If a root word

- 126 -

Copyright © Mometrix Media. You have been licensed one copy of this document for personal use only. Any other reproduction or redistribution is strictly prohibited. All rights reserved.

ends in the letter *y* and is preceded by a consonant, the *y* is changed to *i* before adding the suffix. This is true for all suffixes except those that begin with *i*. For example, *plenty* becomes *plentiful*.

Here are some common suffixes, their meanings, and some examples of their use:

Suffix	Meaning	Examples
age	process, state, rank	passage, bondage
ance	act, condition, fact	acceptance, vigilance
ard	one that does excessively	drunkard, wizard
ate	having, showing	separate, desolate
ation	action, state, result	occupation, starvation
cy	state, condition	accuracy, captaincy
en	cause to be, become	deepen, strengthen
er	one who does	teacher
ess	feminine	waitress, lioness
fic	making, causing	terrific, beatific
fy	make, cause, cause to have	glorify, fortify
ion	action, result, state	union, fusion
ist	doer, believer	monopolist, socialist
ition	action, state, result	sedition, expedition
ity	state, quality, condition	acidity, civility
ize	make, cause to be, treat with	sterilize, mechanize
logue	type of speaking or writing	prologue
ly	like, of the nature of	friendly, positively
or	doer, office, action	juror, elevator, honor
ous	marked by, given to	religious, riotous
ty	quality, state	enmity, activity
ward	in the direction of	backward, homeward

Review Video: Suffixes
Visit mometrix.com/academy and enter code: 212541

Copyright © Mometrix Media. You have been licensed one copy of this document for personal use only. Any other reproduction or redistribution is strictly prohibited. All rights reserved.

Spelling and Punctuation

Spelling rules

<u>Words ending with a consonant</u>

Usually the final consonant is doubled on a word before adding a suffix. This is the rule for single syllable words, words ending with one consonant, and multi-syllable words with the last syllable accented. The following are examples:

- *beg* becomes *begging* (single syllable)
- *shop* becomes *shopped* (single syllable)
- *add* becomes *adding* (already ends in double consonant, do not add another *d*)
- *deter* becomes *deterring* (multi-syllable, accent on last syllable)
- *regret* becomes *regrettable* (multi-syllable, accent on last syllable)
- *compost* becomes *composting* (do not add another *t* because the accent is on the first syllable)

<u>Words ending with *y* or *c*</u>

The general rule for words ending in *y* is to keep the *y* when adding a suffix if the *y* is preceded by a vowel. If the word ends in a consonant and *y* the *y* is changed to an *i* before the suffix is added (unless the suffix itself begins with *i*). The following are examples:

- *pay* becomes *paying* (keep the *y*)
- *bully* becomes *bullied* (change to *i*)
- *bully* becomes *bullying* (keep the *y* because the suffix is *–ing*)

If a word ends with *c* and the suffix begins with an *e, i,* or *y*, the letter *k* is usually added to the end of the word. The following are examples:

- panic becomes panicky
- mimic becomes mimicking

<u>Words containing *ie* or *ei*, and/or ending with *e*</u>

Most words are spelled with an *i* before *e*, except when they follow the letter *c,* **or** sound like *a*. For example, the following words are spelled correctly according to these rules:

- piece, friend, believe (*i* before *e*)
- receive, ceiling, conceited (except after *c*)
- weight, neighborhood, veil (sounds like *a*)

To add a suffix to words ending with the letter *e*, first determine if the *e* is silent. If it is, the *e* will be kept if the added suffix begins with a consonant. If the suffix begins with a vowel, the *e* is dropped. The following are examples:

- *age* becomes *ageless* (keep the *e*)
- *age* becomes *aging* (drop the *e*)

Copyright © Mometrix Media. You have been licensed one copy of this document for personal use only. Any other reproduction or redistribution is strictly prohibited. All rights reserved.

An exception to this rule occurs when the word ends in *ce* or *ge* and the suffix *able* or *ous* is added; these words will retain the letter *e*. The following are examples:

- *courage* becomes *courageous*
- *notice* becomes *noticeable*

Words ending with *ise* or *ize*

A small number of words end with *ise*. Most of the words in the English language with the same sound end in *ize*. The following are examples:

- advertise, advise, arise, chastise, circumcise, and comprise
- compromise, demise, despise, devise, disguise, enterprise, excise, and exercise
- franchise, improvise, incise, merchandise, premise, reprise, and revise
- supervise, surmise, surprise, and televise

Words that end with *ize* include the following:

- accessorize, agonize, authorize, and brutalize
- capitalize, caramelize, categorize, civilize, and demonize
- downsize, empathize, euthanize, idolize, and immunize
- legalize, metabolize, mobilize, organize, and ostracize
- plagiarize, privatize, utilize, and visualize

(Note that some words may technically be spelled with *ise*, especially in British English, but it is more common to use *ize*. Examples include *symbolize/symbolise,* and *baptize/baptise*.)

Words ending with *ceed, sede,* or *cede*

There are only three words that end with *ceed* in the English language: *exceed, proceed,* and *succeed*. There is only one word that ends with *sede*, and that word is *supersede*. Many other words that sound like *sede* actually end with *cede*. The following are examples:

- concede, recede, and precede

Words ending in *able* or *ible*

For words ending in *able* or *ible*, there are no hard and fast rules. The following are examples:

- adjustable, unbeatable, collectable, deliverable, and likeable
- edible, compatible, feasible, sensible, and credible

There are more words ending in *able* than *ible*; this is useful to know if guessing is necessary.

Words ending in *ance* or *ence*

The suffixes *ence, ency,* and *ent* are used in the following cases:

- the suffix is preceded by the letter *c* but sounds like *s* – *innocence*
- the suffix is preceded by the letter *g* but sounds like *j* – *intelligence, negligence*

The suffixes *ance, ancy,* and *ant* are used in the following cases:

- the suffix is preceded by the letter *c* but sounds like *k* – *significant, vacant*
- the suffix is preceded by the letter *g* with a hard sound - *elegant, extravagance*

Copyright © Mometrix Media. You have been licensed one copy of this document for personal use only. Any other reproduction or redistribution is strictly prohibited. All rights reserved.

If the suffix is preceded by other letters, there are no steadfast rules. For example: *finance, elegance,* and *defendant* use the letter *a,* while *respondent, competence,* and *excellent* use the letter *e.*

Words ending in *tion, sion,* or *cian*

Words ending in *tion, sion,* or *cian* all sound like *shun* or *zhun.* There are no rules for which ending is used for words. The following are examples:

- action, agitation, caution, fiction, nation, and motion
- admission, expression, mansion, permission, and television
- electrician, magician, musician, optician, and physician (note that these words tend to describe occupations)

Words with the *ai* or *ia* combination

When deciding if *ai* or *ia* is correct, the combination of *ai* usually sounds like one vowel sound, as in *Britain,* while the vowels in *ia* are pronounced separately, as in *guardian.* The following are examples:

- captain, certain, faint, hair, malaise, and praise (*ai* makes one sound)
- bacteria, beneficiary, diamond, humiliation, and nuptial (*ia* makes two sounds)

Plural forms of nouns

Nouns ending in *ch, sh, s, x,* or *z*

When a noun ends in the letters *ch, sh, s, x,* or *z,* an *es* instead of a singular *s* is added to the end of the word to make it plural. The following are examples:

- *church* becomes *churches*
- *bush* becomes *bushes*
- *bass* becomes *basses*
- *mix* becomes *mixes*
- *buzz* becomes *buzzes*

This is the rule with proper names as well; the Ross family would become the Rosses.

Nouns ending in *y* or *ay/ey/iy/oy/uy*

If a noun ends with a consonant and *y,* the plural is formed by replacing the *y* with *ies.* For example, *fly* becomes *flies* and *puppy* becomes *puppies.* If a noun ends with a vowel and *y,* the plural is formed by adding an *s.* For example, *alley* becomes *alleys* and *boy* becomes *boys.*

Nouns ending in *f* or *fe*

Most nouns ending in *f* or *fe* are pluralized by replacing the *f* with *v* and adding *es.* The following are examples:

- *knife* becomes *knives; self* becomes *selves; wolf* becomes *wolves.*

An exception to this rule is the word *roof; roof* becomes *roofs.*

Nouns ending in *o*

Most nouns ending with a consonant and *o* are pluralized by adding *es.* The following are examples:

- *hero* becomes *heroes; tornado* becomes *tornadoes; potato* becomes *potatoes*

Copyright © Mometrix Media. You have been licensed one copy of this document for personal use only. Any other reproduction or redistribution is strictly prohibited. All rights reserved.

Most nouns ending with a vowel and *o* are pluralized by adding *s*. The following are examples:

- *portfolio* becomes *portfolios*; *radio* becomes *radios*; *shoe* becomes *shoes*.

An exception to these rules is seen with musical terms ending in *o*. These words are pluralized by adding *s* even if they end in a consonant and *o*. The following are examples: *soprano* becomes *sopranos*; *banjo* becomes *banjos*; *piano* becomes *pianos*.

Exceptions to the rules of plurals

Some words do not fall into any specific category for making the singular form plural. They are irregular. Certain words become plural by changing the vowels within the word. The following are examples:

- *woman* becomes *women*; *goose* becomes *geese*; *foot* becomes *feet*

Some words become completely different words in the plural form. The following are examples:

- *mouse* becomes *mice*; *fungus* becomes *fungi*; *alumnus* becomes *alumni*

Some words are the same in both the singular and plural forms. The following are examples:

- *Salmon, species,* and *deer* are all the same whether singular or plural.

Plural forms of letters, numbers, symbols, and compound nouns with hyphens

Letters and numbers become plural by adding an apostrophe and *s*. The following are examples:

- The *L's* are the people whose names begin with the letter *L*.
- They broke the teams down into groups of *3's*.
- The sorority girls were all *KD's*.

A compound noun is a noun that is made up of two or more words; they can be written with hyphens. For example, *mother-in-law* or *court-martial* are compound nouns. To make them plural, an *s* or *es* is added to the main word. The following are examples: *mother-in-law* becomes *mothers-in-law*; *court-martial* becomes *court-martials*.

Capitalization

Sentences, poetry, formal statements, and calendar terms

The first word of every sentence is capitalized. When citing poetry, the first word in every line should be capitalized. For example, the beginning of <u>Annabel Lee</u> by Edgar Allan Poe would be quoted as follows:

It was many and many a year ago,
In a kingdom by the sea....

The first word in formal statements or direct quotations should be capitalized.

The following is an example:

"For immediate release: The XYZ Company has declared bankruptcy."

Copyright © Mometrix Media. You have been licensed one copy of this document for personal use only. Any other reproduction or redistribution is strictly prohibited. All rights reserved.

Calendar terms to be capitalized include the days of the week (Friday, etc.), months of the year (December, etc.), and holidays (Halloween, Easter, etc.).

Proper names, seasons, literary works, and family names

Proper names and titles are capitalized, as are military ranks. The following are examples:

- Jack Carter, Ph.D.
- Princess of Wales
- Senator Max Baucus
- Lieutenant Kathy Johnson

The names of seasons (spring, summer, fall, and winter) are not capitalized unless they are part of a literary quote in which they are capitalized. In literary works such as books, chapters, plays, poems, and articles, the main words are capitalized. Articles (*a, and, the*) are usually not capitalized unless they are the first word. The following provides examples:

The King and I is my favorite play; I also like the book A Time to Kill.

Notice that these are also underlined. Family titles such as *uncle* or *cousin* are not capitalized unless they are part of a proper noun or a title. The following provides examples:

Mom said Uncle Billy is coming for dinner, but he is not bringing his cousin Steve.

Geography

The names of geographical places (states, countries, oceans, etc.) should be capitalized. The following provides examples:

- Houston, Texas is by the Gulf of Mexico; the Rio Grande flows through the western part of the state.

When using directions such as north, south, east, or west, they should be capitalized if they are referring to particular regions. They should not be capitalized if referring to parts of states or when they are points on the compass. The following are examples:

- Louisiana is part of the South.
- I live in western Kentucky.
- John's compass indicated that we are traveling east.

The names of city streets, memorials, or parks should be capitalized if they are used as proper nouns. The following are examples:

- Rose walks past the Lincoln Memorial every day.
- You live on Oak Avenue; that's a nice avenue.

Notice that *avenue* is not capitalized the second time.

History and religion

Historical events such as wars, battles, and treaties and historical documents are capitalized: World War II, Magna Carta, and Battle of Gettysburg. The names of organized associations are also capitalized: Republican Party, United Way, and Sigma Chi.

Copyright © Mometrix Media. You have been licensed one copy of this document for personal use only. Any other reproduction or redistribution is strictly prohibited. All rights reserved.

Words that indicate where something or someone originated are capitalized. The following provides examples:

He is a German from Germany; he also likes German sausage.

The names of religions are capitalized: Catholic Church, Buddhism, and Islam. The names of gods and deities are also capitalized: Messiah, Brahma, and Allah. In most Christian writings, the pronouns *he*, *him*, and *his* are capitalized when they refer to God or Jesus Christ.

Punctuation

Period

A period (.) is put at the end of a declarative sentence (a sentence that states a fact or idea). The following sentence is an example:

The cat crossed the street.

A period is also at the end of an imperative sentence, which is a type of command. The following is an example:

Bring the bag over here.

A period follows an indirect question. The following is an example:

She wants to know how the game works.

A period is also used for abbreviations, such as *Ms., B.C.,* or *Capt.* for *Captain.* A group of periods is called an ellipsis. These are used when quoted material is only partially copied. An ellipsis contains three periods at the beginning of a sentence, three periods in the middle of a sentence, or four periods at the end of a sentence. The following sentence provides an example:

"...Then he picked up the groceries...paid for them...later he went home...."

Comma

A comma (,) has many uses. Things in a list should be separated by commas. The following is an example:

They saw John, Mary, and Drew at the game.

In a complex sentence, the clauses are separated by commas. If both clauses are independent, remove the comma and the connecting word and the sentences should be able to stand alone. The following is an example:

It was August, and it was hot.

Both *It was August* and *It was hot* can stand alone as sentences.

A comma is used to set off the words *yes* and *no*, or to offset a clause or phrase. The following is an example:

Yes, I met Paul yesterday.

- 133 -

Copyright © Mometrix Media. You have been licensed one copy of this document for personal use only. Any other reproduction or redistribution is strictly prohibited. All rights reserved.

A comma separates a city and state (Seattle, Washington) and is used when writing dates (November 1, 1999). A greeting in an informal letter is set off by a comma (Dear Joseph,). A comma is also used when words are quoted. The following is an example:

"One time," I said, "I found fifty dollars."

Colon

The colon (:) is similar to a comma or semicolon but is used when a longer pause is necessary between the phrases. It can sometimes indicate words that need to be emphasized in the sentence.

The following is an example:

When you go to the airport, remember: don't forget your ticket!

A colon is used when writing time (4:25 a.m.) or after a greeting in a formal letter (Dear Sir:). A colon can be used to set off quotes; in that instance, the quote is usually capitalized. The following is an example:

Margaret loved to quote Shakespeare: "To thine own self be true."

Colons are also used by playwrights when writing dialogue.

Semicolon

A semicolon (;) separates two independent clauses if they are not joined by a connective conjunction. The following is an example:

Abby reads books; she likes to watch television too.

The two phrases could have been joined by the word "and" but a semicolon is used instead. A semicolon is also used to join two phrases connected by a conjunctive adverb. Examples of conjunctive adverbs include *therefore, however, thus,* and *furthermore.*

The following is an example:

It was raining; therefore, the baseball game was cancelled.

A semicolon can also be used if a sentence contains many commas. The following is an example:

They were wet, cold, and tired; but they were still in very good spirits.

Hyphen

A hyphen (-) is used to divide a word that will not fit on the line of the sentence. The word should be divided between syllables. The following is an example:

Leslie and Mark want to attend college at the Univer-
sity of Southern Alabama.

Numbers from twenty-one to ninety-nine are written with hyphens (e.g., sixty-seven or thirty-five). Fractions used as adjectives are also written with hyphens (a two-thirds majority in Congress).

If a word begins with any of the following prefixes, a hyphen is used: *great, trans, all, ex,* and *self.* Examples include *great-grandmother, self-aware,* and *ex-wife.* If a prefix precedes a proper noun or adjective, a hyphen is used, such as with *mid-January.*

Copyright © Mometrix Media. You have been licensed one copy of this document for personal use only. Any other reproduction or redistribution is strictly prohibited. All rights reserved.

A hyphen can be used to distinguish words that have different meanings but the same spelling, such as *re-sign* a contract versus *resign* from a job.

Parentheses

Parentheses ( ) are used in pairs to enclose words or phrases that supplement the main sentence. They are placed in the middle and can interrupt the flow. The following is an example:

Brian went to Los Angeles (his favorite city) and went surfing.

If the statement in the parentheses is an entire sentence that can stand on its own, it does not need a separate punctuation mark, unless it is a question; then it would need a question mark. The following is an example:

I saw Susan at the new grocery store (have you been there?) and she asked about you.

Parentheses can also be used to list items. The following is an example:

For the party we need (1) cake, (2) food, and (3) music.

Quotation mark

A pair of quotation marks ("") encloses quoted words or phrases whether the quoted section states what someone said or is a formal quote from a copyrighted work. The following are examples:

- Amy said, "I have a new house."
- In the novel Jane Eyre, Charlotte Bronte wrote, "Reader, I married him."

Quotes are also used for titles of short articles, poems, chapters, songs, or essays. When using slang terms, quotes can be used. The following is an example:

Charlie considers himself a serious "gamer" and has an Xbox.

If a quote is used within a quote, use a single quotation mark. The following is an example:

Mr. Turner said, "Edward R. Murrow used to say, 'Good night, and good luck.'"

Quotation marks are almost always placed after the final punctuation mark (period, question mark, etc.) in a sentence.

Bracket

Brackets ([ ]) can be used to add explanatory or descriptive information to a sentence. The following is an example:

Jay's Place [the new coffee shop] has great espresso.

When quoting material, it is sometimes necessary to change a word or pronoun to fit the structure of the new sentence. Brackets will be used around the new word to show that it is different from the original.

For example, *Jessica noted that her shirt is pink* could be replaced with the following:

Jessica noted, "[my] shirt is pink."

Copyright © Mometrix Media. You have been licensed one copy of this document for personal use only. Any other reproduction or redistribution is strictly prohibited. All rights reserved.

If a quoted word is misspelled, the word *sic* (which literally means *that's how it was*) may be added within brackets. The following is an example:

"Jesse is the best mathmatician [sic] in the club."

Brackets can be complicated and should be used sparingly.

Apostrophe

An apostrophe (') and the letter *s* show possession. They are added after a singular noun. The following is an example:

Susie's car, Steve's idea, and Carl's money were all a part of the plan.

If the possessive is to be made from a word that already ends in the letter *s*, only an apostrophe will be added to avoid too many *s* sounds. The following is an example:

Carlos' hat is over there.

A plural noun can be made possessive: *The children's bookstore is great.* Follow the rule of s with plural nouns. For example, if more than one boy had a basketball, they would be *the boys' basketballs*.

Apostrophes are used with words, letters, or numbers that do not have a specific rule for plurals. The following are examples:

- The t's need to be crossed.
- They went to school in groups of 3's.

A contraction (*can't* or *won't*) uses an apostrophe. Dates can be shortened by using apostrophes, such as *born in '08.*

Question mark

The question mark (?) is used at the end of a sentence that asks a direct question. The following is an example:

How many hours have you been gone?

In the case of an informal, polite request, a period may be used. The following is an example:

Will you please pass the salt.

Exclamation point

An exclamation mark (!) is used when the sentence expresses extreme emotion. The following is an example:

I passed my final exam!

Dash

A dash (—) is used in a sentence when the context or idea suddenly changes pace. It can also indicate an interruption. The following is an example:

Kate chose the red dress—not the black one she just bought—and then went to the dance.

Copyright © Mometrix Media. You have been licensed one copy of this document for personal use only. Any other reproduction or redistribution is strictly prohibited. All rights reserved.

Slash

The slash (/) is used to indicate that the reader has a choice between words. It can be used in some instances in place of the word or. The following is an example:

It was a pass/fail type of test.

Slashes are sometimes used to illustrate gender indifference, such as with *his/her, he/she,* or *him/her.* If used in this way, there are no spaces before and after the slash.

When slashes are used in quoted material, usually poetry, there are spaces before and after the slash. The following is an example:

"Shall I compare thee to a summer's day? / Thou art more lovely and more temperate..."

Commonly Misspelled Words

accidentally	accommodate	accompanied	accompany
achieved	acknowledgment	across	address
aggravate	aisle	ancient	anxiety
apparently	appearance	arctic	argument
arrangement	attendance	auxiliary	awkward
bachelor	barbarian	beggar	beneficiary
biscuit	brilliant	business	cafeteria
calendar	campaign	candidate	ceiling
cemetery	changeable	changing	characteristic
chauffeur	colonel	column	commit
committee	comparative	compel	competent
competition	conceive	congratulations	conqueror
conscious	coolly	correspondent	courtesy
curiosity	cylinder	deceive	deference
deferred	definite	describe	desirable
desperate	develop	diphtheria	disappear
disappoint	disastrous	discipline	discussion
disease	dissatisfied	dissipate	drudgery
ecstasy	efficient	eighth	eligible
embarrass	emphasize	especially	exaggerate
exceed	exhaust	exhilaration	existence
explanation	extraordinary	familiar	fascinate
February	fiery	finally	forehead
foreign	foreigner	foremost	forfeit
ghost	glamorous	government	grammar
grateful	grief	grievous	handkerchief
harass	height	hoping	hurriedly
hygiene	hypocrisy	imminent	incidentally
incredible	independent	indigestible	inevitable
innocence	intelligible	intentionally	intercede
interest	irresistible	judgment	legitimate
liable	library	likelihood	literature
maintenance	maneuver	manual	mathematics
mattress	miniature	mischievous	misspell
momentous	mortgage	neither	nickel

- 137 -

Copyright © Mometrix Media. You have been licensed one copy of this document for personal use only. Any other reproduction or redistribution is strictly prohibited. All rights reserved.

Commonly Misspelled Words

niece	ninety	noticeable	notoriety
obedience	obstacle	occasion	occurrence
omitted	operate	optimistic	organization
outrageous	pageant	pamphlet	parallel
parliament	permissible	perseverance	persuade
physically	physician	possess	possibly
practically	prairie	preceding	prejudice
prevalent	professor	pronunciation	pronouncement
propeller	protein	psychiatrist	psychology
quantity	questionnaire	rally	recede
receive	recognize	recommend	referral
referred	relieve	religious	resistance
restaurant	rhetoric	rhythm	ridiculous
sacrilegious	salary	scarcely	schedule
secretary	sentinel	separate	severely
sheriff	shriek	similar	soliloquy
sophomore	species	strenuous	studying
suffrage	supersede	suppress	surprise
symmetry	temperament	temperature	tendency
tournament	tragedy	transferred	truly
twelfth	tyranny	unanimous	unpleasant
usage	vacuum	valuable	vein
vengeance	vigilance	villain	Wednesday
weird	wholly		

Review Video: Spelling Tips
Visit mometrix.com/academy and enter code: 138869

Copyright © Mometrix Media. You have been licensed one copy of this document for personal use only. Any other reproduction or redistribution is strictly prohibited. All rights reserved.

Structure

Types of sentences

For a sentence to be complete, it must have a subject and a verb or predicate. A complete sentence will express a complete thought, otherwise it is known as a fragment. An example of a fragment is: *As the clock struck midnight.* A complete sentence would be: *As the clock struck midnight, she ran home.* The types of sentences are declarative, imperative, interrogative, and exclamatory.

A declarative sentence states a fact and ends with a period. The following is an example:

The football game starts at seven o'clock.

An imperative sentence tells someone to do something and ends with a period. The following is an example:

Go to the store and buy milk.

An interrogative sentence asks a question and ends with a question mark. The following is an example:

Are you going to the game on Friday?

An exclamatory sentence shows strong emotion and ends with an exclamation point. The following is an example:

I can't believe we won the game!

Modes of sentence patterns

Sentence patterns fall into five common modes with some exceptions. They are:

- Subject + linking verb + subject complement
- Subject + transitive verb + direct object
- Subject + transitive verb + indirect object + direct object
- Subject + transitive verb + direct object + object complement
- Subject + intransitive verb

Common exceptions to these patterns are questions and commands, sentences with delayed subjects, and passive transformations.

Transitions

Transitions are bridges between what has been read and what is about to be read. Transitions smooth the reader's path between sentences and inform the reader of major connections to new ideas forthcoming in the text. Transitional phrases should be used with care, selecting the appropriate phrase for a transition. Tone is another important consideration in using transitional phrases, varying the tone for different audiences. For example, in a scholarly essay, *in summary* would be preferable to the more informal *in short*.

When working with transitional words and phrases, writers usually find a natural flow that indicates when a transition is needed. In reading a draft of the text, it should become apparent where the flow is uneven or rough. At this point, the writer can add transitional elements during

- 139 -

Copyright © Mometrix Media. You have been licensed one copy of this document for personal use only. Any other reproduction or redistribution is strictly prohibited. All rights reserved.

the revision process. Revising can also afford an opportunity to delete transitional devices that seem heavy handed or unnecessary.

Transitional words and phrases are used to transition between paragraphs and also to transition within a single paragraph. Transitions assist the flow of ideas and help to unify an essay. A writer can use certain words to indicate that an example or summary is being presented. The following phrases, among others, can be used as this type of transition: *as a result, as I have said, for example, for instance, in any case, in any event, in brief, in conclusion, in fact, in other words, in short, on the whole,* and *to sum it up.*

Review Video: Transitions
Visit mometrix.com/academy and enter code: 707563

Transitional words

Link similar ideas

When a writer links ideas that are similar in nature, there are a variety of words and phrases he or she can choose, including but not limited to: *also, and, another, besides, equally important, further, furthermore, in addition, likewise, too, similarly, nor, of course,* and *for instance.*

Link dissimilar or contradictory ideas

Writers can link contradictory ideas in an essay by using, among others, the following words and phrases: *although, and yet, even if, conversely, but, however, otherwise, still, yet, instead, in spite of, nevertheless, on the contrary,* and *on the other hand.*

Indicate cause, purpose, or result

Writers may need to indicate that one thing is the cause, purpose, or result of another thing. To show this relationship, writers can use, among others, the following linking words and phrases: *as, as a result, because, consequently, hence, for, for this reason, since, so, then, thus,* and *therefore.*

Indicate time or position

Certain words can be used to indicate the time and position of one thing in relation to another. Writers can use, for example, the following terms to create a timeline of events in an essay: *above, across, afterward, before, beyond, eventually, meanwhile, next, presently, around, at once, at the present time, finally, first, here, second, thereafter,* and *upon.* These words can show the order or placement of items or ideas in an essay.

Commas

Abbreviations, interjections, and direct addresses

Abbreviations, interjections, and direct addresses are all types of sentence interruptions. An interruption is any word or phrase that stops the flow of a sentence. Interruptions should be set off by commas. Abbreviations such as *Jr.* or *Ph.D.* must also be set off by commas. (*Harry Langford, Ph.D., will be hosting the event.*) Interjections are exclamations that lack grammatical connection to a sentence. A comma should be inserted before and after an interjection. (*Oh, you must be joking.*) A direct address occurs when the writer speaks directly to another person. The term used to address the person must be set off by commas. (*No, Mother, I will not lower my voice.*)

Copyright © Mometrix Media. You have been licensed one copy of this document for personal use only. Any other reproduction or redistribution is strictly prohibited. All rights reserved.

Geographical references, transitional words and phrases, and parenthetical words and phrases

Geographical references, transitional words and phrases, and parenthetical words and phrases are all types of sentence interruptions. An interruption is any word or phrase that stops the flow of a sentence. Interruptions should be set off by commas. Geographical references include the names of a city within a state or a specific street address. (*I will visit Detroit, Michigan, in September.*) As in this example, a comma should be placed after the name of the city and another comma should be placed after the name of the state if the sentence continues. Transitional words and phrases include sayings such as *on the other hand, contrary to popular belief*, and *nevertheless*. These expressions must be set off from the rest of the sentence with commas. Parenthetical words and phrases are similar to transitional phrases and must also be set off from the rest of the sentence with commas.

Parallel structure in a sentence

Parallel sentence structure refers to the use of similar word patterns to show that each idea in a sentence has equal importance. Parallel structure can involve single words, phrases, or clauses within a sentence. In the sentence *Susan enjoys painting, singing, and reading*, the words *painting, singing*, and *reading* all end with *-ing*, which creates a parallel structure. The conjunctions *and* and *or* usually signal the need for parallel structure.

Sentence structure

The four major types of sentence structure are:

- Simple sentences: Simple sentences have one independent clause with no subordinate clauses. A simple sentence may contain compound elements—a compound subject, verb, or object, for example—but does not contain more than one full sentence pattern.
- Compound sentences: Compound sentences are composed of two or more independent clauses with no subordinate clauses. The independent clauses are usually joined with a comma and a coordinating conjunction or with a semicolon.
- Complex sentences: A complex sentence is composed of one independent clause with one or more dependent clauses.
- Compound-complex sentences: A compound-complex sentence contains at least two independent clauses and at least one subordinate clause. Sometimes they contain two full sentence patterns that can stand alone. When each independent clause contains a subordinate clause, this makes the sentence both compound and complex.

Simple

A simple sentence is an independent clause that contains a complete subject and a complete predicate. Simple sentences can be very short or long; the length does not indicate the complexity of the sentence. The subject may be singular or compound (more than one subject). The predicate may also be singular or compound. The following are examples:

- Judy watered the lawn. (singular subject, singular predicate)
- Judy and Alan watered the lawn. (compound subject, Judy and Alan)
- Judy watered the lawn and planted flowers. (compound predicate, watered and planted)
- Judy and Alan watered the lawn and planted flowers. (compound subject and predicate)

Compound

A compound sentence consists of two or more simple sentences joined together by a conjunction. Conjunctions can also be called coordinators and include the following: *and, but, or, nor, for, yet,* and

Copyright © Mometrix Media. You have been licensed one copy of this document for personal use only. Any other reproduction or redistribution is strictly prohibited. All rights reserved.

so. A comma is written after the simple sentence and before the conjunction. The following is an example: *I woke up at dawn, so I went outside to watch the sunrise.*

A way to identify a compound sentence is to remove the conjunction and see if the two clauses can stand alone as simple sentences. *In this case, I woke up at dawn* and *I went outside to watch the sunset* can be independent; therefore, the sentence is a compound sentence.

Complex

A complex sentence consists of an independent clause and one or more dependent clauses. The independent clause can exist alone as a sentence while a dependent clause needs to be grouped with an independent clause even though it has its own subject and verb. A dependent clause cannot exist alone as a sentence. Dependent clauses are linked to the independent clause with conjunctions, such as after, *although, as, because, before, that, when, which,* and *while.* The following are examples:

- Although he had the flu, Harry went to work.
- Marcia got married after she finished college.

Notice that the clause can appear before or after the independent phrase.

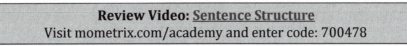

Review Video: Sentence Structure
Visit mometrix.com/academy and enter code: 700478

Paragraph length

The reader's comfort level is paragraphs of between 100 and 200 words. Shorter paragraphs cause too much starting and stopping, and give a choppy effect. Paragraphs that are too long often test the attention span of the reader. Two notable exceptions to this rule exist. In scientific or scholarly papers, longer paragraphs suggest seriousness and depth. In journalistic writing, constraints are placed on paragraph size by the narrow columns in a newspaper format.

The first and last paragraphs of a text will usually be the introduction and conclusion. These special-purpose paragraphs are likely to be shorter than paragraphs in the body of the work. Paragraphs in the body of the essay follow the subject's outline; one paragraph per point in short essays and a group of paragraphs per point in longer works. Some ideas require more development than others, so it is good for a writer to remain flexible. A too-long paragraph may be divided, and shorter ones may be combined.

Coherent paragraphs

A smooth flow of sentences and paragraphs without gaps, shifts, or bumps leads to paragraph coherence. Ties between old and new information can be smoothed by several methods:

- Linking ideas clearly, from the topic sentence to the body of the paragraph, is essential for a smooth transition. The topic sentence states the main point, and this should be followed by specific details, examples, and illustrations that support the topic sentence. The support may be direct or indirect. In indirect support, the illustrations and examples may support a sentence that in turn supports the topic directly.
- The repetition of key words adds coherence to a paragraph. To avoid dull language, variations of the key words may be used.

Copyright © Mometrix Media. You have been licensed one copy of this document for personal use only. Any other reproduction or redistribution is strictly prohibited. All rights reserved.

- Parallel structures are often used within sentences to emphasize the similarity of ideas and connect sentences giving similar information.
- Maintaining a consistent verb tense throughout the paragraph helps. Shifting tenses affects the smooth flow of words and can disrupt the coherence of the paragraph.

Main point of a paragraph

A paragraph should be unified around a main point. A good topic sentence summarizes the paragraph's main point. A topic sentence is more general than subsequent supporting sentences are. Sometime the topic sentence will be used to close the paragraph if earlier sentences give a clear indication of the direction of the paragraph. Sticking to the main point requires deleting or omitting unnecessary sentences that do not advance the main point.

The main point of a paragraph deserves adequate development, which usually means a substantial paragraph. A paragraph of two or three sentences often does not develop a point well enough, particularly if the point is a strong supporting argument of the thesis. An occasional short paragraph is fine, particularly if it is used as a transitional device. A choppy appearance should be avoided.

Examining paragraphs and sentences

Paragraphs are a key structural unit of prose used to break up long stretches of words into more manageable subsets and to indicate a shift in topics or focus. Each paragraph should be examined by identifying the main point of the section and ensuring that every sentence supports or relates to the main theme. Paragraphs should be checked to make sure the organization used in each is appropriate and that the number of sentences is adequate to develop the topic.

Sentences are the building blocks of the written word, and they can be varied by paying attention to sentence length, sentence structure, and sentence openings. These elements should be varied so that writing does not seem boring, repetitive, or choppy. A careful analysis of a piece of writing will expose these stylistic problems, and they can be corrected before the final draft is written. Varying sentence structure and length can make writing more inviting and appealing to a reader.

Essay paragraph types

Explanation: gives examples, facts, and details

Compare and contrast: discusses how things are similar or different

Chronological: arranged according to timing

Spatial: arranged according to location

Emphasis: arranged in order of importance

Cause and effect: arranged from effect to cause or cause to effect

Problem/solution: arranged according to issues and solutions

Topical: arranged according to topics discussed

Copyright © Mometrix Media. You have been licensed one copy of this document for personal use only. Any other reproduction or redistribution is strictly prohibited. All rights reserved.

Comprehensive Practice Tests

This section contains three full-length practice tests.

The table below shows the amount of time and number of questions that are on each practice test. It is recommended that you use a timer when taking the test to properly simulate the test taking conditions.

Reading	Mathematics	Science	English and Language Usage	Total
48 items	34 items	54 items	34 items	170 items
58 minutes	51 minutes	66 minutes	34 minutes	209 minutes

DIRECTIONS: The questions you are about to take are multiple-choice with only one correct answer per question. Read each test item and mark your answer on the appropriate blank on the answer page that precedes each practice test.

When you have completed the practice test, you may check your answers with those on the answer key that follows the test.

Each practice test is followed by detailed answer explanations.

Copyright © Mometrix Media. You have been licensed one copy of this document for personal use only. Any other reproduction or redistribution is strictly prohibited. All rights reserved.

TEAS Practice Test #1

Section 1. Reading

1. Adelaide attempted to <u>assuage</u> her guilt over the piece of cheesecake by limiting herself to salads the following day. Which of the following is the definition for the underlined word in the sentence above?

    a. increase
    b. support
    c. appease
    d. conceal

2. Hilaire's professor instructed him to improve the word choice in his papers. As the professor noted, Hilaire's ideas are good, but he relies too heavily on simple expressions when a more complex word would be appropriate. Which of the following resources will be most useful to Hilaire in this case?

    a. Roget's Thesaurus
    b. Oxford Latin Dictionary
    c. Encyclopedia Britannica
    d. Webster's Dictionary

    <u>The Dewey Decimal Classes</u>

    000 Computer science, information, and general works
    100 Philosophy and psychology
    200 Religion
    300 Social sciences
    400 Languages
    500 Science and mathematics
    600 Technical and applied science
    700 Arts and recreation
    800 Literature
    900 History, geography, and biography

    The next three questions are based on the above.

3. Lise is doing a research project on the various psychological theories that Sigmund Freud developed and on the modern response to those theories. She is not sure where to begin, so she consults the chart of Dewey Decimal Classes. To which section of the library should she go to begin looking for research material?

    a. 100
    b. 200
    c. 300
    d. 900

Copyright © Mometrix Media. You have been licensed one copy of this document for personal use only. Any other reproduction or redistribution is strictly prohibited. All rights reserved.

4. During her research, Lise discovers that Freud's theory of the Oedipal complex was based on ancient Greek mythology that was made famous by Sophocles' play *Oedipus Rex*. To which section of the library should she go if she is interested in reading the play?

    a. 300
    b. 400
    c. 800
    d. 900

5. Also during her research, Lise learns about Freud's Jewish background, and she decides to compare Freud's theories to traditional Judaism. To which section of the library should she go for more information on this subject?

    a. 100
    b. 200
    c. 800
    d. 900

6. Chapter 15: Roman Emperors in the First Century

- Tiberius, 14-37 AD
- Nero, 54-68 AD
- Domitian, 81-96 AD
- Hadrian, 117-138 AD

Analyze the headings above. Which of the following does not belong?

    a. Tiberius, 14-37 AD
    b. Nero, 54-68 AD
    c. Domitian, 81-96 AD
    d. Hadrian, 117-138 AD

7. Although his friends believed him to be enjoying a lavish lifestyle in the large family estate he had inherited, Enzo was in reality <u>impecunious</u>.

Which of the following is the definition for the underlined word in the sentence above?

    a. Penniless
    b. Unfortunate
    c. Emotional
    d. Commanding

Copyright © Mometrix Media. You have been licensed one copy of this document for personal use only. Any other reproduction or redistribution is strictly prohibited. All rights reserved.

8. Follow the numbered instructions to transform the starting word into a different word.

1. Start with the word ESOTERIC
2. Remove both instances of the letter E from the word
3. Remove the letter I from the word
4. Move the letter T from the middle of the word to the end of the word
5. Remove the letter C from the word

What new word has been spelled?

a. SECT
b. SORT
c. SORE
d. TORE

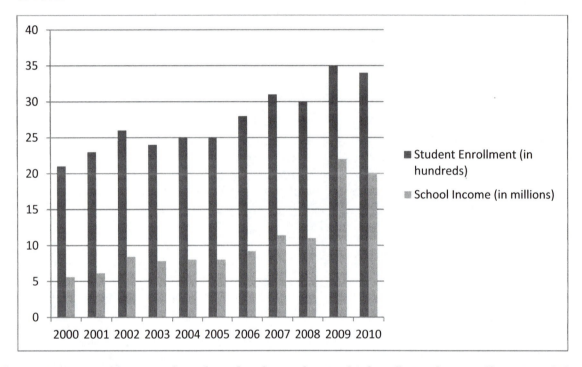

The next two questions are based on the above chart, which reflects the enrollment and the income for a small community college.

9. Based on the chart, approximately how many students attended the community college in the year 2001?

a. 2100
b. 2300
c. 2500
d. 2700

- 147 -

Copyright © Mometrix Media. You have been licensed one copy of this document for personal use only. Any other reproduction or redistribution is strictly prohibited. All rights reserved.

10. In order to offset costs, the college administration decided to increase admission fees. Reviewing the chart above, during which year is it most likely that the college raised the price of admission?

a. 2002
b. 2007
c. 2009
d. 2010

11. The journalist, as part of his ongoing series of articles about the defendant accused of multiple murders, included a note that the defendant had written: "*No matter what they say I am not gilty [sic] of the crime.*" Which of the following does the bracketed expression "*sic*" indicate?

a. An accidental misspelling in the sentence
b. A grammatical error that the editor failed to catch
c. An incorrect usage on the part of the original writer
d. A point of emphasis that the journalist wants readers to see

The Bermuda Triangle

The area known as the Bermuda Triangle has become such a part of popular culture that it can be difficult to separate fact from fiction. The interest first began when five Navy planes vanished in 1945, officially resulting from "causes or reasons unknown." The explanations about other accidents in the Triangle range from the scientific to the supernatural. Researchers have never been able to find anything truly mysterious about what happens in the Bermuda Triangle, if there even is a Bermuda Triangle. What is more, one of the biggest challenges in considering the phenomenon is deciding how much area actually represents the Bermuda Triangle. Most consider the Triangle to stretch from Miami out to Puerto Rico and to include the island of Bermuda. Others expand the area to include all of the Caribbean islands and to extend eastward as far as the Azores, which are closer to Europe than they are to North America.

The problem with having a larger Bermuda Triangle is that it increases the odds of accidents. There is near-constant travel, by ship and by plane, across the Atlantic, and accidents are expected to occur. In fact, the Bermuda Triangle happens to fall within one of the busiest navigational regions in the world, and the reality of greater activity creates the possibility for more to go wrong. Shipping records suggest that there is not a greater than average loss of vessels within the Bermuda Triangle, and many researchers have argued that the reputation of the Triangle makes any accident seem out of the ordinary. In fact, most accidents fall within the expected margin of error. The increase in ships from East Asia no doubt contributes to an increase in accidents. And as for the story of the Navy planes that disappeared within the Triangle, many researchers now conclude that it was the result of mistakes on the part of the pilots who were flying into storm clouds and simply got lost.

The next four questions are based on the passage above.

12. Which of the following describes this type of writing?

a. Narrative
b. Persuasive
c. Expository
d. Technical

Copyright © Mometrix Media. You have been licensed one copy of this document for personal use only. Any other reproduction or redistribution is strictly prohibited. All rights reserved.

13. Which of the following sentences is most representative of a summary sentence for this passage?

a. The problem with having a larger Bermuda Triangle is that it increases the odds of accidents.
b. The area that is called the Bermuda Triangle happens to fall within one of the busiest navigational regions in the world, and the reality of greater activity creates the possibility for more to go wrong.
c. One of the biggest challenges in considering the phenomenon is deciding how much area actually represents the Bermuda Triangle.
d. Researchers have never been able to find anything truly mysterious about what happens in the Bermuda Triangle, if there even is a Bermuda Triangle.

14. With which of the following statements would the author most likely agree?

a. There is no real mystery about the Bermuda Triangle because most events have reasonable explanations.
b. Researchers are wrong to expand the focus of the Triangle to the Azores, because this increases the likelihood of accidents.
c. The official statement of "causes or reasons unknown" in the loss of the Navy planes was a deliberate concealment from the Navy.
d. Reducing the legends about the mysteries of the Bermuda Triangle will help to reduce the number of reported accidents or shipping losses in that region.

15. Which of the following represents an opinion statement on the part of the author?

a. The problem with having a larger Bermuda Triangle is that it increases the odds of accidents.
b. The area known as the Bermuda Triangle has become such a part of popular culture that it can be difficult to sort through the myth and locate the truth.
c. The increase in ships from East Asia no doubt contributes to an increase in accidents.
d. Most consider the Triangle to stretch from Miami to Puerto Rico and include the island of Bermuda.

16. But I don't like the beach, Judith complained. All that sand. It gets in between my toes, in my swimsuit, and in my hair and eyes. Martin suggested an alternative. Then, let's go to the park instead.

The use of italics in the text above indicates which of the following?

a. Dialogue
b. Emphasis
c. Thoughts
d. Anger

17. The guide words at the top of a dictionary page are *intrauterine* and *invest*. Which of the following words is an entry on this page?

a. Intransigent
b. Introspection
c. Investiture
d. Intone

- 149 -

Copyright © Mometrix Media. You have been licensed one copy of this document for personal use only. Any other reproduction or redistribution is strictly prohibited. All rights reserved.

18. The public eagerness to <u>lionize</u> the charming actor after his string of popular films kept his managers busy concealing his shady background and questionable activities.

Which of the following is the definition for the underlined word in the sentence above?
    a. Criticize
    b. Sympathize with
    c. Betray
    d. Glorify

19. Ninette has celiac disease, which means that she cannot eat any product containing gluten. Gluten is a protein present in many grains such as wheat, rye, and barley. Because of her health condition, Ninette has to be careful about what she eats to avoid having an allergic reaction. She will be attending an all-day industry event, and she requested the menu in advance. Here is the menu:

- Breakfast: Fresh coffee or tea, scrambled eggs, bacon or sausage
- Lunch: Spinach salad (dressing available on the side), roasted chicken, steamed rice
- Cocktail Hour: Various beverages, fruit and cheese plate
- Dinner: Spaghetti and sauce, tossed salad, garlic bread

During which of these meals should Ninette be careful to bring her own food?
    a. Breakfast
    b. Lunch
    c. Cocktail Hour
    d. Dinner

20. Chapter 2: Shakespeare Before He Was Famous

- Family Background
- Childhood Experiences
- Education
- Dramatic Works
- Youthful Marriage to Anne Hathaway
- Move to London

Analyze the headings above. Which of the following does not belong?
    a. Family Background
    b. Education
    c. Dramatic Works
    d. Youthful Marriage to Anne Hathaway

Copyright © Mometrix Media. You have been licensed one copy of this document for personal use only. Any other reproduction or redistribution is strictly prohibited. All rights reserved.

21. Letter to the Editor:

> I was disappointed by the August 12th article entitled *"How to Conserve Water."* While the author of the article, Neil Chambers, provided excellent tips, he overlooked the most obvious -- taking shorter showers. Mr. Chambers should consider the recent study by Dr. James Duncan on the subject, which examines the importance of shower length in reducing water use:

>> While water conservation options vary, the most effective might also be one of the simplest. Consumers who take shorter showers can reduce their water usage significantly each year. The standard shower head allows releases more than two gallons of water per minute. By cutting each shower short by only five minutes, consumers can save over twelve gallons of water.

> Water conservationists applaud the newspaper's efforts to direct readers toward opportunities to conserve, but journalists should put a little more effort into research before sending their work to publication.

Which of the following explains the reason for the indentation in the passage above?

a. A quote from another source
b. A conversation between two authorities on a subject
c. A quoted portion from a published article by the author of the letter
d. A disputed claim from the author of the newspaper article

22. With most of the evidence being circumstantial, the defense attorney was successful in his attempt to <u>exculpate</u> his client before the jury. Which of the following is the definition for the underlined word in the sentence above?

a. Dismiss
b. Clear
c. Condemn
d. Forgive

NAME	COMPOSITION (PER 100)	WORLD LITERATURE (PER 100)	TECHNICAL WRITING (PER 100)	LINGUISTICS (PER 100)
Textbook-Mania	$4500	$5150	$6000	$6500
Textbook Central	$4350	$5200	$6100	$6550
Bookstore Supply	$4675	$5000	$5950	$6475
University Textbooks	$4600	$5000	$6100	$6650

Note: Shipping is free for all schools that order 100 textbooks or more.

The next three questions are based on the above table.

Copyright © Mometrix Media. You have been licensed one copy of this document for personal use only. Any other reproduction or redistribution is strictly prohibited. All rights reserved.

23. A school needs to purchase 500 composition textbooks and 500 world literature textbooks.

Which of the textbook suppliers can offer the lowest price?

    a. Textbook Mania
    b. Textbook Central
    c. Bookstore Supply
    d. University Textbooks

24. A school needs to purchase 1000 composition textbooks and 300 linguistics textbooks. Which of the textbook suppliers can offer the lowest price?

    a. Textbook Mania
    b. Textbook Central
    c. Bookstore Supply
    d. University Textbooks

25. A school needs to purchase 400 world literature textbooks and 200 technical writing textbooks. Which of the textbook suppliers can offer the lowest price?

    a. Textbook Mania
    b. Textbook Central
    c. Bookstore Supply
    d. University Textbooks

26. Given his fascination with all things nautical, Blaise could not pass up the opportunity to tour the reproduction 18th-century <u>bark</u> that was docked nearby. Based on the context of the passage above, which of the following is the definition of the underlined word?

    a. The outside surface of a tree
    b. A crisp order
    c. A piece of hard chocolate-coated candy
    d. A sailing vessel

27. A cruise brochure offers a variety of options for Mediterranean cruises. The brochure notes that the ships cruising the Mediterranean pull into the following cities:

- Venice, Italy
- Athens, Greece
- Barcelona, Spain
- Oslo, Norway
- Istanbul, Turkey

Which of these cities is out of place in the list above?

    a. Athens, Greece
    b. Barcelona, Spain
    c. Oslo, Norway
    d. Istanbul, Turkey

Copyright © Mometrix Media. You have been licensed one copy of this document for personal use only. Any other reproduction or redistribution is strictly prohibited. All rights reserved.

28. A brochure provides customers with a list of cities in the United States from which the cruises depart:

- Baltimore, MD
- Boston, MA
- Charleston, SC
- Fort Lauderdale, FL
- _____
- Miami, FL

Consider the pattern in the list of cities above. Which of the following cities belongs in the blank?

a. Tampa, FL
b. Galveston, TX
c. Norfolk, VA
d. New York, NY

Starting Image

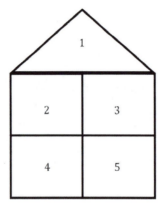

Start with the shape pictured above. Follow the directions to alter its appearance.

- Rotate section 1 90° clockwise and move it to the right side, against sections 3 and 5.
- Remove section 4.
- Move section 2 immediately above section 3.
- Swap section 2 and section 5.
- Remove section 5.
- Draw a circle around the shape, enclosing it completely.

Copyright © Mometrix Media. You have been licensed one copy of this document for personal use only. Any other reproduction or redistribution is strictly prohibited. All rights reserved.

29. Which of the following does the shape now look like?

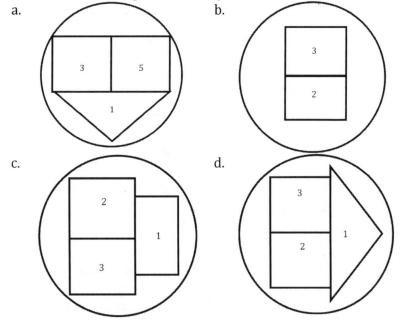

a.
b.
c.
d.

30. Anna is planning a trip to Bretagne, or Brittany, in the northwestern part of France. Since she knows very little about it, she is hoping to find the most up-to-date information with the widest variety of details about hiking trails, beaches, restaurants, and accommodations. Which of the following guides will be the best for her to review?

a. *The Top Ten Places to Visit in Brittany*, published by a non-profit organization in Bretagne looking to draw tourism to the region (2010)
b. *Getting to Know Nantes: Eating, Staying, and Sightseeing in Brittany's Largest City*, published by the French Ministry of Tourism (2009)
c. *Hiking Through Bretagne: The Best Trails for Discovering Northwestern France*, published by a company that specializes in travel for those wanting to experience the outdoors (2008)
d. *The Complete Guide to Brittany*, published by a travel book company that publishes guides for travel throughout Europe (2010)

Despite the aura of challenge that surrounds the making of haggis, Scotland's most famous dish takes some time but is really quite simple to prepare. Start with a sheep's stomach. Wash well, and soak for several hours. At the end of soaking, turn the stomach inside out. Boil one sheep's heart and one sheep's liver for about half an hour. Drain water and chop finely. Chop two or three onions. Toast approximately one cup of oatmeal, and then mix the chopped heart, liver, and onions with several spices: salt, pepper, cayenne, and nutmeg, seasoned to your preference. Add approximately one cup of the broth of your choice. Stuff the sheep's stomach with the mixture, and tie carefully with cooking twine. Make sure the stomach is well sealed. Then, add the stomach to a pot of boiling water, reduce to a simmer, and cook for about three hours. Have a needle ready to prick the stomach gently when it swells--it's better to avoid a haggis explosion!

Copyright © Mometrix Media. You have been licensed one copy of this document for personal use only. Any other reproduction or redistribution is strictly prohibited. All rights reserved.

31. Which of the following best describes the purpose of the passage above?

    a. Narrative
    b. Descriptive
    c. Persuasive
    d. Expository

The following two questions are based on the above image.

32. Edgar needs a new furnace, so he checks the telephone book for a local company that offers furnace installation services. He is also looking for a company that can provide cleaning after installation. Which of the following businesses should he call?

    a. Ferris Furnace
    b. Allen Heating & Air
    c. Everby Furnace
    d. Field's Furnace Installation

Copyright © Mometrix Media. You have been licensed one copy of this document for personal use only. Any other reproduction or redistribution is strictly prohibited. All rights reserved.

33. Pierre's furnace is not working properly, and he needs a repair service. Because it is already 11 PM, he is looking for a furnace repair business that offers 24-hour service. Since he does not know the extent of the damage, Pierre is also hoping for a free estimate. Which of the following businesses should he call?

a. Ferris Furnace
b. Perry Repairs
c. Thomas Refrigeration
d. V&V Furnace Repair

As little as three years before her birth, few would have thought that the child born Princess Alexandrina Victoria would eventually become Britain's longest reigning monarch, Queen Victoria. She was born in 1819, the only child of Edward, Duke of Kent, who was the fourth son of King George III. Ahead of Edward were three brothers, two of whom became king but none of whom produced a legitimate, surviving heir. King George's eldest son, who was eventually crowned King George IV, secretly married a Catholic commoner, Maria Fitzherbert, in 1783. The marriage was never officially recognized, and in 1795, George was persuaded to marry a distant cousin, Caroline of Brunswick. The marriage was bitter, and the two had only one daughter, Princess Charlotte Augusta. She was popular in England where her eventual reign was welcomed, but in a tragic event that shocked the nation, the princess and her stillborn son died in childbirth in 1817.

Realizing the precarious position of the British throne, the remaining sons of King George III were motivated to marry and produce an heir. The first in line was Prince Frederick, the Duke of York. Frederick married Princess Frederica Charlotte of Prussia, but the two had no children. After Prince Frederick was Prince William, the Duke of Clarence. William married Princess Adelaide of Saxe-Meiningen, and they had two sickly daughters, neither of whom survived infancy. Finally, Prince Edward, the Duke of Kent, threw his hat into the ring with his marriage to Princess Victoria of Saxe-Coburg-Saalfeld. The Duke of Kent died less than a year after his daughter's birth, but the surviving Duchess of Kent was not unaware of the future possibilities for her daughter. She took every precaution to ensure that the young Princess Victoria was healthy and safe throughout her childhood.

Princess Victoria's uncle, William, succeeded his brother George IV to become King William IV. The new king recognized his niece as his future heir, but he did not necessarily trust her mother. As a result, he was determined to survive until Victoria's eighteenth birthday to ensure that she could rule in her own right without the regency of the Duchess of Kent. The king's fervent prayers were answered: he died June 20, 1837, less than one month after Victoria turned eighteen. Though young and inexperienced, the young queen recognized the importance of her position and determined to rule fairly and wisely. The improbable princess who became queen ruled for more than sixty-three years, and her reign is considered to be one of the most important in British history.

The next three questions are based on the above passage.

Copyright © Mometrix Media. You have been licensed one copy of this document for personal use only. Any other reproduction or redistribution is strictly prohibited. All rights reserved.

34. Which of the following is a logical conclusion that can be drawn from the information in the passage above?

    a. Victoria's long reign provided the opportunity for her to bring balance to England and right the wrongs that had occurred during the reigns of her uncles.

    b. It was the death of Princess Charlotte Augusta that motivated the remaining princes to marry and start families.

    c. The Duke of Kent had hoped for a son but was delighted with his good fortune in producing the surviving heir that his brothers had failed to produce.

    d. King William IV was unreasonably suspicious of the Duchess of Kent's motivations, as she cared only for her daughter's well-being.

35. What is the author's likely purpose in writing this passage about Queen Victoria?

    a. To persuade the reader to appreciate the accomplishments of Queen Victoria, especially when placed against the failures of her forebears.

    b. To introduce the historical impact of the Victorian Era by introducing to readers the queen who gave that era its name.

    c. To explain how small events in history placed an unlikely princess in line to become the queen of England.

    d. To indicate the role that King George III's many sons played in changing the history of England.

36. Based on the context of the passage, the reader can infer that this information is likely to appear in which of the following types of works?

    a. A scholarly paper

    b. A mystery

    c. A fictional story

    d. A biography

> In 1603, Queen Elizabeth I of England died. She had never married and had no heir, so the throne passed to a distant relative: James Stuart, the son of Elizabeth's cousin and one-time rival for the throne, Mary, Queen of Scots. James was crowned King James I of England. At the time, he was also King James VI of Scotland, and the combination of roles would create a spirit of conflict that haunted the two nations for generations to come.
>
> The conflict developed as a result of rising tensions among the people within the nations, as well as between them. Scholars in the 21st century are far too hasty in dismissing the role of religion in political disputes, but religion undoubtedly played a role in the problems that faced England and Scotland. By the time of James Stuart's succession to the English throne, the English people had firmly embraced the teachings of Protestant theology. Similarly, the Scottish Lowlands was decisively Protestant. In the Scottish Highlands, however, the clans retained their Catholic faith. James acknowledged the Church of England and still sanctioned the largely Protestant translation of the Bible that still bears his name.
>
> James's son King Charles I proved himself to be less committed to the Protestant Church of England. Charles married the Catholic Princess Henrietta Maria of France, and there were suspicions among the English and the Lowland Scots that Charles was quietly a Catholic. Charles's own political troubles extended beyond religion in this case, and he was beheaded in 1649. Eventually, his son King Charles II would be

Copyright © Mometrix Media. You have been licensed one copy of this document for personal use only. Any other reproduction or redistribution is strictly prohibited. All rights reserved.

crowned, and this Charles is believed to have converted secretly to the Catholic Church. Charles II died without a legitimate heir, and his brother James ascended to the throne as King James II.

James was recognized to be a practicing Catholic, and his commitment to Catholicism would prove to be his downfall. James's wife Mary Beatrice lost a number of children during their infancy, and when she became pregnant again in 1687 the public became concerned. If James had a son, that son would undoubtedly be raised a Catholic, and the English people would not stand for this. Mary gave birth to a son, but the story quickly circulated that the royal child had died and the child named James's heir was a foundling smuggled in. James, his wife, and his infant son were forced to flee; and James's Protestant daughter Mary was crowned the queen.

In spite of a strong resemblance to the king, the young James was generally rejected among the English and the Lowland Scots, who referred to him as "the Pretender." But in the Highlands the Catholic princeling was welcomed. He inspired a group known as *Jacobites*, to reflect the Latin version of his name. His own son Charles, known affectionately as Bonnie Prince Charlie, would eventually raise an army and attempt to recapture what he believed to be his throne. The movement was soundly defeated at the Battle of Culloden in 1746, and England and Scotland have remained ostensibly Protestant ever since.

The next seven questions are based on this passage.

37. Which of the following sentences contains an opinion on the part of the author?

a. James was recognized to be a practicing Catholic, and his commitment to Catholicism would prove to be his downfall.
b. James' son King Charles I proved himself to be less committed to the Protestant Church of England.
c. The movement was soundly defeated at the Battle of Culloden in 1746, and England and Scotland have remained ostensibly Protestant ever since.
d. Scholars in the 21st century are far too hasty in dismissing the role of religion in political disputes, but religion undoubtedly played a role in the problems that faced England and Scotland.

38. Which of the following represents the best meaning of the word *foundling*, based on the context in the passage?

a. Orphan
b. Outlaw
c. Charlatan
d. Delinquent

Copyright © Mometrix Media. You have been licensed one copy of this document for personal use only. Any other reproduction or redistribution is strictly prohibited. All rights reserved.

39. Which of the following is a logical conclusion based on the information that is provided within the passage?

a. Like Elizabeth I, Charles II never married and thus never had children.
b. The English people were relieved each time that James II's wife Mary lost another child, as this prevented the chance of a Catholic monarch.
c. Charles I's beheading had less to do with religion than with other political problems that England was facing.
d. Unlike his son and grandsons, King James I had no Catholic leanings and was a faithful follower of the Protestant Church of England.

40. Based on the information that is provided within the passage, which of the following can be inferred about King James II's son?

a. Considering his resemblance to King James II, the young James was very likely the legitimate child of the king and the queen.
b. Given the queen's previous inability to produce a healthy child, the English and the Lowland Scots were right in suspecting the legitimacy of the prince.
c. James "the Pretender" was not as popular among the Highland clans as his son Bonnie Prince Charlie.
d. James was unable to acquire the resources needed to build the army and plan the invasion that his son succeeded in doing.

41. The use of the word *ostensibly* in the final paragraph suggests which of the following?

a. Many of the monarchs of England and Scotland since 1746 have been secretly Catholic.
b. The Catholic faith is unwelcome in England and Scotland, and Catholics have been persecuted over the centuries.
c. The Highland clans of Scotland were required to give up their Catholic faith after the Battle of Culloden in 1746.
d. While Catholics remain within England and Scotland, the two nations profess the Protestant Church of England as the primary church.

42. Which of the following best describes the organization of the information in the passage?

a. Cause-effect
b. Chronological sequence
c. Problem-solution
d. Comparison-contrast

43. Which of the following best describes the author's intent in the passage?

a. To persuade
b. To entertain
c. To express feeling
d. To inform

The instructor of a history class has just finished grading the essay exams from his students, and the results are not good. The essay exam was worth 70% of the final course score. The highest score in the class was a low B, and more than half of the

Copyright © Mometrix Media. You have been licensed one copy of this document for personal use only. Any other reproduction or redistribution is strictly prohibited. All rights reserved.

class of 65 students failed the exam. In view of this, the instructor reconsiders his grading plan for the semester and sends out an email message to all students.

Dear Students:

The scores for the essay exam have been posted in the online course grade book. By now, many of you have probably seen your grade and are a little concerned. (And if you're not concerned, you should be--at least a bit!) At the beginning of the semester, I informed the class that I have a strict grading policy and that all scores will stand unquestioned. With each class comes a new challenge, however, and as any good instructor will tell you, sometimes the original plan has to change. As a result, I propose the following options for students to make up their score:

1) I will present the class with an extra credit project at the next course meeting. The extra credit project will be worth 150% of the point value of the essay exam that has just been completed. While I will not drop the essay exam score, I will give you more than enough of a chance to make up the difference and raise your overall score.
2) I will allow each student to develop his or her own extra credit project. This project may reflect the tenor of option number 1 (above) but will allow the student to create a project more in his or her own line of interest. Bear in mind, however, that this is more of a risk. The scoring for option number 2 will be more subjective, depending on whether or not I feel that the project is a successful alternative to the essay exam. If it is, the student will be awarded up to 150% of the point value of the essay exam.
3) I will provide the class with the option of developing a group project. Students may form groups of 3 to 4 and put together an extra credit project that reflects a stronger response to the questions in the essay exam. This extra credit project will also be worth 150% of the point value of the essay exam. Note that each student will receive an equal score for the project, so there is a risk in this as well. If you are part of a group in which you do most of the work, each member of the group will receive equal credit for it. The purpose of the group project is to allow students to work together and arrive at a stronger response than if each worked individually.

If you are interested in pursuing extra credit to make up for the essay exam, please choose <u>one</u> of the options above. No other extra credit opportunities will be provided for the course.

Good luck!

Dr. Edwards

The next three questions are based on the above passage.

44. Which of the following describes this type of writing?
    a. Technical
    b. Narrative
    c. Persuasive
    d. Expository

Copyright © Mometrix Media. You have been licensed one copy of this document for personal use only. Any other reproduction or redistribution is strictly prohibited. All rights reserved.

45. Which of the following best describes the instructor's purpose in writing this email to his students?

    a. To berate students for the poor scores that they made on the recent essay exam.

    b. To encourage students to continue working hard in spite of failure.

    c. To give students the opportunity to make up the bad score and avoid failing the course.

    d. To admit that the essay exam was likely too difficult for most students.

46. Which of the following offers the best summary for the instructor's motive in sending the email to the students?

    a. By now, many of you have probably seen your grade and are a little concerned. (And if you're not concerned, you should be--at least a bit!)

    b. With each class comes a new challenge, however, and as any good instructor will tell you, sometimes the original plan has to change.

    c. The purpose of the group project is to allow students to work together and arrive at a stronger response than if each worked individually.

    d. At the beginning of the semester, I informed the class that I have a strict grading policy and that all scores will stand unquestioned.

    The following memo was posted to a company message board for all employees to review.

    To all employees:

    It has come to my attention that food items are disappearing from the refrigerator in the break room. Despite the fact that many of the items are unlabeled, they still belong to the individuals who brought them. Because of the food thefts, a number of employees have gone without lunch or have had to purchase a lunch after already bringing one for the day. This is both inconvenient and costly.

    This is also unacceptable. Our company prides itself on hiring employees who respect others, and there is no excuse for taking what does not belong to you. Any employee caught taking an item out of the refrigerator that does not belong to him or her risks termination. (As a quick reminder, we encourage those who bring food items to label those items.) Demonstrate courtesy to your colleagues, and respect what is theirs.

    In other words, if you didn't bring it, don't eat it.

    Alicia Jones

    Human Resources Manager

The next two questions are based on the above passage

47. Which of the following is the human resources manager's intent in the memo?

    a. To persuade

    b. To entertain

    c. To inform

    d. To express feelings

Copyright © Mometrix Media. You have been licensed one copy of this document for personal use only. Any other reproduction or redistribution is strictly prohibited. All rights reserved.

48. Which of the following explains the reason for the parenthetical note about employees labeling their food items?

a. The labeling represents a kind of courtesy to the other employees to show which items belong to whom.

b. The labeling ensures that the company will know whether or not an employee is removing his or her own item.

c. The labeling represents a rule for employees who bring food, and the company can terminate employees that do not label food items.

d. The labeling will enable the company to keep track of what is in the refrigerator and ensure that all employees are eating lunch.

Copyright © Mometrix Media. You have been licensed one copy of this document for personal use only. Any other reproduction or redistribution is strictly prohibited. All rights reserved.

Section 2. Mathematics

1. Which of the following is the percent equivalent of 0.0016?

    a. 16%
    b. 160%
    c. 1.6%
    d. 0.16%

2. Curtis is taking a road trip through Germany, where all distance signs are in metric. He passes a sign that states the city of Dusseldorf is 45 kilometers away. Approximately how far is this in miles?

    a. 42 miles
    b. 37 miles
    c. 28 miles
    d. 16 miles

3. Which of the following is the Roman numeral representation for the year 1768?

    a. MDCCLXVIII
    b. MMCXLVIII
    c. MDCCCXLV
    d. MDCCXLIII

4. It is 18 degrees Celsius at Essie's hotel in London. What is the approximate temperature in degrees Fahrenheit?

    a. 25
    b. 48
    c. 55
    d. 64

5. Pernell's last five consecutive scores on her chemistry exams were as follows: 81, 92, 87, 89, 94. What is the approximate average of her scores?

    a. 81
    b. 84
    c. 89
    d. 91

6. What is the *median* of Pernell's scores, as listed in the question above?

    a. 87
    b. 89
    c. 92
    d. 94

7. Gordon purchased a television when his local electronics store had a sale. The television was offered at 30% off its original price of $472. What was the sale price that Gordon paid?

    a. $141.60
    b. $225.70
    c. $305.30
    d. $330.40

- 163 -

Copyright © Mometrix Media. You have been licensed one copy of this document for personal use only. Any other reproduction or redistribution is strictly prohibited. All rights reserved.

8. $\frac{2}{3} \div \frac{4}{15} \times \frac{5}{8}$

Simplify the expression above. Which of the following is correct?

    a. $1\frac{9}{16}$

    b. $1\frac{1}{4}$

    c. $2\frac{1}{8}$

    d. 2

9. 0.0178 x 2.401

Simplify the expression above. Which of the following is correct?

    a. 2.0358414

    b. 0.0427378

    c. 0.2341695

    d. 0.3483240

10. Murray makes $1143.50 for each pay period, and the payments are deposited into his checking account twice a month. His monthly expenses currently include rent at $900 per month, utilities at $250 per month, car insurance at $45 per month, and the cost of food at $300 per month. Murray is trying to put away some money into a separate savings account each month, but he also wants to make sure he has at least $300 left over from his monthly expenses before putting any money into savings. Calculating all of Murray's monthly expenses, including the $300 he wants to keep in his checking account, how much money can he put into the savings account each month?

    a. $192

    b. $292

    c. $392

    d. $492

Copyright © Mometrix Media. You have been licensed one copy of this document for personal use only. Any other reproduction or redistribution is strictly prohibited. All rights reserved.

11. $4(2x - 6) = 10x - 6$

Solve for x above. Which of the following is correct?

    a. 5
    b. -7
    c. -9
    d. 10

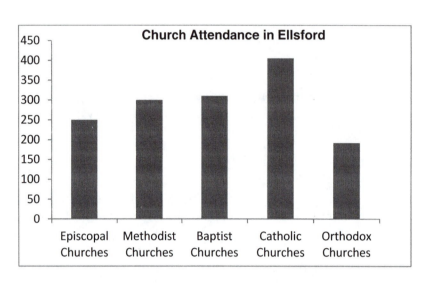

12. The graph above shows the weekly church attendance among residents in the town of Ellsford, with the town having five different denominations: Episcopal, Methodist, Baptist, Catholic, and Orthodox. Approximately what percentage of church-goers in Ellsford attends Catholic churches?

    a. 23%
    b. 28%
    c. 36%
    d. 42%

13. Erma has her eye on two sweaters at her favorite clothing store, but she has been waiting for the store to offer a sale. This week, the store advertises that all clothing purchases, including sweaters, come with an incentive: 25% off a second item of equal or lesser value. One sweater is $50 and the other is $44. If Erma purchases the sweaters during the sale, what will she spend?

    a. $79
    b. $81
    c. $83
    d. $85

14. Sara plans to set up a booth at an industry fair. The cost for the booth is $500. Additionally, she is planning to give each person who visits the booth a pamphlet about her company and a key chain with the company's logo on it. Fair attendance is expected to be around 1500 people, but Sara expects that she will have only half that many people stop by the booth. As a result, she is only planning to bring pamphlets and key chains for 750 people. The cost of each pamphlet is $0.25 and the cost for each key chain is $0.75. What will Sara's overall cost be?

    a. $750
    b. $900
    c. $1000
    d. $1250

Copyright © Mometrix Media. You have been licensed one copy of this document for personal use only. Any other reproduction or redistribution is strictly prohibited. All rights reserved.

15. $4\frac{2}{3} \div 1\frac{1}{6}$

Simplify the expression above. Which of the following is correct?

   a. 2

   b. $3\frac{1}{3}$

   c. 4

   d. $4\frac{1}{2}$

16. $1.034 + 0.275 - 1.294$

Simplify the expression above. Which of the following is correct?

   a. 0.015

   b. 0.15

   c. 1.5

   d. -0.15

17. $(2x + 4)(x - 6)$

Simplify the expression above. Which of the following is correct?

   a. $2x^2 + 8x - 24$

   b. $2x^2 + 8x + 24$

   c. $2x^2 - 8x + 24$

   d. $2x^2 - 8x - 24$

18. On the back of a video case, Digby notices that the listed date of production is MCMXCIV. What is this date in Arabic numerals?

   a. 1991

   b. 1994

   c. 1987

   d. 2003

19. If Stella's current weight is 56 kilograms, which of the following is her approximate weight in pounds? (Note: 1 kilogram is approximately equal to 2.2 pounds.)

   a. 123 pounds

   b. 110 pounds

   c. 156 pounds

   d. 137 pounds

20. Zander is paid $8.50 per hour at his full-time job. He typically works there from 8 AM to 5 PM each weekday, with a one-hour lunch break. The job offers no vacation benefits, so if Zander does not work, he does not get paid. Last week, he worked his full daily schedule of 8 hours each day, except for Wednesday when he left at 3:30 PM. Zander did take his lunch break that day. Which of the following is Zander's pay for the week?

   a. $318.50

   b. $327.25

   c. $335.75

   d. $340

Copyright © Mometrix Media. You have been licensed one copy of this document for personal use only. Any other reproduction or redistribution is strictly prohibited. All rights reserved.

21. $|2x - 7| = 3$

Solve the expression above for x. Which of the following is correct?

    a. $x = 4, 1$
    b. $x = 3, 0$
    c. $x = -2, 6$
    d. $x = 5, 2$

22. Between the years 2000 and 2010, the number of births in the town of Daneville increased from 1432 to 2219. Which of the following is the approximate percent of increase in the number of births during those ten years?

    a. 55%
    b. 36%
    c. 64%
    d. 42%

23. $\frac{1}{4} \times \frac{3}{5} \div 1\frac{1}{8}$

Simplify the expression above. Which of the following is correct?

    a. $\frac{8}{15}$
    b. $\frac{27}{160}$
    c. $\frac{2}{15}$
    d. $\frac{27}{40}$

24. While at the local ice skating rink, Cora went around the rink 27 times total. She slipped and fell 20 of the 27 times she skated around the rink. What approximate percentage of the times around the rink did Cora *not* slip and fall?

    a. 37%
    b. 74%
    c. 26%
    d. 15%

25. For her science project, Justine wants to develop a chart that shows the average monthly rainfall in her town. Which type of chart or graph is most appropriate?

    a. Circle graph
    b. Bar graph
    c. Pie chart
    d. Line graph

26. $3\frac{1}{6} - 1\frac{5}{6}$

Simplify the expression above. Which of the following is correct?

    a. $2\frac{1}{3}$
    b. $1\frac{1}{3}$
    c. $2\frac{1}{9}$
    d. $\frac{5}{6}$

Copyright © Mometrix Media. You have been licensed one copy of this document for personal use only. Any other reproduction or redistribution is strictly prohibited. All rights reserved.

27. Four more than a number, x, is 2 less than $\frac{1}{3}$ of another number, y.

Which of the following algebraic equations correctly represents the sentence above?

    a. $x + 4 = \frac{1}{3}y - 2$

    b. $4x = 2 - \frac{1}{3}y$

    c. $4 - x = 2 + \frac{1}{3}y$

    d. $x + 4 = 2 - \frac{1}{3}y$

28. $\frac{2xy^2 + 16x^2y - 20xy + 8}{4xy}$

Which of the following expressions is equivalent to the one listed above?

    a. $\frac{2}{y} + 4x - 2xy + 2$

    b. $2y + x^2y - 5 + \frac{xy}{2}$

    c. $\frac{y}{2} + 4x - 5 + \frac{2}{xy}$

    d. $\frac{x}{2} + 4xy - 16 + 2$

29. $4x - 6 \geq 2x + 4$

Solve the inequality above for x. Which of the following is correct?

    a. $x \geq 5$

    b. $x \geq 8$

    c. $x \leq 2$

    d. $x \geq 0$

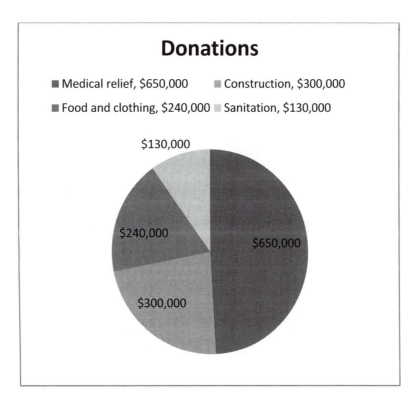

- 168 -

Copyright © Mometrix Media. You have been licensed one copy of this document for personal use only. Any other reproduction or redistribution is strictly prohibited. All rights reserved.

30. After a hurricane struck a Pacific island, donations began flooding into a disaster relief organization. The organization provided the opportunity for donors to specify where they wanted the money to be used, and the organization provided four options. When the organization tallied the funds received, they allotted each to the designated need. Reviewing the chart above, what percentage of the funds was donated to support construction costs?

    a. 49%
    b. 23%
    c. 18%
    d. 10%

31. Margery is planning a vacation, and she has added up the cost. Her round-trip airfare will cost $572. Her hotel cost is $89 per night, and she will be staying at the hotel for five nights. She has allotted a total of $150 for sightseeing during her trip, and she expects to spend about $250 on meals. As she books the hotel, she is told that she will receive a discount of 10% per night off the price of $89 after the first night she stays there. Taking this discount into consideration, what is the amount that Margery expects to spend on her vacation?

    a. $1328.35
    b. $1373.50
    c. $1381.40
    d. $1417.60

32. $\dfrac{7}{3}, \dfrac{9}{2}, \dfrac{10}{9}, \dfrac{7}{8}$

Arrange the numbers above from least to greatest. Which of the following is correct?

    a. $\dfrac{10}{9}, \dfrac{7}{3}, \dfrac{9}{2}, \dfrac{7}{8}$
    b. $\dfrac{9}{2}, \dfrac{7}{3}, \dfrac{10}{9}, \dfrac{7}{8}$
    c. $\dfrac{7}{3}, \dfrac{9}{2}, \dfrac{10}{9}, \dfrac{7}{8}$
    d. $\dfrac{7}{8}, \dfrac{10}{9}, \dfrac{7}{3}, \dfrac{9}{2}$

33. Which of the following is the closest approximation of $\sqrt{30}$?

    a. 5.8
    b. 5.6
    c. 5.5
    d. 5.3

34. $7 + 4^2 - (5 + 6 \times 3) - 10 \times 2$

Simplify the expression above. Which of the following is correct?

    a. -23
    b. -20
    c. 23
    d. 20

Copyright © Mometrix Media. You have been licensed one copy of this document for personal use only. Any other reproduction or redistribution is strictly prohibited. All rights reserved.

Section 3. Science

1. The first four steps of the scientific method are as follows:

       I. Identify the problem
       II. Ask questions
       III. Develop a hypothesis
       IV. Collect data and experiment on that data

Which of the following is the next step in the scientific method?
    a. Observe the data
    b. Analyze the results
    c. Measure the data
    d. Develop a conclusion

2. Which of the following best explains the relationship between science and mathematics?
    a. Mathematics offers different levels that science can use, such as geometry and trigonometry.
    b. Science provides the instruments that mathematicians need to complete calculations.
    c. Both help to improve the technology that is required for people to conduct their lives.
    d. Mathematics provides quantitative results that scientists can apply to theories.

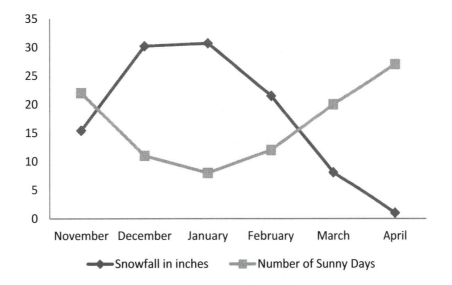

3. The chart above shows the average snowfall in inches for a town on Michigan's Upper Peninsula, during the months November through April. Which of the following can be concluded based on the information that is provided in the chart?
    a. April is not a good month to go skiing in the Upper Peninsula.
    b. Snowfall blocks the sunshine and reduces the number of sunny days.
    c. The fewest sunny days occur in the months with the heaviest snowfall.
    d. There is no connection between the amount of snowfall and the number of sunny days.

Copyright © Mometrix Media. You have been licensed one copy of this document for personal use only. Any other reproduction or redistribution is strictly prohibited. All rights reserved.

4. Reading long books gives Benezet a headache.

War and Peace is a long book.

Reading War and Peace will give Benezet a headache.

Which of the following correctly describes the conclusion that results from the three statements above?

  a. Inductive
  b. Irrational
  c. Relativistic
  d. Deductive

5. Every time Adelaide visits Ireland, it rains in Dublin. So far, Adelaide has visited Ireland seventeen times in the last three years, and she will visit Ireland again next week.

Which of the following is an *inductive* conclusion to the statements above?

  a. Adelaide should avoid Dublin during her visit.
  b. Adelaide should expect rain in Dublin next week.
  c. Adelaide's visits coincide with the rainy season in Ireland.
  d. Adelaide should put off her trip for a week to avoid the rain.

6. The two criteria for classifying epithelial tissue are *cell layers* and _____.

Which of the following completes the sentence above?

  a. Cell composition
  b. Cell absorption
  c. Cell shape
  d. Cell stratification

7. Which of the following types of connective tissue does *not* have its own (and thus limited) blood supply?

  a. Ligaments
  b. Adipose
  c. Bone
  d. Areolar

8. How many organ systems are in the human body?

  a. 12
  b. 15
  c. 9
  d. 11

9. Which element within the respiratory system is responsible for removing foreign matter from the lungs?

  a. Bronchial tubes
  b. Cilia
  c. Trachea
  d. Alveoli

Copyright © Mometrix Media. You have been licensed one copy of this document for personal use only. Any other reproduction or redistribution is strictly prohibited. All rights reserved.

10. Organized from high to low, the hierarchy of the human body's structure is as follows: organism, organ systems, organs, tissues. Which of the following comes next?

    a. Molecules
    b. Atoms
    c. Cells
    d. Muscle

Periodic Table

1 IA																	18 VIIIA
1 **H** 1.01	2 IIA											13 IIIA	14 IVA	15 VA	16 VIA	17 VIIA	2 **He** 4.00
3 **Li** 6.94	4 **Be** 9.01											5 **B** 10.81	6 **C** 12.01	7 **N** 14.01	8 **O** 16.00	9 **F** 19.00	10 **Ne** 20.18
11 **Na** 22.99	12 **Mg** 24.31	3 IIIB	4 IVB	5 VB	6 VIB	7 VIIB	8	9 VIIIB	10	11 IB	12 IIB	13 **Al** 26.98	14 **Si** 28.09	15 **P** 30.97	16 **S** 32.07	17 **Cl** 35.45	18 **Ar** 39.95
19 **K** 39.1	20 **Ca** 40.08	21 **Sc** 44.96	22 **Ti** 47.88	23 **V** 50.94	24 **Cr** 52.00	25 **Mn** 54.94	26 **Fe** 55.85	27 **Co** 58.93	28 **Ni** 58.69	29 **Cu** 63.55	30 **Zn** 65.39	31 **Ga** 69.72	32 **Ge** 72.61	33 **As** 74.92	34 **Se** 78.96	35 **Br** 79.90	36 **Kr** 83.80
37 **Rb** 85.47	38 **Sr** 87.62	39 **Y** 88.91	40 **Zr** 91.22	41 **Nb** 92.91	42 **Mo** 95.94	43 **Tc** (98)	44 **Ru** 101.07	45 **Rh** 102.91	46 **Pd** 106.42	47 **Ag** 107.87	48 **Cd** 112.41	49 **In** 114.82	50 **Sn** 118.71	51 **Sb** 121.76	52 **Te** 127.6	53 **I** 126.9	54 **Xe** 131.29
55 **Cs** 132.9	56 **Ba** 137.3	57 **La*** 138.9	72 **Hf** 178.5	73 **Ta** 180.9	74 **W** 183.9	75 **Re** 186.2	76 **Os** 190.2	77 **Ir** 192.2	78 **Pt** 195.1	79 **Au** 197.0	80 **Hg** 200.6	81 **Tl** 204.4	82 **Pb** 207.2	83 **Bi** 209	84 **Po** (209)	85 **At** (210)	86 **Rn** (222)
87 **Fr** (223)	88 **Ra** (226)	89 **Ac^** (227)	104 **Rf** (261)	105 **Db** (262)	106 **Sg** (263)	107 **Bh** (264)	108 **Hs** (265)	109 **Mt** (268)	110 **Ds** (271)	111 **Rg** (272)							

*	58 **Ce** 140.1	59 **Pr** 140.9	60 **Nd** 144.2	61 **Pm** (145)	62 **Sm** 150.4	63 **Eu** 152.0	64 **Gd** 157.3	65 **Tb** 158.9	66 **Dy** 162.5	67 **Ho** 164.9	68 **Er** 167.3	69 **Tm** 168.9	70 **Yb** 173.0	71 **Lu** 175.0
^	90 **Th** 232.0	91 **Pa** (231)	92 **U** 238.0	93 **Np** (237)	94 **Pu** (244)	95 **Am** (243)	96 **Cm** (247)	97 **Bk** (247)	98 **Cf** (251)	99 **Es** (252)	100 **Fm** (257)	101 **Md** (258)	102 **No** (259)	103 **Lr** (260)

*Note: The row labeled with * is the Lanthanide Series, and the row labeled with ^ is the Actinide Series.*

The next six questions are based on the above chart.

11. On average, how many neutrons does one atom of bromine (Br) have?

    a. 35
    b. 44.90
    c. 45
    d. 79.90

12. On average, how many protons does one atom of zinc (Zn) have?

    a. 30
    b. 35
    c. 35.39
    d. 65.39

Copyright © Mometrix Media. You have been licensed one copy of this document for personal use only. Any other reproduction or redistribution is strictly prohibited. All rights reserved.

13. Which of the following has the highest ionization energy?

    a. Vanadium (V)
    b. Germanium (Ge)
    c. Potassium (K)
    d. Chromium (Cr)

14. Which of the following has the highest electronegativity?

    a. Gallium (Ga)
    b. Thallium (Tl)
    c. Boron (B)
    d. Aluminum (Al)

15. Which of the following would be least likely to chemically bond?

    a. Nitrogen (N)
    b. Sodium (Na)
    c. Calcium (Ca)
    d. Argon (Ar)

16. At 25 °C, there are two elements that exist as liquids: mercury and _____.

    a. Bromine (Br)
    b. Helium (He)
    c. Silicon (Si)
    d. Barium (Ba)

17. Which of the following describes one responsibility of the integumentary system?

    a. Distributing vital substances (such as nutrients) throughout the body
    b. Blocking pathogens that cause disease
    c. Sending leaked fluids from cardiovascular system back to the blood vessels
    d. Storing bodily hormones that influence gender traits

18. When are the *parasympathetic nerves* active within the nervous system?

    a. When an individual experiences a strong emotion, such as fear or excitement
    b. When an individual feels pain or heat
    c. When an individual is either talking or walking
    d. When an individual is either resting or eating

19. Which of the following best describes the relationship between the circulatory system and the integumentary system?

    a. Removal of excess heat from body
    b. Hormonal influence on blood pressure
    c. Regulation of blood's pressure and volume
    d. Development of blood cells within marrow

20. Once blood has been oxygenated, it travels through the pulmonary veins, through the left atrium, and then through the _____ before entering the left ventricle.

    a. Tricuspid valve
    b. Mitral valve
    c. Pulmonary arteries
    d. Aorta

Copyright © Mometrix Media. You have been licensed one copy of this document for personal use only. Any other reproduction or redistribution is strictly prohibited. All rights reserved.

21. *Fungi* are a part of which of the following domains?

    a. Archaea
    b. Archaebacteria
    c. Eubacteria
    d. Eukarya

22. Which of the following are the protein "messengers" that damaged cells release within the immune system to signal the need for repair?

    a. Cytokines
    b. Perforins
    c. Leukocytes
    d. Interferons

23. The _____ of plant cells are larger than those of eukaryotic cells, because they contain water.

    a. Microtubules
    b. Vacuoles
    c. Flagella
    d. Nuclei

24. The three phases of interphase during mitosis are the following: G_1, G_2, and ____.

    a. V
    b. A
    c. S
    d. R

25. Which of the following is the number of possible *codons* within the code for genetic information?

    a. 16
    b. 32
    c. 64
    d. 128

26. Which of the following can cause mutations in human cells?

    a. Ultraviolet light
    b. Phosphate
    c. Proteins
    d. Nucleotides

27. Fill in the blanks below to complete the equation for photosynthesis:

CO_2 + _____ + Sunlight $\rightarrow$ _____ + Oxygen

    a. Glucose, Water
    b. Water, Chlorophyll
    c. Water, Glucose
    d. Chlorophyll, Glucose

Copyright © Mometrix Media. You have been licensed one copy of this document for personal use only. Any other reproduction or redistribution is strictly prohibited. All rights reserved.

28. Which of the following describes the purpose of a vaccine?

    a. Repairing damaged tissues that result from virus and/or cancer
    b. Signaling to the body the presence of a disease-causing pathogen
    c. Identifying the disease-causing pathogens that need to be destroyed
    d. Stimulating an infection to allow the body to produce its own antibodies

29. Which of the following cannot exist in RNA?

    a. Uracil
    b. Thymine
    c. Cytosine
    d. Guanine

30. Taking into account the answer to the question above, which of the following exists in RNA, in place of the substance above?

    a. Thymine
    b. Adenine
    c. Uracil
    d. Cytosine

31. The following four countries are listed in the order of their industrial development, from the greatest to the least amount of industrial development: Japan, Canada, Russia, and Namibia. Which of these countries can be expected to have the highest fertility rates?

    a. Namibia
    b. Canada
    c. Japan
    d. Russia

32. The development of characteristics that allow individuals within a species to survive and reproduce more effectively than others.

Which of the following terms best describes the theory that is defined above?

    a. Mutation
    b. Adaptation
    c. Allele combination
    d. Natural selection

33. In the development of genetic traits, one gene must match to one _____ for the traits to develop correctly.

    a. Codon
    b. Protein
    c. Amino acid
    d. Chromosome

34. Which of the following statements is true about genetic mutations?

    a. Most mutations result from disease.
    b. Mutations are never hereditary.
    c. Mutations due to harmful chemicals are rare.
    d. Most mutations are spontaneous.

Copyright © Mometrix Media. You have been licensed one copy of this document for personal use only. Any other reproduction or redistribution is strictly prohibited. All rights reserved.

35. Positively charged _____ are found *within* the nucleus of an atom, and negatively charged _____ are found *around* the nucleus.

    a. Protons, neutrons
    b. Electrons, neutrons
    c. Protons, electrons
    d. Electrons, protons

36. Which of the following best describes the careful ordering of molecules within solids that have a fixed shape?

    a. Physical bonding
    b. Polar molecules
    c. Metalloid structure
    d. Crystalline order

37. A *weak* bond in DNA often includes a(n) _____ atom.

    a. Oxygen
    b. Nitrogen
    c. Thymine
    d. Hydrogen

38. Which of the following describes the transport network that is responsible for the transference of proteins throughout a cell?

    a. Golgi apparatus
    b. Endoplasmic reticulum
    c. Mitochondria
    d. Nucleolus

39. During the *anaphase* of mitosis, the _____, originally in pairs, separate from their daughters and move to the opposite ends (or poles) of the cell.

    a. Chromosomes
    b. Spindle fibers
    c. Centrioles
    d. Nuclear membranes

40. Which of the following is the *shortest* wavelength in the spectrum of electromagnetic waves?

    a. X-ray
    b. Visible
    c. Gamma
    d. Radio

41. The genetic code for DNA is composed of sequences of cytosine, thymine, guanine, and which of the following?

    a. Bromine
    b. Uracil
    c. Nitrogen
    d. Adenine

Copyright © Mometrix Media. You have been licensed one copy of this document for personal use only. Any other reproduction or redistribution is strictly prohibited. All rights reserved.

42. Which of the following offers the best definition of the *Law of Conservation of Energy*?

    a. Energy stores itself for future displacement and in the process preserves itself.
    b. Energy is displaced in motion and replaced in storage.
    c. Energy is never lost but is transferred from one form to another.
    d. Energy causes items in movement to remain thus unless stopped by another force.

43. A(n) _____ is the physical and visible expression of a genetic trait.

    a. Phenotype
    b. Allele
    c. Gamete
    d. Genotype

44. How many protons would a negatively charted isotope of N-12 have?

    a. 5
    b. 7
    c. 10
    d. 12

45. One or more _____ form during a reaction that results in atoms with unbalanced charges.

    a. Protons
    b. Neutrons
    c. Ions
    d. Electrons

46. A substance is considered *acidic* if it has a pH of less than which of the following?

    a. 12
    b. 9
    c. 7
    d. 4

47. Mutations occur as the result of mutagen-induced changes *or* which of the following?

    a. Duplication of a complete genome
    b. Errors during DNA replication
    c. Excision repair inspections of DNA
    d. Presence of germ cells within DNA

48. Which of the following describes the unit that is used to measure the distance between Earth and stars?

    a. Light-years
    b. Parsecs
    c. Nanometers
    d. Angstroms

49. Which of the following would be an example of potential energy?

    a. A ballet dancer performing stretches
    b A secretary typing at the computer
    c. A ball being thrown from one person to another
    d. A rubber band stretched to its fullest

Copyright © Mometrix Media. You have been licensed one copy of this document for personal use only. Any other reproduction or redistribution is strictly prohibited. All rights reserved.

50. Which of the following best describes one of the roles of RNA?

   a. Manufacturing the proteins needed for DNA
   b. Creating the bonds between the elements that compose DNA
   c. Sending messages about the correct sequence of proteins in DNA
   d. Forming the identifiable "*double helix*" shape of DNA

51. Which of the following do *catalysts* alter to control the rate of a chemical reaction?

   a. Substrate energy
   b. Activation energy
   c. Inhibitor energy
   d. Promoter energy

52. A metallic ion is considered a(n) _____, while a nonmetallic ion is considered a(n) _____.

   a. Metalloid, anion
   b. Anion, cation
   c. Covalent, cation
   d. Cation, anion

53. An unsaturated hydrocarbon with a double bond is considered a(n) _____, while an unsaturated hydrocarbon with a triple bond is considered a(n) _____.

   a. Alkane, alkyne
   b. Alkyne, alkene
   c. Alkene, alkane
   d. Alkene, alkyne

54. The Punnett square shown here indicates a cross between two parents, one with alleles BB and the other with alleles Bb. Select the correct entry for the upper right box in the Punnett square, which is indicated with the letter, *x*:

	B	B
B		x
b		

   a. Bb
   b. bB
   c. BB
   d. bb

- 178 -

Copyright © Mometrix Media. You have been licensed one copy of this document for personal use only. Any other reproduction or redistribution is strictly prohibited. All rights reserved.

Section 4. English and Language Usage

1. Which of the following nouns represents the correct plural form of the word *syllabus*?

    a. Syllabus
    b. Syllaba
    c. Syllabi
    d. Syllabis

2. The Welsh kingdom of Gwynedd existed as an independent state from the early 5th century, when the Romans left Britain, until the late 13th century, when the king of England took control of Wales.

Which of the following functions as an adjective in the sentence above?

    a. Independent
    b. Century
    c. Government
    d. Control

3. Hawaii's Big Island, the largest of the eight primary Hawaiian islands, _____ also the youngest of the islands. Which of the following is the correct verb for the subject of the sentence above?

    a. Are
    b. Is
    c. Was
    d. Were

4. Which of the following sentences shows the correct use of quotation marks?

    a. Grady asked Abe, 'Did you know that an earthquake and a tsunami hit Messina, Italy, in 1908?'
    b. Grady asked Abe, "Did you know that an earthquake and a tsunami hit Messina, Italy, in 1908"?
    c. Grady asked Abe, "Did you know that an earthquake and a tsunami hit Messina, Italy, in 1908?"
    d. Grady asked Abe, " 'Did you know that an earthquake and a tsunami hit Messina, Italy, in 1908'?"

5. Cody's dog lost _____ collar, so _____ mom made him rake the leaves to earn the money for a new one. Which of the following sets of words correctly fill in the blanks in the sentence above?

    a. Its; his
    b. It's; his
    c. His; its
    d. His; it's

6. Donald considered the job offer carefully, but he ultimately decided that the low salary was not _____ given his previous experience. Which of the following is the correct completion of the sentence above?

    a. exceptible
    b. acceptible
    c. acepptable
    d. acceptable

Copyright © Mometrix Media. You have been licensed one copy of this document for personal use only. Any other reproduction or redistribution is strictly prohibited. All rights reserved.

7. I'm usually good about keeping track of my keys. I lost them. I spent hours looking for them. I found them in the freezer.

Which of the following options best combines the sentences above to show style and clarity?

    a. I lost my keys, even though I'm usually good about keeping track of them. I found them in the freezer and spent hours looking for them.
    b. I spent hours looking for my keys and found them in the freezer. I had lost them, even though I'm usually good about keeping track of them.
    c. I'm usually good about keeping track of my keys, but I lost them. After spending hours looking for them, I found them in the freezer.
    d. I'm usually good about keeping track of my keys, but I lost them in the freezer. I had to spend hours looking for them.

8. It was expected by the administration of Maplewood High School that classes would be canceled because of snow. Which of the following best rewrites the sentences above so that the verbs are active instead of passive?

    a. The administration of Maplewood High School expected to cancel classes because of snow.
    b. The snow caused the administration of Maplewood High School to expect that they would have to cancel classes.
    c. It was expected among the administration of Maplewood High School that the snow would cancel classes.
    d. It was the expectation of the Maplewood High School administration that the snow would cause classes to be canceled.

9. After living in Oak Ridge Missouri all her life, Cornelia was excited about her trip to Prague.

Which of the following best shows the correct punctuation of the city and the state within the sentence above?

    a. After living in Oak Ridge, Missouri, all her life, Cornelia was excited about her trip to Prague.
    b. After living in Oak Ridge, Missouri all her life, Cornelia was excited about her trip to Prague.
    c. After living in Oak, Ridge, Missouri all her life, Cornelia was excited about her trip to Prague.
    d. After living in Oak Ridge Missouri all her life, Cornelia was excited about her trip to Prague.

10. Since each member had a different opinion on the issue, the council decided to rest until _____ could discuss the matter further at a later time. Which of the following pronoun(s) best complete(s) the sentence above?

    a. it
    b. he and she
    c. they
    d. each

11. The following words all end in the same suffix, -ism: polytheism, communism, nationalism. This suffix can apply a variety of meanings to words and suggest a range of possibilities, including a doctrine, a condition, a characteristic, or a state of being. Considering the meaning of these three words, how does the suffix -ism apply to all of them?

    a. Doctrine
    b. Condition
    c. Characteristic
    d. State of being

Copyright © Mometrix Media. You have been licensed one copy of this document for personal use only. Any other reproduction or redistribution is strictly prohibited. All rights reserved.

12. Which of the following sentences correctly uses quotes within quotes?

   a. Pastor Bernard read from the book of Genesis: 'And God said, "Let there be light." And there was light.'
   b. Pastor Bernard read from the book of Genesis: "And God said, 'Let there be light.' And there was light."
   c. Pastor Bernard read from the book of Genesis: " 'And God said, Let there be light. And there was light.' "
   d. Pastor Bernard read from the book of Genesis: "And God said, "Let there be light." And there was light."

13. Which of the following is an example of a correctly punctuated sentence?

   a. Beatrice is very intelligent, she just does not apply herself well enough in her classes to make good grades.
   b. Beatrice is very intelligent: she just does not apply herself well enough in her classes to make good grades.
   c. Beatrice is very intelligent she just does not apply herself well enough in her classes to make good grades
   d. Beatrice is very intelligent; she just does not apply herself well enough in her classes to make good grades.

14. Lynton was ready to make a commitment to buying a new car, but he was still unsure about which model would suit him best. Which of the following best removes the nominalization from the sentence above?

   a. Lynton was ready to make a commitment to a new car, but he was still unsure about which model would suit him best.
   b. Lynton was ready to make a commitment to buying a new car, but he was still unsure about the model that would suit him best.
   c. Lynton was ready to commit to buying a new car, but he was still unsure about which model would suit him best.
   d. Lynton was ready to make a commitment to buying a new car, but he was still unsure about which model was best.

15. Which of the following is a compound sentence?

   a. Tabitha and Simon started the day at the zoo and then went to the art museum for the rest of the afternoon.
   b. Tabitha and Simon started the day at the zoo, and then they went to the art museum for the rest of the afternoon.
   c. After starting the day at the zoo, Tabitha and Simon then went to the art museum for the rest of the afternoon.
   d. Tabitha and Simon had a busy day, because they started at the zoo, and then they went to the art museum for the rest of the afternoon.

16. Which of the following follows the rules of capitalization?

   a. Dashiell visited his Cousin Elaine on Tuesday.
   b. Juniper sent a card to Uncle Archibald who has been unwell.
   c. Flicka and her Mother spent the day setting up the rummage sale.
   d. Lowell and his twin Sister look alike but have very different personalities.

- 181 -

Copyright © Mometrix Media. You have been licensed one copy of this document for personal use only. Any other reproduction or redistribution is strictly prohibited. All rights reserved.

17. Historians tend to count Bede as the Father of English History, because he compiled extensive historical details about early England and wrote the Ecclesiastical History of the English People.

Which of the following words does *not* function as a verb in the sentence above?

  a. tend
  b. count
  c. compiled
  d. wrote

18. We cannot allow the budget cuts to _____ the plans to improve education; the futures of _____ children are at stake. Which of the following sets of words correctly fill in the blanks in the sentence above?

  a. effect; your
  b. affect; you're
  c. effect; you're
  d. affect; your

19. The experience of being the survivor of a plane crash left an indelible impression on Johanna, and she suffered from nightmares for years afterwards.

Which of the following best explains the meaning of *indelible* in the sentence above?

  a. candid
  b. permanent
  c. inexpressible
  d. indirect

20. Which of the following sentences contains an incorrect use of capitalization?

  a. For Christmas, we are driving to the South to visit my grandmother in Mississippi.
  b. Last year, we went to East Texas to go camping in Piney Woods.
  c. Next month, we will visit my Aunt Darla who lives just East of us.
  d. When my sister-in-law Susan has her baby, I will take the train north to see her.

21. Which of the following nouns is in the correct plural form?

  a. phenomena
  b. mother-in-laws
  c. deers
  d. rooves

22. Which of the following sentences is grammatically correct?

  a. Krista was not sure who to hold responsible for the broken window.
  b. Krista was not sure whom was responsible for the broken window.
  c. Krista was not sure whom to hold responsible for the broken window.
  d. Krista was not sure on who she should place responsibility for the broken window.

Copyright © Mometrix Media. You have been licensed one copy of this document for personal use only. Any other reproduction or redistribution is strictly prohibited. All rights reserved.

23. Irish politician Constance Markiewicz was the first woman elected to the British House of Commons, but she never served in that capacity due to her activity in forming the Irish Republic.

The word *capacity* functions as which of the following parts of speech in the sentence above?
    a. Verb
    b. Noun
    c. Adverb
    d. Pronoun

24. Which of the following sentences represents the best style and clarity of expression?
    a. Without adequate preparation, the test was likely to be a failure for Zara.
    b. The test was likely to be a failure for Zara without adequate preparation.
    c. Without adequate preparation, Zara expected to fail the test.
    d. Zara expected to fail the test without adequate preparation.

25. Valerie refused to buy the television, because she claimed that the price was exorbitant and _____. Which of the following phrases best completes the meaning of the sentence in the context of the word exorbitant?
    a. the quality too low for the cost
    b. within the expected price range of similar televisions
    c. much better than she had expected it to be
    d. far exceeding the cost of similar televisions

26. Which of the following sentences contains a correct example of subject-verb agreement?
    a. All of the board members are in agreement on the issue.
    b. Each of the students were concerned about the test scores for the final exam.
    c. Neither of the children are at home right now.
    d. Any of the brownie recipes are perfect for the bake sale.

27. Clemence and I went to the library together, and then _____ stopped to get some coffee.

Which of the following phrases correctly fills in the blanks in the sentence above?
    a. her and I
    b. her and me
    c. she and I
    d. me and her

28. *Burton sent the Christmas card to ____ and ____.* Which of the following sets of words correctly fills in the blanks in the sentence above?
    a. her; me
    b. she; me
    c. her; I
    d. she; I

29. Which of the following is a simple sentence?
    a. Phillippa walked the dog, and Primula gave the dog a bath.
    b. Phillippa walked and bathed the dog, and Primula helped.
    c. Phillippa walked the dog, while Primula gave the dog a bath.
    d. Phillippa and Primula walked the dog and gave the dog a bath.

Copyright © Mometrix Media. You have been licensed one copy of this document for personal use only. Any other reproduction or redistribution is strictly prohibited. All rights reserved.

30. After the natural disaster struck the county of Hillsborough in Florida, the president declared a state of emergency for that region and promised immediate aid. Which of the following words or phrases in the sentence above should be capitalized?

    a. county
    b. president
    c. state of emergency
    d. aid

31. After his first three-act drama received great critical acclaim, Erastus was on his way to becoming a respected and established _____ in the community. Which of the following correctly completes the sentence above?

    a. play wright
    b. play write
    c. playwright
    d. play-write

32. Which of the following sentences is most correct in terms of style, clarity, and punctuation?

    a. The possible side effects of the medication that the doctor had prescribed for her was a concern for Lucinda, and she continued to take the medication.
    b. The medication that the doctor prescribed had side effects concerning Lucinda who continued to take it.
    c. Lucinda was concerned about side effects from the medication that her doctor had prescribed, so she continued to take it.
    d. Although Lucinda was concerned about the possible side effects, she continued to take the medication that her doctor had prescribed for her.

33. *The jury reentered the courtroom after reaching ____ decision.* Which of the following correctly completes the sentence above?

    a. it's
    b. they're
    c. its
    d. their

34. Amber was quick to _____ Romy on the way that she had arranged the eclectic pieces of furniture to _____ one another.

Which of the following sets of words correctly fills in the blanks in the sentence above?

    a. compliment; complement
    b. compliment; compliment
    c. complement; compliment
    d. complement; complement

Copyright © Mometrix Media. You have been licensed one copy of this document for personal use only. Any other reproduction or redistribution is strictly prohibited. All rights reserved.

Answer Key and Explanations for Test #1

Reading Answer Explanations

1. C: To *assuage* is to lessen the effects of something, in this case Adelaide's guilt over eating the piece of cheesecake. The context of the sentence also suggests that she feels sorry for eating it and wants to compensate the following day.

2. A: If Hilaire's vocabulary needs a boost, he needs a thesaurus, which provides a range of synonyms (or antonyms) for words. A dictionary is useful for word meanings, but it will not necessarily assist Hilaire in improving the words he already has in his papers. A Latin dictionary makes little sense in this case, since Hilaire needs to find stronger words in English instead of studying word origins or applying a translation. The encyclopedia is also irrelevant, particularly since the professor already approves of Hilaire's work and is not asking him to research further.

3. A: To find information on Freud's psychological theories, Lise should go to class 100.

4. C: In this case, Lise needs to find a work of literature instead of a work of psychology, so she should consult the 800s.

5. B: To study Jewish traditions further, Lise should consult the 200s, which is devoted to books on religion.

6. D: The first century includes the years leading up to 100 AD. That means that all first century emperors will have reigns before 100 AD. Hadrian's reign began in 117 AD, so he belongs in the second century instead of the first.

7. A: The sentence indicates a contrast between the appearance and the reality. Enzo's friends believe him to be wealthy, due to the large home that he inherited, but he is actually penniless.

8. B: The word SORT results from following all of the directions that are provided.

9. B: The enrollment in 2001 falls directly between 2000 and 2500, so 2300 is accurate. Note that the enrollment for 2000 falls much closer to 2000, so 2100 is a best estimate for that year.

10. C: The tuition appears to rise alongside the enrollment, until the year 2009 when it jumps significantly. Since the enrollment between 2008 and 2009 does not justify the immediate jump in income for the school, an increase in tuition costs makes sense.

11. C: The word "sic" is Latin for "as such" or "so." It is used to indicate an error on the part of the original author and is used most often when writers are quoting someone else. If the journalist includes the letter as written by the defendant, this is a natural way to show that the misspelling of "guilty" is the responsibility of the defendant and not a typographical error on the part of the journalist.

12. C: The passage is *expository* in the sense that it looks more closely into the mysteries of the Bermuda Triangle and *exposes* information about what researchers have studied and now believe.

13. D: This sentence is the best summary statement for the entire passage, because it wraps up clearly what the author is saying about the results of studies on the Bermuda Triangle.

Copyright © Mometrix Media. You have been licensed one copy of this document for personal use only. Any other reproduction or redistribution is strictly prohibited. All rights reserved.

14. A: Of all the sentences provided, this is the one with which the author would most likely agree. The passage suggests that most of the "mysteries" of the Bermuda Triangle can be explained in a reasonable way. The passage mentions that some expand the Triangle to the Azores, but this is a point of fact, and the author makes no mention of whether or not this is in error. The author quotes the Navy's response to the disappearance of the planes, but there is no reason to believe the author questions this response. The author raises questions about the many myths surrounding the Triangle, but at no point does the author connect these myths with what are described as accidents that fall "within the expected margin of error."

15. C: The inclusion of the statement about the ships from East Asia is an opinion statement, as the author provides no support or explanation. The other statements within the answer choices offer supporting evidence and explanatory material, making them acceptable for an expository composition.

16. A: In this case, the italics suggest a conversation or a dialogue that is occurring between Judith and Martin. While quotation marks are standard for dialogue, the use of italics here is consistent in representing the conversation effectively.

17. B: Only the word *introspection* can fall between *intrauterine* and *invest*. The words *intransigent* and *intone* come before, and the word *investiture* follows.

18. D: The context of the sentence suggests a positive response from the public, so the word *glorify* makes sense as a definition here. There is nothing about the public's response that suggests they criticize or betray him, and the actor's management working to keep information about him private would indicate that the public is not given the opportunity to sympathize with him.

19. D: The spaghetti and the garlic bread are definitely concerns for Ninette if she is unable to consume products with wheat in them. With all other meals, there appear to be gluten-free options that she can eat.

20. C: A discussion of Shakespeare's dramatic works has no place in a chapter that describes his life before he was famous. All other options make sense in a chapter about his formative years and his experiences prior to moving to London and achieving fame.

21. A: The indented portion of the passage indicates that the writer of the letter to the editor is quoting another source (identified as an article by Dr. James Duncan). For long quotes (longer than three lines), it is standard to indent. Shorter quotes (those shorter than three lines) are typically placed in quotation marks and included within the main text of the paragraph.

22. B: The context of the passage suggests that the defense attorney successfully *cleared* his client. To *dismiss* his client would make little sense here. To *condemn* his client would go against his job description, and to *forgive* is not his role.

23. B: This question and the two that follow require simple multiplication and addition. Since the quantities needed are the same for both texts, one need only find the supplier with the lowest combined price (per 100) for the two texts. Textbook Central's combined price for 100 each of the two texts is $9,550. The closest competitor is University Textbook with a combined price of $9,600. The other two suppliers come in at $9,650 and $9,675. The total for the transaction with Textbook Central is $47,750.

24. B: Once again, Textbook Central prevails. In this case, it is not even necessary to do the calculations. The cost for composition textbooks is $4350 (per 100) and for linguistics textbooks is

Copyright © Mometrix Media. You have been licensed one copy of this document for personal use only. Any other reproduction or redistribution is strictly prohibited. All rights reserved.

$6550 (per 100). The lower cost for the composition textbooks–$150 less per 100 than the closest company in cost–outweighs the slight difference in cost for the linguistics textbooks.

25. C: Bookstore Supply has the lowest cost of the four for the technical writing textbooks, and it has a comparable cost to University Textbook for the world literature textbooks. The slight difference for the technical writing textbooks will make the overall cost lower than University Textbook's and give Bookstore Supply the competitive edge in cost.

26. D: The key words in question 26 are *nautical* and *docked.* This indicates some type of sailing vessel, which is provided in answer choice D.

27. C: It does not require extensive knowledge of geography to know that Oslo, Norway is nowhere near the Mediterranean Sea. Clearly, this city is out of place in the brochure.

28. B: A closer look at the list indicates that the cities are arranged alphabetically by the name of the city. This means that Galveston fits alphabetically between Fort Lauderdale and Miami.

29. D: Answer choice D is the only option that correctly follows the instructions in the question. Sections 4 and 5 are removed; section 1 is placed on the right sides along sections 3 and 2; and there is a circle drawn around the entire shape. Answer choice A places section 1 in the wrong location and fails to switch sections 2 and 5. Answer choice B incorrectly removes section 1 altogether. Answer choice C changes the shape of section 1 to a rectangle and reverses sections 2 and 3.

30. D: Anna is ultimately looking for a good all-around guidebook for the region. *The Top Ten Places to Visit in Brittany* might have some useful information, but it will not provide enough details about hiking trails, beaches, restaurants, and accommodations. *Getting to Know Nantes* limits the information to one city, and Anna's destination in Brittany is not identified. *Hiking Through Bretagne* limits the information to one activity. These three guidebooks might offer great supplemental information, but *The Complete Guide to Brittany* is the most likely to offer *all* of the information that Anna needs for her trip.

31. B: The passage offers details about a process, so it is descriptive in focus. Narrative passages tell a story. Persuasive passages attempt to persuade the reader to believe or agree with something. Expository passages *expose* an idea, theory, etc. and provide analysis. The passage provided simply tells the reader how to do something.

32. C: Everby Furnace is located under both Furnace Cleaning and Furnace Installation, so that is the best place for Edgar to start in looking for a company to do both tasks.

33. D: Only V&V Furnace Repair mentions 24-hour service and free estimates on the work. Thomas Refrigeration mentions "24-hour emergency service" specifically, but any company that offers 24-hour furnace repair service is offering it to assist clients with emergencies.

34. B: The passage does not state this outright, but the author indicates that the younger sons of King George III began considering the option of marrying and producing heirs *after* Princess Charlotte Augusta died. Since she was the heir-apparent, her death left the succession undetermined. The author mentions very little about any "wrongs" that Victoria's uncles committed, so this cannot be a logical conclusion. The passage says nothing about the Duke of Kent's preference for a male heir over a female. (In fact, it was likely that he was delighted to have any heir.) And the author does not provide enough detail about the relationship between the

Copyright © Mometrix Media. You have been licensed one copy of this document for personal use only. Any other reproduction or redistribution is strictly prohibited. All rights reserved.

Duchess of Kent and King William IV to infer logically that his suspicions were "unreasonable" or that the duchess cared only for her daughter's well-being.

35. C: The author actually notes in the last paragraph that Victoria was an "improbable princess who became queen" and the rest of the passage demonstrates how it was a series of small events that changed the course of British succession. The passage is largely factual, so it makes little sense as a persuasive argument. The author mentions the Victorian Era, but the passage is more about Queen Victoria's family background than it is about the era to which she gave her name. And the passage is more about how the events affected Victoria (and through her, England) than it is about the direct effect that George III's sons had on English history.

36. D: This passage is most likely to belong in some kind of biographical reference about Queen Victoria. A scholarly paper would include more analysis instead of just fact. The information in the passage does not fit the genre of mystery at all. And since the passage recounts history, it is not an obvious candidate for a fictional story.

37. D: All other sentences in the passage offer some support or explanation. Only the sentence in answer choice D indicates an unsupported opinion on the part of the author.

38. A: The passage indicates that it was believed the child died and that he was replaced by another child. Since it is unlikely a parent would willingly give up a child, even for such a purpose, the supposed substitution must have been an orphan. The act would have been illegal, but that does not make the child himself an outlaw (answer choice B). An unknowing infant can hardly be accused of being a charlatan (answer choice C), nor is there enough information in the passage to accuse the infant of being a delinquent (answer choice D). It is likely that, if such a fraud was perpetrated, the child was simply an orphan.

39. C: The author actually says, "Charles's own political troubles extended beyond religion in this case, and he was beheaded in 1649." This would indicate that religion was less involved in this situation than in other situations. There is not enough information to infer that Charles II never married; the passage only notes that he had no legitimate children. (In fact, he had more than ten illegitimate children by his mistresses.) And while the chance of a Catholic king frightened many in England, it is reaching beyond logical inference to assume that people were relieved when the royal children died. Finally, the author does not provide enough detail for the reader to assume that James I had *no* Catholic leanings. The author only says that James recognized the importance of committing to the Church of England.

40. A: The author notes, "In spite of a strong resemblance to the king, the young James was generally rejected among the English and the Lowland Scots, who referred to him as "the Pretender." This indicates that there *was* a resemblance, and this increases the likelihood that the child was, in fact, that of James and Mary Beatrice. Answer choice B is too much of an opinion statement that does not have enough support in the passage. The passage essentially refutes answer choice C by pointing out that James "the Pretender" was welcomed in the Highlands. And there is little in the passage to suggest that James was unable to raise an army and mount an attack.

41. D: The context of the passage would suggest that Catholicism is not necessarily absent in England and Scotland but that the Church of England is accepted as primary. The word *ostensibly* means *evidently* or *on the surface*, but this alone is not enough to suggest that many monarchs have secretly been Catholic. The passage offers no indication that Catholics remain unwelcome; and while persecution against Catholics is a historical fact, the passage offers no discussion about it. Additionally, there is not enough information in the passage to arrive at the conclusion that the

Copyright © Mometrix Media. You have been licensed one copy of this document for personal use only. Any other reproduction or redistribution is strictly prohibited. All rights reserved.

Highland clans were required to give up their Catholic faith. It is a possibility, but it cannot be concluded by the use of the word *ostensibly*.

42. B: The passage is composed in a chronological sequence with each king introduced in order of reign.

43. D: The passage is largely informative in focus, and the author provides extensive detail about this period in English and Scottish history. There is little in the passage to suggest persuasion, and the tone of the passage has no indication of a desire to entertain. Additionally, the passage is historical, so the author avoids expressing feelings and instead focuses on factual information (with the exception of the one opinion statement).

44. A: Technical passages focus on presenting specific information and have a tone of formality. Narrative writing focuses on telling a story, and the passage offers no indication of this. Persuasive writing attempts to persuade the reader to agree with a certain position; the instructor offers the students information but leaves the decision up to each student. Expository passages reveal analytical information to the reader. The instructor is more focused on providing the students with information than with offering the students analytical details. (The analysis, it appears, will be up to the students if they choose to complete an extra credit project.)

45. C: Answer choice C fits the tone of the passage best. The instructor is simply offering students the chance to make up the exam score (which is worth 70% of their grade) and thus avoid failing the course. The instructor does not berate students at any point, nor does the instructor admit that the exam was too difficult. Additionally, the instructor offers encouragement to the students should they choose to complete an extra credit project, but that is not the primary purpose of this email.

46. B: This question asks for the best summary of the instructor's motive. In the opening paragraph, the instructor notes that his original grading plan has to change to reflect the exam scores. Because they were low, he now wants to give students a chance to make up for their low scores. Answer choice B thus summarizes his motive effectively. The instructor introduces his email with the notes about the scores being posted, but, given the information that is provided in the message, this is not the sole motive for his writing. Answer choice A limits the motive to the details about the group project, and the instructor provides three options. Answer choice D overlooks the instructor's further note about how the grading policy sometimes has to bend to reflect circumstances.

47. C: The human resources manager is informing employees about the company's new policy regarding food items in the refrigerator and the consequences for breaking that policy. There is no overt persuasion in the passage–beyond the standard persuasion of telling people the rules and expecting them to follow those rules or face the consequences. (As a persuasive passage focuses on convincing someone to agree with or believe something, persuasion does not apply to this passage.) The memo has no tone of entertainment or the expression of feelings; it is simply informing employees of a new policy.

48. B: There is no mistake in the location of the parenthetical note. It directly follows the statement about possible termination for employees who take food items that do not belong to them. This indicates that the labeling will help the company recognize that employees are removing their own food items from the refrigerator. The human resources manager mentions the importance of respect or courtesy, but this is not the best explanation for the parenthetical note. There is no suggestion of termination for employees that do not label their food; the memo notes only that the company encourages labeling. The memo offers no suggestion that the company is interested in

Copyright © Mometrix Media. You have been licensed one copy of this document for personal use only. Any other reproduction or redistribution is strictly prohibited. All rights reserved.

labeling beyond employees being able to eat their own food. There is no reason to believe that the company is trying to ensure that employees actually eat a lunch.

Mathematics Answer Explanations

1. D: To derive a percentage from a decimal, multiply by 100: 0.0016(100) = 0.16%.

2. C: One kilometer is about 0.62 miles, so 45(0.62) is 27.9, or approximately 28 miles.

3. A: In Roman numerals, M is 1000, D is 500, C is 100, L is 50, X is 10, V is 5, and I is 1. For the year 1768, the Roman numeral MDCCLXVIII is correct – representing 1000 + 500 + 200 + 50 + 10 + 5 + 3. MMCXLVIII is 2148 (still yet to be achieved) MDCCCXLV is 1845, and MDCCXLIII is 1743.

4. D: To convert from Celsius to Fahrenheit, start by multiplying by 9 and then dividing by 5. Add 32 to the quotient, and the conversion is complete. For question 4:

$$18(9) = 162$$
$$162/5 = 32.4$$
$$32.4 + 32 = 64.4, \text{ or approximately } 64$$

5. C: To find the average of Pernell's scores, add them up and then divide by the number of scores (5 in this case). In other words,

$$81 + 92 + 87 + 89 + 94 = 443$$
$$443/5 = 88.6, \text{ or approximately } 89$$

6. B: To find the median, list the series of numbers from least to greatest. The middle number represents the median--in this case 81, 87, 89, 92, 94. The number 89 is in the middle, so it is the median.

7. D: The television is 30% off its original price of $472. 30% of 472 is 141.60, and 141.60 subtracted from 472 is 330.40. Thus, Gordon paid $330.40 for the television.

8. A: To simplify, proceed in the order of the operations: $\frac{2}{3} \div \frac{4}{15}$ is $\frac{2}{3} \times \frac{15}{4}$, or $\frac{30}{12}$, which simplifies to $\frac{5}{2}$. Next, multiply $\frac{5}{2}$ by $\frac{5}{8}$. The result is $\frac{25}{16}$, or $1\frac{9}{16}$.

9. B: Question 9 is a simple matter of multiplication. The product is 0.0427378.

10. D: Start by multiplying Murray's payment by 2, since he receives this twice a month: $2287. Subtract all of his expenses, including the $300 he plans to keep in his checking account. The amount of $492 is left over, and this is what Murray can plan to put in his savings account each month, as long as his expenses remain the same.

11. C: Multiplying the equation results in the following:

$$8x - 24 = 10x - 6$$

$$-18 = 2x$$

$$x = -\frac{18}{2}, or - 9$$

- 190 -

Copyright © Mometrix Media. You have been licensed one copy of this document for personal use only. Any other reproduction or redistribution is strictly prohibited. All rights reserved.

12. B: Adding up the number of church-goers in Ellsford results in about 1450 residents who attend a church in the town each week. There are approximately 400 people in Ellsford who attend a Catholic church each week. This number represents about 28% of the 1450 church-goers in the town.

13. C: Erma's sale discount will be applied to the less expensive sweater, so she will receive the $44 sweater for 25% off. This amounts to a discount of $11, so the cost of the sweater will be $33. Added to the cost of the $50 sweater, which is not discounted, Erma's total is $83.

14. D: The combined cost of the pamphlets (750 at $0.25 each) and the key chains (750 at $0.75 each) is $750. With the cost of the booth ($500), Erma will pay a total of $1250.

15. C: Turn both expressions into fractions, and then multiply the first by the reverse of the second:

$$\frac{14}{3} \div \frac{7}{6}$$

$$\frac{14}{3} \times \frac{6}{7}$$

The result is the whole number 4.

16. A: Start by adding the first two expressions, and then subtract 1.294 from the sum:

1.034 + 0.275 = 1.309

1.309 – 1.294

The result is 0.015.

17. D: Multiply in the required order, and then add: $(2x)(x) + (2x)(-6) + (4)(x) + (4)(-6)$. The result is $2x^2 - 8x - 24$.

18. B: Recall that in Roman numerals, M is 1000, D is 500, C is 100, L is 50, X is 10, V is 5, and I is 1. As a result, the year MCMXCIV is 1994. (Note that the I before the V indicates that the I is subtracted from V: 5 – 1, or 4. In the same way, the C before the M also indicates a subtraction, in this case 100 from 1000, or 900.)

19. A: To find the correct answer, simply multiply 56 by 2.2. The result is 123.2, or approximately 123. This is Stella's weight in pounds.

20. B: To find the correct answer, start by adding up what Zander makes for the four full days he works: $8.50 per hours for 32 hours (four full 8-hour days). The result is $272. Then, add up what Zander makes on Wednesday when he leaves at 3:30 but still takes his standard one-hour lunch break. By leaving at 3:30, Zander only works 6.5 hours that day. At $8.50 per hour, this is $55.25 for the day. Added to $272, the result is $327.25.

Copyright © Mometrix Media. You have been licensed one copy of this document for personal use only. Any other reproduction or redistribution is strictly prohibited. All rights reserved.

21. D: Absolute value is determined by the distance between a number and 0 when plotted on a number line. For instance, the absolute value of –5 is 5. To solve the equation in question 21 for x requires the following:

$$|2x - 7| = 3$$

$$2x - 7 = 3, or\ 2x - 7 = -3$$

$$2x - 7 = 3$$

$$2x = 10, so\ x = 5$$

$$\text{OR}$$

$$2x = 4, so\ x = 2$$

The two possible solutions for the absolute value of the equation are 5 and 2.

22. A: Begin by subtracting 1432 from 2219. The result is 787. Then, divide 787 by 1432 to find the percent of increase: 0.549, or 54.9%. Rounded up, this is approximately a 55% increase in births between 2000 and 2010.

23. C: Solve the equation in the order of operations: $\frac{1}{4} \times \frac{3}{5}$, or $\frac{3}{20}$. Follow this up with division, which requires a reversal of the fraction: $\frac{3}{20} \div \frac{9}{8}$, or $\frac{3}{20} \times \frac{8}{9}$, which equals $\frac{24}{180}$. The result simplifies to $\frac{2}{15}$.

24. C: Cora did *not* fall 7 out of 27 times. To find the solution, simply divide 7 by 27 to arrive at 0.259, or 25.9%. Rounded up, this is approximately 26%.

25. D: Justine's graph will be charting the amount of rainfall for each month. Line graph indicate change that occurs over a specified period of time, so this is the best type of graph for Justine to use.

26. B: Since the denominator is the same for both fractions, this is simple subtraction. Start by turning each expression into a fraction: $\frac{19}{6} - \frac{11}{6}$. The result is $\frac{8}{6}$, or $1\frac{2}{6} = 1\frac{1}{3}$.

27. A: The expression "Four more than a number, x" can be interpreted as $x + 4$. This is equal to "2 less than $\frac{1}{3}$ of another number, y," or $\frac{1}{3}y - 2$.

28. C: To solve the equation, start by separating each element:

$$\frac{2xy^2 + 16x^2y - 20xy + 8}{4xy}$$

$$\frac{2xy^2}{4xy}, \text{or } \frac{y}{2}$$

$$\frac{16x^2y}{4xy}, \text{or } 4x$$

$$-\frac{20xy}{4xy}, \text{or } -5$$

$$\frac{8}{4xy}, \text{or } \frac{2}{xy}$$

Copyright © Mometrix Media. You have been licensed one copy of this document for personal use only. Any other reproduction or redistribution is strictly prohibited. All rights reserved.

Combine: $\frac{y}{2} + 4x - 5 + \frac{2}{xy}$.

29. A: To solve, move the terms with x to the same side of the equation and the whole numbers to the other:

$$4x - 6 \geq 2x + 4$$

$$2x \geq 10$$

$$x \geq 5$$

You can test this answer by filling in a number greater than 5 to see if the inequality still holds. For instance with the number 7:

$$4(7) - 6 \geq 2(7) + 4$$

The number 22 (or $28 - 6$) is greater than (though obviously not equal to) 18 (or $14 + 4$), so the inequality works. The only time when the two sides are equal is when $x = 5$.

Note that answer choice B contains a number greater than 5 that also works to make the inequality correct (when the left side of the equation is greater than the right side). The number 8 works only for "greater than," however, and does not solve for "equal to," so answer choice B cannot be the correct answer.

30. B: Start by locating the section of the pie chart that represents construction. It looks close to a quarter of the pie chart, which means that it is probably 23%, but you can verify by adding up the numbers. The total amount of all donations is about \$1.3 million and the amount given for construction is \$0.3 million. $0.3/1.3 = 0.227 \approx 23\%$

31. C: Start by adding up the costs of the trip, excluding the hotel cost: \$572 + \$150 + \$250, or \$972. Then, calculate what Margery will spend on the hotel. The first of her five nights at the hotel will cost her \$89. For each of the other four nights, she will get a discount of 10% per night, or \$8.90. This discount of \$8.90 multiplied by the four nights is \$35.60. The total she would have spent on the five nights without the discount is \$445. With the discount, the amount goes down to \$409.40. Add this amount to the \$972 for a grand total of \$1381.40.

32. D: Turn the fractions into mixed numbers to see the amounts more clearly. The result is that $\frac{7}{8}$ is smaller than $\frac{10}{9}$, or $1\frac{1}{9}$, which is smaller than $\frac{7}{3}$, or $2\frac{1}{3}$, which is smaller than $\frac{9}{2}$, or $4\frac{1}{2}$.

33. C: The square root of 25 is 5, and the square root of 36 is 6. The correct answer to the square root of 30 will have to be close to the mid-point between 5 and 6. As a result, 5.5 is a good place to start testing, and it proves to be correct: $\sqrt{30} = 5.477$. This is approximately 5.5. (In exact terms, 5.5^2 is 30.25, but as this question only asks for the approximation, the answer of 5.5 is correct.) In comparison, 5.3^2 is 28.09; 5.6^2 is 31.36; 5.8^2 is 33.64. None of these is close enough to 30 to be correct.

34. B: Start by calculating the amount in parentheses, completing the multiplication first: $5 + 6 \times 3$, which is $5 + 18$ or 23. Then calculate the product at the end: 10×2, or 20. Calculate the expression 4^2, for a result of 16, and complete the equation:

$$7 + 16 - 23 - 20$$

Copyright © Mometrix Media. You have been licensed one copy of this document for personal use only. Any other reproduction or redistribution is strictly prohibited. All rights reserved.

$$23 - 23 - 20$$

$$0 - 20, or - 20$$

Science Answer Explanations

1. B: There are six steps in the scientific process, the fifth of which is "Analyze the results" (the results of the experiments that were conducted in step four). The results of step four must be analyzed before reaching the final step, "Develop a conclusion."

2. D: Science and mathematics work together with mathematics offering the quantitative results that scientists can use to apply to their theories and thus prove whether or not they are correct.

3. C: The chart shows two specific changes: snowfall levels from November to April and sunny days from November to April. Based on the chart alone, the only information that can be determined is that the fewest sunny days coincide with the months that have the heaviest snowfall. Anything further reaches beyond the immediate facts of the chart and moves into the territory of requiring other facts. As for answer choice D, it uses the word "relationship," which is not required in the question. The question only asks for what can be concluded.

4. D: Deductive reasoning moves from the general to the specific. In this case, the general statement is that Benezet gets a headache from reading long books. The syllogism moves from the general to the specific by noting that *War and Peace* is a long book, therefore Benezet will likely get a headache from reading it.

5. B: Inductive reasoning moves from the specific to the general. In this case, the specific statement is that there is rain in Dublin every time Adelaide visits Ireland. The syllogism in this case moves from the specific to the general by then noting that Adelaide has visited Ireland 17 times in the last 3 years and that she will visit again next week. This is significant, because it raises the likelihood of rain. There is no guarantee of course, but the question merely asks for the inductive conclusion. To conclude the syllogism inductively, the best answer choice notes that Adelaide should expect rain in Dublin next week. All other answer choices move beyond the immediate syllogism and infer other information. (For instance, the first statement does not note that Adelaide actually visits Dublin but rather that she visits Ireland. It can rain in Dublin without Adelaide being there.) It is also possible to infer that Adelaide visits Ireland during the rainy season, but that is not a part of the original statement and therefore not possible as an inductive conclusion to the syllogism.

6. C: *Cell layers* and *cell shape* are the criteria for classifying epithelial tissue.

7. A: Ligaments do not have their own blood supply. As a result, ligament injuries tend to take longer to heal because they have a limited blood supply.

8. D: There are 11 organ systems in the human body: circulatory, digestive, endocrine, integumentary, lymphatic, muscular, nervous, reproductive, respiratory, skeletal, and urinary.

9. B: The cilia are the tiny hairs in the respiratory system that are responsible for removing foreign matter from the lungs. The cilia are located within the bronchial tubes, but it is the cilia that have the responsibility for removing inappropriate materials before they enter the lungs.

10. C: Cells come after tissues and are followed by molecules and then atoms at the very bottom of the hierarchy. Muscles are types of tissues, so muscles do not have a separate place in the hierarchy but instead fall within the types of tissues.

Copyright © Mometrix Media. You have been licensed one copy of this document for personal use only. Any other reproduction or redistribution is strictly prohibited. All rights reserved.

11. B: To determine the average number of neutrons in one atom of an element, subtract the atomic mass from the atomic number. For Bromine (Br), subtract its atomic number (35) from its atomic mass (79.9) to acquire the average number of neutrons, 44.9.

12. A: The number of protons is the same as the element's atomic periodic number: in this case, 30 for Zinc (Zn).

13. B: Ionization energy increases across a period (or row), from left to right. In the period containing the four elements listed in question 13, germanium (Ge) is the furthest to the right and thus has the highest ionization energy, also known as ionization potential.

14. C: Electronegativity increases in a group (or column) as the atomic number decreases–or put another way, the lower the atomic number, then the higher the electronegativity. Among the four elements listed in question 14, Boron (B) has the lowest atomic number (5) and thus the highest electronegativity.

15. D: As one of the noble gases, argon (Ar) is neutral and thus has no electrons for chemical bonding. As a result, it as well as the other noble gases in the period can resist chemical bonding.

16. A: Mercury and bromine are the only elements that are recognized as liquids in their natural state.

17. B: The integumentary system includes skin, hair, and mucous membranes, all of which are responsible–in part, at least–for blocking disease-causing pathogens from entering the blood stream. The circulatory system distributes vital substances through the body. The lymphatic system sends leaked fluids from the cardiovascular system back to the blood vessels. The reproductive system stores bodily hormones that influence gender traits.

18. D: The *parasympathetic nerves* are active when an individual is either resting or eating. The sympathetic nerves are active when an individual experiences a strong emotion, such as fear or excitement. Feeling pain and heat fall under the responsibility of the sensory neurons. Talking and walking fall under the responsibility of the ganglia within the sensory-somatic nervous system.

19. A: The integumentary system (i.e., the skin, hair, mucous membranes, etc.) coordinates with the circulatory system to remove excess heat from the body. The superficial blood vessels (those nearest the surface of the skin) dilate to allow the heat to exit the body. The hormonal influence on blood pressure is the result of the relationship between the circulatory system and the endocrine system. The urinary system is responsible for assisting in the regulation of blood's pressure and volume. The skeletal system is responsible for assisting in the development of blood vessels within the marrow.

20. B: After the blood has gone through the left atrium, it enters the mitral valve before entering the left ventricle.

21. D: There are three domains: Archaea, Eukarya, and Eubacteria. *Fungi*, along with Plantae, Animalia, and Protista, falls within the Eukarya domain.

22. A: Cytokines signal to cells that damaged tissues need to be repaired. Perforins specifically target viruses and cancers. Leukocytes are the white blood cells that respond when tissues need to be repaired. Interferons help in the response to virus attacks by keeping the virus from replicating and spreading within the body.

Copyright © Mometrix Media. You have been licensed one copy of this document for personal use only. Any other reproduction or redistribution is strictly prohibited. All rights reserved.

23. B: The vacuoles function as a type of storage unit for cells. In plant cells, the vacuoles are larger than in eukaryotic cells due to the water content that they require for adequate cell pressure.

24. C: The S phase is the third phase of interphase during mitosis.

25. C: The code is composed of the substances within DNA: adenine (A), cytosine (C), guanine (G), and thymine (T). It is possible to make 64 codons from the combination of these letters.

26. A: Ultraviolet light can cause genetic mutations. Phosphate is a natural part of DNA, as are proteins. In fact, it is the alteration of the natural phosphate structure of the DNA that results in a mutation. Nucleotides also form a natural base within DNA.

27. C: The equation for photosynthesis requires a combination of carbon dioxide (CO_2), water, and sunlight to result in glucose and oxygen.

28. D: The vaccine brings a small amount of an infection into the body to give the body a chance to build up defenses to it by producing antibodies. These antibodies will recognize the disease in the future and prevent contraction of it.

29. B: The substance thymine cannot exist in RNA.

30. C: The substance *uracil* exists in RNA, in place of thymine.

31. A: Scientists have found that fertility rates tend to decrease as societies become more industrialized. As a result, the most industrialized countries typically have low fertility rates, while the least industrialized countries have higher fertility rates. With this in mind, and considering the information provided, Namibia--the least industrialized in the list of nations that is provided--can be expected to have the highest fertility rates.

32. D: Question 32 presents the theory of *natural selection*, or Darwin's theory of the *survival of the fittest*: individuals within a species develop characteristics that allow them to survive and reproduce more effectively (passing on the genes that they carry).

33. B: Each gene must match to a protein for a genetic trait to develop correctly.

34. D: The only true statement among the answer choices is that the majority of mutations are spontaneous. Very few mutations result from disease (although some diseases might result from genetic mutation). Some mutations (such as hemophilia) are indeed hereditary, so they can be passed on through the generations. Harmful chemicals are a known source of genetic mutations, so mutations that result from this source cannot be considered rare.

35. C: Protons are positively charged and found within the nucleus of an atom, while electrons are negatively charged and are found around the nucleus.

36. D: Solids with a fixed shape have a crystalline order that defines and maintains that shape.

37. D: A hydrogen atom creates a weak bond in DNA--in fact, this weak bond is known as a hydrogen bond due to the presence of the hydrogen atom.

38. B: The endoplasmic reticulum is the cell's transport network that moves proteins from one part of the cell to another. The Golgi apparatus assists in the transport but is not the actual transport network. Mitochondria are organelles ("tiny organs") that help in the production of ATP, which the

Copyright © Mometrix Media. You have been licensed one copy of this document for personal use only. Any other reproduction or redistribution is strictly prohibited. All rights reserved.

cells need to operate properly. The nucleolus participates in the production of ribosomes that are needed to generate proteins for the cell.

39. A: The chromosomes separate during anaphase and move to the opposite ends of the cells.

40. C: Gamma rays are the shortest wavelengths in the spectrum. From longest to shortest: radio, microwave, infrared, visible, ultraviolet, x-ray, gamma.

41. D: Adenine is the fourth type of nitrogenous base in DNA. Bromine is not part of DNA construction. Uracil is found in RNA but not in DNA.

42. C: The Law of Conservation of Energy states that energy is never actually lost but instead is transferred back and forth from kinetic to potential. Answer choices A and B do not make much sense, and answer choice D reflects Newton's Second Law instead of the Law of Conservation of Energy.

43. A: The physical expression--such as hair color--is the result of the phenotype. The genotype is the basic genetic code.

44. B: Charge and isotope do not affect the number of protons: protons are determined by the atomic number as shown in the periodic table. Nitrogen (N) has an atomic number of 7, so that is the number of protons that a negatively charted isotope of N-12 has.

45. C: An ion results from an imbalance of charges on an atom after a reaction. A neutral atom has an equal number of protons and electrons so the number of positive charges from the protons is balanced by the amount of negative charges from the electrons. When electrons are transferred between atoms during a chemical reaction, an atom will become positively charged if it has lost electrons or negatively charged if it has gained electrons.

46. C: The number of 7 is the "breaking point" between basic and acidic. Above 7 solutions are considered basic; below 7 solutions are considered acidic. For instance, milk, with a pH of 6.5, is actually considered acidic. Bleach, with a pH of 12.5, is considered basic.

47. B: Mutations result from mutagen-induced changes or errors during DNA replication. That being said, DNA replication is a normal activity, so answer choice A cannot be said to cause mutations. Similarly, excision repair (answer choice C) and the presence of germ cells (answer choice D) are normal within DNA, so neither causes mutations. Errors that occur during these processes, however, might.

48. A: Scientists measure the distance between the earth and the stars (including the sun) in light-years. A light-year is calculated as the distance that light will travel in one year.

49. D: Potential energy is energy that *can* be used but is not currently being used. A ballerina doing stretches is using energy. A secretary typing at a computer is also using energy. Note that a great deal of energy does not have to be used for the energy to be considered *kinetic* or in use (as a result of motion). A ball being thrown from one person to another is in motion and thus possesses kinetic energy. A rubber band stretched to its fullest and held, however, is waiting to spring back and possesses *potential* energy, or the energy that is being stored before use.

50. C: RNA has several roles, one of which is to act as the messenger and deliver information about the correct sequence of proteins in DNA. The ribosomes do the actual manufacturing of the

Copyright © Mometrix Media. You have been licensed one copy of this document for personal use only. Any other reproduction or redistribution is strictly prohibited. All rights reserved.

proteins. Hydrogen, oxygen, and nitrogen work to create the bonds within DNA. And far from having a double helix shape, RNA has what would be considered a more two-dimensional shape.

51. B: Catalysts alter the activation energy during a chemical reaction and therefore control the rate of the reaction. The substrate is the actual surface that enzymes use during a chemical reaction (and there is no such term as *substrate energy*). Inhibitors and promoters participate in the chemical reaction, but it is the activation energy that catalysts alter to control the overall rate as the reaction occurs.

52. D: A metallic ion is called a *cation*, while a nonmetallic ion is called an *anion*. *Metalloid* refers to a type of element that easily accepts or gives off electrons. The term *covalent* refers to a specific type of bond between elements (that is, when atoms share electrons).

53. D: An *alkene* has a double bond, while an *alkyne* has a triple bond. The *alkane* is the saturated hydrocarbon that is altered to produce the unsaturated hydrocarbons with the double or triple bonds. For instance, ethane is the alkane; ethene is the alkene; ethyne is the alkyne.

54. C: Crossing the corresponding alleles from each parent will yield a result of BB in the upper right box of this Punnett square.

English and Language Usage Answer Explanations

1. C: The word *syllabi* is the correct plural form of *syllabus*. The other answer choices reflect incorrect plural forms. Specifically, *syllabus* does not change the form at all, and the Latin root of *syllabus* would require some change. At the same time, *syllaba*--while an accurate plural for some words with Latin roots--is incorrect in this case. And *syllabis* is a double form of the plural, so it cannot be correct.

2. A: The word *independent* is an adjective that modifies the word *state*, describing what kind of state the kingdom of Gwynedd was. The words *century*, *government*, and *control* are all nouns in this context.

3. B: Correct subject-verb agreement would require the singular verb *is* to accompany the singular subject *Big Island*. Readers should not be distracted by the use of *islands* in the appositive phrase just before the verb. The subject-verb relationship is governed by the word that functions as the subject of the sentence, instead of the noun (or, in some cases, the pronoun) that is closest to the verb.

4. C: Answer choice C is correct, because the quotation is a standard quotation (requiring double quotes) as well as a question. Additionally, the question mark belongs inside the quotation marks. Answer choice A correctly places the question mark inside the quotation marks, but the use of single quotes is incorrect for standard quotations. Answer choice B is incorrect, because it places the question mark outside the quotation marks. Answer choice D uses the layered quotes, which are unnecessary in this case, since the sentence presents only one quotation instead of more than one.

5. A: The word *its* is a possessive pronoun the reflects the collar belonging to the dog, and the use of *his* applies to Cody. Answer choice B incorrectly uses the contraction for *it is*. Answer choice C switches the pronouns so that *its* refers to Cody instead of the dog. Answer choice D does the same thing, except with the contraction for *it is* instead of the possessive pronoun.

6. D: *acceptable* is the correct spelling of the word. All other forms represent incorrect spelling of a commonly misspelled word.

Copyright © Mometrix Media. You have been licensed one copy of this document for personal use only. Any other reproduction or redistribution is strictly prohibited. All rights reserved.

7. C: Answer choice C offers the most effective combination of the sentences with the use of the conjunction *but* and the dependent clause starting with *after*. All other answer choices result in choppy or unclear combinations of the four sentences.

8. A: The original sentence contains two passive usages (*was expected* and *would be canceled*). Neither is necessary; both can be adjusted to improve the clarity of the sentence. Answer choice A best adjusts the passive tense to active. Answer choice B awkwardly makes *snow* the subject of the sentence when *administration* is a more effective subject. Answer choice C simply replaces *by* with *among*, but this does nothing to improve the clarity of the sentence. Answer choice D offers a nominalization (*expectation*), which clutters the sentence instead of improves it.

9. A: Correct punctuation requires a comma after both city and state when both fall within the sentence, even when the city and state fall within an opening dependent clause that has a comma after it. All answer choices that do not have a comma after the state as well as the city are incorrect. Answer choice C is incorrect because it adds a comma after *Oak* for no clear reason as the name of the city in full is clearly *Oak Ridge*.

10. C: The word *council* is a collective noun that, in this case, represents a group of individuals functioning individually. As a result, *council* is plural, so it needs the plural pronoun *they*. Within the context of the sentence, *he and she* makes no sense, and *each* is singular in this case, so it does not indicate the plural nature of the council.

11. A: The suffix *-ism* here suggests a doctrine that is followed, whether that be the doctrine of polytheism (a religious doctrine), communism (a social doctrine), or nationalism (a political doctrine).

12. B: Question 12 asks for the correct punctuation of layered quotations. Standard American usage requires the double quotes for the first quotation and the single quotes for any quotes within the original quotes. Answer choice B best reflects this with the phrase "Let there be light" representing the quote within the original quotation. Answer choice A reverses the correct usage. Answer choice C incorrectly makes the entire quotation a quote within an otherwise unidentified quote. Answer choice D uses double quotes within the double quotes, which is incorrect in standard American usage.

13. D: The semicolon correctly joins the two sentences. Answer choice A is incorrect, because it uses a comma splice to join two independent clauses. (To join two independent clauses, a comma needs to be accompanied by a coordinating conjunction.) The colon in answer choice B is incorrect because the information in the second clause does not clearly define or explain the previous clause. Answer choice C is incorrect because it offers no punctuation to separate the two independent clauses and thus creates more confusion than clarity.

14. C: Question 14 asks the student to identify and remove the nominalization. In the original sentence, the nominalization is *commitment*. The easiest way to remove the nominalization is to adjust it to the verb *commit*. As a result, answer choice C is the only correct option because it identifies and removes the nominalization.

15. B: Answer choice B contains two independent clauses that are joined with a comma and the coordinating conjunction *and*. Answer choice A, though it contains a compound subject and a compound verb, is still a simple sentence. Answer choice C opens with a dependent clause, so it is a complex sentence. Answer choice D is a compound-complex sentence because it includes a dependent clause as well as two independent clauses.

Copyright © Mometrix Media. You have been licensed one copy of this document for personal use only. Any other reproduction or redistribution is strictly prohibited. All rights reserved.

16. B: Answer choice B correctly capitalizes *Uncle Archibald*, where *Uncle Archibald* is used as one whole to a specific name, which makes it a proper noun. If the sentence said "her uncle Archibald," then *uncle* would remain lower case. In answer choice A, the word *cousin* needs no capitalization, because it is used to describe Elaine but is not used as part of her name. (The only distinctions are when the word is used within a direct address or opens a sentence.) Similarly, *mother* and *sister* do not need to be capitalized unless they are the first word of the sentence or are used to directly address someone.

17. B: The word *count* is part of an infinitive phrase (*to count*), and infinitive phrases function as adjectives, adverbs, or nouns, so the word *count* cannot be a verb. All other answer choices are verbs.

18. D: The word *affect* is a verb in this context and is the correct usage within the sentence. The possessive pronoun *your* also correctly modifies *children*, so answer choice D is correct. All other answer choices incorrectly apply the words to the sentence.

19. B: The context of the sentence suggests that the trauma of surviving the plane crash left long-term memories that haunted Johanna for many years. As a result, *permanent* is the best meaning of *indelible*. The other meanings make little sense in the context of the sentence. The only possible option is *indirect*, but there is nothing about the sentence to suggest that the nightmares are indirect impressions of a traumatic experience.

20. C: The word *east* in answer choice C is simply a directional indication and does not need to be capitalized in the context of the sentence. All other uses of capitalization are correct in the context of the sentences. The word *South* should be capitalized when it refers to a region of the United States (as indicated by the mention of Mississippi). The word *East* should be capitalized when it refers to the region of Texas. And the word *north* does not need to be capitalized when it is simply a directional indication (as in answer choice D).

21. A: The word *phenomena* is the correct plural form of *phenomenon*, so answer choice A is correct. The correct plural form of *mother-in-law* is *mothers-in-law*. The correct plural form of *deer* is just *deer*. The correct plural form of *roof* is *roofs*.

22. C: The word *whom* correctly indicates the objective case--as in "to hold him/her responsible"--so answer choice C is correct. The word *who* in answer choice A incorrectly indicates the subjective case. Similarly, answer choice B is incorrect because the word *who* is the subjective case (instead of the objective case) here. Answer choice D is incorrect because it incorrectly applies the objective *whom* instead of the subjective *who*.

23. B: The word *capacity* is a noun in this context, so answer choice B is correct. Because the word functions as the object of the preposition, the options of verb and adverb cannot be correct. Answer choice D is incorrect because the word *capacity* is not a pronoun in any context.

24. C: Answer choice C summarizes the ideas within the sentence simply and clearly. Answer choice A moves the ideas around to make them awkward instead of effective. Answer choice B creates a dangling modifier with the phrase without adequate preparation, so it cannot be correct. Similarly, answer choice D makes this phrase a dangling modifier that makes the flow of thought awkward instead of clear.

25. D: The context of the sentence suggests that the word *exorbitant* refers to an excessively high cost, so answer choice D is correct. Answer choice A would be an interesting conclusion to the

Copyright © Mometrix Media. You have been licensed one copy of this document for personal use only. Any other reproduction or redistribution is strictly prohibited. All rights reserved.

sentence, but it does not clearly follow the use of *exorbitant*, so it cannot be correct. Answer choices B and C contradict the suggested meaning of *exorbitant*, so both must be incorrect.

26. A: The pronoun *all* is plural, so it requires the plural verb *are*. The pronouns *each* and *neither* are singular and require singular verbs (not provided in answer choices B and C). The pronoun *any* can be either singular or plural depending on the context of the sentence. In this case, *any* suggests a singular usage, so answer choice D is incorrect with the plural verb.

27. C: The pronouns *she and I* are correctly in the subjective case starting the second independent clause, so answer choice C is correct. All other answer choices contain at least one incorrect objective case usage that cannot function as the subject of the second independent clause.

28. A: Both *her* and *me* are objective case pronouns that accurately function as the object of the preposition *to*. All other answer choices contain at least one incorrect subjective case usage that cannot function as the object of the preposition.

29. D: While answer choice D is arguably the longest of the four sentences, it is actually a simple sentence. It contains a compound subject and a compound verb, but because it represents only one independent clause it still functions as a simple sentence. Answer choices A and B contain two independent clauses and are thus compound sentences. Answer choice C contains a dependent clause, so it is a complex sentence.

30. B: The word *President* should always be capitalized when it refers to the President of the United States, whether or not the President's name is included. All other nouns in this sentence are simple nouns and do not need to be capitalized.

31. C: The word *playwright* is the correct spelling to refer to someone who writes plays. All other forms are incorrect and reflect common confusion about the correct spelling of the word.

32. D: Answer choice D correctly arranges the ideas to reflect the most effective meaning of the sentence. All other answer choices place the ideas in such a way as to create confusion or incorrect punctuation instead of clarity.

33. C: In the context, the collective noun *jury* reflects a unit functioning as one, so the word is singular instead of plural. Answer choice C, the singular possessive pronoun *its*, is correct, while answer choice D (the plural *their*) cannot be correct. The word *it's* is the contraction for *it is*. The word *they're* is the contraction for *they are*.

34. A: Answer choice A correctly places the word *compliment* to refer to Amber's positive remark and *complement* to refer to the excellent way that the pieces of furniture work together.

Copyright © Mometrix Media. You have been licensed one copy of this document for personal use only. Any other reproduction or redistribution is strictly prohibited. All rights reserved.

TEAS Practice Test #2

Section 1. Reading

1. At first, the woman's contractions were only <u>intermittent</u>, so the nurse had trouble determining how far her labor had progressed. Which of the following is the definition for the underlined word?

    a. frequent
    b. irregular
    c. painful
    d. dependable

2. Fearful that the patron might burn himself, Edith made sure to say, "**Hot plate**, sir" when she set the dish on his table. The use of bold font in the text above indicates which of the following?

    a. dialogue
    b. emphasis
    c. thoughts
    d. anger

3. Students who pursue a degree in a humanities discipline (e.g., English, history, philosophy, art, film studies) often have a difficult time finding work after they graduate. Which of the following does the abbreviation "e.g." stand for?

    a. error
    b. correction
    c. addition
    d. example

4. The guide words at the top of a dictionary page are *needs* and *negotiate*. Which of the following words is an entry on this page?

    a. needle
    b. neigh
    c. neglect
    d. nectar

5. Chapter 4: The Fictional Writings of Dorothy L. Sayers

- Plays
- Novels
- Short Stories
- Letters
- Mysteries

Analyze the headings above. Which of the following does not belong?

    a. Novels
    b. Plays
    c. Mysteries
    d. Letters

       Among the first females awarded a degree from Oxford University, Dorothy L.
       Sayers proved to be one of the most versatile writers in post-war England. Sayers

Copyright © Mometrix Media. You have been licensed one copy of this document for personal use only. Any other reproduction or redistribution is strictly prohibited. All rights reserved.

was born in 1893, the only child of an Anglican chaplain, and she received an unexpectedly good education at home. For instance, her study of Latin commenced when she was only six years old. She entered Oxford in 1912, at a time when the university was not granting degrees to women. By 1920, this policy had changed, and Sayers received her degree in medieval literature and modern languages after finishing university. That same year, she also received a master of arts degree.

Sayers's first foray into published writing was a collection of poetry released in 1916. Within a few years, she began work on the detective novels and short stories that would make her famous, due to the creation of the foppish, mystery-solving aristocrat Lord Peter Wimsey. Sayers is also credited with the short story mysteries about the character Montague Egg. In spite of her success as a mystery writer, Sayers continued to balance popular fiction with academic work; her translation of Dante's *Inferno* gained her respect for her ability to convey the poetry in English while still remaining true to the Italian *terza rima*. She also composed a series of twelve plays about the life of Christ, and wrote several essays about education and feminism. In her middle age, Dorothy L. Sayers published several works of Christian apologetics, one of which was so well-received that the archbishop of Canterbury attempted to present her with a doctorate of divinity. Sayers, for reasons known only to her, declined.

The next three questions are based on the above passage.

6. Which of the following describes the type of writing used to create the passage?
    a. narrative
    b. persuasive
    c. expository
    d. technical

7. Which of the following sentences is the best summary of the passage?
    a. Among the first females awarded a degree from Oxford University, Dorothy L. Sayers proved to be one of the most versatile writers in post-war England.
    b. Sayers was born in 1893, the only child of an Anglican chaplain, and she received an unexpectedly good education at home.
    c. Within a few years, she began work on the detective novels and short stories that would make her famous, due to the creation of the foppish, mystery-solving aristocrat Lord Peter Wimsey.
    d. In her middle age, Dorothy L. Sayers published several works of Christian apologetics, one of which was so well-received that the archbishop of Canterbury attempted to present her with a doctorate of divinity.

8. Which of the following sentences contains an opinion statement by the author?
    a. Among the first females awarded a degree from Oxford University, Dorothy L. Sayers proved to be one of the most versatile writers in post-war England.
    b. Sayers was born in 1893, the only child of an Anglican chaplain, and she received an unexpectedly good education at home.
    c. Her translation of Dante's Inferno gained her respect for her ability to convey the poetry in English while still remaining true to the Italian terza rima.
    d. Sayers, for reasons known only to her, declined.

Copyright © Mometrix Media. You have been licensed one copy of this document for personal use only. Any other reproduction or redistribution is strictly prohibited. All rights reserved.

The Dewey Decimal Classes

000 Computer science, information, and general works

100 Philosophy and psychology
200 Religion
300 Social sciences
400 Languages
500 Science and mathematics
600 Technical and applied science
700 Arts and recreation
800 Literature
900 History, geography, and biography

The next four questions are based on the above information.

9. Jorgen is doing a project on the ancient Greek mathematician and poet Eratosthenes. In his initial review, Jorgen learns that Eratosthenes is considered the first person to calculate the circumference of the earth, and that he is considered the first to describe geography as it is studied today. To which section of the library should Jorgen go to find one of the early maps created by Eratosthenes?

    a. 100
    b. 300
    c. 600
    d. 900

10. Due to his many interests and pursuits, Eratosthenes dabbled in a variety of fields, and he is credited with a theory known as the sieve of Eratosthenes. This is an early algorithm used to determine prime numbers. To which section of the library should Jorgen go to find out more about the current applications of the sieve of Eratosthenes?

    a. 000
    b. 100
    c. 400
    d. 500

11. One ancient work claims that Eratosthenes received the nickname "beta" from those who knew him. This is a word that represents the second letter of the Greek alphabet, and it represented Eratosthenes's accomplishments in every area that he studied. To which section of the library should Jorgen go to learn more about the letters of the Greek alphabet and the meaning of the word "beta"?

    a. 200
    b. 400
    c. 700
    d. 900

Copyright © Mometrix Media. You have been licensed one copy of this document for personal use only. Any other reproduction or redistribution is strictly prohibited. All rights reserved.

12. Finally, Jorgen learns that Eratosthenes was fascinated by the story of the Trojan War, and that he attempted to determine the exact dates when this event occurred. Jorgen is unfamiliar with the story of the Fall of Troy, so he decides to look into writings such as *The Iliad* and *The Odyssey*, by Homer. To which section of the library should Jorgen go to locate these works?

    a. 100
    b. 200
    c. 700
    d. 800

13. With all of the planning that preceded her daughter's wedding, Marci decided that picking out a new paint color for her own living room was largely <u>peripheral</u>. Which of the following is the definition for the underlined word?

    a. meaningless
    b. contrived
    c. unimportant
    d. disappointing

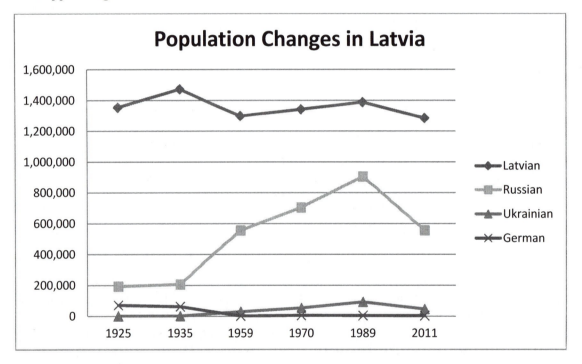

The next four questions are based on the chart above, which reflects the population changes in Latvia during the 20th century as shown through four ethnic groups (Latvian, Russian, Ukrainian, and German).

14. In 2011, the population of Latvia was just over two million people. Of the four ethnic groups shown on the chart above, which represented approximately 25 percent of the total population of Latvia in 2011?

    a. Latvian
    b. Russian
    c. Ukrainian
    d. German

Copyright © Mometrix Media. You have been licensed one copy of this document for personal use only. Any other reproduction or redistribution is strictly prohibited. All rights reserved.

15. According to the chart above, which of the following ethnic groups had the largest percent decrease in population between 1925 and 2011?

    a. Latvian
    b. Russian
    c. Ukrainian
    d. German

16. Between 1925 and 1991, Latvia was part of the Soviet Union. Since 1991, the population of which ethnic group in Latvia appears to have decreased the most?

    a. Latvian
    b. Russian
    c. Ukrainian
    d. German

17. After World War II ended in 1945, large numbers of non-Latvian workers entered the country, primarily to work at construction jobs. Among these non-Latvian ethnic groups, the increase in workers represented a population percentage shift of less than one percent before 1945 to more than three percent by the time of the Soviet Union's collapse. Which ethnic group shown on the chart best represents this shift?

    a. Latvian
    b. Russian
    c. Ukrainian
    d. German

18. Follow the numbered instructions to transform the starting word into a different word.

    1. Start with the word CORPOREAL.
    2. Remove the C from the beginning of the word.
    3. Remove the O from the beginning of the word.
    4. Remove the O from the middle of the word.
    5. Move the E to follow the first R.
    6. Move the L to follow the P.
    7. Remove the second R.
    8. Add the letter Y to the end of the word.

What is the new word?

    a. REALLY
    b. PRETTY
    c. REPLAY
    d. POWER

19. Although not considered the smartest student in her class, Klara was willing to work hard for her grades, and her sedulous commitment to her studies earned her top scores at graduation.

Which of the following is the definition for the underlined word?

    a. diligent
    b. silent
    c. moderate
    d. complicated

Copyright © Mometrix Media. You have been licensed one copy of this document for personal use only. Any other reproduction or redistribution is strictly prohibited. All rights reserved.

20. Flemming is on a new diet that requires him to avoid all dairy products, as well as dairy byproducts. This will be a big change for him, so his doctor gives him information about foods that he might not realize often contain dairy products. These include the following: bread, granola, deli meat, dry breakfast cereal, and energy bars. Which of the following items from Flemming's standard diet will still be safe to eat?

   a. puffed rice cereal
   b. breaded chicken parmesan
   c. sliced turkey sandwich
   d. yogurt made from coconut milk

Car Owner's Manual: Table of Contents:

   I. Vehicle Instruments
   II. Safety Options
   III. Audio, Climate, and Voice Controls
   IV. Pre-Driving and Driving
   V. Routine Maintenance
   VI. Emergencies
   VII. Consumer Resources

The next four questions are based on the above information.

21. To which chapter should Regina turn if she needs to locate information about adjusting the air conditioning in the vehicle?

   a. I
   b. II
   c. III
   d. IV

22. To which chapter should Regina turn if she needs to find out how often the car manufacturer recommends having the oil changed?

   a. IV
   b. V
   c. VI
   d. VII

23. To which chapter should Regina turn if she wants to find out where the nearest dealership is located?

   a. I
   b. III
   c. V
   d. VII

24. To which chapter should Regina turn if she needs to find out what to do if the car begins overheating?

   a. II
   b. III
   c. IV
   d. VI

Copyright © Mometrix Media. You have been licensed one copy of this document for personal use only. Any other reproduction or redistribution is strictly prohibited. All rights reserved.

25. Nora is preparing a large research project for the end of the term, and the instructor has required that all students make sure they are using reliable, scholarly resources in their papers. Of the following resource options, which would not be considered a reliable, scholarly source?

a. Encyclopedia Britannica
b. Wikipedia
c. Science.gov
d. LexisNexis

26. In Sonnet 18, Shakespeare wrote, "Shall I compare thee to a summer's day? / Thou art more lovely and more <u>temperate</u>." Which of the following is the definition for the underlined word?

a. modest
b. conservative
c. agreeable
d. immoderate

27. In the sonnet quoted above, what does the slash between the sentences represent?

a. the end of one stanza and the beginning of another
b. the end of a question and the answer that follows
c. the end of one line of poetry and the start of the next
d. the end of one sentence and the start of the next

Copyright © Mometrix Media. You have been licensed one copy of this document for personal use only. Any other reproduction or redistribution is strictly prohibited. All rights reserved.

The next four questions are based on the above information.

28. Clothilde is looking for an herbal remedy to combat a recent outbreak of eczema. In which chapter should she look for more information?

    a. Chapter 8
    b. Chapter 10
    c. Chapter 11
    d. Chapter 12

29. Clothilde's sister has asked her to recommend an herbal therapy for her five-year-old daughter's chronic cough. In which chapter should Clothilde look for more information?

    a. Chapter 7
    b. Chapter 9
    c. Chapter 10
    d. Chapter 12

Copyright © Mometrix Media. You have been licensed one copy of this document for personal use only. Any other reproduction or redistribution is strictly prohibited. All rights reserved.

30. Clothilde's elderberry plant is nearly overgrown, and she is hoping to trim it back and use the elderflower to prepare a blend of tea, as well as a homemade wine. In which chapter should she look for more information about how to do this?

    a. Chapter 3
    b. Chapter 4
    c. Chapter 5
    d. Chapter 13

31. Clothilde realizes that she failed to maintain her elderberry plant as she should have, and she needs tips about how to keep the plant in good condition to avoid another overgrowth. In which chapter should she look for more information?

    a. Chapter 2
    b. Chapter 3
    c. Chapter 13
    d. Chapter 14

> **LOOKING FOR ROOMMATE – CLEAN HOUSE / QUIET AREA / CLOSE TO UNIVERSITY**
> Need one more female roommate for 3-bd house w/in walking distance of univ. Current occupants quiet, house clean/smoke-free. No pets. Long-term applicants preferred. Rent: $800/mo. Utilities/Internet included. Avail: Aug 15. Call Florence at 985-5687, or send an email to f.carpenter@email.com.

32. Florence receives a number of calls about the roommate advertisement. Of the individuals described below, who seems like the best applicant?

    a. Frances is a research assistant in the science department who has a Yorkshire terrier.
    b. Adelaide works in the humanities department and is looking for a three-month rental.
    c. Cosette is allergic to cigarette smoke and needs a quiet place to study.
    d. Felix is a graduate student in the history department who doesn't have a car.

33. Performing Arts in Museville

- Music
- Opera
- Sculpture
- Dance
- Theater
- Film

Analyze the headings above. Which of the following does not belong?

    a. Opera
    b. Sculpture
    c. Film
    d. Music

Copyright © Mometrix Media. You have been licensed one copy of this document for personal use only. Any other reproduction or redistribution is strictly prohibited. All rights reserved.

COMPANY	ENGLISH BREAKFAST	EARL GREY	DARJEELING	OOLONG	GREEN
Tea Heaven	$25	$27	$26	$32	$30
Wholesale Tea	$24	$24	$24	$26	$27
Tea by The Pound	$22	$25	$30	$28	$29
Tea Express	$25	$28	$26	$29	$30

Note: Prices per 16 oz. (1 pound)

The next two questions are based on the above table.

34. Noella runs a small tea shop and needs to restock. She is running very low on English Breakfast and Darjeeling tea, and she needs two pounds of each. Which company can offer her the best price on the two blends?

   a. Tea Heaven
   b. Wholesale Tea
   c. Tea by The Pound
   d. Tea Express

35. After reviewing her inventory, Noella realizes that she also needs one pound of Earl Grey and two pounds of green tea. Which company can offer her the best price on these two blends?

   a. Tea Heaven
   b. Wholesale Tea
   c. Tea by The Pound
   d. Tea Express

36. The United Nations Statistics Division has divided the continent of Europe into four primary areas: Northern Europe, Southern Europe, Western Europe, and Eastern Europe. Northern Europe is composed of eleven nations that make up Scandinavia, the Baltic states, and Great Britain. According to this definition, which of the following capital cities would not be located in Northern Europe?

   a. Copenhagen
   b. Oslo
   c. London
   d. Kiev

37. The United Nations Statistics Division loosely defines Southern Europe as the area made up of the nations that border the Mediterranean Sea (with the exception of France, which is considered part of Western Europe) and the Black Sea. The single exception to this definition is a nation on the Iberian Peninsula, which borders the Atlantic Ocean but has no Mediterranean coastline. The Iberian Peninsula is also home to Spain, Andorra, and Gibraltar. Which of the following is the other, non-Mediterranean nation on the Iberian Peninsula?

   a. Portugal
   b. Bulgaria
   c. Italy
   d. Cyprus

Copyright © Mometrix Media. You have been licensed one copy of this document for personal use only. Any other reproduction or redistribution is strictly prohibited. All rights reserved.

Dear library patrons:

To ensure that all visitors have the opportunity to use our limited number of computers, we ask that each person restrict himself or herself to 30 minutes on a computer. For those needing to use a computer beyond this time frame, there will be a $3 charge for each 15-minute period.

We thank you in advance for your cooperation.

Pineville Library

The next two questions are based on the above information.

38. Which of the following is a logical conclusion that can be derived from the announcement above?

a. The library is planning to purchase more computers, but cannot afford them yet.
b. The library is facing budget cuts, and is using the Internet fee to compensate for them.
c. The library has added the fee to discourage patrons from spending too long on the computers.
d. The library is offsetting its own Internet service costs by passing on the fee to patrons.

39. Raoul has an upcoming school project, and his own computer is not working. He needs to use the library computer, and he has estimated that he will need to be on the computer for approximately an hour and a half. How much of a fee can Raoul expect to pay for his computer use at the library?

a. $6
b. $9
c. $12
d. $15

Copyright © Mometrix Media. You have been licensed one copy of this document for personal use only. Any other reproduction or redistribution is strictly prohibited. All rights reserved.

371 SALON AND SPA SERVICES

Hair Salons

Angel Cuts 118 *Sparrow*	(345) 485-5717
Hair and a Spare 274 *Finch*	
Extensions	
Handmade Wigs	(345) 485-5547
Perfect Endings 687 *Canary*	(345) 485-5524
Quick Trims 824 *Parakeet*	(345) 485-7569

Nail Salons

Hands to Envy 148 *Canary*	(345) 485-2138
Nails by Manhattan 958 *Avocet*	(345) 485-6748
Natural Nails 285 *Finch*	(345) 485-7691

Tanning Salons

Airbrushed Tans 687 *Avocet*	(345) 485-9482
Cannes Tan 812 *Kittiwake*	(587) 785-5875
Paparazzi-Ready Tans 885 *Sparrow*	(345) 485-4812
Spray Tans Unlimited 671 *Grouse*	(345) 485-7595

Salon and Spa Services

Good Karma Salon & Spa 448 *Ptarmigan*	
Haircuts, Styling, Coloring	
Nails, Tanning, Massages	(345) 485-7824
Holistic Health 986 *Teal*	
Natural Health & Wellness	(345) 485-3333
Sérénité Spa 875 *Tanager*	
Full-Body Relaxation	(345) 485-5846
Total Wellness Day Spa 264 *Avocet*	
Full Spa Svcs Available	(345) 485-8795

CANNES TAN
...WHEN YOU
CAN'T MAKE IT
TO THE RIVIERA
587-785-5875

Angel Cuts
"The Best Haircut in Town"
345-485-5717
Check our website for coupons!

Sérénité Spa – NOW OPEN!
Offering full-body relaxation in a state-of-the-art spa. All spa services available. Call for an appointment with one of our trained aestheticians today!
345-485-5845

Natural Nails
All-Natural Nail Services
-- No harsh chemicals
-- No toxic products
345-485-7691

Hair and a Spare
The best local salon for extensions and wigs made just for you!
Satisfaction guaranteed.
Call today to set up an appointment. Be sure to ask for our first-time customer discount!
(345) 485-5547

The next three questions are based on the above information.

40. Genevieve has recently moved to the area, and she is looking for a salon where she can get a haircut and color, as well as a manicure and pedicure for an upcoming event. Based on the information above, which location is most likely to offer all of these services?

    a. Sérénité Spa
    b. Angel Cuts
    c. Perfect Endings
    d. Good Karma Salon & Spa

41. After considering her options, Genevieve realizes she needs to be careful about where she gets her manicure and pedicure. The last time she had her nails done, she developed an allergic reaction to the nail polish that was used. With this in mind, which location might be the best choice?

    a. Nails by Manhattan
    b. Perfect Endings
    c. Natural Nails
    d. Hands to Envy

Copyright © Mometrix Media. You have been licensed one copy of this document for personal use only. Any other reproduction or redistribution is strictly prohibited. All rights reserved.

42. Based on the addresses shown on the phonebook page, which two businesses are likely in the same shopping center?

    a. Hair and a Spare and Natural Nails
    b. Perfect Endings and Hands to Envy
    c. Nails by Manhattan and Airbrushed Tans
    d. Angel Cuts and Cannes Tan

For lunch, she likes ham and cheese (torn into bites), yogurt, raisins, applesauce, peanut butter sandwiches in the fridge drawer, or any combo of these. She's not a huge eater. Help yourself too. Bread is on counter if you want to make a sandwich.

It's fine if you want to go somewhere, leave us a note of where you are. Make sure she's buckled and drive carefully! Certain fast food places are fun if they have playgrounds and are indoors. It's probably too hot for playground, but whatever you want to do is fine. Take a sippy cup of water and a diaper wherever you go. There's some money here for you in case you decide to go out for lunch with her.

As for nap, try after lunch. She may not sleep, but try anyway. Read her a couple of books first, put cream on her mosquito bites (it's in the den on the buffet), then maybe rock in her chair. Give her a bottle of milk, and refill as needed, but don't let her drink more than $2\frac{1}{2}$ bottles of milk or she'll throw up. Turn on music in her room, leave her in crib with a dry diaper and bottle to try to sleep. She likes a stuffed animal too. Try for 30-45 minutes. You may have to start the tape again. If she won't sleep, that's fine. We just call it "rest time" on those days that naps won't happen.

The next two questions are based on the above passage.

43. To whom is this passage probably being written?

    a. a mother
    b. a father
    c. a babysitter
    d. a nurse

44. You can assume the writer of the passage is:

    a. a mom
    b. a dad
    c. a teacher
    d. a parent

Volleyball is easy to learn and fun to play in a physical education class. With just one net and one ball, an entire class can participate. The object of the game is to get the ball over the net and onto the ground on the other side. At the same time, all players should be in the ready position to keep the ball from hitting the ground on their own side. After the ball has been served, the opposing team may have three hits to get the ball over the net to the other side. Only the serving team may score. If the receiving team wins the volley, the referee calls, "side out" and the receiving team wins the serve. Players should rotate positions so that everyone gets a chance to serve. A game is played to 15 points, but the winning team must win by two points. That means if the score is 14 to 15, the play continues until one team wins by two. A volleyball match consists of three games. The winner of the match is the team that wins two of the three games.

The next four questions are based on the above passage.

Copyright © Mometrix Media. You have been licensed one copy of this document for personal use only. Any other reproduction or redistribution is strictly prohibited. All rights reserved.

45. Who can score in a volleyball game?

   a. the receiving team
   b. the serving team
   c. either team
   d. there is no score

46. How many people can participate in a volleyball game?

   a. 14
   b. 15
   c. half of a class
   d. an entire class

47. What is something that a referee might call in a volleyball game?

   a. "side out"
   b. "time out"
   c. "out of order"
   d. "be careful"

48. What equipment is needed for volleyball?

   a. a referee, a goal, a ball
   b. a goal, a ball, a net
   c. a net, a ball
   d. two balls, one net

Copyright © Mometrix Media. You have been licensed one copy of this document for personal use only. Any other reproduction or redistribution is strictly prohibited. All rights reserved.

Section 2. Mathematics

1. Within a certain nursing program, 25% of the class wanted to work with infants, 60% of the class wanted to work with the elderly, 10% of the class wanted to assist general practitioners in private practices, and the rest were undecided. What fraction of the class wanted to work with the elderly?

    a. $\frac{1}{4}$

    b. $\frac{1}{10}$

    c. $\frac{3}{5}$

    d. $\frac{1}{20}$

2. Veronica has to create the holiday schedule for the neonatal unit at her hospital. She knows that 35% of the staff members will not be available because they are taking vacation days during the holiday. Of the remaining staff members who will be available, only 20% are certified to work in the neonatal unit. What percentage of the TOTAL staff is certified and available to work in the neonatal unit during the holiday?

    a. 7%

    b. 13%

    c. 65%

    d. 80%

3. A patient requires a 30% decrease in the dosage of his medication. His current dosage is 340 mg. What will his dosage be after the decrease?

    a. 70 mg

    b. 238 mg

    c. 270 mg

    d. 340 mg

4. A study about anorexia was conducted on 100 patients. Within that patient population 70% were women, and 10% of the men were overweight as children. How many male patients in the study were NOT overweight as children?

    a. 3

    b. 10

    c. 27

    d. 30

5. University Q has an extremely competitive nursing program. Historically, $\frac{3}{4}$ of the students in each incoming class major in nursing but only $\frac{1}{5}$ of those who major in nursing actually complete the program. If this year's incoming class has 100 students, how many students will complete the nursing program?

    a. 75

    b. 20

    c. 15

    d. 5

> Four nurse midwives open a joint practice together. They use a portion of the income to pay for various expenses for the practice. Each nurse midwife contributes $2000 per month.

- 216 -

Copyright © Mometrix Media. You have been licensed one copy of this document for personal use only. Any other reproduction or redistribution is strictly prohibited. All rights reserved.

The next five questions are based on the above information.

6. The first midwife uses $\frac{2}{5}$ of her monthly contribution to pay the rent and utilities for the office space. She saves half of the remainder for incidental expenditures, and uses the rest of the money to purchase medical supplies. How much money does she spend on medical supplies each month?

    a. $600
    b. $800
    c. $1000
    d. $1200

7. The second midwife allocates $\frac{1}{2}$ of her funds to pay an office administrator, plus another $\frac{1}{10}$ for office supplies. What is the total fraction of the second midwife's budget that is spent on the office administrator and office supplies?

    a. $\frac{3}{5}$
    b. $\frac{2}{12}$
    c. $\frac{2}{20}$
    d. $\frac{1}{20}$

8. Each month, the third midwife pays $900 for malpractice insurance. Then she pays $200 for a cleaning service to sanitize the office. Finally, she pays $100 for advertising. How much money does the third midwife have left after paying these expenses?

    a. $1200
    b. $1100
    c. $900
    d. $800

9. The fourth midwife is saving to buy an office building for the practice. So each month she puts money aside in a special savings account. The ratio of her monthly savings to the rent is 1:2. If the rent is $800 per month, how much money does she put into the special savings account each month?

    a. $100
    b. $200
    c. $400
    d. $1600

10. All four midwives decided to combine their money to purchase an ultrasound machine. The first midwife gave $501.93 towards the purchase of the machine. The second contributed $498.05; the third gave $499.92, and the fourth gave $500.02. Estimate the total amount of money the midwives used to purchase the machine.

    a. $1000
    b. $1500
    c. $2000
    d. $2500

Copyright © Mometrix Media. You have been licensed one copy of this document for personal use only. Any other reproduction or redistribution is strictly prohibited. All rights reserved.

11. A patient was taking 310 mg of antidepressant each day. However, the doctor determined that this dosage was too high and reduced the dosage by a fifth. Further observation revealed the dose was still too high, so he reduced it again by 20 mg. What is the final dosage of the patient's antidepressant?

    a. 20 mg
    b. 42 mg
    c. 228 mg
    d. 248 mg

12. A lab technician took 100 hairs from a patient to conduct several tests. The technician used $\frac{1}{7}$ of the hairs for a drug test. How many hairs were used for the drug test? Round your answer to the nearest hundredth.

    a. 14.00
    b. 14.20
    c. 14.29
    d. 14.30

13. A patient was transferred from a hospital in Europe to an American hospital in order to undergo a rare operation. The patient's medical chart lists his age in Roman numerals as XXIV. How old is the patient?

    a. 24
    b. 21
    c. 11
    d. 4

14. Susan is extremely excited about starting her first job as a nurse. Her gross annual salary is $40,000. Susan contributes 10% of her salary **before** taxes to a retirement account. Then she pays 25% of her remaining salary in state and federal taxes. Finally, she pays $30 per month for health insurance. What is Susan's annual take-home pay?

    a. $25640
    b. $25970
    c. $26640
    d. $26970

15. Susan decided to celebrate getting her first nursing job by purchasing a new outfit. She bought a dress for $69.99 and a pair of shoes for $39.99. She also bought accessories for $34.67. What was the total cost of Susan's outfit, including accessories?

    a. $69.99
    b. $75.31
    c. $109.98
    d. $144.65

Copyright © Mometrix Media. You have been licensed one copy of this document for personal use only. Any other reproduction or redistribution is strictly prohibited. All rights reserved.

16. Use the following table from a checking account statement to determine the ending balance in the account.

    a. $88.50
    b. $239.16
    c. $300.00
    d. $511.50

Transaction description	Amount
Beginning balance	$300.00
Purchase coffee at cafe	$3.56
Pay utility bill	$132.61
Deposit money in ATM	$75.33
Ending balance	??

17. Complete the following equation:

$$2 + (2)(2) - 2 \div 2 = ?$$

    a. 5
    b. 3
    c. 2
    d. 1

18. The emergency room manager at a certain hospital will host a celebration for the doctors and staff because they met the quarterly wait-time goals. For each person who RSVPs for the celebration, the manager will order 2 cupcakes, 1 can of soda, and 1 serving of fruit salad. Each cupcake costs $1.75. A can of soda costs $0.75, and a serving of fruit salad costs $2.50. If 50 people RSVP for the event, how much will the emergency room manager spend on cupcakes?

    a. $87.50
    b. $125.00
    c. $175.00
    d. $337.50

19. As part of a study, a set of patients will be divided into three groups: $\frac{4}{15}$ of the patients will be in Group Alpha, $\frac{2}{5}$ of the patients will be in Group Beta, and $\frac{1}{3}$ of the patients will be in Group Gamma. Order the groups from smallest to largest, according to the number of patients in each group.

    a. Group Alpha, Group Beta, Group Gamma
    b. Group Alpha, Group Gamma, Group Beta
    c. Group Gamma, Group Alpha, Group Beta
    d. Group Gamma, Group Beta, Group Alpha

20. Solve the following equation:

$$2x + 6 = 14$$

    a. x = 4
    b. x = 8
    c. x = 10
    d. x = 13

Copyright © Mometrix Media. You have been licensed one copy of this document for personal use only. Any other reproduction or redistribution is strictly prohibited. All rights reserved.

21. Add polynomial #1 and polynomial #2.

Polynomial #1: $4x + 2x + 2y + 4y$

Polynomial #2: $8y + 6y + 4x + 2x$

   a. 12xy + 8xy + 6xy + 6xy
   b. 32xy
   c. 12y + 20x
   d. 12x + 20y

22. During week 1, Nurse Cameron worked 5 shifts. During week 2, she worked twice as many shifts as she did during week 1. During week 3, she added 4 shifts to the number of shifts she worked during week 2. Which equation below describes the number of shifts Nurse Cameron worked during week 3?

   a. shifts $= (2)(5) + 4$
   b. shifts $= (4)(5) + 2$
   c. shifts $= 5 + 2 + 4$
   d. shifts $= (5)(2)(4)$

23. Solve the following expression.

$$|(3)(-4)| + (3)(4) - 1$$

   a. -1
   b. 1
   c. 23
   d. 24

Copyright © Mometrix Media. You have been licensed one copy of this document for personal use only. Any other reproduction or redistribution is strictly prohibited. All rights reserved.

24. Which graph accurately describes the data presented in the table below?

Hospital Staff	Average hours worked per week
Administrators	40
Nurses	55
Residents	80
Physicians	35

a.

b.

c.

d.

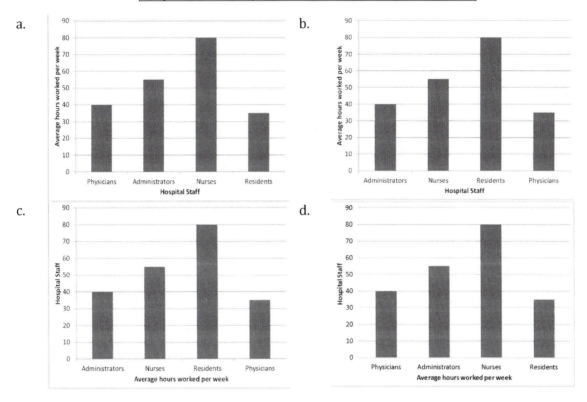

25. According to the circle graph below, which group works the most amount of time?

a. Residents
b. Physicians
c. Administrators
d. Nurses

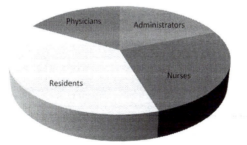

Copyright © Mometrix Media. You have been licensed one copy of this document for personal use only. Any other reproduction or redistribution is strictly prohibited. All rights reserved.

26. What are the dependent and independent variables in the graph below?

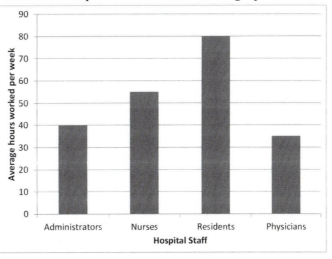

a. The dependent variable is Nurses. The independent variable is Physicians.
b. The dependent variable is Physicians. The independent variable is Nurses.
c. The dependent variable is Hospital Staff. The independent variable is Average hours worked per week.
d. The dependent variable is Average hours worked per week. The independent variable is Hospital Staff.

27. How many milligrams are in 5 grams?

a. 5 g = 0.005 mg
b. 5 g = 50 mg
c. 5 g = 500 mg
d. 5 g = 5000 mg

28. About how much does an apple weigh?

a. 1 mg
b. 0.001 g
c. 100 g
d. 1000 kg

29. A charter bus driver drove at an average speed of 65 mph for 305 miles. If he stops at a gas station for 15 minutes, then drives another 162 miles at an average speed of 80 mph, how long, will it have been since he began the trip?

a. 0.96 hours
b. 6.44 hours
c. 6.69 hours
d. 6.97 hours

Copyright © Mometrix Media. You have been licensed one copy of this document for personal use only. Any other reproduction or redistribution is strictly prohibited. All rights reserved.

30. Use the figure below to determine the distance between marks 1 and 4. The marks are evenly spaced two centimeters apart.

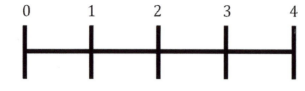

    a. 2 cm
    b. 6 cm
    c. 8 cm
    d. 10 cm

31. Two even integers and one odd integer are multiplied together. Which of the following could be their product?

    a. 3.75
    b. 9
    c. 16.2
    d. 24

32. There are $\frac{80\ mg}{0.8\ ml}$ in Acetaminophen Concentrated Infant Drops. If the proper dosage for a four year old child is 240 mg, how many milliliters should the child receive?

    a. 0.8 ml
    b. 1.6 ml
    c. 2.4 ml
    d. 3.2 ml

33. Using the chart below, which equation describes the relationship between x and y?

    a. x = 3y
    b. y = 3x
    c. $y = \frac{1}{3}x$
    d. $\frac{x}{y} = 3$

x	y
2	6
3	9
4	12
5	15

34. On a highway map, the scale indicates that 1 inch represents 45 miles. If the distance on the map is 3.2 inches, how far is the actual distance?

    a. 45 miles
    b. 54 miles
    c. 112 miles
    d. 144 miles

Copyright © Mometrix Media. You have been licensed one copy of this document for personal use only. Any other reproduction or redistribution is strictly prohibited. All rights reserved.

Section 3. Science

1. Which item below is part of the circulatory system?

    a. Kidneys
    b. Lungs
    c. Heart
    d. Stomach

2. Which item below is NOT part of the digestive system?

    a. Stomach
    b. Brain
    c. Mouth
    d. Esophagus

3. Which item below best describes the primary function of the nervous system?

    a. The nervous system is the center of communication in the body.
    b. The nervous system is primarily responsible for helping the body breathe.
    c. The nervous system transports blood throughout the body.
    d. The nervous system helps the body break down food.

4. Which of the following systems is primarily responsible for helping the body breathe?

    a. Nervous system
    b. Circulatory system
    c. Digestive system
    d. Respiratory system

5. Which system helps fight illness?

    a. Immune system
    b. Digestive system
    c. Nervous system
    d. Urinary system

6. Which item in the following list is NOT one of the major types of bones in the human body?

    a. Dense bone
    b. Long bone
    c. Short bone
    d. Irregular bone

7. Which of the following bone types is embedded in tendons?

    a. Long bones
    b. Sesamoid bones
    c. Flat bones
    d. Vertical bones

8. Which of the following factors could cause population growth in the United States?

    a. Fatal disease
    b. Migration from the United States to Europe
    c. Increased birth rate
    d. Increased death rate

Copyright © Mometrix Media. You have been licensed one copy of this document for personal use only. Any other reproduction or redistribution is strictly prohibited. All rights reserved.

9. Which of the following does NOT affect fertility in women?

    a. Smoking
    b. Stress
    c. Alcohol consumption
    d. All the above factors affect fertility in women.

10. If scientists created a cure for cancer, how would the population most likely be affected?

    a. The population would decrease.
    b. The population would increase.
    c. The population would remain the same.
    d. The population would end.

11. Each year, 3% of the people in country Q move to a different country. However, 1% of the people move back the next year. How is the population of country Q most likely affected by this movement of its citizens?

    a. The population decreases.
    b. The population increases.
    c. The population remains unchanged.
    d. The population is overcrowded.

12. Which of the following scenarios best illustrates the process of natural selection?

    a. When food was no longer available on the ground, the giraffes with long necks were able to eat leaves from tall trees. These giraffes survived and reproduced, creating more giraffes with long necks. After some time, all giraffes had long necks.
    b. When food was no longer available on the ground, the giraffes looked to other animals to give them food each day.
    c. When food was no longer available on the ground, the giraffes wondered how they would eat.
    d. When food was no longer available on the ground, the giraffes became extinct.

13. The term "*Homo sapiens*" belongs to which two categories of the biological classification?

    a. *Homo* is the kingdom and *sapiens* designates the phylum.
    b. *Homo* is the phylum and *sapiens* designates the kingdom.
    c. *Homo* is the species and *sapiens* designates the genus.
    d. *Homo* is the genus and *sapiens* designates the species.

14. Which part of the cell is often called the cell "power house" because it provides energy for cellular functions?

    a. Nucleus
    b. Cell membrane
    c. Mitochondria
    d. Cytoplasm

15. What function do ribosomes serve within the cell?

    a. Ribosomes are responsible for cell movement.
    b. Ribosomes aid in protein synthesis.
    c. Ribosomes help protect the cell from its environment.
    d. Ribosomes have enzymes that help with digestion.

Copyright © Mometrix Media. You have been licensed one copy of this document for personal use only. Any other reproduction or redistribution is strictly prohibited. All rights reserved.

16. What is the most likely reason that cells differentiate?

   a. Cells differentiate to avoid looking like all the cells around them.
   b. Cells differentiate so that simple, non-specialized cells can become highly specialized cells.
   c. Cells differentiate so that multicellular organisms will remain the same size.
   d. Cells differentiate for no apparent reason.

17. How is meiosis similar to mitosis?

   a. Both produce daughter cells that are genetically identical.
   b. Both produce daughter cells that are genetically different.
   c. Both occur in humans, other animals, and plants.
   d. Both occur asexually.

18. Which of the following statements is TRUE?

   a. Photosynthesis occurs in both plants and animals.
   b. Respiration occurs in both plants and animals.
   c. Photosynthesis occurs only in animals, while respiration occurs only in plants.
   d. Photosynthesis occurs only in plants, while respiration occurs only in animals.

19. How do DNA and RNA function together as part of the human genome?

   a. DNA carries genetic information from RNA to the cell cytoplasm.
   b. RNA carries genetic information from DNA to the cell cytoplasm.
   c. DNA and RNA carry genetic information from the cell nucleus to the cytoplasm.
   d. DNA and RNA do not interact within the cell.

20. Which statement below best describes genetic mutations?

   a. Genetic mutations are changes in DNA that occur systematically at fast rates.
   b. Genetic mutations are changes in DNA that occur spontaneously at low rates.
   c. Genetic mutations occur when DNA remains the same over relatively short time intervals.
   d. Genetic mutations occur when DNA remains the same over relatively long time intervals.

21. What process should the DNA within a cell undergo before cell replication?

   a. The DNA should quadruple so that daughter cells have more than enough DNA material after cell division.
   b. The DNA should triple so that daughter cells have three times the amount of DNA material after cell division.
   c. The DNA should replicate so that daughter cells have the same amount of DNA material after cell division.
   d. The DNA should split so that daughter cells have half the amount of DNA material after cell division.

22. What basic molecular unit enables hereditary information to be transmitted from parent to offspring?

   a. Genes
   b. Blood
   c. Organs
   d. Hair

Copyright © Mometrix Media. You have been licensed one copy of this document for personal use only. Any other reproduction or redistribution is strictly prohibited. All rights reserved.

23. Which statement most accurately compares and contrasts the structures of DNA and RNA?

    a. Both DNA and RNA have 4 nucleotide bases. Three of the bases are the same but the fourth base is thymine in DNA and uracil in RNA.
    b. Both DNA and RNA have the same 4 nucleotide bases. However, the nucleotides bond differently in the DNA when compared to RNA.
    c. Both DNA and RNA have 6 nucleotide bases. However, the shape of DNA is a triple helix and the shape of RNA is a double helix.
    d. Both DNA and RNA have a double helix structure. However, DNA contains 6 nucleotide bases and RNA contains 4 nucleotide bases.

24. Which of the following characteristics is part of a person's genotype?

    a. Brown eyes that appear hazel in the sunlight
    b. CFTR genes that causes cystic fibrosis
    c. Black hair that grows rapidly
    d. Being a fast runner

Let B represent the dominant gene for a full head of hair, and let b represent the recessive gene for male pattern baldness. The following Punnett square represents the offspring of two people with recessive genes for baldness.

	B	b
B	Possibility 1	Possibility 2
b	Possibility 3	Possibility 4

The next two questions are based on the above information.

25. According to the Punnett square, which possibility would produce an offspring with male pattern baldness?

    a. Possibility 1
    b. Possibility 2
    c. Possibility 3
    d. Possibility 4

26. According to the Punnett square, which possibility would produce an offspring with a full head of hair?

    a. Possibility 1
    b. Possibility 2
    c. Possibility 3
    d. All of the above.

27. Which of the following celestial bodies serves as a major external source of heat, light, and energy for Earth?

    a. Mars
    b. The Big Dipper
    c. The sun
    d. The moon

Copyright © Mometrix Media. You have been licensed one copy of this document for personal use only. Any other reproduction or redistribution is strictly prohibited. All rights reserved.

28. Which of the following reactions is an example of oxidation?

a. Copper loses 2 electrons.
b. Copper gains 2 electrons.
c. Copper loses 2 neutrons.
d. Copper gains 2 neutrons.

29. Chemical C is a catalyst in the reaction between chemical A and chemical B. What is the effect of chemical C?

a. Chemical C increases the rate of the reaction between A and B.
b. Chemical C decreases the rate of the reaction between A and B.
c. Chemical C converts A from an acid to a base.
d. Chemical C converts A from a base to an acid.

30. What type of molecules are enzymes?

a. Water molecules
b. Protein molecules
c. Tripolar molecules
d. Inorganic molecules

31. Fill in the blanks in this sentence: Acids have a pH that is _____ while bases have a pH that is ___.

a. Acids have a pH that is <u>less than 7</u> while bases have a pH that is <u>equal to 7</u>.
b. Acids have a pH that is <u>equal to 7</u> while bases have a pH that is <u>greater than 7</u>.
c. Acids have a pH that is <u>less than 7</u> while bases have a pH that is <u>greater than 7</u>.
d. Acids have a pH that is <u>greater than 7</u> while bases have a pH that is <u>less than 7</u>.

32. What type of chemical bond connects the sodium and chlorine atoms in a molecule of salt?

a. Ionic bond
b. Covalent bond
c. Coordinated bond
d. Salty bond

33. Which of the following statements is NOT a chemical property of water?

a. Water molecules contain hydrogen and oxygen atoms.
b. Water has a pH of 7.
c. Water molecules have covalent bonds.
d. Water molecules have ionic bonds.

34. Consider the following statements about a ball. Which of these statements describes the ball possessing the most kinetic energy?

a. A ball is sitting on top of a hill.
b. A ball is rolling down a hill.
c. A ball is resting in a bucket.
d. A ball is being held in someone's hand.

Copyright © Mometrix Media. You have been licensed one copy of this document for personal use only. Any other reproduction or redistribution is strictly prohibited. All rights reserved.

35. An atom has 5 protons, 5 neutrons, and 6 electrons. What is the electric charge of this atom?

    a. Neutral
    b. Positive
    c. Negative
    d. Undetermined

36. Which of the following statements most accurately describes the major components of an atom?

    a. Positrons and negatrons are located in the atomic nucleus while neutrons orbit the nucleus.
    b. Positrons and neutrons are located in the atomic nucleus while negatrons orbit the nucleus.
    c. Protons and electrons are located in the atomic nucleus while neutrons orbit the nucleus.
    d. Protons and neutrons are located in the atomic nucleus while electrons orbit the nucleus.

37. What type of chemical bond is formed when electrons are shared between atoms?

    a. Covalent bond
    b. Ionic bond
    c. Dipolar bond
    d. Molecular bond

38. The table below contains information from the periodic table of elements.

Element	Atomic number	Approximate atomic weight
H	1	1
He	2	4
Li	3	7
Be	4	9

Which pattern below best describes the elements listed in the table?

    a. The elements are arranged in order by weight with H being the heaviest atom and Be being the lightest atom.
    b. The elements are arranged in order by electron charge with H having the most electrons and Be having the fewest electrons.
    c. The elements are arranged in order by protons with H having the most protons and Be having the fewest protons.
    d. The elements are arranged in order by protons with H having the fewest protons and Be having the most protons.

39. Which statement best describes the difference between a liquid and a solid?

    a. Atoms in a liquid have a fixed structure, but solids maintain the shape of their container.
    b. Liquids maintain the shape of their container, but atoms in a solid have a fixed structure.
    c. Atoms in a solid flow easily, but atoms in a liquid do not flow.
    d. Solids and liquids are made of different kinds of atoms.

40. The process of changing from a liquid to a gas is called _____?

    a. Freezing
    b. Condensation
    c. Vaporization
    d. Sublimation

Copyright © Mometrix Media. You have been licensed one copy of this document for personal use only. Any other reproduction or redistribution is strictly prohibited. All rights reserved.

41. A nurse wants to investigate how different environmental factors affect her patients' body temperatures. Which tool would be the most helpful when the nurse conducts her investigation?

    a. Scale
    b. Yard stick
    c. Thermometer
    d. Blood pressure monitor

42. A scientific study has over 2000 data points. Which of the following methods is most likely to help the researcher gain usable information from the data?

    a. Use statistical analysis to understand trends in the data.
    b. Look at each individual data point, and try to create a trend.
    c. Eliminate 90% of the data so that the sample size is more manageable.
    d. Stare at the data until a pattern pops out.

43. Many years ago, people believed that flies were created from spoiled food because spoiled food that was left out in the open often contained fly larvae. So a scientist placed fresh food in a sealed container for an extended period of time. The food spoiled, but no fly larvae were found in the food that was sealed. Based on this evidence, what is the most likely reason that spoiled food left out in the open often contained fly larvae?

    a. The spoiled food evolved into fly larvae.
    b. Since the food was left out in the open, flies would lay eggs in the food.
    c. Fly larvae were spontaneously generated by the spoiled food.
    d. People only imagined they saw fly larvae in the spoiled food.

44. The average life expectancy in the 21st century is about 75 years. The average life expectancy in the 19th century was about 40 years. What is a possible explanation for the longer life expectancy in the present age?

    a. Advances in medical technology enable people to live longer.
    b. Knowledge about how basic cleanliness can help avoid illness has enabled people to live longer.
    c. The creation of various vaccines has enabled people to live longer.
    d. All of the statements above offer reasonable explanations for longer life expectancy.

45. A doctor needs to convince his boss to approve a test for a patient. Which statement below best communicates a scientific argument that justifies the need for the test?

    a. The patient looks like he needs this test.
    b. The doctor feels that the patient needs this test.
    c. The patient's symptoms and health history suggest that this test will enable the correct diagnosis to help the patient.
    d. The patient has excellent insurance that will pay for several tests, and the doctor would like to run as many tests as possible.

46. A hospital board wants to investigate how long people wait to see a doctor when visiting the emergency room (ER). Which statement provides the best reason to conduct this investigation?

    a. The board can use ER wait times to help themselves feel good.
    b. The board can use ER wait times to determine if the ER is understaffed.
    c. The board can use ER wait times for advertising purposes.
    d. There is no sound reason to conduct this investigation.

Copyright © Mometrix Media. You have been licensed one copy of this document for personal use only. Any other reproduction or redistribution is strictly prohibited. All rights reserved.

47. Which of the following statements provides the best reason to include technology in scientific research?

    a. Technology can provide the ability to efficiently and effectively collect and analyze an extremely large amount of data.

    b. Technology can be used to create nice pictures of the research results.

    c. Technology can help researchers spend more time with their families.

    d. Technology should not be included in scientific research.

48. Which of the following statements is NOT a reason to include mathematics in scientific research?

    a. Researchers can use mathematics to sway research outcomes in whatever direction they choose.

    b. Statistical mathematics can help researchers discover patterns and trends in large amounts of data.

    c.   Mathematics enables data analysis to be objective instead of subjective.

    d.   Researchers can use mathematics to help define measurable research goals.

49. Which of the following structures has the lowest blood pressure?

    a. Arteries

    b. Arteriole

    c. Venule

    d. Vein

50. Which of the heart chambers is the most muscular?

    a. Left atrium

    b. Right atrium

    c. Left ventricle

    d. Right ventricle

51. Which part of the brain interprets sensory information?

    a. Cerebrum

    b. Hindbrain

    c. Cerebellum

    d. Medulla oblongata

52. Which of the following proteins is produced by cartilage?

    a. Actin

    b. Estrogen

    c. Collagen

    d. Myosin

53. Which component of the nervous system is responsible for lowering the heart rate?

    a. Central nervous system

    b. Sympathetic nervous system

    c. Parasympathetic nervous system

    d. Distal nervous system

Copyright © Mometrix Media. You have been licensed one copy of this document for personal use only. Any other reproduction or redistribution is strictly prohibited. All rights reserved.

54. How much air does an adult inhale in an average breath?

    a. 500 mL
    b. 750 mL
    c. 1000 mL
    d. 1250 mL

Copyright © Mometrix Media. You have been licensed one copy of this document for personal use only. Any other reproduction or redistribution is strictly prohibited. All rights reserved.

Section 4. English and Language Usage

1. Which of the following sentences shows the correct way to separate the items in the series?

    a. These are actual cities in the United States: Unalaska, Alaska; Yreka, California; Two Egg, Florida; and Boring, Maryland.

    b. These are actual cities in the United States: Unalaska; Alaska, Yreka; California, Two Egg; Florid, and Boring; Maryland.

    c. These are actual cities in the United States: Unalaska, Alaska, Yreka, California, Two Egg, Florida, and Boring, Maryland.

    d. These are actual cities in the United States: Unalaska Alaska, Yreka California, Two Egg Florida, and Boring Maryland.

2. Adella knows how high the stakes are in her trading job at the investment bank, so she is very ____ about following the rules and fulfilling all of the requirements. Which of the following words should be placed in the blank?

    a. conscientous
    b. consientious
    c. conscientious
    d. consciencious

3. ____ going on vacation to ____ house on Lake Chelan, and they plan to water ski and parasail while ____. Which of the following sets of words would correctly complete the sentence?

    a. Their; there; they're
    b. They're; their; there
    c. They're; there; their
    d. There; they're; their

4. Which of the following sentences demonstrates the correct use of an apostrophe?

    a. Lyle works for the courthouse, and among his responsibilities is getting the jurors meal's.
    b. Lyle works for the courthouse, and among his responsibilities is getting the juror's meals.
    c. Lyle works for the courthouse, and among his responsibilities is getting the jurors' meals.
    d. Lyle works for the courthouse, and among his responsibilities is getting the jurors meals'.

5. Which of the following is a complex sentence?

    a. Milton's favorite meal is spaghetti and meatballs, along with a side salad and garlic toast.
    b. Before Ernestine purchases a book, she always checks to see if the library has it.
    c. Desiree prefers warm, sunny weather, but her twin sister Destiny likes a crisp, cold day.
    d. Ethel, Ben, and Alice are working together on a school project about deteriorating dams.

6. Finlay flatly refused to take part in the piano recital, so his parents had to cajole him with the promise of a trip to his favorite toy store. Which of the following is the best definition of cajole as it is used in the sentence?

    a. prevent
    b. threaten
    c. insist
    d. coax

Copyright © Mometrix Media. You have been licensed one copy of this document for personal use only. Any other reproduction or redistribution is strictly prohibited. All rights reserved.

7. Which of the following nouns is the correct plural form of the word *tempo*?

    a. tempo
    b. tempae
    c. tempi
    d. tempos

8. Which of the following sentences follows the rules of capitalization?

    a. Kristia knows that her Aunt Jo will be visiting, but she is not sure if her uncle will be there as well.
    b. During a visit to the monastery, Jess interviewed brother Mark about the daily prayer schedule.
    c. Leah spoke to cousin Martha about her summer plans to drive from Colorado to Arizona.
    d. Justinia will be staying with family in the outer banks during the early Fall.

9. To register a vehicle, each person will need ____ proof of insurance, proof of a passed safety inspection, and a completed registration application. Which of the following choices best completes the sentence?

    a. their
    b. its
    c. the
    d. his or her

10. Which of the following sentences does NOT use correct punctuation to separate independent clauses?

    a. Anne likes to add salsa to her scrambled eggs; Gordon unaccountably likes his with peanut butter.
    b. Anne likes to add salsa to her scrambled eggs, however Gordon unaccountably likes his with peanut butter.
    c. Anne likes to add salsa to her scrambled eggs. Gordon unaccountably likes his with peanut butter.
    d. Anne likes to add salsa to her scrambled eggs, but Gordon unaccountably likes his with peanut butter.

11. Fenella wanted to attend the concert. She also wanted to attend the reception at the art gallery. She tried to find a way to do both in one evening. She failed. Which of the following options best combines these sentences? Consider both style and clarity when choosing a response.

    a. Although Fenella wanted to attend the concert, she also wanted to attend the reception at the art gallery, so she tried to find a way to do both in one evening. She failed.
    b. Fenella wanted to attend both the concert and the reception at the art gallery, but she failed to find a way to do both in one evening.
    c. Fenella failed to find a way to attend both the concert and the reception at the art gallery.
    d. Because Fenella wanted to attend both the concert and the reception at the art gallery, she tried to find a way to do both in one evening. Unfortunately, she failed.

12. Which of the following nouns is the correct plural form of the word *human*?

    a. humans
    b. humen
    c. human's
    d. humans'

Copyright © Mometrix Media. You have been licensed one copy of this document for personal use only. Any other reproduction or redistribution is strictly prohibited. All rights reserved.

13. The word *permeate*, meaning "to penetrate or pervade," is made up of two parts with a Latin origin: the root *meare*, which means "to pass," and the prefix *per-*. Based on the current definition of the word *permeate*, which of the following is the most likely meaning of the prefix *per-*?

    a. across
    b. by
    c. with
    d. through

14. The following words share a common Greek-based suffix: *anthropology, cosmetology, etymology,* and *genealogy*. What is the most likely meaning of the suffix *-logy*?

    a. record
    b. study
    c. affinity
    d. fear

15. *Jacob had been worried about the speech, but in the end he did well.* Which of the following words functions as an adverb in the sentence?

    a. worried
    b. about
    c. but
    d. well

16. Most doctors _____ that there _____ a lot of reasons to add a daily multivitamin to the diet.

Which of the following sets of words correctly completes the sentence?

    a. agree; is
    b. agree; are
    c. agrees; is
    d. agrees; are

17. Which of the following sentences contains a correct example of subject-verb agreement?

    a. Neither Jeanne nor Pauline like the dinner options on the menu.
    b. All of the council likes the compromise that they have reached about property taxes.
    c. The faculty of the math department were unable to agree on the curriculum changes.
    d. Both Clara and Don feels that they need to be more proactive in checking on the contractors.

18. The guest speaker was undoubtedly an erudite scholar, but his comments on nomological determinism seemed to go over the heads of the students in the audience. Which of the following best explains the meaning of erudite in the sentence?

    a. authentic
    b. arrogant
    c. faulty
    d. knowledgeable

19. *Wearing white to a funeral is considered by many to be _____.* Which of the following correctly completes the sentence?

    a. sacrelegious
    b. sacriligious
    c. sacrilegious
    d. sacreligious

Copyright © Mometrix Media. You have been licensed one copy of this document for personal use only. Any other reproduction or redistribution is strictly prohibited. All rights reserved.

20. Which of the following demonstrates the correct use of a hyphen?

    a. super-sede
    b. cross-word
    c. self-evident
    d. super-market

21. Due to concerns about overspending, the city council conducted an investigation into the budget and then facilitated a discourse among local residents about ways to cut spending. Which of the following best removes the nominalization from the sentence?

    a. Due to concerns about overspending, the city council facilitated a discourse among local residents after conducting an investigation into the budget.
    b. Concerned about overspending, the city council investigated the budget and then discussed ways to cut spending with residents.
    c. Concerned about overspending, the city council investigated the budget and then opened the floor up to local residents about ways to cut spending.
    d. Due to concerns about overspending, the city council reviewed the budget and then turned over the decision about ways to cut spending to residents.

22. Which of the following is a simple sentence?

    a. Ben likes baseball, but Joseph likes basketball.
    b. It looks like rain; be sure to bring an umbrella.
    c. Although he was tired, Edgar still attended the recital.
    d. Marjorie and Thomas planned an exciting trip to Maui.

23. *Anne-Charlotte and I will be driving together to the picnic this weekend.* Which of the following words functions as a pronoun in the sentence?

    a. be
    b. this
    c. together
    d. I

24. Which of the following demonstrates the correct use of quotation marks?

    a. The professor read aloud from the first chapter of *David Copperfield*, entitled "I am Born."
    b. The professor read aloud from the first chapter of "*David Copperfield*," entitled I am Born.
    c. The professor read aloud from the first chapter of *David Copperfield*, entitled 'I am Born.'
    d. The professor read aloud from the first chapter of "*David Copperfield*," entitled 'I am Born.'

25. Which of the following sentences is the best in terms of style, clarity, and conciseness?

    a. Ava has a leap year birthday; she is really twenty, and her friends like to joke that she is only five years old.
    b. Because Ava has a leap year birthday, her friends like to joke that she is only five years old when she is really twenty.
    c. Ava is twenty years old, her friends like to joke that she is five because she has a leap year birthday.
    d. Although Ava has a leap year birthday, she is twenty years old, but her friends like to joke that she is five.

Copyright © Mometrix Media. You have been licensed one copy of this document for personal use only. Any other reproduction or redistribution is strictly prohibited. All rights reserved.

26. The housekeeper Mrs. Vanderbroek had a fixed daily routine for running the manor, and was not particularly amenable to any suggested changes. Which of the following best explains the meaning of amenable as it is used in the sentence?

    a. capable
    b. agreeable
    c. obstinate
    d. critical

27. A quick review of all available housing options indicated that Casper had little choice but to rent for now and wait for a better time to buy. Which of the following words does not function as an adjective in the sentence?

    a. quick
    b. available
    c. little
    d. rent

28. Roan and _____ were so angry about the gag gift that they refused to speak to Elsie and _____ for two months.

    a. she; I
    b. she; me
    c. her; I
    d. her; me

29. Tamara had a problem with her furnace. She checked the phonebook for repair shops. She called two different repair shops. They were closest to her home. The first quoted a very high price. The second quoted a more reasonable price. Which of the following options best combines the sentences? Consider style, clarity, and conciseness when selecting your response.

    a. Tamara had a problem with her furnace, so she checked the phonebook for repair shops. She called two different shops that were closest to her home. Although the first quoted a very high price, the second quoted a more reasonable price.
    b. After discovering that she had a problem with her furnace, Tamara checked the phone book for repair shops and called two different shops. These two were closest to her home. It turned out that the first quoted a very high price, but the second was more reasonable.
    c. Of the two furnace repair shops that Tamara called, the first quoted a very high price, but the second quoted a more reasonable price. Tamara needed to have her furnace repaired after discovering that there was a problem with it.
    d. When Tamara had a problem with her furnace, she checked the phonebook for repair shops that were closest to her home and called two different shops. The first quoted a very high price, but the second was more reasonable.

30. The Constitution mentions the right to _____ arms, but one common mistake is to spell this as though the Founding Fathers were ensuring the right to go sleeveless. Which of the following words correctly completes the sentence?

    a. bear
    b. bare
    c. barre
    d. baire

Copyright © Mometrix Media. You have been licensed one copy of this document for personal use only. Any other reproduction or redistribution is strictly prohibited. All rights reserved.

31. Which word is NOT used correctly in the context of the following sentence?

There is no real distinction among the two treatment protocols recommended online.

    a. real
    b. among
    c. protocols
    d. online

Choose the meaning of the underlined words in the sentences below.

32. Her concern for him was <u>sincere.</u>

    a. intense
    b. genuine
    c. brief
    d. misunderstood

33. He is a very <u>courteous</u> young man.

    a. handsome
    b. polite
    c. inconsiderate
    d. odd

34. Spanish is a difficult language to <u>comprehend</u>.

    a. learn
    b. speak
    c. understand
    d. appreciate

Copyright © Mometrix Media. You have been licensed one copy of this document for personal use only. Any other reproduction or redistribution is strictly prohibited. All rights reserved.

Answer Key and Explanations for Test #2

Reading Answer Explanations

1. B: The word *intermittent* suggests that something occurs at imprecise intervals, so answer choice B is the best synonym. Answer choices A and D suggest the exact opposite of the meaning indicated in the sentence. Answer choice C likely reflects another element of the woman's labor, but it has nothing to do with the meaning of the word *intermittent*.

2. B: The context of the sentence suggests that Edith is emphasizing the temperature of the plate. In this sentence, dialogue is conveyed with the quotation marks, and part of the quotation is not in a bold font. The bold font must mean something other than dialogue, so answer choice A cannot be correct. The sentence clearly indicates that Edith speaks to the man, so answer choice C makes little sense. Additionally, there is no reason to believe that Edith is angry. Rather, she is concerned about the man's safety. Therefore, answer choice D is incorrect.

3. D: In this sentence, the information in parentheses appears to be examples of humanities disciplines. (Additionally, the abbreviation "e.g." stands for the Latin phrase *exempli gratia*, meaning "for example.") Thus, answer choice D is the correct option. There is no reason to believe that the information in parentheses is either an error or a correction, so answer choices A and C are incorrect. While answer choice C has promise – suggesting that the information in parentheses is an addition to information already provided – it is not as strong as option D, since option D provides the more logical explanation about the parenthetical details being examples.

4. C: Only the word *neglect* can fall between the guide words *needs* and *negotiate* on a dictionary page. The words *needle* and *nectar* would come before *needs*, and the word *neigh* would follow *negotiate*.

5. D: The chapter title refers to the *fictional* works of Dorothy L. Sayers, and letters generally do not fall under the category of fiction. Novels, plays, and mysteries, however, usually do.

6. C: An expository passage seeks to *expose* information by explaining or defining it in detail. As this passage focuses on describing the written works of Dorothy L. Sayers, it may safely be considered expository. The author is not necessarily telling a story, something one might expect from a strictly narrative passage. (Additionally, the author's main point, that of explaining why Sayers was such a versatile writer, represents a kind of thesis statement for shaping the overall focus of the passage. A narrative passage would focus more on simply telling the story of Sayers's life.) At no point is the author attempting to persuade the reader about anything, and there is nothing particularly technical about the passage. Rather, it is a focused look at Sayers's educational background and how she developed into a writer of many genres; this makes it solidly expository.

7. A: As indicated in the answer explanation above, the main focus of the passage is Sayers's versatility as a writer. The first paragraph notes this and then begins discussing her education, introducing the experience that would inform her later accomplishments. The second paragraph then follows this up with specifics about the types of writing she did. Answer choice B would be correct if the passage were more narrative than expository. Answer choices C and D focus on specific works for which Sayers is remembered, but both are too limited to be considered a representative summary of the entire passage.

Copyright © Mometrix Media. You have been licensed one copy of this document for personal use only. Any other reproduction or redistribution is strictly prohibited. All rights reserved.

8. B: The mention of an "unexpectedly good education" represents an opinion on the part of the author. As the author does not follow this up with an explanation about *why* such an education would be unexpectedly good, the statement is simply a moment of bias on the author's part, rather than an element within the larger argument. There is no bias in the other answer choices. Answer choices A and C are factual statements about Sayers's life and work. Answer choice D, while it might hint vaguely at disapproval on the author's part (who might, perhaps, wish to know Sayers's reasons), is not necessarily a statement containing bias. It is indeed true that Sayers turned down the doctorate of divinity, and it is also true that her reasons for doing so are unknown. Only answer choice B conveys an opinion of the author.

9. D: A search for early maps by one of the first people to study geography would certainly take Jorgen to the 900 section of the library: History, geography, and biography. For this particular study, there is no reason for Jorgen to look among books on philosophy and psychology, social sciences, or technical and applied science.

10. D: The sieve of Eratosthenes is a mathematical tool, so Jorgen should go to the science and mathematics section. While the sieve might be used in certain computer applications, there is no specific indication of this. As a result, answer choice D is a better option than answer choice A. Also, Jorgen has no reason to check the philosophy and psychology or languages sections to find out more about a mathematical topic.

11. B: Section 400 is the section on languages, so it is a good place to look for more information about the letters of the Greek alphabet. Jorgen would be unlikely to find anything useful in the sections on religion, arts and recreation, or history, geography, and biography. (It is arguable, of course, that the use of Greek letters in relation to Christianity – Christ as the "alpha" and the "omega," or the beginning and the end – make the religion section a possible place to look for the meaning of "beta." But, this is certainly not the first place Jorgen should look, as the information would be buried in a book about Christianity. Checking for a Greek language guide would be far quicker.)

12. D: Section 800 features works of literature, so that is the best place for Jorgen to begin looking for *The Iliad* and *The Odyssey*. The philosophy and psychology section will likely contain references to these works, but Jorgen would still have to go to the literature section to obtain the works themselves. The same thing can be said about the religion and arts and recreation sections.

13. C: While planning her daughter's wedding, Marci is likely to find picking out a paint color for the living room *unimportant*. Therefore, answer choice C is the most logical option. Choosing a paint color might also be meaningless at the moment, but it is not without meaning altogether. It is simply not as important. Answer choice A infers more than the sentence implies. Answer choice B could be forced into the sentence (if Marci was looking for a distraction from the stress of wedding planning, for instance), but it is not natural, and it is certainly not a synonym for *peripheral*. Answer choice D makes little sense in the context of the sentence.

14. B: Latvia's total population was around two million in 2011. Twenty-five percent of this number is about 500,000 people. The Russian population is closest to this number. The chart indicates that the Latvian population was around 1,300,000 in 2011; the Ukrainian population was well under 200,000; the German population was even lower than the Ukrainian population.

15. D: According to the chart, the Latvian and German populations are the only ones that decreased. In terms of sheer numbers, the Latvian population decrease exceeded the German population decrease by around 2,000 people. But in terms of percentage, which is what the question asks

- 240 -

Copyright © Mometrix Media. You have been licensed one copy of this document for personal use only. Any other reproduction or redistribution is strictly prohibited. All rights reserved.

about, the German population decrease is far greater. An ethnic group that declines from around 70,000 people to just over 3,000 people has decreased by over 90 percent. The Latvian population, on the other hand, decreased by only about five percent.

16. B: The Russian population of Latvia decreased the most since 1991. The Latvian population decreased slightly, but not to the same degree. The Ukrainian population decreased by an even smaller percentage since 1991. The German population remained relatively unchanged between 1991 and 2011.

17. C: On the chart, the only ethnic group that represents approximately one percent of the population after World War II and approximately three percent by 1991 is the Ukrainian population. The Latvian and Russian populations represent much larger percentages of the total population of Latvia. The German population decreased significantly during this time period.

18. C: As the final step indicates, the new word should end in *Y*. This immediately eliminates answer choice D. Answer choice A adds an *L* when a second one is not required, and answer choice B adds two *Ts* to a word that has none. Only answer choice C follows all of the directions to spell the new word: REPLAY.

19. A: Klara's success is clearly the result of diligence, so answer choice A must be correct. It is possible that her diligence was also silent, but the sentence does not indicate this. Answer choice B, then, cannot be correct. A moderate commitment by an average student would not lead to exemplary results, so answer choice C is incorrect. Answer choice D makes no sense in the context of the sentence.

20. D: Puffed rice is a dry breakfast cereal, and therefore contains (or might contain) a dairy product. Breaded chicken parmesan contains both bread crumbs and parmesan cheese; the cheese is certainly a dairy product, and bread is on the warning list from the doctor. A sliced turkey sandwich contains deli meat and bread, both of which are discouraged by Flemming's doctor. Yogurt made from coconut milk, however, is meant to be a dairy-free alternative, so it should be a safe choice for Flemming.

21. C: Chapter III of the manual contains information about adjusting the climate within the vehicle, so it is here that Regina will find the instructions she needs to adjust the air conditioning. Chapter I would be the best choice if the manual did *not* also include Chapter III. The chapter on safety options would probably not contain information about how to operate the air conditioning, so answer choice B is incorrect. Regina should definitely adjust the air conditioning before she begins driving, but the information needed to do this is not likely to be found in Chapter IV.

22. B: Chapter V discusses routine maintenance, and oil changes fall firmly in this category. With this chapter available, there is no reason for Regina to check the chapters on pre-driving and driving, emergencies, or consumer resources.

23. D: A list of dealerships is most likely to be found in the section on consumer resources. With this chapter available, there is no reason for Regina to check the chapters on vehicle instruments; audio, climate, and voice controls; or routine maintenance.

24. D: An overheating vehicle is definitely an emergency, so Regina would need to consult Chapter VI. The other chapters contain useful information that Regina will need once her vehicle is back in working order, but until then she should focus on the information in the chapter about emergency situations.

Copyright © Mometrix Media. You have been licensed one copy of this document for personal use only. Any other reproduction or redistribution is strictly prohibited. All rights reserved.

25. B: As most students discover, Wikipedia is not considered a reliable source or a particularly scholarly one. The Encyclopedia Britannica is, however, as are Science.gov (which would contain officially recognized information provided by a government organization) and LexisNexis (a reputable site containing legal and educational resources).

26. C: The word *temperate* can have a number of meanings, including "modest" and "conservative." In the context of the poem, however, the best meaning is "agreeable," because the poet is clearly saying that his beloved is lovelier and more agreeable than a summer day. The meaning of "immoderate" is the opposite of that suggested by the word *temperate* in the poem.

27. C: The slash between the sentences indicates the break in the lines of poetry. The reader knows this is a poem, because question 26 refers to the lines as part of a sonnet. The most obvious reason to separate the sentences would be to note where the poet has divided the lines. There is not enough of the sonnet to suggest that the slash indicates different stanzas. (In addition, a Shakespearean sonnet does not typically have stanzas as they are most often recognized in poetry.) The question mark on its own indicates a question; the slash is not needed to indicate this, or to indicate that the statement that follows is a direct answer to the question. Similarly, the end punctuation indicates the end of each sentence. A slash is not necessary for this. (Otherwise, there would be a slash at the end of both sentences, instead of one between the two.)

28. D: Eczema is a topical condition, so Chapter 12 (section D) would be the most appropriate place to look. Eczema is not specific to either men or women, nor is it specific to adults, so Chapter 8 would not be the best place to look. Finally, eczema is neither a respiratory condition nor a digestive condition.

29. A: This question asks the reader to consider the distinction between a recognized respiratory condition (Chapter 10) and a children's condition (Chapter 7). In this case, the first and best place to check is Chapter 7, because it addresses conditions specific to children, and it describes herbs that may be useful in treating these conditions. Herbs, like pharmaceuticals, need to be used carefully, and the type of herbal remedy that would be used to treat an adult respiratory condition is not necessarily the same one that would be used to treat a respiratory condition in a child. Additionally, the dosage would certainly be different, so the chapter on children's conditions is the correct place to look. Chapters 9 and 12 (immunity and detox, respectively) would not contain useful information for this particular situation.

30. C: Chapter 5 contains information about using herbs in beverages. Since Clothilde is looking for ways to use the elderflower to make tea and wine, this chapter should be useful. Chapter 3 would not likely contain information that would be useful in this situation. Chapter 4 discusses using herbs in food, so Clothilde is unlikely to find anything in this section about beverages. Chapter 13 would certainly be the place to look in the index of herbs, but this chapter would most likely contain a listing of the herb and a summary of its properties, rather than recommendations for how to use it in tea or wine making.

31. B: Chapter 3 contains information about caring for herbs, so it is the first place Clothilde should look. The herb is clearly already planted, so Chapter 2 will not be of much use in this case. Again, Chapter 13 would certainly be the place to look in the index of herbs, but this chapter would most likely contain a listing of the herb and a summary of its properties, rather than recommendations for maintaining the plant. Chapter 14, the alphabetical listing for herbs J-O, is unlikely to contain any information either about caring for herbs in general or about the elderberry in particular.

Copyright © Mometrix Media. You have been licensed one copy of this document for personal use only. Any other reproduction or redistribution is strictly prohibited. All rights reserved.

32. C: Only Cosette fulfills all of the clearly stated requirements in the ad. She does not smoke (and is, in fact, allergic to cigarette smoke), and she needs a quiet place to study in a house that is advertised as having quiet occupants. Also implied is Cosette's need to be close to the university, since she is likely going to be studying for classes. Frances has a dog, and this is not allowed according to the ad. Adelaide is looking for a short-term lease, and the other occupants prefer a long-term renter. Felix is male, and the other occupants are looking for a female renter.

33. B: Sculpture is not typically classified as a performing art.

34. B: For two pounds of each type of tea, Wholesale Tea's price would be $96, which is the best price. Tea Heaven's price would be $102. Tea by The Pound's price would be $104. Tea Express's price would be the same as Tea Heaven's price: $102.

35. B: Wholesale Tea would have the best price for these specific blends. The price for one pound of Earl Grey and two pounds of green tea would be $78. Tea Heaven's price would be $87. Tea by The Pound's price would be $83. Tea Express's price would be $88.

36. D: Kiev is the capital of Ukraine, which is not part of Northern Europe according to the information provided in the question. (It is not one of the Scandinavian countries, it is not one of the Baltic states, and it is certainly not part of Great Britain.) Copenhagen is the capital of Denmark, and Oslo is the capital of Norway. Both of these regions are part of Scandinavia. London is the capital of England in Great Britain.

37. A: Portugal is the other country on the Iberian Peninsula. It is unique among countries in Southern Europe because it does not have a coastline along the Mediterranean Sea or the Black Sea. The western and southern coasts of Portugal border the Atlantic Ocean. Italy and Cyprus are not on the Iberian Peninsula, and both have Mediterranean coasts. Bulgaria is also not on the Iberian Peninsula, and its eastern coast borders the Black Sea.

38. C: The only logical conclusion that can be made based on the announcement is that the library has applied a fee to Internet usage beyond 30 minutes to discourage patrons from spending too long on the computers. There is nothing in the announcement to suggest that the library plans to add more computers. The announcement mentions a limited number of computers, but there is no indication that there are plans to change this fact. The announcement makes no mention of the library's budget, so it is impossible to infer that the library is facing budget cuts or that the library is compensating for budget cuts with the fee. Similarly, the announcement says nothing about the library's Internet costs, so it is impossible to conclude logically that the library is attempting to offset its own Internet fees.

39. C: Raoul will need the computer for a total of 90 minutes. The first 30 minutes are free, so Raoul will need to be prepared to pay for 60 minutes. This is equal to four intervals of 15 minutes. Each 15-minute interval costs $3, so Raoul will need to pay $12 for his Internet usage at the library.

40. D: Good Karma Salon & Spa specifically notes that it offers haircuts, coloring, and nail services. Based on the information in the telephone book, then, this will likely be the best choice for Genevieve. The Sérénité Spa advertisement states that the business offers "all spa services," but does not specify what those services are in the same way that the Good Karma Salon & Spa advertisement does. Angel Cuts and Perfect Endings appear in the hair salon section. Therefore, while they likely offer haircuts and coloring, they may not offer nail services. Furthermore, there is nothing in these ads to suggest that manicures and pedicures are offered at these locations.

Copyright © Mometrix Media. You have been licensed one copy of this document for personal use only. Any other reproduction or redistribution is strictly prohibited. All rights reserved.

41. C: Natural Nails advertises that it uses no harsh chemicals or toxic products, so this is Genevieve's best option to avoid another allergic reaction. Nails by Manhattan and Hands to Envy make no comment about the chemical content of their products, so Genevieve should probably avoid these places. Perfect Endings is a hair salon, not a nail salon.

42. A: Hair and a Spare is located at 274 Finch, while Natural Nails is located at 285 Finch. These businesses would almost certainly be in the same shopping center, if not right next door to each other. Perfect Endings and Hands to Envy are located on the same street, but the address numbers are so far apart that these two businesses are likely not in the same shopping center. The same is true for Nails by Manhattan and Airbrushed Tans. Angel Cuts and Cannes Tan are located on different streets.

43. C: Although it never specifically addresses the babysitter, the directions are clearly instructions for how to take care of a little girl. A mother or father would not need this information written down in such detail, but a babysitter might. You can infer the answer in this case.

44. D: You cannot assume gender, and the note never indicates whether the writer is male or female. You can tell that the writer is the main caretaker of the child in question, so "parent" is the best choice in this case. A teacher or nurse might be able to write such a note, but parent is probably more likely, making it the best choice.

45. B: The information in the passage lets you know that only the serving team can score. This rule is different in different leagues, so it is important to read the passage instead of going by what you know from your own life.

46. D: Although any number of people could play in a volleyball game, the passage mentions that the entire class could participate in a game. Do all of them have to participate? No. But that wasn't the question.

47. A: The referee might yell any number of things, but only "side out" is mentioned in the passage.

48. C: In volleyball, all that is needed in terms of equipment is a ball and a net.

Mathematics Answer Explanations

1. C: According to the problem statement, 60% of the class wanted to work with the elderly. Therefore, convert 60% to a fraction by using the following steps:

$$60\% = \frac{60}{100}$$

Now simplify the above fraction using a greatest common factor of 20.

$$\frac{60}{100} = \frac{3}{5}$$

2. B: Since 35% of the staff will take vacation days, only 100% – 35% = 65% of the staff is available to work. Of the remaining 65%, only 20% are certified to work in the neonatal unit. Therefore multiply 65% by 20% using these steps:

Copyright © Mometrix Media. You have been licensed one copy of this document for personal use only. Any other reproduction or redistribution is strictly prohibited. All rights reserved.

Convert 65% and 20% into decimals by dividing both numbers by 100.

$$\frac{65}{100} = 0.65 \text{ and } \frac{20}{100} = 0.20$$

Now multiply 0.65 by 0.20 to get

$$(0.65)(0.20) = 0.13$$

Now convert 0.13 to a percentage by multiplying by 100.

$$(0.13)(100) = 13\%$$

3. B: The patient's dosage must decrease by 30%. So calculate 30% of 340:

$$(0.30)(340 \text{ mg}) = 102 \text{ mg}$$

Now subtract the 30% decrease from the original dosage.

$$340 \text{ mg} - 102 \text{ mg} = 238 \text{ mg}$$

4. C: Since 70% of the patients in the study were women, 30% of the patients were men. Calculate the number of male patients by multiplying 100 by 0.30.

$$(100)(0.30) = 30$$

Of the 30 male patients in the study, 10% were overweight as children. So 90% were not overweight. Multiply 30 by 0.90 to get the final answer.

$$(30)(0.90) = 27$$

5. C: If the incoming class has 100 students, then $\frac{3}{4}$ of those students will major in nursing.

$$(100)\left(\frac{3}{4}\right) = 75$$

So 75 students will major in nursing but only $\frac{1}{5}$ of that 75 will complete the nursing program.

$$(75)\left(\frac{1}{5}\right) = 15$$

Therefore, 15 students will complete the program.

6. A: The first midwife contributes $2000 per month, and she uses $\frac{2}{5}$ of that amount for rent and utilities.

$$(\$2000)\left(\frac{2}{5}\right) = \$800$$

So the midwife pays $800 for rent and utilities, which leaves her with

$$\$2000 - \$800 = \$1200$$

Copyright © Mometrix Media. You have been licensed one copy of this document for personal use only. Any other reproduction or redistribution is strictly prohibited. All rights reserved.

The midwife divides the remaining $1200 in half.

$$\frac{\$1200}{2} = \$600$$

The midwife saves $600 and buys medical supplies with the remaining $600.

7. A: The second midwife allocates $\frac{1}{2}$ of her funds for an office administrator plus another $\frac{1}{10}$ for office supplies. So add $\frac{1}{2}$ and $\frac{1}{10}$ by first finding a common denominator.

$$\frac{1}{2} = \frac{5}{10}$$

$$\frac{5}{10} + \frac{1}{10} = \frac{6}{10}$$

Now simplify $\frac{6}{10}$ by using the greatest common factor of 6 and 10, which is 2.

$$6 \div 2 = 3 \text{ and } 10 \div 2 = 5$$

Therefore, $\frac{6}{10} = \frac{3}{5}$.

8. D: First add all expenses for the third midwife. Then subtract her total expenses from $2000.

$$\$900 + \$200 + \$100 = \$1200$$

$$\$2000 - \$1200 = \$800$$

9. C: The ratio of her savings to the rent is 1:2, which means that for every $2 she pays in rent, she saves $1 for the purchase of an office building. To calculate the amount the fourth midwife saves for the purchase of a building, divide $800 by 2.

$$\frac{\$800}{2} = \$400$$

10. C: Each midwife contributed about $500 towards the ultrasound purchase.

$$\$500 + \$500 + \$500 + \$500 = \$2000$$

11. C: To obtain the new dosage, subtract 1/5th of 310 mg from the original dosage of 310 mg, then subtract 20 mg.

$$310 \text{ mg} - \left(310 \times \frac{1}{5}\right) \text{mg} - 20 \text{ mg} = 228 \text{ mg}$$

12. C: Find $\frac{1}{7}$ of 100 by multiplying

$$(100)\left(\frac{1}{7}\right) = \frac{100}{7} = 14.2857$$

Copyright © Mometrix Media. You have been licensed one copy of this document for personal use only. Any other reproduction or redistribution is strictly prohibited. All rights reserved.

$\frac{100}{7}$ is an improper fraction. Convert the fraction to a decimal and round to the nearest hundredth to get 14.29.

13. A: The Roman numeral system requires adding or subtracting the individual digits in order to obtain the full number. The X equals 10. So XX means add 10 + 10 to get 20. The I equals 1 and V equals 5. However, since the I is placed directly before the V, subtract 5 – 1 to get 4. Finally, add 20 + 4 to get 24.

14. C: Susan receives $40,000. First she contributes 10% of her salary to a retirement account.

$$(\$40{,}000)(0.10) = \$4{,}000$$

$$\$40{,}000 - \$4{,}000 = \$36{,}000$$

After contributing to her retirement account, Susan has $36,000 left. Then she pays 25% in taxes.

$$(\$36{,}000)(0.25) = \$9{,}000$$

$$\$36{,}000 - \$9{,}000 = \$27{,}000$$

After paying taxes, Susan has $27,000 left. Finally, she pays $30 each month for health insurance. Calculate the annual amount Susan pays for health insurance, and subtract this amount from her remaining salary.

$$(\$30)(12) = \$360$$

$$\$27{,}000 - \$360 = \$26{,}640$$

15. D: To determine the total cost of Susan's outfit, add all her purchases.

$$\$69.99 + \$39.99 + \$34.76 = \$144.65$$

16. B: The beginning balance for the account was $300.00. Then two purchases were made. So subtract those purchase amounts from the beginning balance.

$$\$300.00 - \$3.56 - \$132.61 = \$163.83$$

Next, a deposit was made into the account. So add the amount of the deposit to get the ending balance.

$$\$163.83 + \$75.33 = \$239.16$$

17. A: Apply the order of operations to solve this problem. Multiplication and division are computed first from left to right. Then addition and subtraction are computed next from left to right.

$$2 + (2)(2) - 2 \div 2 =$$
$$2 + 4 - 2 \div 2 =$$
$$2 + 4 - 1 =$$
$$6 - 1 =$$
$$5$$

Copyright © Mometrix Media. You have been licensed one copy of this document for personal use only. Any other reproduction or redistribution is strictly prohibited. All rights reserved.

18. C: The office manager will order 2 cupcakes for each person and 50 people will attend the event.

$$(2)(50) = 100$$

Therefore, the manager will order 100 cupcakes. Each cupcake costs $1.75. Calculate the total cost for cupcakes.

$$(100)(\$1.75) = \$175.00$$

19. B: Compare and order the rational numbers by finding a common denominator for all three fractions. The least common denominator for 3, 5, and 15 is 15. Now convert the fractions with different denominators into fractions with a common denominator.

$$\frac{4}{15} = \frac{4}{15}$$
$$\frac{2}{5} = \frac{6}{15}$$
$$\frac{1}{3} = \frac{5}{15}$$

Now that all three fractions have the same denominator, order them from smallest to largest by comparing the numerators.

$$\frac{4}{15} < \frac{5}{15} < \frac{6}{15}$$

Since $\frac{4}{15}$ of the patients are in Group Alpha, this group has the smallest number of patients. The next largest group has $\frac{5}{15}$ of the patients, which is Group Gamma. The largest group has $\frac{6}{15}$ of the patients, which is Group Beta.

20. A: Solve the equation for x.

$$2x + 6 = 14$$
$$2x = 14 - 6$$
$$2x = 8$$
$$x = \frac{8}{2}$$
$$x = 4$$

21. D: Add the polynomials by combining all the like terms, which have the same variable. In other words, combine all the x terms and then combine all the y terms.

$$4x + 2x + 4x + 2x = 12x$$

$$8y + 6y + 2y + 4y = 20y$$

Since $12x$ and $20y$ are different terms, the final answer is

$$12x + 20y$$

Copyright © Mometrix Media. You have been licensed one copy of this document for personal use only. Any other reproduction or redistribution is strictly prohibited. All rights reserved.

22. A: During week 1, Nurse Cameron worked 5 shifts.

$$\text{shifts for week 1} = 5$$

During week 2, she worked twice as many shifts as she did during week 1.

$$\text{shifts for week 2} = (2)(5)$$

During week 3, she added 4 shifts to the number of shifts she worked during week 2.

$$\text{shifts for week 3} = (2)(5) + 4$$

23. C: Use the order of operations to solve this problem. Also remember that the absolute value of a number is always positive.

$$|(3)(-4)| + (3)(4) - 1 =$$
$$|-12| + (3)(4) - 1 =$$
$$12 + 12 - 1 =$$
$$24 - 1 =$$
$$23$$

24. B: The graph presented in choice B has the correct data and correct axes. Choice A has incorrect data. For example, physicians do not work 40 hours per week. Choice C has incorrect labels for the axes. The label, "Average hours worked per week," refers to numbers, and the label, "Hospital Staff," refers to people. Choice C has incorrect data and incorrect axes labels.

25. A: The section marked "Residents" takes up the largest amount of the circle graph. Therefore, the residents work the most amount of time.

26. D: The variables are the objects the graph measures. In this case, the graph measures the Hospital Staff and the Average hours worked per week. The dependent variable changes with the independent variable. Here, the average hours worked per week depends on the particular type of hospital staff. Therefore, the dependent variable is Average hours worked per week and the dependent variable is Hospital Staff.

27. D: The prefix, milli-, means 1000th. In this case,

$$1\,\text{g} = 1000\,\text{mg}$$

Therefore,

$$(5)(1\,\text{g}) = (5)(1000\,\text{mg})$$

$$5\,\text{g} = (5)(1000\,\text{mg})$$

$$5\,\text{g} = 5000\,\text{mg}$$

28. C: A small apple weighs about 100 g. Choice A, 1 mg, is much too small, and 0.001 g is the same as 1 mg. Choice D, 1000 kg, is much too large.

Copyright © Mometrix Media. You have been licensed one copy of this document for personal use only. Any other reproduction or redistribution is strictly prohibited. All rights reserved.

29. D. To calculate the total time taken, divide the distance driven by the speed it was driven at:

$$305 \text{ mi} \div 65 \text{ mph} = 305 \text{ miles} \times \frac{1 \text{ hour}}{65 \text{ miles}} = 4.69 \text{ hours}$$

$$162 \text{ mi} \div 80 \text{ mph} = 162 \text{ miles} \times \frac{1 \text{ hour}}{80 \text{ miles}} = 2.03 \text{ hours}$$

Convert the minutes spent at the gas station to hours: $15 \text{ min} \times \frac{1 \text{ hour}}{60 \text{ minutes}} = 0.25 \text{ hours}$

Find the total time taken on the trip by summing all the times: $4.69 + 2.03 + 0.25 = 6.97 \text{ hours}$

30. B: Each segment between marks in the figure is 2 cm long, and 3 segments are between 1 and 4. Therefore the total distance between 1 and 4 is

$$(2 \text{ cm})(3) = 6 \text{ cm}$$

31. D: Integers include all positive and negative whole numbers and the number zero. The product of three integers must be an integer, so you can eliminate any answer choice that is not a whole number: choices (A) and (C). The product of two even integers is even. The product of even and odd integers is even. The only even choice is 24.

32. C: Divide the mg the child should receive by the number of mg in 0.8 ml to determine how many 0.8 ml doses the child should receive: $\frac{240}{80} = 3$. Multiply the number of doses by 0.8 to determine how many ml the child should receive: $3 \times 0.8 = 2.4 \text{ ml}$

33. B: The chart indicates that each x value must be tripled to equal the corresponding y value, so $y = 3x$. One way you can determine this is by plugging corresponding pairs of x and y into the answer choices.

34. D: Use the following proportion: $\frac{1 \, in}{45 \, miles} = \frac{3.2 \, in}{x \, miles}$

Cross multiply: $x = (45)(3.2) = 144$ miles

Science Answer Explanations

1. C: The circulatory system circulates materials throughout the entire body. The heart is part of this system, since it is responsible for pumping blood that carries these materials. The kidneys are part of the urinary system. The lungs belong to the respiratory system, and the stomach is part of the digestive system.

2. B: The digestive system helps the body process food. The stomach, mouth, and esophagus all participate in food digestion. The brain, however, is part of the nervous system.

3. A: The nervous system is the body's communication center. The body uses the respiratory system to breathe, and blood is transported by the circulatory system. The digestive system breaks down food for the body.

4. D: The respiratory system uses the lungs, diaphragm, trachea, and bronchi to help the body breathe. The nervous system is the body's center of communication. The circulatory system transports materials through the body, and the digestive system processes food.

Copyright © Mometrix Media. You have been licensed one copy of this document for personal use only. Any other reproduction or redistribution is strictly prohibited. All rights reserved.

5. A: The immune system helps protect the body from bacteria, viruses, infections, and other elements that could cause illness. The digestive and nervous systems are discussed in the explanations for questions 3 and 4. The urinary system helps the body expel liquid waste.

6. A: The human body has five types of bones: long bones, short bones, irregular bones, flat bones, and sesamoid bones. While bones may be dense, this is not a major category of bones in the body.

7. B: Sesamoid bones are embedded in tendons. Choice D, vertical bones, is not a major bone type. Long bones contain a long shaft, and flat bones are thin and curved.

8. C: An increase in the birth rate would lead to growth in the population. Fatal disease, migration to Europe, and increased death rate would cause the population to decline.

9. D: Among other factors, fertility in women is adversely affected by smoking, stress, and alcohol consumption. Therefore, women who desire optimum fertility should consume alcohol in moderation, refrain from smoking, and avoid stressful situations.

10. B: If scientists created a cure for cancer, people who otherwise would have died from cancer would continue to live. Therefore, the population would most likely increase.

11. A: Each year, 3% of the population in country Q leaves but only 1% returns. Therefore, more people leave each year than move back, and the population steadily declines.

12. A: The process of natural selection describes how animals survive by adapting to their environment. The animals that survive produce offspring who have the same survival skills. In this case, the giraffes with long necks were able to survive by eating a food source that may not have been available to animals that usually ate food near the ground. The giraffes with long necks then produced offspring with long necks who could eat from this higher food source.

13. D: The term "*Homo sapiens*" is used by scientists to classify humans. In the biological classification system, *Homo* is the genus and *sapiens* designates the species.

14. C: Mitochondria are often called the power house of the cell because they provide energy for the cell to function. The nucleus is the control center for the cell. The cell membrane surrounds the cell and separates the cell from its environment. Cytoplasm is the thick fluid within the cell membrane that surrounds the nucleus and contains organelles.

15. B: Ribosomes are organelles that help synthesize proteins within the cell. Cilia and flagella are responsible for cell movement. The cell membrane helps the cell maintain its shape and protects it from the environment. Lysosomes have digestive enzymes.

16. B: Cells differentiate so that simple, less specialized cells can become highly specialized cells. For example, humans are multicellular organisms who undergo cell differentiation numerous times. Cells begin as simple zygotes after fertilization and then differentiate to form a myriad of complex tissues and systems before birth.

17. C: Both meiosis and mitosis occur in humans, other animals, and plants. Mitosis produces cells that are genetically identical, and meiosis produces cells that are genetically different. Only mitosis occurs asexually.

18. B: Photosynthesis describes the process plants use to generate food from sunlight, carbon dioxide, and water. It does not occur in animals. Respiration is the process by which oxygen is used to release energy from glucose, producing carbon dioxide. It occurs in both plants and animals,

- 251 -

Copyright © Mometrix Media. You have been licensed one copy of this document for personal use only. Any other reproduction or redistribution is strictly prohibited. All rights reserved.

though in plants the amount of oxygen produced by photosynthesis is generally more than that used by respiration.

19. B: DNA is the primary carrier of genetic information in most cells. RNA serves as a messenger that transmits genetic information from DNA to the cytoplasm of the cell.

20. B: Genetic mutations are changes in DNA that occur spontaneously at low rates. Genetic mutations rarely occur at fast rates. If the DNA remains the same, no mutation occurs.

21. C: After cell division, the daughter cells should be exact copies of the parent cells. Therefore, the DNA should replicate, or make an exact copy of itself, so that each daughter cell will have the full amount of DNA.

22. A: Genes are the molecular units that enable parents to pass hereditary traits on to their offspring. The blood, organs, and hair all contain the genes that makeup the offspring, but these are not basic molecular units.

23. A: Both DNA and RNA are made up of 4 nucleotide bases. Both DNA and RNA contain cytosine, guanine, and adenine. However, DNA contains thymine and RNA contains uracil. Choice B is incorrect because DNA and RNA do not have the same 4 nucleotides, and choices C and D are incorrect because neither DNA nor RNA contains 6 nucleotides. Furthermore, DNA has a double helix structure, and RNA has a single helix structure.

24. B: The genotype describes a person's genetic makeup. The phenotype describes a person's observable characteristics. Among the choices, the CFTR gene refers to genetic makeup while the other choices all describe traits that are observable.

25. D: The complete Punnett square is shown below.

	B	b
B	BB	Bb
b	Bb	bb

Because male pattern baldness is a recessive gene, the offspring would need the *bb* gene combination in order to inherit this trait. Possibility 4 corresponds to the *bb* gene combination.

26. D: Refer to the complete Punnett square in the explanation for question 25. Because male pattern baldness is recessive, the offspring would need the *bb* gene combination in order to inherit this trait. Therefore, any offspring with the *B* gene will have a full head of hair. Possibilities 1, 2, and 3 all have the *B* gene.

27. C: The sun is the celestial body that serves as a major external source of heat, light, and energy for Earth. Mars is a planet and the Big Dipper is a constellation. The moon only reflects the light of the sun and is not an energy source for Earth.

28. A: Oxidation is half of a redox (oxidation-reduction) reaction. Oxidation refers to losing electrons and reduction refers to gaining electrons. The two reactions always occur in pairs. In this case, an example of an oxidation reaction is copper losing 2 electrons.

Copyright © Mometrix Media. You have been licensed one copy of this document for personal use only. Any other reproduction or redistribution is strictly prohibited. All rights reserved.

29. A: A catalyst increases the rate of a chemical reaction without becoming part of the net reaction. Therefore, chemical C increases the rate of the reaction between A and B. The catalyst does not change the chemicals within the reaction.

30. B: Enzymes are protein molecules produced by living organisms. Enzymes serve as catalysts for certain biological reactions.

31. C: The pH of acids is less than 7, and the pH of bases is greater than 7. A substance with a pH equal to 7 is neutral.

32. A: An ionic bond occurs between atoms when one atom donates valence electrons to another atom that receives those electrons. In this case, sodium donates an electron to chlorine, forming an ionic bond between the two atoms.

33. D: Water molecules contain hydrogen and oxygen atoms that are covalently bonded. Water molecules do not have ionic bonds. Also, water has a neutral pH of 7.

34. B: In general, the faster an object is moving, the more kinetic energy it possesses. In choices A, C, and D, the ball is not moving, so it has no kinetic energy. In choice B, the ball is in motion, so it does have some kinetic energy in this case.

35. C: The atom is negatively charged. Neutrons have no charge. Protons have positive charge and electrons have negative charge equal in magnitude to the positive charge of the proton. Because the atom has more electrons than protons, the atom has a negative charge.

36. D: The nucleus contains protons and neutrons while electrons orbit the nucleus of the atom. Positrons are not a major component of an atom, and "negatron" is just an obsolete term for an electron.

37. A: A covalent bond is formed between atoms that share electrons. For example, the hydrogen and oxygen atoms in water have covalent bonds because they share their valence electrons.

38. D: The atomic number equals the number of protons and the number of electrons in an atom. Since Be has an atomic number of 4, it has 4 protons and 4 electrons. H has the fewest protons and electrons, as denoted by its atomic number of 1.

39. B: Liquids are free flowing and take on the shape of their container. Solids are rigid and fixed. Therefore, the atoms in a solid have a fixed structure.

40. C: Vaporization is the process of changing from a liquid to a gas. For instance, water vaporizes when boiled to create steam. Freezing is the process of changing from a liquid to a solid. Condensation describes changing from a gas to a liquid, and sublimation is the process of changing from a solid to a gas.

41. C: The nurse wants to investigate her patients' body temperatures. A thermometer is the only tool in the list that will help measure the temperature of a person's body.

42. A: The researcher should use statistical analysis to understand trends in the data. Different statistics tools can help manage and examine large data sets. The researcher would probably miss important correlations by looking at the individual data points, and eliminating most of the data would defeat the purpose of conducting the study. Simply staring at the data would not be helpful.

Copyright © Mometrix Media. You have been licensed one copy of this document for personal use only. Any other reproduction or redistribution is strictly prohibited. All rights reserved.

43. B: Based on the evidence, the most likely explanation for fly larvae in the spoiled food is that flies laid their eggs in the food. When the food was left out in the open, the flies had access to it and laid their eggs. However, when the food was in a sealed container, the flies could not lay their eggs in the food. Hence, the spoiled food in the sealed container had no fly larvae.

44. D: Longer life expectancy could be explained by any or all of the alternatives presented. Advances in medical technology, basic cleanliness, and vaccines could all help people live longer in the 21st century.

45. C: A scientific argument should be based on measurable and observable facts such as the patient's current symptoms and health history. Discussing the patient's appearance or the doctor's feelings does not communicate a scientific argument. While insurance may be a factor in most healthcare systems, the status of the patient's insurance does not communicate a scientific argument that justifies the need for the test.

46. B: The best reason to conduct this investigation is so the board can determine if the ER is understaffed. Although the board may want to feel good, this is not a good reason to conduct an investigation. While advertising may be important to the success of the hospital, having the proper staff in the emergency is more critical than advertising.

47. A: Technology should be used in scientific research for several reasons. Among the items in this list, the best reason is the large amount of data that technology allows researchers to collect and analyze. While technology does allow researchers to create nice pictures and spend more time with their families, these reasons are secondary to data collection and analysis.

48. A: Although some unscrupulous researchers may use mathematics to sway research outcomes, this is not a reason to include math in scientific research. Creating measurable research goals, seeking objective data analysis, and discovering trends and patterns are all good reasons to include mathematics in scientific research.

49. D: Of the given structures, veins have the lowest blood pressure. *Veins* carry oxygen-poor blood from the outlying parts of the body to the heart. An *artery* carries oxygen-rich blood from the heart to the peripheral parts of the body. An *arteriole* extends from an artery to a capillary. A *venule* is a tiny vein that extends from a capillary to a larger vein.

50. C: Of the four heart chambers, the left ventricle is the most muscular. When it contracts, it pushes blood out to the organs and extremities of the body. The right ventricle pushes blood into the lungs. The atria, on the other hand, receive blood from the outlying parts of the body and transport it into the ventricles. The basic process works as follows: Oxygen-poor blood fills the right atrium and is pumped into the right ventricle, from which it is pumped into the pulmonary artery and on to the lungs. In the lungs, this blood is oxygenated. The blood then reenters the heart at the left atrium, which when full pumps into the left ventricle. When the left ventricle is full, blood is pushed into the aorta and on to the organs and extremities of the body.

51. A: The *cerebrum* is the part of the brain that interprets sensory information. It is the largest part of the brain. The cerebrum is divided into two hemispheres, connected by a thin band of tissue called the corpus callosum. The *cerebellum* is positioned at the back of the head, between the brain stem and the cerebrum. It controls both voluntary and involuntary movements. The *medulla oblongata* forms the base of the brain. This part of the brain is responsible for blood flow and breathing, among other things.

Copyright © Mometrix Media. You have been licensed one copy of this document for personal use only. Any other reproduction or redistribution is strictly prohibited. All rights reserved.

52. C: *Collagen* is the protein produced by cartilage. Bone, tendon, and cartilage are all mainly composed of collagen. *Actin* and *myosin* are the proteins responsible for muscle contractions. Actin makes up the thinner fibers in muscle tissue, while myosin makes up the thicker fibers. Myosin is the most numerous cell protein in human muscle. *Estrogen* is one of the steroid hormones produced mainly by the ovaries. Estrogen motivates the menstrual cycle and the development of female sex characteristics.

53. C: The *parasympathetic nervous system* is responsible for lowering the heart rate. It slows down the heart rate, dilates the blood vessels, and increases the secretions of the digestive system. The *central nervous system* is composed of the brain and the spinal cord. The *sympathetic nervous system* is a part of the autonomic nervous system; its role is to oppose the actions taken by the parasympathetic nervous system. So, the sympathetic nervous system accelerates the heart, contracts the blood vessels, and decreases the secretions of the digestive system.

54. A: An adult inhales 500 mL of air in an average breath. Interestingly, humans can inhale about eight times as much air in a single breath as they do in an average breath. People tend to take a larger breath after making a larger inhalation. This is one reason that many breathing therapies, for instance those incorporated into yoga practice, focus on making a complete exhalation. The process of respiration is managed by the autonomic nervous system. The body requires a constant replenishing of oxygen, so even brief interruptions in respiration can be damaging or fatal.

English and Language Usage Answer Explanations

1. A: Semicolons are used to separate items in a series when those items contain internal commas, such as in a listing of cities and states. Answer choice A correctly demonstrates this. Answer choice B places the semicolon between the city and its state, instead of between *each* listing of the city and its state, and this is incorrect. A comma is always used to separate a single instance of a city and a state. Answer choice C separate the items in the series with commas, but this creates confusion for the reader, since there are already commas between each city and its state. Answer choice D places commas between each item in the series, but fails to include the necessary comma between each city and its state.

2. C: The word *conscientious* tends to fall into the "frequently misspelled category," and answer choice C demonstrates the correct spelling of the word. The other answer choices fail to spell the word accurately.

3. B: Answer choice B presents the correct order of words for the sentence: <u>They're</u> [They are] going on vacation to <u>their</u> [possessive pronoun] house on Lake Chelan, and they plan to water ski and parasail while <u>there</u> [adverb indicating location]. The other answer choices place these words in incorrect order.

4. C: When a plural word is made possessive, the standard rule is to place the apostrophe after the final *s*, as in *jurors'*. Answer choice C correctly demonstrates this. Answer choices A and D place the possessive apostrophe within *meals* (*meal's* and *meals'*), and these forms of the word do not make sense within the context of the sentence. Answer choice B places the possessive apostrophe before the final *s*, as in *juror's*, which indicates only a single juror. This form is incorrect in the context of the sentence.

5. B: A complex sentence contains a single independent clause in addition to a dependent clause. Answer choice B opens with the dependent clause *Before Ernestine purchases a book* and ends with the independent clause *she always checks to see if the library has it*. Answer choice A is a simple

- 255 -

Copyright © Mometrix Media. You have been licensed one copy of this document for personal use only. Any other reproduction or redistribution is strictly prohibited. All rights reserved.

sentence, as it has no dependent clause. Answer choice C is a compound sentence, because it has two independent clauses. Answer choice D is also a simple sentence, although it has a compound subject.

6. D: In the context of the sentence, it appears that Finlay's parents are attempting to *coax* him by promising a trip to his favorite toy store. Answer choice A makes little sense, as the sentence indicates Finlay's parents want him to participate in the recital. Answer choice B might work, but the promise of a trip to the toy store seems more like a reward than a punishment. Answer choice C makes no sense when added to the sentence in place of the word *cajole*.

7. C: The correct plural form of *tempo* is *tempi*. This word has an Italian root, and thus follows the pattern of other, similar words that end in -*i* in their plural form. Note also that *tempo*, meaning time, is simply the Italian form of the Latin *tempus*. (Recall the Latin expression *tempus fugit*, or "time flies.") Other Latin-based nouns ending in -*us* also take the -*i* ending when made plural: *octopus > octopi*, *syllabus > syllabi*, etc.

8. A: In answer choice A, *Aunt Jo* is correctly capitalized, because *aunt* identifies a specific person. The word *uncle* is not capitalized in this sentence, because the uncle's name is not added. Answer choice B fails to capitalize *Brother Mark*, as the expression clearly identifies a monk. Answer choice C fails to capitalize *Cousin Martha*. *Cousin* should be capitalized, because the word identifies a specific individual. Answer choice D fails to capitalize *Outer Banks*, which is the proper noun for a region; answer choice D also incorrectly capitalizes *Fall*. Seasons are not capitalized.

9. D: The correct pronoun for the antecedent *person* is *his or her*. The plural *their* in answer choice A is incorrect, because the word *person* is singular. Answer choice B cannot be correct, because a person is not identified as *it* in the English language. The article *the*, answer choice C, makes little sense in the context of the sentence.

10. B: Answer choice B demonstrates a comma splice, which is the use of a comma to join two independent clauses. Note that *however* is not a conjunction, and cannot join two sentences like other coordinating conjunctions (e.g., *and*, *but*, *or*, etc.) can. Answer choice A correctly uses a semicolon between the independent clauses. Answer choice C correctly uses a period between the independent clauses. Answer choice D correctly uses a comma and the coordinating conjunction *but* to join the independent clauses.

11. B: Answer choice B combines the sentences in the best way. The sentences are combined into a single sentence, and all of the details are still included. Answer choices A and D do a good job of combining the sentences, but still consist of more than one sentence. Answer choice C combines the sentences, but leaves out the part about how she "tried to find a way to attend both." There is no clear reason to leave this out, so answer choice C is not the best choice.

12. A: The correct plural form of *human* is *humans*. Despite the fact that it contains the form *man*, the plural form is not *humen*, as indicated in answer choice B. Answer choices C and D both contain apostrophes, which are not necessary in standard plural forms.

13. D: If the root *meare* means "to pass," and the word *permeate* means "to penetrate or pervade," the most likely meaning of the prefix *per-* is "through." This would yield a literal word meaning of "to pass through," which is similar in meaning to the original: "to penetrate or pervade." The phrase "to pass across" does not match the original Latin origins. Similarly, "to pass by" and "to pass with" are not consistent with the meaning of "passing through."

Copyright © Mometrix Media. You have been licensed one copy of this document for personal use only. Any other reproduction or redistribution is strictly prohibited. All rights reserved.

14. B: Anthropology is the study of human culture. Cosmetology is the study of cosmetic techniques. Etymology is the study of word meanings. Genealogy is the study of family history. All of these words would indicate that the suffix -*logy* refers to the study of something. It cannot refer to a record, since that indicates something in the past, and the words in question describe activities that are ongoing. An affinity for something is not the same as a committed study of it, and each item in the question represents its own dedicated field. The suffix for "fear" is -*phobia*.

15. D: An adverb modifies a verb, and in the sentence, the word *well* modifies the verb *did* by indicating *how* Jacob did with his speech. The word *worried* is a verb. The word *about* is a preposition. The word *but* is a conjunction.

16. B: The correct version of the sentence is as follows: "Most doctors agree that there are a lot of reasons to add a daily multivitamin to the diet." Both blanks need plural verbs: the verb *agree* to modify the plural *doctors*, and the verb *are* to modify the plural *a lot*. All other answer choices include at least one singular verb, and these are therefore incorrect in the context of the sentence.

17. C: It is correct to pair a plural verb with a collective noun when that noun indicates a plural context. In answer choice C, it is clear that the faculty members are acting individually in their disagreement, so the plural verb makes sense. In answer choice A, the pronoun *neither* is singular, so the verb that accompanies it should also be singular. In answer choice B, the pronoun *all* is plural, so the accompanying verb should be plural. Similarly, in answer choice D, the pronoun *both* is plural, so the verb that accompanies it should also be plural.

18. D: The sentence suggests that the scholar was very *knowledgeable* about his subject matter; it is just that his presentation went over the students' heads. The word *authentic* suggests an external guarantee of correctness, which makes little sense in the context of the sentence. The word *arrogant* might be accurate, except that there is nothing in the sentence to suggest the guest speaker deliberately spoke over the students' heads. It is simply that his knowledge was not presented effectively given the audience. Finally, there is nothing in the sentence to suggest that the guest speaker was *faulty* in any way. Rather, he knew so much that he failed to connect with an audience that was less knowledgeable.

19. C: The word *sacrilegious* indicates a violation of sacred expectations, and wearing white to a funeral would be something that would violate the sacred expectations of many. The other answer choices are spelled incorrectly, particularly *sacreligious*, which spells the word with the correct spelling of *religious*. This is not correct, as the spelling is adjusted when joined to the other root.

20. C: Of the answer choices, the only prefix that requires hyphenation is *self-*. The other answer choices are words containing prefixes that do not require hyphens.

21. B: Answer choice B includes all of the necessary information while still removing the nominalization. All of the other answer choices either include nominalization or extended phrases that make the statement longer and more confusing than necessary. Additionally, answer choice D claims that the city council let residents make the decision; the original sentence claims only that the city council asked for comments from residents. Therefore, answer choice D adds inaccurate information.

22. D: Answer choice D has a plural subject, but is still a simple sentence. Answer choice A is a compound sentence, as it is composed of two independent clauses. Answer choice B consists of two independent sentences that are joined by a semicolon. (The punctuation is correct, and creates two simple sentences, not one.) Answer choice C contains a dependent clause, so it is a complex sentence.

Copyright © Mometrix Media. You have been licensed one copy of this document for personal use only. Any other reproduction or redistribution is strictly prohibited. All rights reserved.

23. D: Answer choice D is a pronoun: the subjective case *I*. Answer choice A is a helping verb. Answer choice B is an adjective. Answer choice C is an adverb.

24. A: A book title should be italicized, but the chapter titles (if the chapters *are* titled) should be placed in double quotation marks. (Double quotation marks are correct for all standard quotations in American English.) Answer choice A correctly demonstrates this. All of the other answer choices incorrectly place the book title in quotation marks, or place the chapter title in single quotation marks.

25. B: Answer choice B is the clearest and the most concise. Answer choices A and C include more than one independent clause. As the statement can function as a single independent clause, this is unnecessary. Answer choice D works, but it is not the best option in terms of style, clarity, and concision. The coordinating conjunction with the added independent clause makes the sentence more unwieldy than answer choice B.

26. B: The context of the sentence suggests that Mrs. Vanderbroek would not be delighted about any changes to her routine. Thus, answer choice B makes the most sense. Answer choice A has promise, but it does not exactly fit the meaning of the sentence. It is not that Mrs. Vanderbroek would be incapable of accepting change, but rather that she would not welcome it. Answer choices C and D indicate Mrs. Vanderbroek's overall response to changes, but they do not work as synonyms for the word *amenable*.

27. D: The words *quick*, *available*, and *little* are all adjectives in the sentence. *Quick* modifies *review*; *available* modifies *housing options*; *little* modifies *choice*. The word *rent* is part of the infinitive (i.e. verbal) phrase *to rent*.

28. B: Based on the context of the sentence, the word in the first blank should be in the subjective case, while the word in the second blank should be in the objective case. Only answer choice B indicates this. Answer choice A places both words in the subjective case; answer choice D places both words in the objective case. Answer choice C reverses the correct order of the words. The first is in the objective case, and the second is in the subjective case.

29. D: Answer choice D combines the six sentences into two primary sentences, and this answer choice fulfills the requirement for a combination that is "as concise as possible." Answer choice C is also two primary sentences, but they reverse the flow of thought and make the sentence less sensible. Answer choices A and B are both three primary sentences, and thus are not as concise as possible.

30. A: The form *bear* is correct in this context, because it suggests the right to carry or own arms. The form *bare* indicates an uncovered limb. The word *barre* is the French form of *bar*, and is typically used to describe a ballet barre where dancers train. The word *baire* is an alternative colloquial form that refers to a mosquito net in some parts of the United States.

31. B: The preposition *among* is not used correctly in the sentence. In this case, the word *between* would be more appropriate. *Among* and *between* both mean *in the midst of some other things*. However, *between* is used when there are only two other things, and *among* is used when there are more than two. For example, it would be correct to say *between first and second base* or *among several friends*. In this sentence, the preposition *among* is inappropriate for describing placement amid *two treatment protocols*.

32. B: To say something is sincere means that it is genuine or real. For example, saying someone showed sincere concern means that their concern was genuine, and not fake.

Copyright © Mometrix Media. You have been licensed one copy of this document for personal use only. Any other reproduction or redistribution is strictly prohibited. All rights reserved.

33. B: Describing somebody as courteous implies that they are polite and well-mannered. Polite and courteous both convey the same meaning.

34. C: If you say that you comprehend something, it is the same as saying you understand it. For example, saying you comprehend what another person is saying is the same as saying you understand them.

Copyright © Mometrix Media. You have been licensed one copy of this document for personal use only. Any other reproduction or redistribution is strictly prohibited. All rights reserved.

TEAS Practice Test #3

Section 1. Reading

1. Ernestine has a short research project to complete, and her assigned topic is the history of the Globe Theatre in London. Which of the following sources would be the best starting point for Ernestine's research?

    a. Roget's Thesaurus
    b. Oxford Latin Dictionary
    c. Encyclopedia Britannica
    d. Webster's Dictionary

2. List of Romance Languages

- Latin
- French
- Spanish
- Romanian
- American
- Portuguese

Analyze the headings above. Which of the following does not belong?

    a. Spanish
    b. American
    c. French
    d. Portuguese

3. The guide words at the top of a dictionary page are *considerable* and *conspicuous*. Which of the following words is an entry on this page?

    a. consonantal
    b. consumption
    c. conserve
    d. conquistador

4. Considering the dictionary guide words above, which of the following words most likely appears on the *previous* page of the dictionary?

    a. consonantal
    b. consumption
    c. conserve
    d. conquistador

5. The heavy spring rain resulted in a <u>plethora</u> of zucchini in Kit's garden, and left her desperately giving the vegetables to anyone who was interested. Which of the following is the definition for the underlined word in the sentence?

    a. irritation
    b. quantity
    c. abundance
    d. waste

Copyright © Mometrix Media. You have been licensed one copy of this document for personal use only. Any other reproduction or redistribution is strictly prohibited. All rights reserved.

6. Follow the numbered instructions to transform the starting word into a different word.

1. Start with the word PREVARICATE.
2. Remove the P.
3. Replace the first A with the final E.
4. Remove the I from the word.
5. Remove the C from the word.
6. Remove the A from the word.

What is the new word?
- a. REVEST
- b. REVERT
- c. REVIEW
- d. REVERSE

7. Ethan works in his company's purchasing department, and he needs to purchase 500 pens to give away to customers. He finds the following information about purchasing pens in bulk.

Company	Specialty Pens	Office in Bulk	Office Warehouse	Ballpoint & Lead
Price per unit	$.97 per pen	$45 per 50 pens	$95 per 100 pens	$1 per pen OR $99 per 100 pens

Based on the information above, which company will have the best price for 500 pens?
- a. Specialty Pens
- b. Office in Bulk
- c. Office Warehouse
- d. Ballpoint & Lead

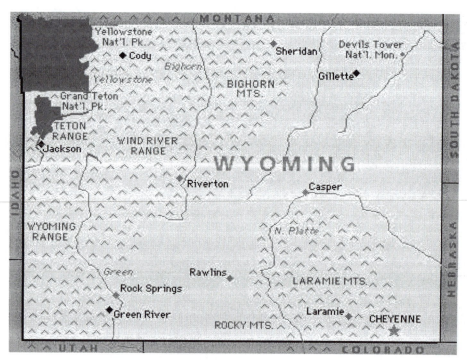

The next four questions are based on the image above.

- 261 -

Copyright © Mometrix Media. You have been licensed one copy of this document for personal use only. Any other reproduction or redistribution is strictly prohibited. All rights reserved.

8. On the map above, the symbol /\ indicates mountains. How many different mountain ranges are in the state of Wyoming?

   a. 3
   b. 4
   c. 5
   d. 6

9. On the map above, the star symbol indicates the state capital. Which city is the capital of Wyoming?

   a. Laramie
   b. Cheyenne
   c. Jackson
   d. Sheridan

10. On the map above, how many national parks are shown in the state of Wyoming?

   a. 2
   b. 3
   c. 4
   d. 5

11. On the map above, which states are south of Wyoming?

   a. Utah and Idaho
   b. Colorado and Utah
   c. Montana and Colorado
   d. Colorado and Nebraska

12. The warning against smoking may have been <u>tacit</u>, but Beryl instinctively knew that her mother wanted her to avoid picking up the habit. Which of the following is the definition for the underlined word in the sentence?

   a. complicated
   b. empty
   c. wordy
   d. unstated

> They were known as "The Five": a group of Russian musicians who eschewed rigidly formal classical training and set out on their own to give a new artistic sound to classical music in Russia. Mily Balakirev and Cesar Cui are considered the founders of the movement, but the three who later joined them have become far more famous and respected outside, and perhaps even inside, of Russia. Modest Mussorgsky, with his passion for themes of Russian folklore and nationalism, is remembered for the piano piece *Pictures and an Exhibition*, as well as for the passionate opera *Boris Godunov*. Nikolai Rimsky-Korsakov, who spent his early years as a naval officer, had a penchant for infusing his works with the sounds of the sea. But, he might be best remembered for the hauntingly beautiful symphonic suite *Scheherazade*. Alexander Borodin balanced a career as a skilled and highly respected chemist with his interest in classical music. He produced a number of symphonies, as well as the opera *Prince Igor*. Despite their lack of formal training and their unorthodox approach to producing classical music, The Five had an influence that reached far beyond their time. Composers such as Alexander Glazunov, Sergei Prokofiev, and Igor Stravinsky studied under Rimsky-Korsakov. Additionally, the mid-twentieth century composer

Copyright © Mometrix Media. You have been licensed one copy of this document for personal use only. Any other reproduction or redistribution is strictly prohibited. All rights reserved.

Dmitri Shostakovich studied under Glazunov, creating a legacy of musical understanding that persisted well beyond the era of The Five.

The next three questions are based on the information above.

13. Which of the following describes the type of writing used in the passage?

    a. narrative
    b. persuasive
    c. expository
    d. technical

14. Which of the following is the best summary sentence for the passage?

    a. Composers such as Alexander Glazunov, Sergei Prokofiev, and Igor Stravinsky studied under Rimsky-Korsakov.
    b. Despite their lack of formal training and their unorthodox approach to producing classical music, The Five had an influence that reached far beyond their time.
    c. They were known as "The Five": a group of Russian musicians who eschewed rigidly formal classical training and set out on their own to give a new artistic sound to classical music in Russia.
    d. Mily Balakirev and Cesar Cui are considered the founders of the movement, but the three who later joined them have become far more famous and respected outside, and perhaps even inside, of Russia.

15. Based on the information in the passage, which of the composers among The Five would the author likely agree was the most influential?

    a. Alexander Glazunov
    b. Modest Mussorgsky
    c. Nikolai Rimsky-Korsakov
    d. Cesar Cui

    A dictionary entry includes the following information for the word *collar*:

    col·lar [**kol**-er] *n* [Middle English, *coler*, fr. Old French *colier*, fr. Latin *collare* neckband, fr. *collum* neck]

The next three questions are based on the information above.

16. The symbol in the middle of the word *collar* indicates which of the following?

    a. emphasis
    b. spelling
    c. origin
    d. syllables

17. The bold font used in the first half of the word indicates which of the following?

    a. emphasis
    b. spelling
    c. origin
    d. syllables

Copyright © Mometrix Media. You have been licensed one copy of this document for personal use only. Any other reproduction or redistribution is strictly prohibited. All rights reserved.

18. Based on the information in the dictionary entry, what is the earliest language origin of the word *collar*?

    a. English
    b. Middle English
    c. Old French
    d. Latin

19. Seeing the cookie crumbs on the child's face, Ena could not believe he would tell such a <u>barefaced</u> lie and claim he had not eaten any cookies. Which of the following is the definition for the underlined word in the sentence?

    a. effective
    b. arrogant
    c. shameless
    d. hostile

    Monarchs of England: House of Stuart

- James I (reigned 1603-1625)
- Charles I (reigned 1625-1649)
- Oliver Cromwell (lord protector 1653-1658)
- Charles II (reigned 1660-1685)
- James II (reigned 1685-1688)
- Mary II (reigned 1689-1694)
- William III (reigned 1689-1702)
- Anne (reigned 1702-1714)

The next two questions are based on the information above.

20. Analyze the headings above using the information provided in the title. Which of the following does not belong?

    a. William III
    b. Anne
    c. Charles II
    d. Oliver Cromwell

21. In the headings listed above, there are two occasions when a break occurs in the House of Stuart, and dates are missing. Before the reign of which of the following two monarchs do these breaks occur?

    a. Charles I and Charles II
    b. Charles II and Mary II
    c. Charles II and James II
    d. William III and Anne

Copyright © Mometrix Media. You have been licensed one copy of this document for personal use only. Any other reproduction or redistribution is strictly prohibited. All rights reserved.

Starting in 1856, Alfred, Lord Tennyson began publishing his compilation of Arthurian legends that became known as *Idylls of the King*. These poems were based on the earlier Medieval collection *Le Morte d'Arthur*, by Sir Thomas Malory, which dated to the middle of the 15th century. Malory's work, which is believed to be largely a translation of older French stories, was written in prose style. It combined the earlier tales into a single grouping for English readers. As the title suggests, Malory's focus was largely on the epic nature of Arthur's life. Malory discussed his birth, his rise as a prince and warrior, his quests as a knight, and his eventual death. Malory also included chapters on knights such as Lancelot and Gareth, and he discussed the relationships between Tristan and Isolde, and Lancelot and Guinevere. Instead of embracing the romance angle, however, Malory focused more on the moral elements within these stories.

Tennyson, though heavily influenced by Malory, took a different approach to the Arthurian stories. For one, he wrote them in poetry form, not prose. Additionally, Tennyson, as a Victorian poet, was more interested in the romantic qualities of the stories, and included the distinct elements of nature and elegy. *Idylls of the King* has a softer focus overall. For instance, in Malory's work, Guinevere faces execution for her adultery, and is only spared when Lancelot rides in to rescue her. In Tennyson's work, Arthur chooses to forgive Guinevere, and she chooses to spend the rest of her days doing good works in a convent. Some literary scholars believe that Tennyson was writing an allegory about social problems and the need for social justice that

existed during Tennyson's own time. Charles Dickens is remembered for doing the same thing in his novels about the abuses of lower-class children in Victorian England.

The next four questions are based on the information above.

22. Which of the following describes the structure of the above passage?

   a. problem-solution
   b. sequence
   c. comparison-contrast
   d. cause-effect

23. The author of the passage notes several distinctions between Tennyson and Malory. Which of the following is not identified as a difference between the two authors?

   a. Malory wrote prose, while Tennyson wrote poetry.
   b. Malory wrote during the Medieval era, while Tennyson wrote during the Victorian era.
   c. Malory was more focused on heroism and morality, while Tennyson was more focused on nature and elegy.
   d. Malory wrote stories about Gareth, Tristan, and Isolde, while Tennyson focused only on Arthur, Lancelot, and Guinevere.

Copyright © Mometrix Media. You have been licensed one copy of this document for personal use only. Any other reproduction or redistribution is strictly prohibited. All rights reserved.

24. Which of the following sentences distracts the reader from the main focus of the passage?

a. Malory's work, which is believed to be largely a translation of older French stories, was written in prose style.

b. Instead of embracing the romance angle, however, Malory focused more on the moral elements within these stories.

c. In Tennyson's work, Arthur chooses to forgive Guinevere, and she chooses to spend the rest of her days doing good works in a convent.

d. Charles Dickens is remembered for doing the same thing in his novels about the abuses of lower-class children in Victorian England.

25. With which of the following statements would the author of the passage most likely agree?

a. Malory and Tennyson shaped their approach to the Arthurian legends based on the defining qualities of their respective eras.

b. Because *Le Morte d'Arthur* is more of a translation than a literary creation, *Idylls of the King* is a superior work.

c. By undermining the moral qualities that Malory highlighted, Tennyson failed to appreciate the larger purpose of the stories in a Medieval context.

d. Ultimately, Malory's influence on Tennyson was minimal, because Tennyson took a different approach and infused his poems with the mood of his day.

26. Regina has a severe allergy to dairy products. She is going to attend a work-related function during which lunch will be served. She requests to see the menu before the function to make sure there is something she will be able to eat. For lunch, the organizers will be serving soup, bread, and a light salad. The following soup options are available:

- Cream of potato soup
- Lentil soup
- Broccoli cheese soup
- Cream of tomato soup

Which of the above options is most likely the best choice for Regina?

a. Cream of potato

b. Lentil soup

c. Broccoli cheese soup

d. Cream of tomato soup

Copyright © Mometrix Media. You have been licensed one copy of this document for personal use only. Any other reproduction or redistribution is strictly prohibited. All rights reserved.

World War I Casualties: European Allies (1914-1918)

Country	Military Deaths	Military Wounded	Civilian Deaths (war/famine/disease)	Total Population	Percent of Population Lost
Belgium	58,637	44,686	62,000	7,400,000	1.63
France	1,397,800	4,266,000	300,000	39,600,000	4.29
Italy	651,000	953,886	589,000	35,600,000	3.48
Romania	250,000	120,000	450,000	7,500,000	9.33
Russia	2,254,369	4,950,000	1,500,000	175,100,000	2.14
United Kingdom	886,939	1,663,435	109,000	45,400,000	2.19

Sources: Commonwealth War Graves Commission, La Population de la France pendant de la guerre, United Kingdom War Office, United States War Department

The next four questions are based on the information above.

27. In terms of the percentage of its entire population, which of the following nations suffered the greatest loss during World War I?

    a. France
    b. Italy
    c. Romania
    d. Russia

28. In terms of numbers alone, which of the following nations suffered the greatest loss during World War I?

    a. Belgium
    b. Romania
    c. Russia
    d. United Kingdom

29. As a percentage of its total population, which of the following nations suffered the greatest loss of civilians during World War I?

    a. Belgium
    b. Italy
    c. Romania
    d. Russia

30. Based on the information provided about civilian deaths, which of the following most likely contributed to the largest number of civilian deaths during World War I?

    a. the sinking of the RMS *Lusitania* in 1915
    b. the trench warfare system that resulted in the "war of attrition"
    c. the development of mustard gas for the battlefield
    d. the Spanish Influenza epidemic of 1918

Copyright © Mometrix Media. You have been licensed one copy of this document for personal use only. Any other reproduction or redistribution is strictly prohibited. All rights reserved.

Announcement for all faculty members:

It has come to the university's attention that there is crowding in the faculty canteen between the hours of 11 a.m. and 1 p.m., an issue that is due to the increase in staff numbers in several faculty departments. A number of faculty members have complained that they stood in line so long that they were unable to get lunch, or did not have time to eat lunch. To offset the crowding, the university has polled the various departments about schedules, and has settled on a recommended roster for when the members of each department should visit the faculty canteen for lunch:

- Business Dept: 10.30 a.m.-11.30 a.m.
- Art Dept: 10.45 a.m.-11.45 a.m.
- Math and Science Dept: 12 p.m.-1 p.m.
- Social Sciences Dept: 12.30 p.m.-1.30 p.m.
- Humanities Dept: 1 p.m.-2 p.m.

We ask that all faculty members respect this schedule. Faculty will be expected to display a department badge before entering the canteen for lunch.

The next two questions are based on the information above.

31. Based on the information in the announcement, what might the reader assume about how the university determined the lunch schedule?

a. The university arranged the schedule alphabetically, according to the name of each department.
b. The university checked with the departments in advance to make sure faculty members would be amenable to the change.
c. The university checked to see when the most faculty members from each department would be entering the canteen.
d. The university was most concerned about crowding in the canteen, and simply decided to establish different times for each department.

32. Which best describes the final two sentences of the announcement?

a. a friendly reminder to all faculty members to bring a badge to the canteen
b. a word of caution to faculty members about trying to enter the canteen at the wrong time
c. an implied suggestion that faculty members should consider getting lunch elsewhere
d. an indication of university sanctions for faculty members who enter the canteen outside the schedule

During the summer, Angela read the following classics: *The Great Gatsby*, by F. Scott Fitzgerald; *Brave New World*, by Aldous Huxley; *A Passage to India*, by E.M. Forster; and "The Cask of Amontillado," by Edgar Allen Poe.

The next two questions are based on the sentence above.

Copyright © Mometrix Media. You have been licensed one copy of this document for personal use only. Any other reproduction or redistribution is strictly prohibited. All rights reserved.

33. In the statement above, several items are italicized, while only one is placed in quotation marks. According to the rules of punctuation, the following should be placed in quotation marks: article titles, book chapters, short stories, and episodes of television shows. Considering the list of works that Angela read, into which category does "The Cask of Amontillado" most likely fit?

   a. newspaper article
   b. book chapter
   c. short story
   d. television show episode

34. What is the purpose of the italics used for several of the works identified in the sentence above?

   a. to indicate a full-length published book
   b. to indicate a work of classic literature
   c. to indicate recommended summer reading
   d. to indicate books that Angela completed

35. Based on the student's <u>florid</u> complexion, Vivienne knew that his nerves were getting the better of him before the debate. Which of the following is the definition for the underlined word in the sentence?

   a. rambling
   b. flushed
   c. unclear
   d. weak

36. In a book review published in a large national newspaper, the reviewer said the book was "most likely to be enjoyed only by those with puerile fantasies." Based on this description, what can be inferred about the reviewer's opinion?

   a. The reviewer strongly recommends the book for young adults.
   b. The reviewer believes the book is inappropriate for children.
   c. The reviewer considers the book to have wide audience appeal.
   d. The reviewer feels that the book would not appeal to mature adults.

Thomas and his sister are planning to see a new science fiction film, but they have to work around their schedules. Both are free for a showing before 6 p.m. or after 10 p.m. Here are the current show times for cinemas in their area:

   - Twin Theatres: 6:15 p.m., 7:20 p.m., and 8:40 p.m.
   - Reveler Cinema: 5:45 p.m. and 7:15 p.m.
   - Big Screen 14: 6:00 p.m., 6:45 p.m., 9:10 p.m., and 10:05 p.m.
   - Best Seat in The House: 8:20 p.m., 9:55 p.m., and 11:25 p.m.

The next two questions are based on the information above.

37. Which of these cinemas does not have an option that will work for Thomas and his sister?

   a. Twin Theatres
   b. Reveler Cinema
   c. Big Screen 14
   d. Best Seat in The House

Copyright © Mometrix Media. You have been licensed one copy of this document for personal use only. Any other reproduction or redistribution is strictly prohibited. All rights reserved.

38. After an unexpected rearrangement of their schedules, Thomas and his sister realize that they will have to squeeze in the film after 10.30 p.m. Given this new information, which cinema is the best option?

    a. Twin Theatres
    b. Reveler Cinema
    c. Big Screen 14
    d. Best Seat in The House

In an effort to conserve water, the town of Audley has asked residents and businesses to water their lawns just one day a week. It has provided the following schedule based on addresses:

- Monday: addresses ending in 0 and 9
- Tuesday: addresses ending in 1 and 8
- Wednesday: addresses ending in 2 and 7
- Thursday: addresses ending in 3 and 6
- Friday: addresses ending in 5
- Saturday: addresses ending in 4

Businesses with suite numbers should use the final number in the suite number to determine their watering schedule.

The next three questions are based on the information above.

39. The Morgan family lives at 5487 South Elm Street. On which day of the week will they be able to water their lawn?

    a. Tuesday
    b. Wednesday
    c. Thursday
    d. Saturday

40. Everby Title Company is located at 48752 Beech Avenue, Suite 853. On which day of the week will the company be able to water its lawn?

    a. Monday
    b. Wednesday
    c. Thursday
    d. Sunday

41. The watering schedule has only one number for both Friday and Saturday. Based on the information provided, what is the most logical reason for this?

    a. There are more addresses ending with these numbers than with the other numbers.
    b. All businesses have addresses ending in these numbers, and they consume the most water.
    c. The residents at these addresses are the most likely to consume more water.
    d. The city is more concerned about water usage in the latter part of the week.

42. Sybilla is currently working three jobs in an effort to <u>aggrandize</u> herself financially and pay off her college debts. Which of the following is the definition for the underlined word in the sentence?

    a. add
    b. develop
    c. strengthen
    d. dispute

Copyright © Mometrix Media. You have been licensed one copy of this document for personal use only. Any other reproduction or redistribution is strictly prohibited. All rights reserved.

Passage 1:

Fairy tales, fictional stories that involve magical occurrences and imaginary creatures like trolls, elves, giants, and talking animals, are found in similar forms throughout the world. This occurs when a story with an origin in a particular location spreads geographically to, over time, far-flung lands. All variations of the same story must logically come from a single source. As language, ideas, and goods travel from place to place through the movement of peoples, stories that catch human imagination travel as well through human retelling.

Passage 2:

Fairy tales capture basic, fundamental human desires and fears. They represent the most essential form of fictionalized human experience: the bad characters are pure evil, the good characters are pure good, the romance of royalty (and of commoners becoming royalty) is celebrated, etc. Given the nature of the fairy tale genre, it is not surprising that many different cultures come up with similar versions of the same essential story.

The next four questions are based on the two passages above.

43. On what point would the authors of both passages agree?

    a. Fairy tales share a common origin.
    b. The same fairy tale may develop independently in a number of different cultures.
    c. There are often common elements in fairy tales from different cultures.
    d. Fairy tales capture basic human fears.

44. What does the "nature of the fairy tale genre" refer to in Passage 2?

    a. The representation of basic human experience
    b. Good characters being pure good and bad characters being pure evil
    c. Different cultures coming up with similar versions of the same story
    d. Commoners becoming royalty

45. Which of the following is not an example of something the author of Passage 1 claims travels from place to place through human movement?

    a. Fairy tales
    b. Language
    c. Ideas
    d. Foods

46. Which of the following is not an example of something that the author of Passage 1 states might be found in a fairy tale?

    a. Trolls
    b. Witches
    c. Talking animals
    d. Giants

Copyright © Mometrix Media. You have been licensed one copy of this document for personal use only. Any other reproduction or redistribution is strictly prohibited. All rights reserved.

What outdoorsy, family adventure can you have on a hot, summer day? How about spelunking? If you live in an area that is anywhere near a guided, lit cave, find out the hours of operation and hit the road towards it as soon as you can. Hitch up the double jogging stroller and make your way out into the wilderness, preferably with a guide, and discover the wonders of the cool, dark earth even while it is sweltering hot in the outside world. It will be 58 degrees in that cave, and you can explore inside for as long as you please. Best part? The absolutely awesome naps that the kids will take after such an exciting adventure! Be sure to bring:
Bottled water
Light-up tennis shoes if you have them (they look fabulous in the dark)
Flashlights or glow sticks just for fun
Jackets
Changes of clothes in case of getting muddy and/or dirty

The next two questions are based on the passage above.

47. Based on the information given, what is spelunking?

a. going in a cave
b. an outdoor adventure
c. walking with a double stroller
d. a hot, summer day

48. Given the style of writing for the passage, which of the following magazines would be the best fit for this article?

a. *Scientific Spelunking*
b. *Family Fun Days*
c. *Technical Caving in America*
d. *Mud Magazine*

Copyright © Mometrix Media. You have been licensed one copy of this document for personal use only. Any other reproduction or redistribution is strictly prohibited. All rights reserved.

Section 2. Mathematics

1. Dr. Maya asked Nurse Andrew to recommend patients for a study about high blood pressure and high cholesterol. When Nurse Andrew analyzed his patients, he saw that $\frac{1}{10}$ of his patients had high blood pressure and normal cholesterol, $\frac{3}{5}$ had high blood pressure and high cholesterol, $\frac{1}{4}$ had normal blood pressure and high cholesterol, and $\frac{1}{20}$ had normal blood pressure and normal cholesterol. What percentage of his patients did Nurse Andrew recommend for the study?

    a. 5%
    b. 10%
    c. 25%
    d. 60%

2. Dr. Lee saw that 30% of all his patients developed an infection after taking a certain antibiotic. He further noticed that 5% of that 30% required hospitalization to recover from the infection. What percentage of Dr. Lee's patients were hospitalized after taking the antibiotic?

    a. 1.5%
    b. 5%
    c. 15%
    d. 30%

3. A patient requires a 30% increase in the dosage of her medication. Her current dosage is 270 mg. What will her dosage be after the increase?

    a. 81 mg
    b. 270 mg
    c. 300 mg
    d. 351 mg

4. A study about bulimia was conducted on 500 patients. Within that patient population 60% were women, and 20% of the men experienced some kind of childhood trauma. How many male patients in the study did NOT experience a childhood trauma?

    a. 40
    b. 100
    c. 160
    d. 200

5. University X requires some of its nursing students to take an exam before being admitted into the nursing program. In this year's class, $\frac{1}{2}$ the nursing students were required to take the exam and $\frac{3}{5}$ of those who took the exam passed the exam. If this year's class has 200 students, how many students passed the exam?

    a. 120
    b. 100
    c. 60
    d. 50

Copyright © Mometrix Media. You have been licensed one copy of this document for personal use only. Any other reproduction or redistribution is strictly prohibited. All rights reserved.

Four roommates must use their financial aid checks to pay their living expenses. Each student receives $1000 per month.

The next five questions are based on the information above.

6. The first roommate uses $\frac{1}{4}$ of his financial aid check for the rent and utilities. Then he divides the remainder in half so that he can save $\frac{1}{2}$ the remainder. He lives off the rest. How much money does the student live off of each month?

    a. $250
    b. $375
    c. $500
    d. $1000

7. The second roommate budgets $\frac{1}{5}$ of his check for dining out plus another $\frac{1}{4}$ of his check for social activities. What is the total fraction of the second roommate's financial aid check that is spent on dining out and social activities?

    a. $\frac{1}{20}$
    b. $\frac{9}{20}$
    c. $\frac{1}{9}$
    d. $\frac{2}{9}$

8. Each month, the third roommate pays $250 for rent and utilities. Then he pays $100 for his car and insurance. Finally, he invests $25. How much money does the third roommate have left after paying these expenses?

    a. $975
    b. $750
    c. $650
    d. $625

9. The fourth roommate is saving to buy a house. So each month he puts money aside in a special house savings account. The ratio of his monthly house savings to his rent is 1:3. If he pays $270 per month in rent, how much money does he put into his house savings account each month?

    a. $90
    b. $270
    c. $730
    d. $810

10. Three of the roommates decided to combine their money to purchase a single birthday gift for their fourth roommate. The first roommate donated $12.03. The second roommate contributed $11.96, and the third roommate gave $12.06. Estimate the total amount of money the roommates used to purchase the gift.

    a. $34
    b. $35
    c. $36
    d. $37

Copyright © Mometrix Media. You have been licensed one copy of this document for personal use only. Any other reproduction or redistribution is strictly prohibited. All rights reserved.

11. A patient was exercising for 45 minutes a day. However, the doctor determined that this amount of exercise was dangerous for the patient's heart. So the doctor recommended that the patient reduce his daily exercising routine by 7 minutes. How long is the patient's new daily exercising routine?

    a. 38 minutes
    b. 45 minutes
    c. 52 minutes
    d. 60 minutes

12. A lab technician took 500 milliliters of blood from a patient. The technician used $\frac{1}{6}$ of the blood for further tests. How many milliliters of blood were used for further tests? Round your answer to the nearest hundredth.

    a. 83.00
    b. 83.30
    c. 83.33
    d. 83.34

13. A patient's medical records were faxed from a hospital in the Middle East to a hospital in the USA. The patient's weight was listed in Roman numerals as LXIV kilograms. How much does the patient weigh?

    a. 34 kg
    b. 44 kg
    c. 54 kg
    d. 64 kg

14. Veronica was recently promoted to department manager for the oncology department at a local hospital. Her gross annual salary is $70,000. Veronica contributes 15% of her salary **before** taxes to a retirement account. Then she pays 30% of her remaining salary in state and federal taxes. Finally, she pays $70 per month for health insurance for her entire family. What is Veronica's annual take-home pay?

    a. $37,660
    b. $38,430
    c. $40,810
    d. $41,580

15. Veronica decided to celebrate her promotion by purchasing a new car. The base price for the car was $40,210. She paid an additional $3,015 for a surround sound system and $5,218 for a maintenance package. What was the total price of Veronica's new car?

    a. $50,210
    b. $48,443
    c. $43,225
    d. $40,210

Copyright © Mometrix Media. You have been licensed one copy of this document for personal use only. Any other reproduction or redistribution is strictly prohibited. All rights reserved.

16. Use the following table from a savings account statement to determine the ending balance in the account.

Transaction description	Amount
Beginning balance	$503.81
Deposit money with bank teller	$125.00
Withdrawal using ATM	$215.00
Monthly interest earned	$5.38
Ending balance	??

    a. $419.19
    b. $503.81
    c. $599.19
    d. $849.19

17. Complete the following equation:

$$2 + (2)(4) - 4 \div 2 = ?$$

    a. 3
    b. 5
    c. 6
    d. 8

18. The pediatric ward of a hospital is hosting a holiday party for the children and their families. For each group of 4 people who RSVP for the party, the hospital staff will order 1 medium pizza and 8 holiday cupcakes. Each medium pizza costs $9.50, and each cupcake costs $2.75. If 160 people RSVP for the event, how much money will the hospital staff spend on pizza?

    a. $380
    b. $880
    c. $950
    d. $1520

19. Based on their prescribing habits, a set of doctors was divided into three groups: $\frac{1}{3}$ of the doctors were placed in Group X because they always prescribed medication. $\frac{5}{12}$ of the doctors were placed in Group Y because they never prescribed medication. $\frac{1}{4}$ of the doctors were placed in Group Z because they sometimes prescribed medication. Order the groups from largest to smallest, according to the number of doctors in each group.

    a. Group X, Group Y, Group Z
    b. Group Z, Group Y, Group X
    c. Group Z, Group X, Group Y
    d. Group Y, Group X, Group Z

20. Solve the following equation:

$$\frac{2y}{10} + 5 = 25$$

    a. $y = 25$
    b. $y = 100$
    c. $y = 150$
    d. $y = 200$

Copyright © Mometrix Media. You have been licensed one copy of this document for personal use only. Any other reproduction or redistribution is strictly prohibited. All rights reserved.

21. Subtract polynomial #2 from polynomial #1.

Polynomial #1: $8x + 7y + 6z$

Polynomial #2: $3z + 4y + 5x$

    a. $5x + 3y + z$
    b. $5xz + 3y + xz$
    c. $3x + 3y + 3z$
    d. $11x + 11y + 11z$

22. During January, Dr. Lewis worked 20 shifts. During February, she worked three times as many shifts as she did during January. During March, she worked half the number of shifts she worked during February. Which equation below describes the number of shifts Dr. Lewis worked in March?

    a. $\text{shifts} = 20 + 3 + \frac{1}{2}$
    b. $\text{shifts} = (20)(3)\left(\frac{1}{2}\right)$
    c. $\text{shifts} = (20)(3) + \frac{1}{2}$
    d. $\text{shifts} = 20 + (3)\left(\frac{1}{2}\right)$

23. Solve the following expression.

$$|2 - 10| + (2)(10) - 5$$

    a. 7
    b. 15
    c. 20
    d. 23

24. Which circle graph accurately describes the data presented in the table below?

Nurse specialties	Number of nurses
Anesthesia	60
Midwifery	30
Pediatrics	175
Geriatrics	100

a.　　　　　　　　　　　b.

c.　　　　　　　　　　　d.

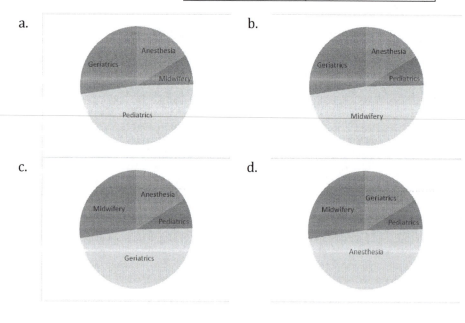

Copyright © Mometrix Media. You have been licensed one copy of this document for personal use only. Any other reproduction or redistribution is strictly prohibited. All rights reserved.

25. According to the bar graph below, which specialty has the least number of nurses?

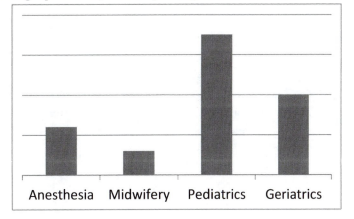

- a. Anesthesia
- b. Midwifery
- c. Pediatrics
- d. Geriatrics

26. What is the independent variable in the graph below?

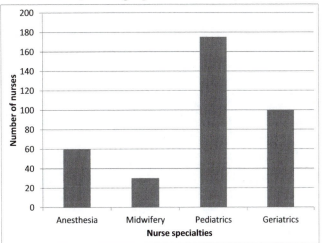

- a. Anesthesia
- b. Geriatrics
- c. Nurse specialties
- d. Number of nurses

27. How many centimeters are in 7 meters?
- a. 7 m = 7 cm
- b. 7 m = 70 cm
- c. 7 m = 700 cm
- d. 7 m = 7000 cm

Copyright © Mometrix Media. You have been licensed one copy of this document for personal use only. Any other reproduction or redistribution is strictly prohibited. All rights reserved.

28. About how long is the average human eyelash?

    a. 1 nanometer
    b. 1 centimeter
    c. 1 meter
    d. 1 kilometer

29. A farmer plans to install fencing around a certain field. If each side of the hexagonal field is 320 feet long, and fencing costs $1.75 per foot, how much will the farmer need to spend on fencing material to fence the perimeter of the field?

    a. $2,240
    b. $2,800
    c. $3,360
    d. $4,480

30. Use the figure below to determine the distance between marks 1 and 3. Each segment between marks is the same length.

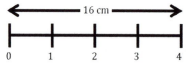

    a. 2 cm
    b. 4 cm
    c. 8 cm
    d. 16 cm

Copyright © Mometrix Media. You have been licensed one copy of this document for personal use only. Any other reproduction or redistribution is strictly prohibited. All rights reserved.

City X (250)	Profession	City Y (183)
74	**Doctor**	55
121	Registered Nurse	87
14	Administrator	9
15	Maintenance	11
6	Pharmacist	5
4	Radiologist	2
2	Physical Therapist	2
1	Speech Pathologist	1
13	Other	11
	Gender	
153	Male	93
97	Female	90
	Age	
24	Youngest	22
73	Oldest	77
	Ethnicity	
51	African American	42
50	Asian American	27
45	Hispanic American	35
47	Caucasian	37
57	Other	42
	Years on Staff	
64	0-5	32
63	5-10	41
57	10-15	67
47	15-20	30
14	20-25	19
5	More than 25	5
	Number of Patient Complaints	
202	0	161
43	1--4	21
5	5-10	1
0	More than 10	0

Profile of Staff at Mercy Hospital in City X and Mercy Hospital in City Y
Total Combined Staff: 433

The next four questions are based on the previous information.

Copyright © Mometrix Media. You have been licensed one copy of this document for personal use only. Any other reproduction or redistribution is strictly prohibited. All rights reserved.

31. Which percentage is greatest?

    a. The percentage of Asian Americans to staff as a whole in City X?
    b. The percentage of staff members who have been on staff 10-15 years to staff as a whole in City X?
    c. The percentage of Doctors to staff as a whole in City X and City Y?
    d. The percentage of staff with 1-4 complaints to staff as a whole in City Y?

32. If all Caucasian staff members in City Y have been on staff between 5-10 years, how many non-Caucasian staff members in City Y have been on staff 5-10 years?

    a. 0
    b. 4
    c. 37
    d. 41

33. Approximately what percentage more staff members in City Y are female than in City X?

    a. 5
    b. 10
    c. 15
    d. 20

34. According to the chart, the percentage of staff who have received zero complaints is

    a. greater in City X than in City Y
    b. greater in City Y than in City X
    c. the same in City X and in City Y
    d. growing in both City X and City Y

Copyright © Mometrix Media. You have been licensed one copy of this document for personal use only. Any other reproduction or redistribution is strictly prohibited. All rights reserved.

Section 3. Science

1. Which of the following items is NOT part of the circulatory system?

    a. Kidneys
    b. Heart
    c. Blood
    d. Blood vessels

2. Which of the following items belongs to the digestive system?

    a. Spine
    b. Lungs
    c. Brain
    d. Stomach

3. Which system below is the center of communication for the body?

    a. Respiratory system
    b. Nervous system
    c. Digestive system
    d. Circulatory system

4. Which item below best describes the primary function of the respiratory system?

    a. The respiratory system helps carry blood throughout the body.
    b. The respiratory system helps break down food for the body.
    c. The respiratory system helps the body breathe.
    d. The respiratory system helps send messages throughout the body.

5. Which of the following items is NOT a primary function of a healthy immune system?

    a. The immune system helps the body avoid infections.
    b. The immune system detects infections.
    c. The immune system eliminates infections.
    d. The immune system creates infections.

6. The spine and hips belong to which of the following bone types?

    a. Curvy bones
    b. Irregular bones
    c. Flat bones
    d. Long bones

7. Long bones are one of the five major types of bone in the human body. All of the following bones are long bones, EXCEPT

    a. Thighs
    b. Forearms
    c. Ankles
    d. Fingers

Copyright © Mometrix Media. You have been licensed one copy of this document for personal use only. Any other reproduction or redistribution is strictly prohibited. All rights reserved.

8. The population of the United States is directly influenced by all the following factors EXCEPT:

    a. Education
    b. Immigration
    c. Births
    d. Deaths

9. Which of the following factors would have NO influence on birth rates within a given population?

    a. The age of the women in the population
    b. The health of the women in the population
    c. The fertility of the women in the population
    d. All of these factors would influence birth rates within a given population.

10. Which of the following would most likely cause the population of the United States to increase?

    a. Women stop having children so they can focus on their careers.
    b. The government forces all adult males to join the military.
    c. Scientists discontinue all research to find cures for deadly diseases.
    d. Scientists create a cure for cancer.

11. Within a certain population, every time 1 person dies, 2 babies are born. How is this population most likely changing over time?

    a. The population is decreasing.
    b. The population is increasing.
    c. The population is remaining the same.
    d. The population has reached a steady state.

12. Which of the following scenarios does NOT describe the process of natural selection?

    a. The fastest zebras avoid being eaten by predators. Therefore, they live to produce offspring that are also fast runners.
    b. The polar bears with the thickest fur coats survive the harsh winters. Therefore, they live to produce offspring who also have thick fur coats.
    c. Animals that are born blind are soon eaten by predators. Therefore, they do not live to produce other animals that may be born blind.
    d. All of the above scenarios describe the process of natural selection.

13. Consider the categories of the biological classification system. Which choice below lists categories from broadest to most specific?

    a. Phylum, kingdom, genus, species
    b. Kingdom, phylum, genus, species
    c. Genus, kingdom, phylum, species
    d. Genus, species, phylum, kingdom

14. Which part of the cell serves as the control center for all cell activity?

    a. Nucleus
    b. Cell membrane
    c. Cytoplasm
    d. Mitochondria

Copyright © Mometrix Media. You have been licensed one copy of this document for personal use only. Any other reproduction or redistribution is strictly prohibited. All rights reserved.

15. What are the cellular functions of cilia and flagella?

    a. Cilia and flagella are responsible for cell movement.
    b. Cilia and flagella synthesize proteins.
    c. Cilia and flagella help protect the cell from its environment.
    d. Cilia and flagella have enzymes that help with digestion.

16. What is the process by which simple cells become highly specialized cells?

    a. Cellular complication
    b. Cellular specialization
    c. Cellular differentiation
    d. Cellular modification

17. How does meiosis differ from mitosis?

    a. Meiosis is used to repair the body. Mitosis is used to break down the body.
    b. Meiosis is used for asexual reproduction of single-celled organisms. Mitosis is used for sexual reproduction of multicellular organisms.
    c. Meiosis only occurs in humans. Mitosis only occurs in plants.
    d. Meiosis produces cells that are genetically different. Mitosis produces cells that are genetically identical.

18. Which statement best describes how photosynthesis is different from respiration?

    a. Photosynthesis occurs in animals, but respiration occurs in plants.
    b. During photosynthesis, oxygen is given off, but during respiration, oxygen is taken in.
    c. Photosynthesis requires oxygen, but respiration requires carbon dioxide.
    d. Photosynthesis uses darkness, but respiration uses sunlight.

19. How does the structure of RNA differ from the structure of DNA?

    a. RNA contains 4 nucleotides while DNA contains 6 nucleotides.
    b. RNA contains a double helix while DNA contains a single helix.
    c. RNA contains a single helix while DNA contains a double helix.
    d. The structure of RNA is exactly the same as the structure of DNA.

20. Which type of cell must mutate in order to change an organism's offspring?

    a. Germ cell
    b. Marrow cell
    c. Tissue cell
    d. Ovarian cell

21. How does RNA work with DNA during cell replication?

    a. RNA primes DNA to triple so that daughter cells will have an abundance of DNA material.
    b. DNA primes RNA to triple so that daughter cells will have an abundance of RNA material.
    c. DNA primes RNA replication so that daughter cells will have the same amount of RNA as the parent cell.
    d. RNA primes DNA replication so that daughter cells will have the same amount of DNA as the parent cell.

Copyright © Mometrix Media. You have been licensed one copy of this document for personal use only. Any other reproduction or redistribution is strictly prohibited. All rights reserved.

22. What functions do genes serve in the relationship between parents and offspring?

    a. Genes enable hereditary information to be passed from parents to offspring.
    b. Genes prohibit hereditary information from being passed from parents to offspring.
    c. Genes enable environmental factors to affect parents and offspring.
    d. Genes serve no function in the relationship between parents and offspring.

23. Which statement best describes the structural relationships among chromosomes, genes, and DNA?

    a. A chromosome contains the four genes that make up the DNA double helix.
    b. A gene contains many chromosomes that make up DNA.
    c. A chromosome is a single piece of DNA that contains many genes.
    d. Chromosomes, genes, and DNA have no structural relationships.

24. What does the phenotype describe about an individual?

    a. The phenotype describes a person's genetic makeup.
    b. The phenotype describes a person's observable characteristics.
    c. The phenotype describes a person's environmental factors.
    d. The phenotype describes all the phenomena a person has experienced since birth.

A person with the T gene will be tall and a person with the S gene will be short. A person with the B gene will have black hair and a person with the R gene will have red hair. Now consider the Punnett square below.

	T	S
R	Possibility 1	Possibility 2
B	Possibility 3	Possibility 4

The next two questions are based on the information above.

25. What are the characteristics of the person with genes from possibility 1?
    a. Short with black hair
    b. Short with red hair
    c. Tall with black hair
    d. Tall with red hair

26. Which possibility would produce a short offspring with black hair?
    a. Possibility 1
    b. Possibility 2
    c. Possibility 3
    d. Possibility 4

27. Which of the following statements about the sun is FALSE?
    a. The sun is a major external source of heat for Earth.
    b. The sun is a major external source of light for Earth.
    c. The sun is only a minor source of light for Earth since a lot of Earth's light comes from the moon.
    d. Energy from the sun can be used for solar power.

Copyright © Mometrix Media. You have been licensed one copy of this document for personal use only. Any other reproduction or redistribution is strictly prohibited. All rights reserved.

28. Which of the following is an example of an oxidation-reduction (redox) reaction?

   a. Copper loses 2 electrons and silver loses 4 electrons.
   b. Copper loses 2 electrons and silver gains 2 electrons.
   c. Copper gains 2 electrons and silver loses 2 protons.
   d. Copper gains 2 neutrons and silver loses 2 protons.

29. A chemist wants to increase the rate of a reaction between two chemicals. What should he add to the reaction to increase the rate?

   a. A catalyst
   b. An acid
   c. A base
   d. A neutralizer

30. Fill in the blanks in this sentence: Enzymes are _____ molecules that serve as _____ for certain biological reactions.

   a. Enzymes are irrelevant molecules that serve as suppressors for certain biological reactions.
   b. Enzymes are acidic molecules that serve as catalysts for certain biological reactions.
   c. Enzymes are lipid molecules that serve as catalysts for certain biological reactions.
   d. Enzymes are protein molecules that serve as catalysts for certain biological reactions.

31. A lab technician wants to identify an unknown substance. A litmus paper test reveals the pH of the substance is 2. What type of substance is this?

   a. Carcinogen
   b. Water
   c. Acid
   d. Base

32. What type of chemical bond connects the oxygen and hydrogen atoms in a molecule of water?

   a. Static bond
   b. Aquatic bond
   c. Ionic bond
   d. Covalent bond

33. Which of the following statements describes a chemical property of water?

   a. Water has a pH of 1.
   b. A water molecule contains 2 hydrogen atoms and 1 oxygen atom.
   c. A water molecule contains 2 oxygen atoms and 1 hydrogen atom.
   d. The chemical formula for water is HO_2.

34. A man swings a golf club using the following steps:

Step 1: He raises the golf club above his shoulder and stops with club held in midair.
Step 2: He rapidly lowers the golf club.
Step 3: He hits the golf ball.

At which step in the swing does the golf club have the most potential energy?

   a. Step 1
   b. Step 2
   c. Step 3
   d. The potential energy is the same at all steps.

Copyright © Mometrix Media. You have been licensed one copy of this document for personal use only. Any other reproduction or redistribution is strictly prohibited. All rights reserved.

35. An atom has 2 protons, 4 neutrons, and 2 electrons. What is the approximate atomic mass of this atom?

    a. 2
    b. 4
    c. 6
    d. 8

36. What are the three major components of an atom?

    a. Positrons, negatrons, and decepticons
    b. Protons, neutrons, and electrons
    c. Molecules, dipoles, and bonds
    d. Proteins, dipoles, and lipids

37. What type of bond is formed when electrons are transferred between atoms?

    a. Transfer bond
    b. Static bond
    c. Covalent bond
    d. Ionic bond

38. The table below contains information from the periodic table of elements.

Element	Atomic number	Approximate atomic weight
B	5	11
C	6	12
N	7	14
O	8	16

Which pattern below best describes the masses of the elements listed in the table?

    a. The elements are listed in random order, C being the heaviest element and N being the lightest element.
    b. The elements are listed in decreasing order, B being the heaviest element and O being the lightest element.
    c. The elements are listed in increasing order, B being the lightest element and O being the heaviest element.
    d. All the elements weigh the same, so the order is irrelevant.

39. Which of the following statements best describes the similarities between gases and liquids?

    a. Gases and liquids both take on the shape of their container.
    b. Gases and liquids both have a fixed shape.
    c. Atoms in a gas and atoms in a liquid are both lighter than air molecules.
    d. Gases have no similarities with liquids.

40. Which statement below best describes the process of condensation?

    a. Condensation is the process of changing from a gas to a liquid.
    b. Condensation is the process of changing from a liquid to a gas.
    c. Condensation is the process of changing from a solid to a liquid.
    d. Condensation is the process of changing from a solid to a gas.

Copyright © Mometrix Media. You have been licensed one copy of this document for personal use only. Any other reproduction or redistribution is strictly prohibited. All rights reserved.

41. A researcher is conducting a survey on the connections between smoking and premature aging. Which of the following questions should the researcher ask survey participants?

    a. Do you enjoy taking surveys?
    b. Are you married?
    c. Do you exercise?
    d. Do you smoke?

42. An organization wants to improve communication between children who are adopted and their biological families. The organization also wants to protect everyone's privacy. Which method below would most improve communication between these two parties?

    a. Create a large book with names, addresses, and other personal information so that adopted children can search for their biological families.
    b. Establish a secure Internet site that helps match adopted children with their biological families.
    c. Publish information in the newspaper about adopted children and their biological families so that people who read the paper can communicate with each other.
    d. Use word of mouth communication so that adopted children can pass messages to their biological families.

43. Every child in a certain family suffers from autism. Based on this evidence, what possible conclusion can be drawn about autism?

    a. Autism may be lethal.
    b. Autism may be genetic.
    c. Autism is related to traditional nuclear family structures.
    d. No conclusion can be drawn based on this evidence.

44. Women were more likely to die in childbirth in the 18th century than in the 21st century. What is a possible explanation for why women are less likely to die in childbirth in the present age?

    a. Doctors are better equipped to perform cesarean sections.
    b. Doctors have more tools to monitor mothers during childbirth, so complications can be detected much earlier.
    c. Doctors wash their hands well to avoid transferring germs and infections.
    d. All of the statements above offer reasonable explanations for decreases in mortality during childbirth.

45. A dietitian wants to convince a patient to lose weight. Which statement below best communicates a scientific argument that justifies the need for weight loss?

    a. Losing weight can lower blood pressure, increase energy level, and promote overall health.
    b. Society tends to treat overweight people unfairly.
    c. Members of the opposite sex are more interested in people who maintain a healthy weight.
    d. Losing weight is easy to do.

46. A researcher wants to investigate the relationship between family income and quality of medical care. Which statement provides the best reason to conduct this investigation?

    a. The researcher can learn more about wealthy people and ask them for money.
    b. The investigation can help target healthy people so that they can remain healthy.
    c. Results of this investigation may identify a group of people who do not receive quality medical care so that these people could receive better medical treatments.
    d. There is no reason to conduct this investigation.

Copyright © Mometrix Media. You have been licensed one copy of this document for personal use only. Any other reproduction or redistribution is strictly prohibited. All rights reserved.

47. Which of the following statements provides the best reason to include mathematics in scientific research?

    a. Mathematics allows researchers to take an emotional approach to data analysis.
    b. Mathematics allows researchers to take an objective approach to data analysis.
    c. Mathematics allows researchers to take an unrealistic approach to data analysis.
    d. Mathematics allows researchers to take an artistic approach to data analysis.

48. All of the following statements are reasons to include technology in scientific research EXCEPT:

    a. Technology can allow researchers to access a large number of research participants.
    b. Technology can allow researchers to fabricate research results.
    c. Technology can allow researchers to analyze a large amount of data.
    d. Technology can allow researchers to conduct a wide variety of different experiments.

49. What is the name for the reactant that is entirely consumed by the reaction?

    a. Limiting reactant
    b. Reducing agent
    c. Reaction intermediate
    d. Reagent

50. What is the name for the horizontal rows of the periodic table?

    a. Groups
    b. Periods
    c. Families
    d. Sets

51. What is the mass (in grams) of 7.35 mol water?

    a. 10.7 g
    b. 18 g
    c. 132 g
    d. 180.6 g

52. What is 119°K in degrees Celsius?

    a. 32°C
    b. −154°C
    c. 154°C
    d. −32°C

53. How many different types of tissue are there in the human body?

    a. 4
    b. 6
    c. 8
    d. 10

54. What is the name of the outermost layer of skin?

    a. Dermis
    b. Epidermis
    c. Subcutaneous tissue
    d. Hypodermis

Copyright © Mometrix Media. You have been licensed one copy of this document for personal use only. Any other reproduction or redistribution is strictly prohibited. All rights reserved.

Section 4. English and Language Usage

1. The Declaration of Independence contains these famous lines: "When in the Course of human events it becomes necessary for one people to dissolve the political bands which have connected them with another...a decent respect to the opinions of mankind requires that they should declare the causes which impel them to the separation." Which of the following best explains the purpose of the ellipses in the passage?

    a. to indicate emphasis
    b. to indicate excluded material
    c. to indicate quoted material
    d. to indicate more than one point of view

2. The soldier was awarded the ____ for his display of courage, strength, and ____ in battle. Which of the following words correctly completes the sentence?

    a. metal; mettle
    b. medal; metal
    c. medal; mettle
    d. mettle; metal

3. The teacher reminded the class that each student was responsible for ____ work and that any cheating or plagiarizing would be swiftly punished. Which of the following correctly completes the sentence?

    a. their
    b. his
    c. his or her
    d. one's

4. Thomas Macaulay once commented that "Few of the many wise apothegms which have been uttered have prevented a single foolish action." Which of the following best explains the meaning of apothegms as it is used in the sentence?

    a. advice
    b. preferences
    c. quotes
    d. sayings

5. A childhood reading of *Tales from Shakespeare* permanently ____ Helene's interest in studying the Great Bard. Which of the following correctly completes the sentence?

    a. piqued
    b. peaked
    c. peked
    d. peeked

Copyright © Mometrix Media. You have been licensed one copy of this document for personal use only. Any other reproduction or redistribution is strictly prohibited. All rights reserved.

6. Which of the following demonstrates correct punctuation?

    a. Graham still needs the following items for his class: a sable brush, soft pastels, a sketchbook, and an easel.

    b. Graham still needs the following items for his class, a sable brush, soft pastels, a sketchbook, and an easel.

    c. Graham still needs the following items for his class: a sable brush; soft pastels; a sketchbook; and an easel.

    d. Graham still needs the following items for his class – a sable brush; soft pastels; a sketchbook; and an easel.

7. The French and Indian War was not an isolated war in North America. It was part of a larger war that Europe was fighting. Europeans called it the Seven Years' War. Which of the following options best combines the sentences? Consider style, clarity, and conciseness when choosing your response.

    a. The French and Indian War did not occur in North America but was rather a small part of the larger European war known as the Seven Years' War.

    b. What Europeans called the Seven Years' War was called the French and Indian War in North America. It was part of a larger war that Europe was fighting.

    c. The French and Indian War was not an isolated war in North America but was rather part of a larger war that Europe was fighting, known among Europeans as the Seven Years' War.

    d. While North America was fighting the French and Indian War, the Europeans were fighting a much larger war known as the Seven Years' War.

8. During the Seven Years' War, England and France fought over the control of the North American colonies, as well as the trade routes to those colonies. Which of the following words functions as a verb in the sentence?

    a. fought
    b. control
    c. trade
    d. those

9. Which of the following is a simple sentence?

    a. Following the French and Indian War, Spain gave up Florida to England.
    b. England returned part of Cuba to Spain, while France gave up part of Louisiana.
    c. France lost most of its Caribbean islands, and England gained dominance over them.
    d. Because every nation lost something, no clear victor was declared.

10. Which of the following sentences follows the rules of capitalization?

    a. One major conflict in the Seven Years' War occurred between the Prussian Hohenzollern Family and the Austrian Hapsburg Family.
    b. The Hapsburg family was considered to be the rulers of the Holy Roman empire.
    c. At the start of the war, Maria Theresa was the empress of Austria and was strengthening Austria's military.
    d. Frederick the Great of Prussia had recently acquired the former Austrian Province of Silesia.

Copyright © Mometrix Media. You have been licensed one copy of this document for personal use only. Any other reproduction or redistribution is strictly prohibited. All rights reserved.

11. Which of the following sentences demonstrates the correct use of quotation marks?

    a. Maria Theresa was the mother of Marie Antoinette, the French queen remembered for saying, 'Let them eat cake.'
    b. Maria Theresa was the mother of Marie Antoinette, the French queen remembered for saying, 'Let them eat cake'.
    c. Maria Theresa was the mother of Marie Antoinette, the French queen remembered for saying, "Let them eat cake."
    d. Maria Theresa was the mother of Marie Antoinette, the French queen remembered for saying, "Let them eat cake".

12. Which of the following sentences contains a correct example of subject-verb agreement?

    a. Some of the post-rally fervor have already died down.
    b. Gary, as well as his three children, are coming to visit later today.
    c. Are neither Robert nor his parents planning to see the presentation?
    d. We waited patiently while a herd of moose was crossing the mountain highway.

13. *I tried to call Lisle earlier, but I could not get her on the phone.* Which of the following words functions as an adverb in the sentence?

    a. call
    b. earlier
    c. could
    d. phone

14. The Hapsburg rule of the Austro-Hungarian Empire effectively ended with the reign of Franz Joseph I (1848-1916). Which of the following best explains the purpose of the parentheses in the sentence?

    a. to indicate the page numbers in the book where this information might be found
    b. to tell the reader when the Austro-Hungarian empire collapsed
    c. to identify information that was located using another source
    d. to set off useful information that does not fit directly into the flow of the sentence

15. Which of the following sentences is grammatically correct?

    a. The person who left the trash in the hallway needs to pick it up now.
    b. Nobody needs to turn in their projects before the end of the month.
    c. Every new instructor should stop by the main office to pick up one's room key.
    d. Both Simeon and Ruth are generous with his or her time.

16. *I never know when you are joking about something.* What is the point of view indicated by the underlined words in the sentence?

    a. third; second
    b. second; first
    c. first; second
    d. first; third

Copyright © Mometrix Media. You have been licensed one copy of this document for personal use only. Any other reproduction or redistribution is strictly prohibited. All rights reserved.

17. Maud will try to be there by 4:00, but she will _____ be there no later than 4.30. Which of the following correctly completes the sentence?

    a. defiantly
    b. definitely
    c. defanately
    d. definetly

18. *Walking is a very good exercise that the majority of people can incorporate into their daily lives.* A verbal is a verb form that is used as a different part of speech. In the above sentence, which part of speech is the word *walking* used as?

    a. noun
    b. adverb
    c. adjective
    d. conjunction

19. In the fairy tale Sleeping Beauty, the story opens with the christening of a princess. All of the fairies are invited except one; when this fairy realizes that she has been overlooked, she utters a malediction upon the princess that results in the princess pricking her finger on a spindle and falling asleep for one hundred years. Which of the following best explains the meaning of malediction as it is used in the passage?

    a. enchantment
    b. remedy
    c. promise
    d. curse

20. The story of Sleeping Beauty is similar to many fairy tales. Its origins are unknown. It is believed to be a combination of different versions of an old story. One of the most familiar versions comes from the French collection of fairy tales by Charles Perrault. The German Brothers Grimm also incorporated elements into their version.

Which of the following options best arranges the sentences above without losing the meaning of the passage? Consider style and clarity when choosing a response.

    a. The story of *Sleeping Beauty* is similar to many fairy tales, because its origins are unknown. It is believed to be a combination of different versions of an old story. One of the most familiar versions comes from the French collection of fairy tales by Charles Perrault. The German Brothers Grimm also incorporated elements into their publication.
    b. The origins of *Sleeping Beauty* are unknown, but like many fairy tales it is believed to be a combination of different forms of an old story. The most familiar version is that of the French Charles Perrault. Another familiar version comes from the German Brothers Grimm.
    c. Like many fairy tales, the origins of *Sleeping Beauty* are unknown, and it is believed to be a combination of different versions of an old story. One of the most familiar versions comes from the French collection of fairy tales by Charles Perrault, while the German Brothers Grimm also incorporated elements into their publication.
    d. One of the most familiar versions of *Sleeping Beauty* comes from the French collection of fairy tales by Charles Perrault, and the German Brothers Grimm also incorporated elements into their publication. But the story of *Sleeping Beauty* is similar to that of many fairy tales. Its origins are unknown, and it is believed to be a combination of different forms of an old story.

Copyright © Mometrix Media. You have been licensed one copy of this document for personal use only. Any other reproduction or redistribution is strictly prohibited. All rights reserved.

21. Which of the following sentences demonstrates the correct use of an apostrophe?

a. In one version of the story, there are seven fairy's invited to the christening, while in another version there are twelve fairy's.
b. Some historians' believe that the number twelve represents the shift from a lunar year of thirteen months to a solar year of twelve months.
c. Other historians claim that the symbolism in the fairy tale is more about nature and the shifting season's.
d. Regardless of its meaning, the fairy tale remains popular and has been immortalized in Tchaikovsky's music for the ballet.

22. The teacher spoke firmly to the class: "If you want to succeed in this course, be willing to work hard and turn in work on time." Which of the following points of view is indicated by the underlined word in the sentence?

a. first-person singular
b. third-person plural
c. second-person plural
d. third-person singular

23. Which of the following is not a simple sentence?

a. Agatha Christie was the author of more than sixty detective novels.
b. Her most famous detectives were Hercule Poirot and Miss Marple.
c. She also wrote over fifteen collections of short stories about these detectives.
d. Most readers favor Poirot, but Christie preferred Miss Marple.

24. Hercule Poirot is remembered not only for his genius in solving mysteries, but also for his fastidious habits and his commitment to personal grooming. Which of the following best explains the meaning of fastidious as it is used in the sentence?

a. fussy
b. lazy
c. old-fashioned
d. hilarious

25. The elderly Miss Marple, on the other hand, is remembered for solving the mysteries she encounters by making seemingly extraneous connections to life in her small village. Which of the following best explains the meaning of extraneous as it is used in the sentence?

a. sophisticated
b. irrelevant
c. diligent
d. useful

26. At a party, Thornton is usually the first one on the dance floor, but unfortunately he has no ____. Which of the following correctly completes the sentence?

a. rhythym
b. rythym
c. rhthym
d. rhythm

Copyright © Mometrix Media. You have been licensed one copy of this document for personal use only. Any other reproduction or redistribution is strictly prohibited. All rights reserved.

27. *In* Modern American Usage, *Wilson Follett noted the following example of a dangling modifier: "Leaping to the saddle, his horse bolted."* Which of the following sentences removes the dangling modifier from the above sentence while retaining style and clarity?

    a. His horse bolted as it leaped to the saddle.
    b. When he leaped to the saddle, his horse bolted.
    c. His horse bolting, he leaped to the saddle.
    d. He leaped to the saddle, his horse bolted.

28. *You'll have to ask Hilda; the choice is ____.* Which of the following correctly completes the sentence?

    a. hers
    b. her's
    c. hers'
    d. hers's

29. The word *anaesthetic* refers to medication that causes a temporary loss of feeling or sensation. This word is made up of two primary Greek parts: the root *aesthet* and the prefix *an-*. The root word *aesthet* means "feeling." Based on the meaning of the word in medical usage, which is the most likely meaning of the prefix *an-*?

    a. without
    b. against
    c. away
    d. before

30. The years leading up to the American Civil War are often referred to using the term *antebellum*. This word is composed of two primary Latin parts: the root *bellum*, which means "war," and the prefix *ante-*. Based on the contextual usage of this word, what is the most likely meaning of the prefix *ante-*?

    a. again
    b. good
    c. before
    d. together

31. _____ went to the movies after having dinner at Lenny's.

    a. Her and I
    b. Her and me
    c. She and I
    d. She and me

32. Which word is NOT spelled correctly in the following sentence?

Dr. Vargas was surprised that the prescription had effected Ron's fatigue so dramatically.

    a. surprised
    b. prescription
    c. effected
    d. fatigue

Copyright © Mometrix Media. You have been licensed one copy of this document for personal use only. Any other reproduction or redistribution is strictly prohibited. All rights reserved.

33. Which word is NOT spelled correctly in the following sentence?

The climate hear is inappropriate for snow sports such as skiing.

> a. climate
> b. hear
> c. inappropriate
> d. skiing

34. Which word is NOT used correctly in the following sentence?

Before you walk any further, beware of the approaching traffic.

> a. before
> b. further
> c. beware
> d. approaching

Copyright © Mometrix Media. You have been licensed one copy of this document for personal use only. Any other reproduction or redistribution is strictly prohibited. All rights reserved.

Answer Key and Explanations for Test #3

Reading Answer Explanations

1. C: The best starting point for a research project on the Globe Theatre of London would be the Encyclopedia Britannica. A thesaurus is an excellent place to find synonyms, while a dictionary is an excellent place to find word meanings. However, neither would contain information about the history of the Globe Theatre. (While writing, Ernestine might find herself in need of a better word or a word meaning; in this case, the thesaurus and dictionary will be useful.) A Latin dictionary would not be useful for researching the history of the Globe Theatre.

2. B: The student does not have to be familiar with the Romance languages to know that "American" is a nationality, not a language. (The primary language spoken in America is usually considered to be English.) Based on this information alone, choice B can be selected as the correct answer. The other languages listed in the answer choices (Spanish, French, and Portuguese) are both recognized languages and Romance languages.

3. A: The word *consonantal* would fall between the words *considerable* and *conspicuous* on a dictionary page. The word *consumption* would follow *conspicuous*, while the words *conserve* and *conquistador* would precede *considerable*.

4. C: Of the answer choices given, the word that would most likely appear on the previous dictionary page is *conserve*, which is alphabetically closer to *considerable* than *conquistador* is. Both *considerable* and *conserve* begin with *cons-*. The vowel that follows is different. The word *conquistador*, however, has only *con-* in common with *considerable*. This leaves far more room for words (and potentially pages) in between these two entries. The word *consonantal* would fall between the words *considerable* and *conspicuous* on a dictionary page. The word *consumption* would follow *conspicuous*.

5. C: The correct answer is *abundance.* The sentence suggests that Kit has more zucchini than she needs, and is therefore trying to offload zucchini on anyone who might want some. The *plethora* might lead to a mild *irritation*, but the words are definitely not synonyms. (In some cases, a *plethora* is certainly not an irritation.) The word *plethora* is related to a *quantity*, but it is a specific type of quantity: an excess. Because the word *quantity* can also describe a lack of something, these words are not synonyms. Kit is obviously trying to avoid *waste*, but the words *plethora* and *waste* are not synonyms. *Waste* would also not be a natural replacement for *plethora* in the sentence.

6. B: When the directions are followed correctly, the new word is REVERT. The words REVEST and REVERSE require the addition of an S. (REVERSE also requires a second E.) The word REVIEW requires the addition of an I (which has been removed) and a W.

7. B: If Ethan buys his pens from Office in Bulk, he will pay $450 for 500 pens. At Specialty Pens, he would pay $485; at Office Warehouse, he would pay $475; at Ballpoint & Lead, he would pay $495.

8. D: The symbol /\ appears numerous times on the map, so the best way to determine the actual number of mountain ranges is to use the text on the map. In the state of Wyoming, six separate ranges are identified: the Wyoming Range, the Teton Range, the Wind River Range, the Bighorn Mountains, the Rocky Mountains (which are part of a much larger mountain range that crosses a number of states), and the Laramie Mountains. All of the other answer choices identify too few ranges. (From a purely technical perspective, all of these smaller ranges are actually part of the

Copyright © Mometrix Media. You have been licensed one copy of this document for personal use only. Any other reproduction or redistribution is strictly prohibited. All rights reserved.

larger range of Rocky Mountains that shapes this part of the United States. Because the map identifies the separate ranges, however, it is accurate to recognize the distinctions. What is more, there is nothing on the map to indicate that all of these ranges are part of the Rockies, so the test taker may count each one separately.)

9. B: On the map, the star symbol is underneath the city of Cheyenne, which is the capital. The other answer choices – Laramie, Jackson, and Sheridan – are not identified as the capital city.

10. A: Two national parks are identified on the map: Grand Teton National Park and Yellowstone National Park. There is also a national monument (Devils Tower National Monument), but since the question says nothing about national monuments and specifies national *parks*, answer choice B can be ruled out. Choices C and D are both too high.

11. B: Colorado and Utah lie along Wyoming's southern border. Idaho lies to the west; Nebraska and South Dakota lie to the east; Montana lies along the northern border.

12. D: If Beryl knew something instinctively, it is safe to say that her mother's warning was not stated outright. Therefore, answer choice D is the best option. Answer choice A makes little sense. Answer choice B makes sense only if Beryl suspects her mother does not care whether or not she smokes. Answer choice C has a meaning that is the opposite of the one implied in the sentence.

13. C: The passage is expository, because it *exposes* or reveals information about the topic. A narrative passage tells a story; this passage does not. A technical passage provides the reader with instructions or details about completing a certain activity; this passage does not. A persuasive passage attempts to convince the reader to agree with the author's viewpoint about a topic. There is nothing persuasive about this passage.

14. B: Answer choice B, the second-to-last sentence in the passage, best summarizes the main point of the passage: that although The Five might not have had solid formal training, they influenced Russian music, and that influence extended beyond their own era. Answer choice A is too specific, and focuses on those who were influenced rather than on the actual composers who made up The Five. Because it is the opening sentence of the passage, answer choice C is a good option. However, answer choice B gets more to the heart of the topic. Answer choice C leaves out the information about long-term influence, so it is not the best option for a summary sentence. Answer choice D focuses on only two of The Five, so it cannot be a summary statement for the entire passage.

15. C: The final two sentences of the passage suggest that answer C is the best choice: "Composers such as Alexander Glazunov, Sergei Prokofiev, and Igor Stravinsky studied under Rimsky-Korsakov. Additionally, the mid-twentieth century composer Dmitri Shostakovich studied under Glazunov, creating a legacy of musical understanding that persisted well beyond the era of The Five." While the author does not explicitly state that Rimsky-Korsakov was the most influential, he is the only composer who is specifically linked to later composers. These noted composers include Rimsky-Korsakov's own students (Glazunov, Prokofiev, and Stravinsky) and one of his student's students (Shostakovich). Based on this, it is reasonable to conclude that the author would agree that Rimsky-Korsakov was the most influential of "The Five." While the other individuals listed in the answer choices had a definite influence on music and composed notable works, none of them is specifically linked to later composers in the passage.

16. D: The symbol that divides the word *collar* in half indicates the syllables, which in this case are *col* and *lar*. The symbol cannot indicate emphasis, because the word is simply divided in half. The spelling of the word is clear by looking at it, so there is no need to split the word in half to indicate

Copyright © Mometrix Media. You have been licensed one copy of this document for personal use only. Any other reproduction or redistribution is strictly prohibited. All rights reserved.

spelling. And while origin is indicated later in the dictionary entry, there is nothing about the initial presentation of the word to suggest that the symbol in the middle indicates the word's origin.

17. A: The bold font indicates that the first part of the word is emphasized when the word is pronounced: **col**-lar instead of col-**lar**. A bold font is never a part of a word's spelling, so there is no need to bold any part of the word to indicate spelling. The bold font does nothing to indicate the word's origin. While the bold font does appear in one part of the word and not the other, this does not in itself indicate the syllables in the way the symbol between the two halves of the word does. For instance, the word could be written **col**lar, and this would still suggest emphasis rather than indicate the word's syllables.

18. D: The earliest word in the information about the word's origin is *collum*. All other origins appear to date back to this word. *Collum*, which led to a Latin word (*collare*), led to the Old French form *colier*, which eventually became the Middle English form *coler*. This later evolved into the Modern English word *collar*. The earliest language origin indicated is Latin.

19. C: Since the crime is fairly obvious, Ena is surprised that the child's lie is so *shameless*. Answer choice A is incorrect, because there is nothing *effective* about the child's lie. The child may be *arrogant* in assuming he will get away with lying, but this option is not as strong as answer choice C. There is nothing in the sentence to suggest that the child's lie is *hostile*, so answer choice D makes little sense.

20. D: The heading notes that the information is related to *monarchs* within the *Stuart* family. There are two significant problems with Oliver Cromwell being included in this list: (1) he is not a Stuart (since his last name is Cromwell), and (2) he is identified as a "lord protector" instead of someone who reigned in England. The test taker does not have to be familiar with English history to spot this anomaly. All of the other answer choices are reigning monarchs of the Stuart family.

21. B: The reign of Charles I ended in 1649. Between 1653 and 1658, Oliver Cromwell is noted as "lord protector," and then there is another break of two years before Charles II assumes the throne in 1660. Additionally, James II's reign ends in 1688, but Mary II does not assume the throne until 1689. For all of the other monarchs listed (except Charles II), the starting date of their reign coincides with the ending date of the previous monarch's reign, so this break – albeit brief – is still considered a break. (Historically, James II was forced to abdicate in late December of 1688 after what many believed to be the faked birth of a male heir, and his daughter, Mary, did not take over for a few weeks after this. She ruled alongside her husband, William III. This was truly a short break in the monarchy, but it was definitely a break. It represented a period during which England was without a recognized monarch.)

22. C: Throughout the passage, the author compares and contrasts the Arthurian writings of Malory and Tennyson, so the structure of the passage is clearly comparison-contrast. No problem is presented, so no solution must be posited. A passage written using a sequence structure would be focused on presenting information for the reader to follow in order (i.e. a "how-to" essay). The author essentially goes back and forth between Malory and Tennyson, so this passage does not employ a sequence structure. While there are some statements indicating cause and effect – Tennyson is said to have been influenced by Malory, for instance – the focus of the passage is more on comparing the two authors.

23. D: The following differences between Malory and Tennyson are noted in the passage: 1) Malory wrote in prose, while Tennyson wrote in poetry. 2) Malory wrote during the Medieval era, while Tennyson wrote during the Victorian era. 3) Malory was more focused on heroism and morality,

Copyright © Mometrix Media. You have been licensed one copy of this document for personal use only. Any other reproduction or redistribution is strictly prohibited. All rights reserved.

while Tennyson was more focused on nature and elegy. The author of the passage mentions that Malory wrote about Gareth, Tristan, and Isolde, but there is not enough information in the passage to argue that Tennyson did *not*.

24. D: The passage is primarily about Malory and Tennyson. The author includes useful information toward the end of the passage to indicate what Tennyson's contemporary influences might have been (that is, "social problems and the need for social justice" within his own era). The information about Charles Dickens, however, seems to come out of nowhere. It does not merit a place in the passage, since the author says nothing about a similar author in Malory's time, which would make the comparison complete. As a result, the information about Dickens is irrelevant. The other answer choices, however, contain useful information that develops the author's main point.

25. A: In the first paragraph, the author notes that Malory was a Medieval writer who "focused more on the moral elements within these stories." This statement would also be true of Medieval literature in general. In the second paragraph, the author says that it has been argued that Tennyson "was writing an allegory about social problems and the need for social justice that existed during Tennyson's own time." This writing would also reflect the interests and defining qualities of the author's era. Therefore, answer choice A is correct. The author of the passage compares and contrasts the two writers' works, but there is nothing in the passage to suggest that he or she is taking a stand on which writer's work is superior. As a result, answer choices B and C are incorrect. Answer choice D counters the information at the start of the second paragraph that says Tennyson was "heavily influenced" by Malory. Even though Tennyson might have put his own spin on the Arthurian legends, he was still clearly influenced by Malory.

26. B: Without seeing an ingredient list for each soup, the best the test taker can do is look at the names and determine whether or not any form of dairy is likely included in the soup. The cheese in the broccoli cheese soup, as well as the cream in both the tomato and potato soup are likely to be problematic for Regina, as they are all dairy products. No dairy products are listed in "lentil soup," so this may be assumed to be the safest choice. (In traditional Mediterranean and Middle Eastern preparation, lentil soup does not typically include dairy products.)

27. C: The final column in the chart indicates the percentage of each country's population that was lost. For Romania, this percentage is 9.33. The percentages for the other choices are half of this or less. Of the nations listed in the chart, Romania certainly fared the worst in terms of the percentage of the population that was lost, even if the actual numbers are lower than they are for other nations.

28. C: Looking only at the numbers, the casualties in Russia are staggeringly high: 2,254,369 military deaths, 4,950,000 military wounded, and 1,500,000 civilian deaths. The fact that these numbers represent only 2.14 percent of Russia's population speaks to how many people were in Russia at the time. (According to the chart, the total population was 175,100,000.) The casualty numbers for the United Kingdom are also high, but nowhere near as high as they are for Russia. The numbers for Belgium and Romania are also high. In Romania, these losses represent a large percentage of the population. Russia, however, suffered the highest number of casualties, which is the focus of the question.

29. C: In Romania, civilian deaths are listed at 450,000. This represents 6 percent of the total population of 7,500,000. The civilian deaths in Belgium represent less than 1 percent of the total population. This is also true for Russia, despite the higher actual number of deaths. In Italy, civilian deaths represent a little over 1.5 percent of the population, which is still far below the percentage for Romania.

- 300 -

Copyright © Mometrix Media. You have been licensed one copy of this document for personal use only. Any other reproduction or redistribution is strictly prohibited. All rights reserved.

30. D: The chart notes that civilian deaths are ones that are due to war, famine, and disease. Answer choice A is certainly related to war. However, the sinking of the RMS *Lusitania*, while tragic and certainly a cause of civilian deaths, would not have caused such a large number of casualties. Answer choices B and C reference events that seem exclusive to the battlefield: the trench warfare system and the mustard gas used on the battlefield. While civilians were certainly affected by these events, these answer choices seem to exclude civilian involvement. Both specifically mention battlefield activity. If an answer choice had mentioned the bombing or gassing of towns, however, this would have suggested civilian involvement. The Spanish Influenza epidemic is the most logical choice, in large part because it fits the "disease" category very well. The fact that the epidemic struck Europe at the end of the war (note the dates of the war that are included at the top of the chart) and affected what must have been an already weakened population makes this event a likely cause of a significant number of civilian deaths during World War I.

31. C: The announcement includes the following sentence: "To offset the crowding, the university has polled the various departments about schedules, and has settled on a recommended roster for when the members of each department should visit the faculty canteen for lunch." This suggests that the university made every effort to find out the schedules for each department and create a lunch arrangement that would give the members of each department the best opportunity possible to visit the canteen. The list is clearly not arranged alphabetically, so answer choice A is incorrect. The university definitely contacted the departments, as noted in the announcement. However, since the announcement mentions respecting the schedule and says nothing about an approval process, it is difficult to determine whether or not the university is worried about whether the faculty members will be amenable to the new lunch roster. Therefore, answer choice B can be eliminated. Finally, answer choice D seems to contradict the information in the announcement, so it too is incorrect. If the university contacted the departments about faculty schedules, the university obviously put some thought into the schedule. Answer choice D would suggest an arbitrary decision about scheduling, with no thought given to current faculty department schedules.

32. B: The final two sentences are as follows: "We ask that all faculty members respect this schedule. Faculty will be expected to display a department badge before entering the canteen for lunch." The overall recommendation is that faculty members should honor the schedule, with the added implication that faculty members will either not be allowed to enter the canteen outside of the posted lunch roster or that departments will be notified if the faculty members do make this effort. No doubt the announcement is also a recommendation to bring the badge, but there is an undercurrent of warning in it that goes beyond a "friendly reminder." Therefore, answer choice A is incorrect. There is nothing in the announcement or in the two final sentences to suggest that the university wants faculty members to eat lunch elsewhere, so answer choice C is incorrect. Answer choice D is a good option, but it infers just a little too much from the final two sentences. While university sanctions might very well be imposed on faculty members who don't follow the schedule, these two sentences alone are simply a word of caution to faculty members that the schedule needs to be respected. Answer choice D goes too far, so it too is incorrect.

33. C: Angela's reading list appears to consist of classic works of literature, as the opening statement notes that she "read the following classics." This means that "The Cask of Amontillado" by Edgar Allen Poe is unlikely to be a newspaper article, a book chapter by itself that is separate from the rest of the book, or a television show episode. Based on the information provided, it is most likely a short story.

34. A: The italics indicate full-length published books. The italics cannot represent works of classic literature. This is because according to the sentence, "The Cask of Amontillado" is also a classic. However, it is not italicized. Similarly, the italics cannot represent Angela's summer reading or the

Copyright © Mometrix Media. You have been licensed one copy of this document for personal use only. Any other reproduction or redistribution is strictly prohibited. All rights reserved.

books that she has completed, because the item in quotation marks is also on Angela's summer reading list. (Additionally, in the case of answer choice D, the sentence states that Angela "read" these works, so the sentence itself indicates they have all been completed.)

35. B: If the student's nerves are getting the better of him, it is likely that he is either very pale or very flushed. Because *flushed* is one of the options, it is the correct choice. A complexion cannot be *rambling*, so answer choice A is incorrect. Answer choice C has a hint of promise, but it makes the sentence more confusing, so it too is incorrect. It is difficult to know what is meant by the phrase "*weak* complexion," so answer choice D is too unclear to be correct.

36. D: Even if the test taker is unfamiliar with the meaning of *puerile*, the word *fantasies* should suggest something childish. The overall tone indicates an attitude of distaste toward the book. Consider the following wording in particular: "most likely to be enjoyed only by those with puerile fantasies." *Only* limits the audience, and *puerile fantasies* limits it even further. Answer choice A is incorrect, because the author makes no recommendations, and comments only on who might enjoy the book. Answer choice B is possible, but the tone would suggest that the *puerile fantasies* are not so much natural (as an appreciation for fantasy literature would be to children), but rather unique to a limited audience of adults. Answer choice C is incorrect, because the overall implication of the statement is that the book will appeal to a very limited audience. This leaves answer choice D, which is the best option: the author of the review believes the book would not appeal to mature adults.

37. A: Only Twin Theatres does not have a showing before 6 p.m. or after 10 p.m. The other cinemas have at least one showing before or after these times.

38. D: The only showing available after 10.30 p.m. is the 11.25 p.m. showing at Best Seat in The House. None of the other cinemas has a showing after 10.30 p.m.

39. B: Residents with addresses ending in 7 may water on Wednesdays, so the Morgan family should set up its watering schedule for this day of the week. The other days are for people with addresses that end in numbers other than 7.

40. C: The final sentence of the announcement notes the following: "Businesses with suite numbers should use the final number in the suite number to determine their watering schedule." No doubt this is due to the fact that businesses with suite numbers will have the same street address as a number of other businesses. Using the suite number will help spread out the watering schedule. In the case of the Everby Title Company, the suite address ends in 3, so the watering day is Thursday. Based on the information in the announcement, the other answer choices can be eliminated.

41. A: There is no explanation regarding the organization of the schedule, nor does the announcement say anything about why there is only one number assigned to Friday and Saturday. The announcement does say that the watering limitations reflect an "effort to conserve water," so the best inference is that the city has found that there are more addresses ending in these numbers (4 and 5), and has therefore adjusted the schedule accordingly. There is no way to determine from the announcement whether or not all businesses end in these numbers, or whether or not businesses consume more water, so answer choice B is incorrect. It is impossible to determine from the announcement if residents at these addresses consume more water, so answer choice C is incorrect. Similarly, there is nothing in the announcement to indicate that the city is more concerned about water usage in the latter part of the week – or why the part of the week would make a difference – so answer choice D is incorrect. The announcement only notes a goal of water

Copyright © Mometrix Media. You have been licensed one copy of this document for personal use only. Any other reproduction or redistribution is strictly prohibited. All rights reserved.

conservation, and that water usage will be allotted by address. Therefore, the most logical assumption is that there are more addresses ending in 4 and 5 than in the other numbers.

42. C: Sybilla is clearly trying to improve her financial situation, so the word *strengthen* makes the most sense. The word *add* captures the idea, but it does not fit into the sentence as a synonym for *aggrandize*. The word *develop* has promise, but it does not capture the meaning in the same way as *strengthen* does when used in place of *aggrandize*. The word *dispute* makes no sense in the context of the sentence.

43. C: Since both authors are explaining in the passages how the same story may come to be in different cultures, it is clear they both accept that there are often common elements in fairy tales from different cultures.

44. A: The author of Passage 2 claims that the essence and nature of fairy tales is their representation of basic human experience. It is this assertion that leads the author to believe that the same story could develop independently in different places.

45. D: The author does not mention the movement of food in the passage.

46. B: The author never mentions witches in the passage.

47. A: The passage suggests that spelunking is an outdoorsy, family adventure, then goes on to describe the adventure of going to a cave. If you do not already know that spelunking is another word for caving, you can infer this information based on reading the passage.

48. B: The article's style is not technical or scientific in the least. It is a simple and lighthearted article about something a family could do together. It is adventurous, but *Adventures for Men* is not a good choice since the fun is for the whole family. *Mud Magazine* might have been the next best choice, but *Family Fun Days* is clearly better. Your job is to choose the best choice of the options given.

Mathematics Answer Explanations

1. D: Nurse Andrew had to recommend patients for a study about high blood pressure and high cholesterol. According to the problem statement, $\frac{3}{5}$ of his patients fit this category. Therefore, convert $\frac{3}{5}$ to a percentage using these steps:

$$3 \div 5 = 0.60 \text{ and } (0.60)(100) = 60\%$$

2. A: Dr. Lee noticed that 5% of 30% of his patients were hospitalized. So multiply 30% by 5% using these steps:

Convert 30% and 5% into decimals by dividing both numbers by 100.

$$\frac{30}{100} = 0.30 \text{ and } \frac{5}{100} = 0.05$$

Now multiply 0.30 by 0.05 to get

$$(0.30)(0.05) = 0.015$$

- 303 -

Copyright © Mometrix Media. You have been licensed one copy of this document for personal use only. Any other reproduction or redistribution is strictly prohibited. All rights reserved.

Now convert 0.015 to a percentage by multiplying by 100.

$$(0.015)(100) = 1.5\%$$

3. D: The patient's dosage must increase by 30%. So calculate 30% of 270:

$$(0.30)(270 \text{ mg}) = 81 \text{ mg}$$

Now add the 30% increase to the original dosage.

$$270 \text{ mg} + 81 \text{ mg} = 351 \text{ mg}$$

4. C: Since 60% of the patients in the study were women, 40% of the patients were men. Calculate the number of male patients by multiplying 500 by 0.40.

$$(500)(0.40) = 200$$

Of the 200 male patients in the study, 20% experienced some trauma as a child. So 80% did not experience a childhood trauma. Multiply 200 by 0.80 to get the final answer.

$$(200)(0.80) = 160$$

5. C: If the incoming class has 200 students, then $\frac{1}{2}$ of those students were required to take the exam.

$$(200)\left(\frac{1}{2}\right) = 100$$

So 100 students took the exam but only $\frac{3}{5}$ of that 100 passed the exam.

$$(100)\left(\frac{3}{5}\right) = 60$$

Therefore 60 students passed the exam.

6. B: The first roommate receives $1000 per month, and he uses $\frac{1}{4}$ of that amount for rent and utilities.

$$(\$1000)\left(\frac{1}{4}\right) = \$250$$

So the student pays $250 for rent and utilities, which leaves him with

$$\$1000 - \$250 = \$750$$

The student divides the remaining $750 in half.

$$\frac{\$750}{2} = \$375$$

The student saves $375 and lives off the remaining $375.

Copyright © Mometrix Media. You have been licensed one copy of this document for personal use only. Any other reproduction or redistribution is strictly prohibited. All rights reserved.

7. B: The second roommate budgets $\frac{1}{5}$ of his check for dining out plus another $\frac{1}{4}$ of his check for social activities. So add $\frac{1}{5}$ and $\frac{1}{4}$ by first finding a common denominator.

$$\frac{1}{5} = \frac{4}{20} \text{ and } \frac{1}{4} = \frac{5}{20}$$

$$\frac{4}{20} + \frac{5}{20} = \frac{9}{20}$$

8. D: First add all expenses for the third roommate. Then subtract his total expenses from $1000.

$$\$250 + \$100 + \$25 = \$375$$

$$\$1000 - \$375 = \$625$$

9. A: The ratio of his savings to his rent is 1:3, which means that for every $3 he pays in rent, he saves $1 for the purchase of a house. So to calculate the amount the fourth roommate saves for the purchase of a house, divide $270 by 3.

$$\frac{\$270}{3} = \$90$$

10. C: Each roommate donated about $12 towards the gift purchase.

$$\$12 + \$12 + \$12 = \$36$$

11. A: To obtain the length of the new routine, subtract 7 minutes from the length of the original routine, which was 45 minutes.

$$45 \text{ minutes} - 7 \text{ minutes} = 38 \text{ minutes}$$

12. C: Find $\frac{1}{6}$ of 500 by multiplying

$$(500)\left(\frac{1}{6}\right) = \frac{500}{6} = 83.3333$$

$\frac{500}{6}$ is an improper fraction. Convert the fraction to a decimal and round to the nearest hundredth to get 83.33.

13. D: The Roman numeral system requires adding or subtracting the individual digits in order to obtain the full number. The L equals 50 and X equals 10. So LX means add 50 + 10 to get 60. The I equals 1 and V equals 5. However, since the I is placed directly before the V, subtract 5 – 1 to get 4. Finally, add 60 + 4 to get 64.

14. C: Veronica receives $70,000. First she contributes 15% of her salary to a retirement account.

$$(\$70,000)(0.15) = 10,500$$

$$\$70,000 - \$10,500 = \$59,500$$

Copyright © Mometrix Media. You have been licensed one copy of this document for personal use only. Any other reproduction or redistribution is strictly prohibited. All rights reserved.

After contributing to her retirement account, Veronica has $59,500 left. Then she pays 30% in taxes.

$$(\$59{,}500)(0.30) = \$17{,}850$$

$$\$59{,}500 - \$17{,}850 = \$41{,}650$$

After paying taxes, Veronica has $41,650 left. Finally, she pays $70 each month for health insurance. Calculate the annual amount Veronica pays for health insurance, and subtract this amount from her remaining salary.

$$(\$70)(12) = \$840$$

$$\$41{,}750 - \$840 = \$40{,}810$$

15. B: To determine the total cost of Veronica's new car, add all her expenditures.

$$\$40{,}210 + \$3{,}015 + \$5{,}218 = \$48{,}443$$

16. A: The beginning balance for the account was $503.81. Then one deposit was made. So add the amount of that deposit to the beginning balance.

$$\$503.81 + 125.00 = \$628.81$$

Next, an ATM was used to withdraw money from the account. So subtract the amount of the withdrawal from the new balance.

$$\$628.81 - \$215.00 = \$413.81$$

Finally, add the monthly interest earned to obtain the ending balance.

$$\$413.81 + \$5.38 = 419.19$$

17. D: Apply the order of operations to solve this problem. Multiplication and division are computed first from left to right. Then addition and subtraction are computed next from left to right.

$$2 + (2)(4) - 4 \div 2 =$$
$$2 + 8 - 4 \div 2 =$$
$$2 + 8 - 2 =$$
$$10 - 2 =$$
$$8 =$$

18. A: The hospital staff will order 1 pizza for each group of 4 people, and 160 people will attend the event.

$$160 \div 4 = 40$$

Therefore, the staff will order 40 pizzas. Each pizza costs $9.50. Calculate the total cost for pizzas.

$$(40)(\$9.50) = \$380$$

Copyright © Mometrix Media. You have been licensed one copy of this document for personal use only. Any other reproduction or redistribution is strictly prohibited. All rights reserved.

19. D: Compare and order the rational numbers by finding a common denominator for all three fractions. The least common denominator for 3, 12, and 4 is 12. Now convert the fractions with different denominators into fractions with the same denominator.

$$\frac{1}{3} = \frac{4}{12}$$

$$\frac{5}{12} = \frac{5}{12}$$

$$\frac{1}{4} = \frac{3}{12}$$

Now that all three fractions have the same denominator, order them from largest to smallest by comparing the numerators.

$$\frac{5}{12} > \frac{4}{12} > \frac{3}{12}$$

Since $\frac{5}{12}$ of the doctors are in Group Y, this group has the largest number of doctors. The next largest group has $\frac{4}{12}$ of the doctors, which is Group X. The smallest group has $\frac{3}{12}$ of the doctors, which is Group Z.

20. B: Solve the equation for y.

$$\frac{2y}{10} + 5 = 25$$

$$\frac{2y}{10} = 25 - 5$$

$$\frac{2y}{10} = 20$$

$$2y = (20)(10)$$

$$2y = 200$$

$$y = \frac{200}{2}$$

$$y = 100$$

21. C: Subtract the polynomials by subtracting all the like terms, which have the same variable.

$$8x - 5x = 3x$$

$$7y - 4y = 3y$$

$$6z - 3z = 3z$$

Since 3x, 3y, and 3z are all different terms, the final answer is

$$3x + 3y + 3z$$

- 307 -

Copyright © Mometrix Media. You have been licensed one copy of this document for personal use only. Any other reproduction or redistribution is strictly prohibited. All rights reserved.

22. B: During January, Dr. Lewis worked 20 shifts.

$$\text{shifts for January} = 20$$

During February, she worked three times as many shifts as she did during January.

$$\text{shifts for February} = (20)(3)$$

During March, she worked half the number of shifts she worked in February.

$$\text{shifts for March} = (20)(3)\left(\frac{1}{2}\right)$$

23. D: Use the order of operations to solve this problem. Also remember that the absolute value of a number is always positive.

$$|2 - 10| + (2)(10) - 5 =$$

$$|-8| + (2)(10) - 5 =$$

$$8 + 20 - 5 =$$

$$28 - 5 =$$

$$23$$

24. A: Using the table to list the nurse specialties from largest to smallest gives this order: pediatrics, geriatrics, anesthesia, and midwifery. Therefore, pediatrics should represent the largest slice of the circle graph and midwifery should represent the smallest. Only the graph in choice A fits these criteria.

25. B: The bar for midwifery is shortest of the four. Therefore, midwifery is the specialty with the least number of nurses.

26. C: The variables are the objects the graph measures. In this case, the graph measures the nurse specialties and the number of nurses for each specialty. The dependent variable changes with the independent variable. Here, the number of nurses depends on the particular nurse specialty. Therefore, the independent variable is nurse specialties.

27. C: The prefix, centi-, means 100th. In this case,

$$1 \text{ m} = 100 \text{ cm}$$

Therefore,

$$(7)(1 \text{ m}) = (7)(100 \text{ cm})$$

$$7 \text{ m} = (7)(100 \text{ cm})$$

$$7 \text{ m} = 700 \text{ cm}$$

28. B: A human eyelash is about one centimeter long. Nanometers are much too short to describe an eyelash. Meters and kilometers are much too long.

Copyright © Mometrix Media. You have been licensed one copy of this document for personal use only. Any other reproduction or redistribution is strictly prohibited. All rights reserved.

29. C: A hexagonal field has 6 sides. Each side is 320 feet long, so multiply 320 by 6 to get the perimeter of the field: 320 × 6 = 1920 feet. At $1.75 per foot, the perimeter fence will cost 1920 × 1.75 = $3360.

30. C: The entire length of the figure is 16 cm and the figure has 4 segments. Therefore, each segment is 4 cm long.

$$16 \text{ cm} \div 4 = 4 \text{ cm}$$

Two segments are between segments 1 and 3. Therefore,

$$(2)(4 \text{ cm}) = 8 \text{ cm}$$

31. C: To find each percentage, divide the first number by the second number, then multiply by 100. So the percentage in answer A is $\left(\frac{50}{250}\right) \times 100 = 20$, the percentage in answer B is $\left(\frac{57}{250}\right) \times 100 = 22.8$, the percentage in answer C is $\left[\frac{(74+55)}{433}\right] \times 100 = \left(\frac{129}{433}\right) \times 100 = 29.8$, the percentage in answer D is $\left(\frac{21}{183}\right) \times 100 = 11.5$, and the percentage in answer E is $\left(\frac{5}{183}\right) \times 100 = 2.7$.

32. B: There are 37 Caucasian staff members in City Y. If we subtract this from the number of employees with 5-10 years of service in City Y (41), we see that 4 of those staff members must be non-Caucasian.

33 B: The percentage of female staff members in City Y is $\left(\frac{90}{183}\right) \times 100 = 49.2$. In City X, it is $\left(\frac{97}{250}\right) \times 100 = 38.8$. Subtracting, we see that the difference between these percentages is approximately 10.

34. B: The percentage of staff members with zero complaints in City X is $\left(\frac{202}{250}\right) \times 100 = 80.8$. In City Y, the percentage is $\left(\frac{161}{183}\right) \times 100 = 88.0$.

Science Answer Explanations

1. A: The circulatory system circulates materials throughout the entire body. The heart, blood, and blood vessels are part of the circulatory system. The kidneys, however, are part of the urinary system.

2. D: The digestive system helps the body process food and the stomach is the only item in the list that helps the body with digestive functions. The spine is part of the skeletal system, the brain is part of the nervous system, and the lungs are part of the respiratory system.

3. B: The nervous system is the center of communication for the body. The respiratory system helps the body breathe. The digestive system helps break down food, and the circulatory system carries vital materials to all the areas of the body.

4. C: The respiratory system uses the lungs, diaphragm, trachea, and bronchi to help the body breathe. The circulatory system carries blood. Food is broken down by the digestive system, and the central nervous system sends messages throughout the body.

5. D: The immune system helps the body avoid, detect, and eliminate infections. A healthy immune system should not, however, create infections.

Copyright © Mometrix Media. You have been licensed one copy of this document for personal use only. Any other reproduction or redistribution is strictly prohibited. All rights reserved.

6. B: The human body has 5 types of bone. The spine and hips are irregular bones because they do not fit the other major bone types, which are long, short, flat, and sesamoid. Choice A, curvy bones, does not describe one of the major bone types.

7. C: Most bones in the limbs are long bones, including the thighs, forearms, and fingers. The ankles, however, are not long bones because they do not have a shaft that is longer than it is wide.

8. A: Education does not directly influence the population of the United States since education does not determine how many people live in the country. Immigration, births, and deaths directly affect the number of people in the United States at any point in time.

9. D: Birth rates within a given population are influenced by the age, health, and fertility of the women within that population. In order for the population to have high birth rates, many women must be healthy, fertile, and of child bearing age.

10. D: If scientists find a cure for cancer, those who would have died from the disease would live longer. Therefore the population would most likely increase. All the other choices would most likely cause the population to decrease or would have no direct effect.

11. B: Each time 1 person dies, 2 babies are born to take that person's place. Therefore, the population is increasing. In order for the population to decrease, more people would have to die than be born. The population is changing and therefore has not reached a steady state.

12. D: The process of natural selection describes how animals survive by adapting to their environment. The animals that survive produce offspring who have the same advantageous traits and survival skills. Conversely, animals that lack such traits and skills do not live to produce offspring that may also lack them. In this case, the first two scenarios present fast zebras and polar bears with thick coats. In both cases, these animals possess traits that allow them to survive and reproduce. The third choice demonstrates how natural selection eliminates animals that lack the advantageous trait of sight.

13. B: The choices list four categories of the biological classification system. Within these four choices, the kingdom is the broadest category and the phylum is a bit more specific. The genus narrows down the classification even further, and the species is the narrowest of all the major categories.

14. A: The nucleus is the control center for the cell. The cell membrane surrounds the cell and separates the cell from its environment. Cytoplasm is the thick fluid within the cell membrane that surrounds the nucleus and contains organelles. Mitochondria are often called the power house of the cell because they provide energy for the cell to function.

15. A: Cilia and flagella are responsible for cell movement. Ribosomes are organelles that help synthesize proteins within the cell. The cell membrane helps the cell maintain its shape and protects it from the environment. Lysosomes have digestive enzymes.

16. C: Cellular differentiation is the process by which simple, less specialized cells become highly specialized, complex cells. For example, humans are multicellular organisms who undergo cell differentiation numerous times. Cells begin as simple zygotes after fertilization and then differentiate to form a myriad of complex tissues and systems before birth.

17. D: Meiosis produces cells that are genetically different, having half the number of chromosomes of the parent cells. Mitosis produces cells that are genetically identical; daughter cells have the

Copyright © Mometrix Media. You have been licensed one copy of this document for personal use only. Any other reproduction or redistribution is strictly prohibited. All rights reserved.

exact same number of chromosomes as parent cells. Mitosis is useful for repairing the body while meiosis is useful for sexual reproduction.

18. B: Photosynthesis describes the process plants use to generate food from sunlight, carbon dioxide, and water. Oxygen is given off as a byproduct of photosynthesis. Animals and plants use respiration to take oxygen into the body, and carbon dioxide is a waste product of respiration.

19. C: The structure of RNA is a single helix containing 4 nucleotides. DNA, on the other hand, is a double helix containing 4 nucleotides.

20. A: The germ cell is an embryonic cell that can develop into a gamete. Therefore, only mutations in the germ cells or the gametes themselves can change an organism's offspring.

21. D: After cell division, the daughter cells should be exact copies of the parent cells. Therefore, the DNA should replicate, or make an exact copy of itself. RNA primes DNA replication.

22. A: Genes store hereditary information and thus allow hereditary traits to be passed from parents to offspring. Genes do not prohibit hereditary transmission, and genes are not known to enable any type of environmental factors.

23. C: A chromosome is a single piece of DNA that contains many genes. Genes do not, therefore, contain many chromosomes. Furthermore, the DNA double helix contains four nucleotides, not four genes.

24. B: The phenotype describes a person's observable characteristics. The genotype describes a person's genetic makeup. Environmental factors and various phenomena are not part of the phenotype.

25. D: The complete Punnett square is shown below.

	T	S
R	TR	SR
B	TB	SB

Possibility 1 corresponds to a person with the *TR* gene combination, which means the person is tall with red hair.

26. D: Refer to the complete Punnett square in the explanation for question 25. Possibility 4 corresponds to the *SB* pair of genes, which is short with black hair.

27. C: The sun is a major external source of both light and heat for Earth. Also, the sun's energy can be used for solar power. The moon only reflects the light of the sun and is not a major light source for Earth.

28. B: Oxidation refers to losing electrons, and reduction refers to gaining electrons. The two reactions always occur in pairs. In this case, the best example of a redox reaction is copper losing 2 electrons and silver gaining 2 electrons.

29. A: A catalyst increases the rate of a chemical reaction without becoming part of the reaction. Therefore, the chemist should add a catalyst. Adding an acid, base, or neutralizer may not affect the reaction rate.

Copyright © Mometrix Media. You have been licensed one copy of this document for personal use only. Any other reproduction or redistribution is strictly prohibited. All rights reserved.

30. D: Enzymes are protein molecules that serve as catalysts for certain biological reactions. Enzymes are not acids or lipids. Enzymes are definitely relevant for living organisms and do not suppress reactions.

31. C: The substance is an acid because the pH is less than 7. Pure water has a pH near 7, and bases have a pH above 7. Carcinogens cause cancer, which cannot be gauged by a pH test.

32. D: A covalent bond is one in which atoms share valence electrons. Within a water molecule, one oxygen atom and two hydrogen atoms share valence electrons to yield the H_2O structure.

33. B: A water molecule contains 2 hydrogen atoms and 1 oxygen atom. Therefore the chemical formula for water is H_2O. Also, the pH of water is 7.

34. A: Potential energy is energy that is stored due to an object's position. In this case, the golf club has the most potential energy when it is highest off the ground at step 1. The potential energy is released and becomes kinetic energy in step 2. Then energy is transferred from the club to the ball in step 3.

35. C: The atomic mass of an atom is approximately equal to the number of protons plus the number of neutrons. The weight of the electrons has little effect on the overall atomic mass.

36. B: The three major components of an atom are protons, neutrons, and electrons. Protons and neutrons have positive and neutral charges while electrons are negatively charged. Protons and neutrons reside in the atomic nucleus and make up the vast majority of the atomic weight. Electrons orbit the atomic nucleus and their mass is negligible.

37. D: Ionic bonds are formed when electrons are transferred between atoms. For instance, the sodium and chlorine atoms in salt have ionic bonds because electrons are transferred from sodium to chlorine.

38. C: The atomic weight tells the mass of the element. In the table, B is the lightest element, weighing 11 atomic mass units, and O is the heaviest element, weighing 16 atomic mass units.

39. A: Both gases and liquids are free flowing with no defined shape. Therefore, both gases and liquids take on the shape of their container.

40. A: Condensation is the process of changing from a gas to a liquid. For instance, gaseous water molecules in the air condense to form liquid rain drops. Vaporization describes changing from liquid to gas. Melting is the process of changing from solid to liquid and sublimation describes changing from solid to gas.

41. D: The researcher wants to correlate smoking with premature aging. Therefore, she needs to know if the survey participants smoke. If the participant does not smoke, the data may not be relevant to the research study.

42. B: Establishing a secure Internet site could help match adopted children with the biological families and still protect everyone's privacy. The other methods are impractical and would not provide privacy protection.

43. B: The evidence says that every child in a certain family suffers from autism. All of these children have genetic commonalities. Therefore, autism may be genetic. The evidence does not mention whether the children died from autism. Therefore, no conclusion can be drawn that

Copyright © Mometrix Media. You have been licensed one copy of this document for personal use only. Any other reproduction or redistribution is strictly prohibited. All rights reserved.

autism may be lethal. Furthermore, the sample size of the evidence is much too small to suggest that autism is related to traditional nuclear family structures.

44. D: Decreased mortality during childbirth could be explained by any or all of the statements presented. Safer cesarean sections, health monitoring tools, and hand washing could all improve a woman's chances of surviving childbirth.

45. A: A scientific argument should discuss outcomes that are objective and measureable, such as blood pressure, energy level, and overall health. The other choices present arguments that are subjective and based on emotions instead of facts.

46. C: Conducting this investigation may reveal a group of people who need higher quality medical care. Asking wealthy people for money does not help the researcher learn more about their quality of medical care. Although helping healthy people to stay healthy is important, helping those with poor medical care is more critical.

47. B: Mathematics is inherently objective. Therefore, mathematics allows researchers to take an objective approach to analyzing their data. Scientific research does not typically include data analysis that is emotional, unrealistic, or artistic.

48. B: Fabricating research results is not a reason to include technology. Accessing large amounts of data, analyzing data, and conducting a variety of experiments are all ways that technology can benefit scientific research.

49. A: A limiting reactant is entirely used up by the chemical reaction. Limiting reactants control the extent of the reaction and determine the quantity of the product. A reducing agent is a substance that reduces the amount of another substance by losing electrons. A reagent is any substance used in a chemical reaction. Some of the most common reagents in the laboratory are sodium hydroxide and hydrochloric acid. The behavior and properties of these substances are known, so they can be effectively used to produce predictable reactions in an experiment.

50. B: The horizontal rows of the periodic table are called periods. The vertical columns of the periodic table are known as groups or families. All of the elements in a group have similar properties. The relationships between the elements in each period are similar as you move from left to right. The periodic table was developed by Dmitri Mendeleev to organize the known elements according to their similarities. New elements can be added to the periodic table without necessitating a redesign.

51. C: The mass of 7.35 mol water is 132 grams. You should be able to find the mass of various chemical compounds when you are given the number of mols. The information required to perform this function is included on the periodic table. To solve this problem, find the molecular mass of water by finding the respective weights of hydrogen and oxygen. Remember that water contains two hydrogen molecules and one oxygen molecule. The molecular mass of hydrogen is roughly 1, and the molecular mass of oxygen is roughly 16. A molecule of water, then, has approximately 18 grams of mass. Multiply this by 7.35 mol, and you will obtain the answer 132.3, which is closest to answer choice c.

52. B: 119°K is equivalent to –154 degrees Celsius. It is likely that you will have to perform at least one temperature conversion on the exam. To convert degrees Kelvin to degrees Celsius, simply subtract 273. To convert degrees Celsius to degrees Kelvin, simply add 273. To convert degrees Kelvin into degrees Fahrenheit, multiply by $\frac{9}{5}$ and subtract 460. To convert degrees Fahrenheit to

Copyright © Mometrix Media. You have been licensed one copy of this document for personal use only. Any other reproduction or redistribution is strictly prohibited. All rights reserved.

degrees Kelvin, add 460 and then multiply by $\frac{5}{9}$. To convert degrees Celsius to degrees Fahrenheit, multiply by $\frac{9}{5}$ and then add 32. To convert degrees Fahrenheit to degrees Celsius, subtract 32 and then multiply by $\frac{5}{9}$.

53. A: There are four different types of tissue in the human body: epithelial, connective, muscle, and nerve. *Epithelial* tissue lines the internal and external surfaces of the body. It is like a sheet, consisting of squamous, cuboidal, and columnar cells. They can expand and contract, like on the inner lining of the bladder. *Connective* tissue provides the structure of the body, as well as the links between various body parts. Tendons, ligaments, cartilage, and bone are all examples of connective tissue. *Muscle* tissue is composed of tiny fibers, which contract to move the skeleton. There are three types of muscle tissue: smooth, cardiac, and skeletal. *Nerve* tissue makes up the nervous system; it is composed of nerve cells, nerve fibers, neuroglia, and dendrites.

54. B: The epidermis is the outermost layer of skin. The thickness of this layer of skin varies over different parts of the body. For instance, the epidermis on the eyelids is very thin, while the epidermis over the soles of the feet is much thicker. The dermis lies directly beneath the epidermis. It is composed of collagen, elastic tissue, and reticular fibers. Beneath the dermis lies the subcutaneous tissue, which consists of fat, blood vessels, and nerves. The subcutaneous tissue contributes to the regulation of body temperature. The hypodermis is the layer of cells underneath the dermis; it is generally considered to be a part of the subcutaneous tissue.

English and Language Usage Answer Explanations

1. B: Ellipses are frequently used in quotations to indicate that material has been excluded. This is certainly the case in the quoted passage in question 1. A brief section from the Declaration of Independence has been removed from the quote, and this exclusion is indicated by the ellipses. Ellipses do not indicate emphasis; they indicate that something is not included. Quotation marks indicate quoted material. Ellipses, while often used in quoted material, are not exclusive to, nor do they indicate, quoted material. Ellipses may be used regardless of the point of view, so they do not indicate a single point of view or more than one point of view.

2. C: The soldier would have received a *medal* for his display of courage, strength, and *mettle*, which is a slightly archaic (but still relevant) word that suggests bravery in the face of danger. The other answer choices contain one or more incorrect words.

3. C: The word *each* is singular, and this quality is emphasized by the singular *student*. As a result, the accompanying pronoun should be the singular *his or her*. If spoken, this sentence might contain the plural *their*, which would be more common for speech patterns. But, this is certainly not correct, and should not be used in writing. The singular *his* by itself is considered inappropriate and exclusive, and would only be correct if the context of the sentence indicated a class full of male students (which it does not). The word *one's* reads awkwardly in the sentence, and does more to confuse its meaning than to add to it.

4. D: The context suggests that Thomas Macaulay thought that people seldom apply wise sayings to avoid foolishness. The plural word in the sentence suggests the need for a plural synonym, so *advice* does not work. The word *preferences* does not make much sense in the sentence. While the statement itself is a quote – and wise sayings are usually quoted – the word *quotes* is not a synonym for *apothegms*, and is therefore not the best choice.

Copyright © Mometrix Media. You have been licensed one copy of this document for personal use only. Any other reproduction or redistribution is strictly prohibited. All rights reserved.

5. A: The word *piqued* is the correct choice, and is used to describe a heightened interest in something. The word *peaked* would be appropriate to describe height or the highest reach (e.g., *his blood pressure* peaked, *and then came back down*). The word *peke* is frequently used to describe a Pekingese breed of dog; therefore, *peked* does not make sense in the context of this sentence. The word *peeked* would suggest someone looking around the corner to see something.

6. A: Answer choice A includes all of the correct elements of punctuation needed to make this sentence clear and readable. In particular, there is a colon after the phrase "the following items for his class"; this indicates that a series of items will be listed. As these items do not contain internal commas, they may be separated by commas, so the rest of the punctuation in answer choice A is correct. Answer choice B uses a comma instead of a colon in front of the introductory phrase, making the series of items difficult to distinguish. Answer choice C uses semicolons instead of commas between the items in the series. The semicolons are not necessary, and make the sentence more confusing to read instead of clearer. Answer choice D uses a dash, which is not a correct way to introduce a series of items.

7. C: Answer choice C combines all of the information in the passage into a single coherent sentence. Answer choice A inexplicably states that the French and Indian War did not occur in North America, but the passage does not indicate this. Instead, the passage notes that the French and Indian War was not an isolated conflict, that it *did* occur in North America, and that it was also part of the larger Seven Years' War Europe was fighting. Answer choice B contains correct information, but is choppy rather than fluid and coherent. Answer choice B is more than one sentence, and it lacks the style and clarity of answer choice C. Answer choice D contains correct information, but it fails to explain – as stated in the original passage – that the French and Indian War was actually part of the larger Seven Years' War. Answer choice D implies that the French and Indian War was unrelated to the Seven Years' War, which contradicts the passage.

8. A: Of the answer choices, the only word that functions as a verb is *fought*. The word *control* is a noun in this sentence. The word *trade* functions either as an adjective to modify *routes*, or as a part of the single noun phrase *trade routes*. The word *those* functions as an adjective.

9. A: Only answer choice A is a simple sentence. It contains an opening phrase, but as this is a phrase instead of a dependent clause, the sentence is simple. Answer choices B and D contain a dependent clause, which makes these sentences complex. Answer choice C contains two independent clauses, which make the sentence compound.

10. C: In answer choice C, the word *empress* does not need to be capitalized, because it is not being used as a title. Instead, it is simply a description of Maria Theresa's role as empress over Austria. Answer choice A incorrectly capitalizes the word *family* twice. Answer choice B fails to capitalize the word *empire* in *Holy Roman Empire*. Answer choice D incorrectly capitalizes *province*, which is not being used as a proper noun in the sentence.

11. C: Answer choice C correctly uses double quotation marks and places the period within the quotation marks. Answer choice A uses single quotation marks. Answer choice B uses single quotation marks, and incorrectly places the period outside the quotation marks. Answer choice D correctly uses double quotation marks, but incorrectly places the period outside of them.

12. D: As the herd is apparently moving in unison across the highway, the collective noun *herd* is singular, and thus takes a singular verb. (If, however, the moose were stampeding at random, each moose in a different direction, the collective noun *herd* would be considered plural.) In answer choice A, the pronoun *some* can be either singular or plural, depending on the prepositional phrase

Copyright © Mometrix Media. You have been licensed one copy of this document for personal use only. Any other reproduction or redistribution is strictly prohibited. All rights reserved.

that follows it. Because the phrase contains the singular *fervor*, the sentence needs a singular verb. (On the other hand, the phrase *some of the people* would require a plural verb, because of the plural *people*.) In answer choice B, *Gary* is the primary subject, and requires a singular verb, regardless of the phrase *as well as his three children* that sits between Gary and the verb. In answer choice C, the opening verb in this interrogative sentence is determined by whether the noun following the pronoun *neither* is singular or plural. In this case, the singular *Robert* requires that the opening verb be *is*. Note that if the order were reversed, the sentence would be correct with *are: Are neither his parents nor Robert planning to see the presentation*? This is fairly awkward, though, so the other form would be more common.

13. B: The word *earlier* is an adverb that modifies the verb *tried* and answers the adverb question *when*? The word *call* is part of the infinitive (i.e. noun) phrase *to call*. The word *could* is a helping verb that accompanies the verb *get*. The word *phone* functions as a noun in this sentence.

14. D: In question 14, the parenthetical statement includes information that is useful – in this case the years of Franz Joseph I's reign – but does not fit into the flow of the sentence. The writer has chosen to include the years of Franz Joseph I's reign in parentheses, instead of using a dependent clause along the lines of "...the reign of Franz Joseph I, who ruled from 1848 to 1916." The parentheses provide information that the reader would likely want to know without interrupting the flow of the sentence. There is nothing about the parenthetical remark to indicate that the numbers refer to the pages of a book; instead, the numbers make much more sense as dates. The information in answer choice B is essentially implied; if the empire collapsed after his reign, it is safe to say that 1916 marks the date of its collapse. But, this is not really the purpose of the parentheses. The purpose is to offset useful information without interrupting the flow of the sentence. It is likely that all of the information in the sentence came from one source, so the parentheses do not indicate outside material in this case.

15. A: In answer choice A, the subjective case pronoun *who* (rather than *whom*) correctly follows *person*. Additionally, the singular subject *person* is accompanied by the singular verb *needs*. In answer choice B, *nobody* is singular, and needs the singular *his or her* to follow it instead of *their*. In answer choice C, the use of *one's* is incorrect; it should be *his, hers,* or *his or her*. In answer choice D, however, the use of *his or her* is not correct because of the structure of the sentence. The mention of the plural *Simeon and Ruth* makes the plural *their* correct.

16. C: Answer choice C correctly identifies that *I* is the first person and *you* is the second person. The order is also correct. The other answer choices either include an incorrect point of view or place the points of view in incorrect order.

17. B: The word *definitely* is often spelled incorrectly. (It does not help that the Spell Check option of word processing programs often overwrites any misspellings with *defiantly*.) Only answer choice B demonstrates the correct spelling. The other answer choices are either spelled incorrectly or, in the case of *defiantly*, simply indicate the wrong word.

18. A: In the sentence provided, the word *walking* is a gerund (which functions as a noun) and the subject. In this sentence, the word *walking* is not being used as an adverb, an adjective, or a conjunction. Its use as an adverb in any context would be fairly unlikely; its use as a conjunction would be virtually impossible.

19. D: The use of *malediction* in the sentence, combined with the obvious wrath of the fairy who was not invited to the princess's christening, would suggest that what the fairy utters is a *curse*. No doubt some *enchantment* is involved, but this particular word does not capture the sense of

Copyright © Mometrix Media. You have been licensed one copy of this document for personal use only. Any other reproduction or redistribution is strictly prohibited. All rights reserved.

impending evil that is implied. A *remedy* will be needed to counter the effects of the curse, but this is clearly not the meaning of *malediction*. It is logical that the *malediction* is also a promise of evil to come, but the word *promise* fails to capture the negativity that is implied.

20. C: Only answer choice C arranges the sentences in such a way as to maintain the original meaning of the passage, while also illustrating style and clarity. Answer choice A contains some of the information from the passage, but leaves most of it untouched. Answer choice B contains good information, but it also tweaks the original passage to suggest ideas that are not necessarily there. The original claims that Perrault's version is *one of the most familiar*. Answer choice B claims that it is *the* most familiar. The final sentence in answer choice B adds in details about the Brothers Grimm having provided their own version of the story. But, the original passage indicates that the fairy tale we know today contains elements from Perrault as well as the Brothers Grimm. Answer choice B fails to indicate this clearly. Answer choice D reverses the order of the information in the passage, but to little effect. If anything, answer choice D appears to be more about Perrault and the Brothers Grimm than about the origins of *Sleeping Beauty*. As this is not the main topic of the passage, choice D is not an effective revision.

21. D: Answer choice D correctly uses an apostrophe to indicate the possessive element within the sentence. Answer choice A incorrectly changes the plural word *fairies* into the possessive word *fairy's*. Similarly, answer choice B makes the plural *historians* possessive, and answer choice C makes the plural *seasons* possessive by changing it to the singular possessive *season's*. None of these words is possessive in the context of their respective sentences, so only answer choice D is correct.

22. C: The word *you* is always second person, and it is either singular or plural depending on its context. In the sentence provided, the teacher is speaking to a class, and the class is likely to be made up of more than one person. Therefore, the *you* in the sentence is second-person plural. The other answer choices identify the wrong point of view, and answer choices A and D incorrectly identify the word as singular.

23. D: Answer choice D contains two independent clauses, so it is a compound sentence, not a simple sentence. All of the other answer choices are simple sentences.

24. A: Someone who is committed to personal grooming is likely to be *fussy*, and this is the meaning of the word *fastidious*. The word *lazy* makes little sense in the context of the sentence. No doubt some of Poirot's activities are both *old-fashioned* and *hilarious*, but neither of these words fit the context of the sentence, and thus cannot be synonyms for *fastidious*.

25. B: The sentence indicates that the connections Miss Marple makes are *seemingly extraneous*. However, the sentence also states that she uses this information to solve mysteries. This would suggest that the word *extraneous* means *irrelevant*. Answer choice A indicates the very opposite of what the sentence implies. Answer choice C makes little sense in the context of the sentence. Answer choice D would work but for the adverb *seemingly*; this indicates that the connections appear to be irrelevant, but are actually not. With *seemingly* in the sentence, the meaning completely changes if *useful* is added in place of *extraneous*.

26. D: This is another word that is frequently misspelled. *Rhythm* is the correct spelling. All of the other answer choices add an unnecessary *y* and add or leave out an *h*.

27. B: For the sentence to read correctly, it must be clear that someone is leaping into the saddle when the horse bolts. In its original form, the only party identified in the sentence is the horse, and a horse cannot leap into a saddle. Answer choice B includes the mention of a second party (an unnamed *he*), who does the leaping as the horse does the bolting. Answer choice A creates an

Copyright © Mometrix Media. You have been licensed one copy of this document for personal use only. Any other reproduction or redistribution is strictly prohibited. All rights reserved.

amusing picture, but it fails to make sense of the original sentence. Answer choice C is an interesting take on the sentence, but it places the action of the sentence in an odd order. It is more likely that the bolting occurred immediately after the leaping, and not the other way around, as indicated in answer choice C. (One cannot exactly leap into a saddle after the horse has already taken off.) Answer choice D is technically correct in terms of the information it provides, but it turns a single sentence into two sentences, and it incorrectly joins them with a comma splice.

28. A: The possessive pronoun *hers* is spelled without any apostrophes. Only answer choice A correctly indicates this. The other answer choices attempt to insert an apostrophe and/or an extra *s* into the word.

29. A: If an anaesthetic creates a temporary loss of feeling or sensation, and *aesthet* means "feeling," then *an-* must mean "without." Therefore, anaesthetic means "without feeling." The other prefix meanings do not create as clear a connection to the recognized meaning of the full word *anaesthetic*. To be "against feeling" makes little sense. To be "away feeling" is meaningless. To be "before feeling" would be appropriate to describe the moments before the anaesthetic wears off, but this is a qualification rather than a clear definition.

30. C: If the years leading up to the American Civil War are described as *antebellum*, and *bellum* means "war," the only possible meaning of *ante-* is "before." *Antebellum*, therefore, means "before war." The other prefixes do little to break the word down to a sensible meaning. "Again war" and "together war" are meaningless. "Good war" does nothing to explain why the pre-Civil War years were called *antebellum*, particularly when considering the atrocities of war that were soon to follow.

31. C: The phrase *she and I* makes the sentence grammatically correct. The blank needs to be filled by the subject of the sentence. The subject of a sentence or clause is the person, place, or thing that performs the verb. There are a couple of ways to determine that this sentence needs a subject. To begin with, the blank is at the beginning of the sentence, where the subject most often is found. Also, when you read the sentence, you will notice that it is unclear who went to the movies. Because you are looking for the subject, you need the nominative pronouns *she and I*.

32. C: The word *effected* is not spelled correctly in this sentence. In order to answer this question, you need to know the difference between *affect* and *effect*. The former is a verb and the latter is a noun. In other words, *affect* is something that you do and *effect* is something that is. In this sentence, the speaker is describing something that the prescription medication *did*. Therefore, the appropriate word is a verb. *Effect*, however, is a noun. For this reason, instead of *effected* the author should have used the word *affected*.

33. B: The word *hear* is not spelled correctly in this sentence. The speaker has mixed up the homophones *hear* and *here*. *Homophones* are words that sound the same but are spelled differently and have a different meaning. Homophones are not to be confused with *homonyms*, which are spelled the same but have a different meaning. In question 5, the author is trying to describe the place where the climate is; that is, he or she is describing the climate *here*. Unfortunately, the author uses the word *hear*, which is a verb meaning "to listen."

34. B: The word *further* is not used correctly in this sentence. Here, the word *farther* would be more appropriate. The distinction between *further* and *farther* is likely to appear in at least one question on the exam. For the purposes of the examination, you just need to know that *farther* can be used to describe physical distance, while *further* cannot. In this sentence, the speaker is describing a distance to be walked, which is a physical distance. For this reason, the word *further* is incorrect.

- 318 -

Copyright © Mometrix Media. You have been licensed one copy of this document for personal use only. Any other reproduction or redistribution is strictly prohibited. All rights reserved.

How to Overcome Test Anxiety

Just the thought of taking a test is enough to make most people a little nervous. A test is an important event that can have a long-term impact on your future, so it's important to take it seriously and it's natural to feel anxious about performing well. But just because anxiety is normal, that doesn't mean that it's helpful in test taking, or that you should simply accept it as part of your life. Anxiety can have a variety of effects. These effects can be mild, like making you feel slightly nervous, or severe, like blocking your ability to focus or remember even a simple detail.

If you experience test anxiety—whether severe or mild—it's important to know how to beat it. To discover this, first you need to understand what causes test anxiety.

Causes of Test Anxiety

While we often think of anxiety as an uncontrollable emotional state, it can actually be caused by simple, practical things. One of the most common causes of test anxiety is that a person does not feel adequately prepared for their test. This feeling can be the result of many different issues such as poor study habits or lack of organization, but the most common culprit is time management. Starting to study too late, failing to organize your study time to cover all of the material, or being distracted while you study will mean that you're not well prepared for the test. This may lead to cramming the night before, which will cause you to be physically and mentally exhausted for the test. Poor time management also contributes to feelings of stress, fear, and hopelessness as you realize you are not well prepared but don't know what to do about it.

Other times, test anxiety is not related to your preparation for the test but comes from unresolved fear. This may be a past failure on a test, or poor performance on tests in general. It may come from comparing yourself to others who seem to be performing better or from the stress of living up to expectations. Anxiety may be driven by fears of the future—how failure on this test would affect your educational and career goals. These fears are often completely irrational, but they can still negatively impact your test performance.

> **Review Video:** 3 Reasons You Have Test Anxiety
> Visit mometrix.com/academy and enter code: 428468

Copyright © Mometrix Media. You have been licensed one copy of this document for personal use only. Any other reproduction or redistribution is strictly prohibited. All rights reserved.

Elements of Test Anxiety

As mentioned earlier, test anxiety is considered to be an emotional state, but it has physical and mental components as well. Sometimes you may not even realize that you are suffering from test anxiety until you notice the physical symptoms. These can include trembling hands, rapid heartbeat, sweating, nausea, and tense muscles. Extreme anxiety may lead to fainting or vomiting. Obviously, any of these symptoms can have a negative impact on testing. It is important to recognize them as soon as they begin to occur so that you can address the problem before it damages your performance.

> **Review Video:** 3 Ways to Tell You Have Test Anxiety
> Visit mometrix.com/academy and enter code: 927847

The mental components of test anxiety include trouble focusing and inability to remember learned information. During a test, your mind is on high alert, which can help you recall information and stay focused for an extended period of time. However, anxiety interferes with your mind's natural processes, causing you to blank out, even on the questions you know well. The strain of testing during anxiety makes it difficult to stay focused, especially on a test that may take several hours. Extreme anxiety can take a huge mental toll, making it difficult not only to recall test information but even to understand the test questions or pull your thoughts together.

> **Review Video:** How Test Anxiety Affects Memory
> Visit mometrix.com/academy and enter code: 609003

Effects of Test Anxiety

Test anxiety is like a disease—if left untreated, it will get progressively worse. Anxiety leads to poor performance, and this reinforces the feelings of fear and failure, which in turn lead to poor performances on subsequent tests. It can grow from a mild nervousness to a crippling condition. If allowed to progress, test anxiety can have a big impact on your schooling, and consequently on your future.

Test anxiety can spread to other parts of your life. Anxiety on tests can become anxiety in any stressful situation, and blanking on a test can turn into panicking in a job situation. But fortunately, you don't have to let anxiety rule your testing and determine your grades. There are a number of relatively simple steps you can take to move past anxiety and function normally on a test and in the rest of life.

> **Review Video:** How Test Anxiety Impacts Your Grades
> Visit mometrix.com/academy and enter code: 939819

Copyright © Mometrix Media. You have been licensed one copy of this document for personal use only. Any other reproduction or redistribution is strictly prohibited. All rights reserved.

Physical Steps for Beating Test Anxiety

While test anxiety is a serious problem, the good news is that it can be overcome. It doesn't have to control your ability to think and remember information. While it may take time, you can begin taking steps today to beat anxiety.

Just as your first hint that you may be struggling with anxiety comes from the physical symptoms, the first step to treating it is also physical. Rest is crucial for having a clear, strong mind. If you are tired, it is much easier to give in to anxiety. But if you establish good sleep habits, your body and mind will be ready to perform optimally, without the strain of exhaustion. Additionally, sleeping well helps you to retain information better, so you're more likely to recall the answers when you see the test questions.

Getting good sleep means more than going to bed on time. It's important to allow your brain time to relax. Take study breaks from time to time so it doesn't get overworked, and don't study right before bed. Take time to rest your mind before trying to rest your body, or you may find it difficult to fall asleep.

> **Review Video: <u>The Importance of Sleep for Your Brain</u>**
> Visit mometrix.com/academy and enter code: 319338

Along with sleep, other aspects of physical health are important in preparing for a test. Good nutrition is vital for good brain function. Sugary foods and drinks may give a burst of energy but this burst is followed by a crash, both physically and emotionally. Instead, fuel your body with protein and vitamin-rich foods.

Also, drink plenty of water. Dehydration can lead to headaches and exhaustion, especially if your brain is already under stress from the rigors of the test. Particularly if your test is a long one, drink water during the breaks. And if possible, take an energy-boosting snack to eat between sections.

> **Review Video: <u>How Diet Can Affect your Mood</u>**
> Visit mometrix.com/academy and enter code: 624317

Along with sleep and diet, a third important part of physical health is exercise. Maintaining a steady workout schedule is helpful, but even taking 5-minute study breaks to walk can help get your blood pumping faster and clear your head. Exercise also releases endorphins, which contribute to a positive feeling and can help combat test anxiety.

When you nurture your physical health, you are also contributing to your mental health. If your body is healthy, your mind is much more likely to be healthy as well. So take time to rest, nourish your body with healthy food and water, and get moving as much as possible. Taking these physical steps will make you stronger and more able to take the mental steps necessary to overcome test anxiety.

> **Review Video: <u>How to Stay Healthy and Prevent Test Anxiety</u>**
> Visit mometrix.com/academy and enter code: 877894

Copyright © Mometrix Media. You have been licensed one copy of this document for personal use only. Any other reproduction or redistribution is strictly prohibited. All rights reserved.

Mental Steps for Beating Test Anxiety

Working on the mental side of test anxiety can be more challenging, but as with the physical side, there are clear steps you can take to overcome it. As mentioned earlier, test anxiety often stems from lack of preparation, so the obvious solution is to prepare for the test. Effective studying may be the most important weapon you have for beating test anxiety, but you can and should employ several other mental tools to combat fear.

First, boost your confidence by reminding yourself of past success—tests or projects that you aced. If you're putting as much effort into preparing for this test as you did for those, there's no reason you should expect to fail here. Work hard to prepare; then trust your preparation.

Second, surround yourself with encouraging people. It can be helpful to find a study group, but be sure that the people you're around will encourage a positive attitude. If you spend time with others who are anxious or cynical, this will only contribute to your own anxiety. Look for others who are motivated to study hard from a desire to succeed, not from a fear of failure.

Third, reward yourself. A test is physically and mentally tiring, even without anxiety, and it can be helpful to have something to look forward to. Plan an activity following the test, regardless of the outcome, such as going to a movie or getting ice cream.

When you are taking the test, if you find yourself beginning to feel anxious, remind yourself that you know the material. Visualize successfully completing the test. Then take a few deep, relaxing breaths and return to it. Work through the questions carefully but with confidence, knowing that you are capable of succeeding.

Developing a healthy mental approach to test taking will also aid in other areas of life. Test anxiety affects more than just the actual test—it can be damaging to your mental health and even contribute to depression. It's important to beat test anxiety before it becomes a problem for more than testing.

> **Review Video: Test Anxiety and Depression**
> Visit mometrix.com/academy and enter code: 904704

Copyright © Mometrix Media. You have been licensed one copy of this document for personal use only. Any other reproduction or redistribution is strictly prohibited. All rights reserved.

Study Strategy

Being prepared for the test is necessary to combat anxiety, but what does being prepared look like? You may study for hours on end and still not feel prepared. What you need is a strategy for test prep. The next few pages outline our recommended steps to help you plan out and conquer the challenge of preparation.

Step 1: Scope Out the Test

Learn everything you can about the format (multiple choice, essay, etc.) and what will be on the test. Gather any study materials, course outlines, or sample exams that may be available. Not only will this help you to prepare, but knowing what to expect can help to alleviate test anxiety.

Step 2: Map Out the Material

Look through the textbook or study guide and make note of how many chapters or sections it has. Then divide these over the time you have. For example, if a book has 15 chapters and you have five days to study, you need to cover three chapters each day. Even better, if you have the time, leave an extra day at the end for overall review after you have gone through the material in depth.

If time is limited, you may need to prioritize the material. Look through it and make note of which sections you think you already have a good grasp on, and which need review. While you are studying, skim quickly through the familiar sections and take more time on the challenging parts. Write out your plan so you don't get lost as you go. Having a written plan also helps you feel more in control of the study, so anxiety is less likely to arise from feeling overwhelmed at the amount to cover. A sample plan may look like this:

- Day 1: Skim chapters 1–4, study chapter 5 (especially pages 31–33)
- Day 2: Study chapters 6–7, skim chapters 8–9
- Day 3: Skim chapter 10, study chapters 11–12 (especially pages 87–90)
- Day 4: Study chapters 13–15
- Day 5: Overall review (focus most on chapters 5, 6, and 12), take practice test

Step 3: Gather Your Tools

Decide what study method works best for you. Do you prefer to highlight in the book as you study and then go back over the highlighted portions? Or do you type out notes of the important information? Or is it helpful to make flashcards that you can carry with you? Assemble the pens, index cards, highlighters, post-it notes, and any other materials you may need so you won't be distracted by getting up to find things while you study.

If you're having a hard time retaining the information or organizing your notes, experiment with different methods. For example, try color-coding by subject with colored pens, highlighters, or post-it notes. If you learn better by hearing, try recording yourself reading your notes so you can listen while in the car, working out, or simply sitting at your desk. Ask a friend to quiz you from your flashcards, or try teaching someone the material to solidify it in your mind.

Step 4: Create Your Environment

It's important to avoid distractions while you study. This includes both the obvious distractions like visitors and the subtle distractions like an uncomfortable chair (or a too-comfortable couch that makes you want to fall asleep). Set up the best study environment possible: good lighting and a

Copyright © Mometrix Media. You have been licensed one copy of this document for personal use only. Any other reproduction or redistribution is strictly prohibited. All rights reserved.

comfortable work area. If background music helps you focus, you may want to turn it on, but otherwise keep the room quiet. If you are using a computer to take notes, be sure you don't have any other windows open, especially applications like social media, games, or anything else that could distract you. Silence your phone and turn off notifications. Be sure to keep water close by so you stay hydrated while you study (but avoid unhealthy drinks and snacks).

Also, take into account the best time of day to study. Are you freshest first thing in the morning? Try to set aside some time then to work through the material. Is your mind clearer in the afternoon or evening? Schedule your study session then. Another method is to study at the same time of day that you will take the test, so that your brain gets used to working on the material at that time and will be ready to focus at test time.

Step 5: Study!

Once you have done all the study preparation, it's time to settle into the actual studying. Sit down, take a few moments to settle your mind so you can focus, and begin to follow your study plan. Don't give in to distractions or let yourself procrastinate. This is your time to prepare so you'll be ready to fearlessly approach the test. Make the most of the time and stay focused.

Of course, you don't want to burn out. If you study too long you may find that you're not retaining the information very well. Take regular study breaks. For example, taking five minutes out of every hour to walk briskly, breathing deeply and swinging your arms, can help your mind stay fresh.

As you get to the end of each chapter or section, it's a good idea to do a quick review. Remind yourself of what you learned and work on any difficult parts. When you feel that you've mastered the material, move on to the next part. At the end of your study session, briefly skim through your notes again.

But while review is helpful, cramming last minute is NOT. If at all possible, work ahead so that you won't need to fit all your study into the last day. Cramming overloads your brain with more information than it can process and retain, and your tired mind may struggle to recall even previously learned information when it is overwhelmed with last-minute study. Also, the urgent nature of cramming and the stress placed on your brain contribute to anxiety. You'll be more likely to go to the test feeling unprepared and having trouble thinking clearly.

So don't cram, and don't stay up late before the test, even just to review your notes at a leisurely pace. Your brain needs rest more than it needs to go over the information again. In fact, plan to finish your studies by noon or early afternoon the day before the test. Give your brain the rest of the day to relax or focus on other things, and get a good night's sleep. Then you will be fresh for the test and better able to recall what you've studied.

Step 6: Take a practice test

Many courses offer sample tests, either online or in the study materials. This is an excellent resource to check whether you have mastered the material, as well as to prepare for the test format and environment.

Check the test format ahead of time: the number of questions, the type (multiple choice, free response, etc.), and the time limit. Then create a plan for working through them. For example, if you have 30 minutes to take a 60-question test, your limit is 30 seconds per question. Spend less time on the questions you know well so that you can take more time on the difficult ones.

Copyright © Mometrix Media. You have been licensed one copy of this document for personal use only. Any other reproduction or redistribution is strictly prohibited. All rights reserved.

If you have time to take several practice tests, take the first one open book, with no time limit. Work through the questions at your own pace and make sure you fully understand them. Gradually work up to taking a test under test conditions: sit at a desk with all study materials put away and set a timer. Pace yourself to make sure you finish the test with time to spare and go back to check your answers if you have time.

After each test, check your answers. On the questions you missed, be sure you understand why you missed them. Did you misread the question (tests can use tricky wording)? Did you forget the information? Or was it something you hadn't learned? Go back and study any shaky areas that the practice tests reveal.

Taking these tests not only helps with your grade, but also aids in combating test anxiety. If you're already used to the test conditions, you're less likely to worry about it, and working through tests until you're scoring well gives you a confidence boost. Go through the practice tests until you feel comfortable, and then you can go into the test knowing that you're ready for it.

Test Tips

On test day, you should be confident, knowing that you've prepared well and are ready to answer the questions. But aside from preparation, there are several test day strategies you can employ to maximize your performance.

First, as stated before, get a good night's sleep the night before the test (and for several nights before that, if possible). Go into the test with a fresh, alert mind rather than staying up late to study.

Try not to change too much about your normal routine on the day of the test. It's important to eat a nutritious breakfast, but if you normally don't eat breakfast at all, consider eating just a protein bar. If you're a coffee drinker, go ahead and have your normal coffee. Just make sure you time it so that the caffeine doesn't wear off right in the middle of your test. Avoid sugary beverages, and drink enough water to stay hydrated but not so much that you need a restroom break 10 minutes into the test. If your test isn't first thing in the morning, consider going for a walk or doing a light workout before the test to get your blood flowing.

Allow yourself enough time to get ready, and leave for the test with plenty of time to spare so you won't have the anxiety of scrambling to arrive in time. Another reason to be early is to select a good seat. It's helpful to sit away from doors and windows, which can be distracting. Find a good seat, get out your supplies, and settle your mind before the test begins.

When the test begins, start by going over the instructions carefully, even if you already know what to expect. Make sure you avoid any careless mistakes by following the directions.

Then begin working through the questions, pacing yourself as you've practiced. If you're not sure on an answer, don't spend too much time on it, and don't let it shake your confidence. Either skip it and come back later, or eliminate as many wrong answers as possible and guess among the remaining ones. Don't dwell on these questions as you continue—put them out of your mind and focus on what lies ahead.

Be sure to read all of the answer choices, even if you're sure the first one is the right answer. Sometimes you'll find a better one if you keep reading. But don't second-guess yourself if you do immediately know the answer. Your gut instinct is usually right. Don't let test anxiety rob you of the information you know.

Copyright © Mometrix Media. You have been licensed one copy of this document for personal use only. Any other reproduction or redistribution is strictly prohibited. All rights reserved.

If you have time at the end of the test (and if the test format allows), go back and review your answers. Be cautious about changing any, since your first instinct tends to be correct, but make sure you didn't misread any of the questions or accidentally mark the wrong answer choice. Look over any you skipped and make an educated guess.

At the end, leave the test feeling confident. You've done your best, so don't waste time worrying about your performance or wishing you could change anything. Instead, celebrate the successful completion of this test. And finally, use this test to learn how to deal with anxiety even better next time.

> **Review Video: 5 Tips to Beat Test Anxiety**
> Visit mometrix.com/academy and enter code: 570656

Important Qualification

Not all anxiety is created equal. If your test anxiety is causing major issues in your life beyond the classroom or testing center, or if you are experiencing troubling physical symptoms related to your anxiety, it may be a sign of a serious physiological or psychological condition. If this sounds like your situation, we strongly encourage you to seek professional help.

Copyright © Mometrix Media. You have been licensed one copy of this document for personal use only. Any other reproduction or redistribution is strictly prohibited. All rights reserved.

Thank You

We at Mometrix would like to extend our heartfelt thanks to you, our friend and patron, for allowing us to play a part in your journey. It is a privilege to serve people from all walks of life who are unified in their commitment to building the best future they can for themselves.

The preparation you devote to these important testing milestones may be the most valuable educational opportunity you have for making a real difference in your life. We encourage you to put your heart into it—that feeling of succeeding, overcoming, and yes, conquering will be well worth the hours you've invested.

We want to hear your story, your struggles and your successes, and if you see any opportunities for us to improve our materials so we can help others even more effectively in the future, please share that with us as well. **The team at Mometrix would be absolutely thrilled to hear from you!** So please, send us an email (support@mometrix.com) and let's stay in touch.

If you'd like some additional help, check out these other resources we offer for your exam:

http://mometrixflashcards.com/TEAS

Copyright © Mometrix Media. You have been licensed one copy of this document for personal use only. Any other reproduction or redistribution is strictly prohibited. All rights reserved.

Additional Bonus Material

Due to our efforts to try to keep this book to a manageable length, we've created a link that will give you access to all of your additional bonus material.

Please visit https://www.mometrix.com/bonus948/teas to access the information.

Copyright © Mometrix Media. You have been licensed one copy of this document for personal use only. Any other reproduction or redistribution is strictly prohibited. All rights reserved.